Taste of Home
TEST KITCHEN
FAVORITES

TASTE OF HOME BOOKS • RDA ENTHUSIAST BRANDS, LLC • MILWAUKEE, WI

Taste *of* Home

International Standard Book Numbers:
D 978-1-62145-717-6
U 978-1-62145-718-3
International Standard Serial Number:
2690-3792
Component Numbers:
D 119700104H
U 119700106H

Executive Editor: Mark Hagen
Senior Art Director: Raeann Thompson
Editor: Amy Glander
Designer: Jazmin Delgado
Deputy Editor, Copy Desk: Dulcie Shoener
Contributing Copy Editor: Deb Warlaumont Mulvey

Cover Photography: *Taste of Home* Photo Studio

Pictured on front cover:
Green Onion Rolls, p. 67
Key Lime Blondie Bars, p. 202
Yummy Corn Chip Salad, p. 81
Oreo Cupcakes with Cookies & Cream Frosting, p. 233
Buffalo Chicken Enchiladas, p. 128

Pictured on title page:
The Best Marinara Sauce, p. 176

Pictured on back cover:
Crunchy Chili Cilantro Lime Roasted Shrimp, p. 116
Apricot & Macadamia Eggnog Bread, p. 76
Frozen Brandy Old-Fashioneds, p. 31
Curry-Rubbed Roast Chicken, p. 143

Printed in USA

1 3 5 7 9 10 8 6 4 2

More ways to connect with us:

Welcome to Our Kitchen

DISHING WITH

Sarah Farmer
Taste of Home
Executive Culinary Director

This year I celebrated my 17th anniversary at *Taste of Home*. Since 2004 I've edited, tested, tasted, styled, filmed, developed and demo'd a lot of recipes. It's probably no surprise that I have hundreds of favorites. My collection is messy—the recipes are crinkled, smudged, scribbled on and worn from using them time and time again. I treasure them all, including the ones I've saved in my expanding Digital Recipe Box at toh.com. (Tip: If you haven't tried this feature on our website yet, I encourage you to do so. You'll love it!)

My most-loved recipes are those that fall in the "comfort" zone—warm, cozy and hearty. Nearest and dearest to my heart is The Best Ever Chili, page 11. I developed this recipe using fresh chili powder I brought back from my honeymoon in Santa Fe. It's rich and beefy, with layers of flavors for depth and dimension. I think it's important for recipes to incorporate different textures, which is why, in my family, we serve this chili over cooked macaroni noodles with dollops of silky sour cream on top (to cut through the heat a bit) and lots of corn chips for crunch and a salty kick. This chili uses a long list of ingredients, but it's well worth the effort.

Our Test Kitchen team members rave about their personal faves as well. They love talking about the dishes they've developed, tweaked and tasted over the years. Some of these recipes were created by our staff, but most were shared with us from our community of home cooks. In this book you'll find a mix of our everyday go-tos and our ultimate favorites, including some of the top contenders from our first-ever Recipe of the Year contest. (Find the winning recipe for 2020, Loaded Huevos Rancheros with Roasted Poblano Peppers, on page 58.)

What other types of recipes are we craving these days? We cherish luscious desserts along with all the gooey, cheesy classics *Taste of Home* is famous

for. But we also love fresh, healthy, and quick and easy dishes, too. This year, we're tested more recipes that are global-inspired and made with plant-based ingredients. (We know something is trending when we start seeing it pop up in the recipes you share.) Whether it's meaty or meatless, decadent or dairy-free, air-fried or country-fried, our Test Kitchen touches all kinds of fantastic recipes that feed the soul, connect us to family and friends, and make us happy! Thank you for your recipes, tips and heartwarming stories. Please, keep them coming! Our collection of favorites is never-ending!

Happy cooking,

Take a Peek Inside Our Test Kitchen

Family cooks sharing their all-time best recipes—that's long been the hallmark of *Taste of Home*. And while we couldn't do what we do without these gracious home cooks, it's our Test Kitchen team that makes sure each recipe we share will turn out perfect. Here's a peek into some of what goes on behind the scenes.

What kind of education or professional credentials do the Taste of Home *Test Kitchen staffers have?*
Our Test Kitchen professionals are trained and trusted experts. We have earned degrees in varied fields that relate to food or publishing: food science, culinary arts, nutrition and wellness, art and design, and dietetics. We have more than 200 years of combined professional culinary experience.

What do you look for in new recipes submissions?
We embrace recipes that have a little something extra to offer—a classic recipe with a new flavor spin, for example, or something slightly different from what is already in our extensive collection. The recipe must also have easy-to-follow instructions.

What three ingredients does the kitchen use most?
We have 229,000 recipes in our database from all kinds of cooking styles and cuisines. Our top-rated recipes are consistently down-home dishes that warm the soul. It's no surprise that cheese, with a total of 13,000 ounces, takes the lead as the most-used ingredient in the past year. Flour weighs in at 7,200 pounds. Butter is right up there with 382 pounds. We also use mass quantities of milk, eggs, olive oil and everyone's favorite ingredient—bacon!

What about all the groceries?
Over the course of a year, we process more than 400 grocery orders and prep 24,000 ingredients. Our grocery inventory, ordering and shopping process is significant and requires hours of dedicated work each week from Test Kitchen team members. We rely on our recipe management database to help. This remarkable tool keeps multiple grocery lists organized, collating every ingredient for every recipe scheduled for testing, photography or video, by grocery departments like fresh produce, meats, staples, canned and packaged, dairy, deli, frozen, etc.

From there, our prep kitchen team produces shoppable lists and schedules them on different shopping days. (We don't want to buy perishable produce on Monday if it's not needed until Friday.) Some orders are placed online through a local grocery store that makes weekly deliveries. Others are picked up at stores throughout the week by our prep kitchen staff. We even have a shopping van with our *Taste of Home* logo on it!

Who washes all the dishes?
In the blink of an eye, towering stacks of dirty dishes pile up in the Test Kitchen, prep kitchens and even our photo studio. We are so thankful to have a team of two fabulous full-time employees responsible for keeping our pots, pans, measuring cups and all sorts of cooking tools and equipment cleaned and organized. The dishwashers loop around the kitchens and studios throughout the day, loading up their carts with bins of dirty dishes for cleaning at the wash station. We couldn't keep up the pace without them!

CONTENTS

FAVORITE...

STAFF RECIPES 6

SNACKS 22

BREAKFASTS 42

BREADS, BISCUITS & MORE 62

SOUPS, SALADS & SANDWICHES............................ 78

FISH, SEAFOOD & MEATLESS 100

BEEF, CHICKEN & PORK 122

SIDE DISHES 148

ODDS & ENDS 170

COOKIES, BROWNIES & BARS....................................186

CAKES & PIES 208

DESSERTS 230

INDEX..252

EQUIVALENTS & SUBSTITUTIONS 255

CUTTING TECHNIQUES..............................256

THE BEST EVER CHILI
PAGE 11

Staff Recipes

At *Taste of Home*, we're all about authentic family-pleasing meals. Here are some of our very own recipes—the dishes we've tasted, tested and perfected in our own home kitchens. Whether you're feeding a crowd or just your own hungry crew, dig in to these staff creations that capture the essence of home cooking.

DISHING WITH

Rashanda Cobbins
Food Editor

Summer corn is one of my favorite vegetables, so when it's in season I make this easy soup in the slow cooker.

MEXICAN STREET
CORN CHOWDER

MEXICAN STREET CORN CHOWDER

—Rashanda Cobbins, Food Editor

Prep: 35 min. • **Cook:** 3½ hrs.
Makes: 8 servings (2¼ qt.)

- 10 ears fresh corn (about 5½ cups)
- 1¼ to 2 cups water
- 6 bacon strips, chopped
- 2 small onions, chopped
- 2 small green peppers, chopped
- 1 jalapeno pepper, seeded and finely chopped
- 1 tsp. ground chipotle pepper
- 2 tsp. salt
- ¾ tsp. ground cumin
- ¼ tsp. pepper
- 1 cup heavy whipping cream
- 1 medium lime, zested and juiced
  Optional: Fresh cilantro, lime wedges, sliced jalapeno, chopped bell pepper and crumbled cotija cheese

1. Cut corn off cobs. Rub the edge of a knife over each cob to "milk" it; add enough water to cob juice to equal 2 cups. Add corn and liquid to a 5-qt. slow cooker.
2. In a large skillet, cook bacon over medium heat until crisp, 5-7 minutes. Remove with a slotted spoon; drain bacon on paper towels. Discard drippings, reserving 2 Tbsp. in pan. Add the onion, green pepper and jalapeno to skillet; cook and stir over medium-high heat until soft, 3-4 minutes. Add seasonings and cook 1 minute more; transfer to slow cooker. Cook on low 3½-4 hours, until corn is tender and mixture has thickened slightly.
3. Stir in cream and lime zest and juice. Puree mixture with an immersion blender to desired consistency. Garnish with reserved bacon. If desired, top with cilantro and serve with, lime wedges, jalapeno, bell pepper and cojita cheese.
1 cup: 287 cal., 18g fat (9g sat. fat), 43mg chol., 743mg sod., 29g carb. (10g sugars, 4g fiber), 8g pro.

PORK & CHEESY
MACARONI SLIDERS

PORK & CHEESY MACARONI SLIDERS

I love sliders! This sweet and savory recipe was created out of leftover ingredients that I had in my fridge. They're perfect for both weeknight meals and special occasions.
—Rashanda Cobbins, Food Editor

Prep: 30 min. • **Bake:** 10 min.
Makes: 12 servings

- 1 cup uncooked cavatappi pasta
- 1 Tbsp. butter
- 1½ tsp. all-purpose flour
- ¼ tsp. pepper
- ½ cup 2% milk
- ¾ cup shredded sharp cheddar cheese
- 1 pkg. (18 oz.) Hawaiian sweet rolls
- 1 carton (16 oz.) refrigerated fully cooked barbecue shredded pork, warmed
- 2 Tbsp. melted butter
- 1 Tbsp. honey
- ½ tsp. ground mustard
- 1 jalapeno pepper, sliced, optional

1. Preheat oven to 375°. Cook the pasta according to package directions.
2. Meanwhile, in a small saucepan, melt butter over medium heat. Stir in flour and pepper until smooth; gradually whisk in milk. Bring to a boil, stirring constantly; cook and stir until thickened, 3-5 minutes. Stir in the cheese until melted. Drain pasta; stir into cheese sauce. Set aside.
3. Place roll bottoms in a greased 13x9-in. baking dish. Layer with pork, pasta mixture and roll tops. Combine melted butter, honey and mustard. Brush over roll tops.
4. Bake until tops are golden brown and filling is hot, 10-12 minutes. If desired, top with jalapeno pepper slices.
1 slider: 305 cal., 10g fat (6g sat. fat), 48mg chol., 466mg sod., 39g carb. (17g sugars, 2g fiber), 14g pro.

VEGAN PEANUT
BUTTER COOKIES

VEGAN PEANUT BUTTER COOKIES

Even without butter or eggs, these peanut butter cookies are soft and chewy. No one will be able to tell they're vegan! If you want a little extra texture, feel free to use chunky peanut butter or add a quarter-cup crushed peanuts to the dough.
—Katie Bandurski, Associate Digital Editor

- -

Prep: 15 min. • **Bake:** 10 min. + cooling
Makes: 3 dozen

- 1 cup creamy peanut butter
- ½ cup sugar
- ½ cup packed brown sugar
- 1 Tbsp. vanilla extract
- ⅓ cup unsweetened almond milk
- 1 cup all-purpose flour
- 1 tsp. baking soda
- ½ tsp. baking powder
- ½ tsp. salt

1. Preheat oven to 350°. In a large bowl, cream the peanut butter, sugars and vanilla until light and fluffy, about 4 minutes. Beat in the almond milk. In another bowl, whisk flour, baking soda, baking powder and salt; gradually beat into creamed mixture.
2. Shape level tablespoonfuls into balls. Place 2 in. apart on parchment-lined baking sheets; flatten with a fork. Bake until set, 8-10 minutes. Cool on pan 5 minutes before removing to wire racks to cool completely.
1 cookie: 79 cal., 4g fat (1g sat. fat), 0 chol., 107mg sod., 10g carb. (7g sugars, 0 fiber), 2g pro.

TEST KITCHEN TIP
Letting the cookies rest once they're out of the oven is very important. Since they contain no butter or eggs, they need a little time to firm up. If you remove them from the pan too early, they'll crumble.

EASY CHOCOLATE SOUFFLES

Try these easy-to-make souffles for your next dinner party. The mini servings have a maximum portion of deliciousness!
—Sarah Farmer, Executive Culinary Director

- -

Prep: 20 min. • **Bake:** 15 min.
Makes: 6 servings

- 4 large eggs
- 6 tsp. plus 1 Tbsp. sugar, divided
- 1 cup light corn syrup
- ½ cup baking cocoa
- 1 tsp. vanilla extract
  Confectioners' sugar

1. Separate the eggs; let stand at room temperature for 30 minutes. Coat six 6-oz. souffle dishes with cooking spray. Sprinkle 1 tsp. of sugar into each dish, tilting to cover the bottom and sides; set aside.
2. Preheat oven to 375°. In a large bowl, whisk corn syrup, cocoa, egg yolks and vanilla until blended; set aside. In a large bowl with clean beaters, beat egg whites on medium speed until soft peaks form. Gradually beat in remaining sugar on high until stiff peaks form. Gently fold a fourth of the egg white mixture into chocolate mixture; fold in remaining egg white mixture.
3. Spoon batter into prepared dishes. Bake 15-20 minutes or until a toothpick inserted in the center comes out clean. Dust with confectioners' sugar. Serve warm.
1 serving: 250 cal., 4g fat (1g sat. fat), 142mg chol., 108mg sod., 53g carb. (34g sugars, 1g fiber), 5g pro.

THE BEST EVER CHILI
—Sarah Farmer, Executive Culinary Director

Prep: 20 min. • **Cook:** 1 hour 20 min.
Makes: 8 servings

- 3 dried ancho or guajillo chiles
- 1 to 2 cups boiling water
- 2 Tbsp. tomato paste
- 3 garlic cloves
- ¼ cup chili powder
- 1½ tsp. smoked paprika
- 2 tsp. ground cumin
- 1 lb. ground beef
- 1½ tsp. Montreal steak seasoning
- 2 lbs. beef tri-tip roast, cut into ½-in. cubes
- 2 tsp. salt, divided
- 2 tsp. coarsely ground pepper, divided
- 2 Tbsp. canola oil, divided
- 1 large onion, chopped (about 2 cups)
- 1 poblano pepper, seeded and chopped
- 1 tsp. dried oregano
- 1½ tsp. crushed red pepper flakes
- 3 cups beef stock
- 1 bottle (12 oz.) beer
- 2 cans (14½ oz. each) fire-roasted diced tomatoes, undrained
- 1 can (16 oz.) kidney beans, drained
- 3 Tbsp. masa harina
  Optional: American cheese slices, sour cream, shredded cheddar cheese, diced red onion and corn chips

1. Combine chiles and enough boiling water to cover; let stand until softened, about 15 minutes. Drain, reserving ⅓ cup of the soaking liquid. Discard stems and seeds. Process chiles, tomato paste, garlic and reserved liquid until smooth.

2. In a small skillet, toast chili powder, paprika and cumin over medium heat until aromatic, 3-4 minutes; remove and set aside. In a Dutch oven, cook and stir ground beef and steak seasoning over medium-high heat until beef is no longer pink, about 5 minutes; remove and drain.

3. Sprinkle steak cubes with 1 tsp. each salt and pepper. In same Dutch oven, brown beef in batches in 1 Tbsp. oil over medium-high heat; remove and set aside. Saute onion and poblano pepper in the remaining 1 Tbsp. oil until tender, about 5 minutes. Stir in toasted spices, oregano and pepper flakes. Add the cooked meats along with beef stock, beer, tomatoes, beans, remaining salt and pepper, and chile paste mixture. Cook over medium heat 20 minutes; reduce heat to low. Stir in masa harina and simmer 30-45 minutes longer. Serve with desired toppings.

Freeze option: Freeze the cooled chili in freezer containers. To use, partially thaw in refrigerator overnight. Heat through in a saucepan, stirring occasionally; add a little broth or water if necessary.

1¾ cups: 473 cal., 20g fat (6g sat. fat), 103mg chol., 1554mg sod., 29g carb. (8g sugars, 7g fiber), 41g pro.

THE BEST
EVER CHILI

DISHING WITH

Sarah Farmer
Executive Culinary Director

My dad and my father-in-law are the gurus in our chili-loving clan. But after my honeymoon to New Mexico, inspired by the fresh and fragrant chili peppers at the Santa Fe farmers market, I felt it was time to introduce them to my spicy, meaty version with a touch of masa harina.

PEANUT BUTTER PRETZEL SHAKE

—Beth Tomkiw, Chief Content Officer

- -

Takes: 15 min. • **Makes:** 4 servings

3	Tbsp. hot fudge ice cream topping
4	miniature pretzels, coarsely crumbled
2	Tbsp. chopped salted peanuts
4	Peanut Butter Pretzel Bars plus additional for topping, optional (see recipe on page 195)
1½	cups vanilla ice cream
1	cup 2% milk
½	cup whipped cream

1. Spread hot fudge topping around rim of a tall glass; sprinkle with pretzels and peanuts. Freeze until ready to fill.

2. In a blender, add 4 Peanut Butter Pretzel Bars, ice cream and milk. Cover; blend until smooth. Pour into prepared glasses. Top with whipped cream. If desired, thread more pretzel bars on skewers; serve in shakes.

1 shake (without toppings): 665 cal., 41g fat (20g sat. fat), 74mg chol., 600mg sod., 69g carb. (45g sugars, 3g fiber), 12g pro.

DISHING WITH

Beth Tomkiw
Chief Content Officer

Social media sites like Instagram and Pinterest are home to all kinds of creative taste temptations, like the #freakshakes that inspired me to make (and consume) this ice-creamy peanut butter pretzel shake. While I certainly wouldn't advocate a steady diet of crazy milkshakes, indulging in one every once in a while is a treat we all deserve. After all, sweets make life sweeter.

PEANUT BUTTER PRETZEL SHAKE

DUTCH-OVEN RAISIN WALNUT BREAD

Looking for the perfect snack? Try a slice of this bread studded with raisins and walnuts.
—Catherine Ward, Prep Kitchen Manager

- -

Prep: 15 min. + rising
Bake: 50 min. + cooling
Makes: 1 loaf (32 slices)

- 6 to 7 cups (125 grams per cup) all-purpose flour
- ¼ cup sugar
- 2 tsp. active dry yeast
- 2 tsp. ground cinnamon
- 2 tsp. salt
- 1 cup raisins
- 1 cup chopped walnuts
- 3 cups cool water (70° to 75°)

1. In a large bowl, whisk 6 cups flour, sugar, yeast, cinnamon and salt. Stir in raisins and walnuts; add water and enough remaining flour to form a moist, shaggy dough. Do not knead. Cover and let rise in a cool place until doubled, 7-8 hours.
2. Preheat oven to 450°; place a Dutch oven with lid onto center rack and heat for at least 30 minutes. Once Dutch oven is heated, turn dough onto a generously floured surface. Using a metal scraper or spatula, quickly shape into a round loaf. Gently place on top of a piece of parchment.
3. Using a sharp knife, make a slash (¼ in. deep) across the top of the loaf. Using the parchment, immediately lower bread into heated Dutch oven. Cover; bake 30 minutes. Uncover and bake until the bread is deep golden brown and sounds hollow when tapped, about 20-30 minutes longer, partially covering if browning too much. Remove loaf from pan and cool completely on wire rack.
1 slice: 130 cal., 3g fat (0 sat. fat), 0 chol., 149mg sod., 24g carb. (4g sugars, 1g fiber), 3g pro.

> **TEST KITCHEN TIP**
> This is a soft, gentle dough that should be baked immediately after shaping. Preheating the Dutch oven prior to shaping, and working with the dough quickly, are keys to success.

DUTCH-OVEN BREAD

Warm homemade bread makes an average day extraordinary. Enjoy this beautiful crusty loaf as is, or stir in a few extras like cheese, garlic, herbs and dried fruits.
—Catherine Ward, Prep Kitchen Manager

- -

Prep: 15 min. + rising
Bake: 45 min. + cooling
Makes: 1 loaf (16 slices)

- 3 to 3½ cups (125 grams per cup) all-purpose flour
- 1 tsp. active dry yeast
- 1 tsp. salt
- 1½ cups water (70° to 75°)

1. In a large bowl, whisk 3 cups flour, yeast and salt. Stir in water and enough remaining flour to form a moist, shaggy dough. Do not knead. Cover and let rise in a cool place until doubled, 7-8 hours. Preheat oven to 450°; place a Dutch oven with lid onto center rack and heat for at least 30 minutes. Once Dutch oven is heated, turn dough onto a generously floured surface. Using a metal scraper or spatula, quickly shape into a round loaf. Gently place on top of a piece of parchment.
2. Using a sharp knife, make a slash (¼ in. deep) across the top of the loaf. Using the parchment, immediately lower bread into heated Dutch oven. Cover; bake 30 minutes. Uncover and bake until loaf is deep golden brown and sounds hollow when tapped, about 15-20 minutes longer, partially covering if browning too much. Remove loaf from pan and cool completely on wire rack.
1 slice: 86 cal., 0 fat (0 sat. fat), 0 chol., 148mg sod., 18g carb. (0 sugars, 1g fiber), 3g pro.

DUTCH-OVEN BREAD

CHICKEN WITH PEACH-AVOCADO SALSA

This fresh dinner is pure summer—juicy peaches, creamy avocado, grilled chicken and a kick of hot sauce and lime. Make the salsa ahead to get it on the table even faster.
—Shannon Norris, Senior Food Stylist

- -

Takes: 30 min. • **Makes:** 4 servings

- 1 medium peach, peeled and chopped
- 1 medium ripe avocado, peeled and cubed
- ½ cup chopped sweet red pepper
- 3 Tbsp. finely chopped red onion
- 1 Tbsp. minced fresh basil
- 1 Tbsp. lime juice
- 1 tsp. hot pepper sauce
- ½ tsp. grated lime zest
- ¾ tsp. salt, divided
- ½ tsp. pepper, divided
- 4 boneless skinless chicken breast halves (6 oz. each)

1. For salsa, in a small bowl, combine the peaches, avocado, red pepper, onion, basil, lime juice, hot sauce, lime zest, ¼ tsp. salt and ¼ tsp. pepper.

2. Sprinkle chicken with remaining salt and pepper. On a lightly greased grill rack, grill the chicken, covered, over medium heat for 5 minutes. Turn; grill until a thermometer reads 165°, about 7-9 minutes longer. Serve with salsa.

1 chicken breast half with ½ cup salsa: 265 cal., 9g fat (2g sat. fat), 94mg chol., 536mg sod., 9g carb. (4g sugars, 3g fiber), 36g pro. **Diabetic exchanges:** 5 lean meat, 1 fat, ½ starch.

THE BEST SWEET POTATO PIE

—Shannon Norris, Senior Food Stylist

- -

Prep: 1½ hours+chilling
Bake: 35 min. + cooling • **Makes:** 8 servings

CRUST:

- 1 large egg yolk
- ¼ to ½ cup ice water, divided
- 2½ cups all-purpose flour
- 3 Tbsp. sugar
- ½ tsp. salt
- ½ cup cold shortening, cubed
- ½ cup cold butter, cubed

FILLING:

- 2½ lbs. sweet potatoes
- ⅔ cup packed brown sugar
- ½ cup sour cream
- 3 large eggs, lightly beaten
- ⅓ cup butter, melted
- 1 Tbsp. bourbon
- 2 tsp. vanilla extract
- 1½ tsp. ground cinnamon
- ½ tsp. ground nutmeg
- ½ tsp. salt
  Optional toppings: Whipped cream and sugared cranberries

1. In a small bowl, mix egg yolk with ¼ cup ice water; set aside. Place the flour, sugar and salt in a food processor; pulse until blended. Add the shortening and butter; pulse until shortening and butter are the size of peas. While pulsing, add egg yolk mixture. Add just enough of remaining ice water to form moist crumbs. Divide dough in half. Shape each into a disk; wrap and refrigerate dough for 1 hour or overnight.

2. Preheat oven to 400°. Scrub sweet potatoes; place in a 13x9-in. baking pan with 1½ cups water. Bake until tender, 45-50 minutes. Meanwhile, on a lightly floured surface, roll 1 disk of dough to a ⅛-in.-thick circle; transfer to a 9-in. deep-dish pie plate. Trim pastry to ½ in. beyond rim of plate; flute edge. Roll remaining disk to ⅛-in. thickness; cut into desired shapes with floured 1-in. cookie cutters. Place on a parchment-lined baking sheet. Refrigerate crust and cutouts for at least 30 minutes.

3. Peel potatoes when they are cool enough to handle; place in a food processor. Pulse to coarsely mash. Add brown sugar and the next 8 ingredients; blend until smooth. Pour filling into chilled crust. Bake on lowest oven rack 15 minutes. Reduce oven setting to 350°; bake until the center is just set, 20-25 minutes. Bake pastry cutouts on an upper oven rack until golden brown, 10-12 minutes. Cool on a wire rack; decorate pie with crust cutouts and toppings as desired.

1 piece: 726 cal., 37g fat (18g sat. fat), 147mg chol., 500mg sod., 88g carb. (38g sugars, 6g fiber), 10g pro.

CHICKEN WITH PEACH-AVOCADO SALSA

DISHING WITH

Shannon Norris
Senior Food Stylist

I love this recipe's rich, sweet potato flavor and irresistibly buttery crust. Sour cream makes the filling super smooth, and the brown sugar and spices make it extra cozy. There's no doubt that this is the best sweet potato pie!

THE BEST SWEET
POTATO PIE

THE BEST
HUMMUS

DISHING WITH

James Schend
Deputy Editor, Culinary

Hummus is my go-to appetizer when I need something quick, easy and impressive. Over the years I've picked up a number of tricks that make this the best hummus you'll ever have.

THE BEST HUMMUS
—James Schend, Deputy Editor, Culinary

- -

Prep: 25 min. • **Cook:** 20 min. + chilling
Makes: 1½ cups

- 1   can (15 oz.) chickpeas, rinsed and drained
- ½   tsp. baking soda
- ¼   cup fresh lemon juice
- 1   Tbsp. minced garlic
- ½   tsp. kosher salt
- ½   tsp. ground cumin
- ½   cup tahini
- 2   Tbsp. extra virgin olive oil
- ¼   cup cold water
       Optional: Olive oil, roasted chickpeas, toasted sesame seeds, ground sumac

1. Place chickpeas in a large saucepan; add water to cover by 1 in. Gently rub chickpeas together to loosen outer skin. Pour off water and any skins that are floating. Repeat 2-3 times until no skins float to the surface; drain. Return to saucepan; add baking soda and enough water to cover by 1 in. Bring to a boil; reduce heat. Simmer, uncovered, until chickpeas are very tender and just starting to fall apart, 20-25 minutes.

2. Meanwhile, in a blender, process lemon juice, garlic and salt until almost a paste. Let stand 10 minutes; strain, discarding solids. Stir in cumin. In a small bowl, stir together tahini and olive oil.

3. Add chickpeas to blender; add cold water. Loosely cover and process until completely smooth. Add lemon mixture and process. With blender running, slowly add tahini mixture, scraping sides of blender as needed. Adjust seasoning with additional salt and cumin if desired.

4. Transfer mixture to a serving bowl; cover and refrigerate for at least 30 minutes. If desired, top with additional olive oil and assorted toppings.

¼ cup: 250 cal., 19g fat (3g sat. fat), 0 chol., 361mg sod., 15g carb. (2g sugars, 5g fiber), 7g pro.

BACON-WRAPPED AVOCADO WEDGES

We all know almost everything is improved with bacon, and avocado is no exception. Since it's made in an air fryer, this appetizer is one to remember. It will definitely impress your friends!

—James Schend, Deputy Editor, Culinary

Takes: 30 min. • **Makes:** 1 dozen

- 2 medium ripe avocados
- 12 bacon strips

SAUCE
- ½ cup mayonnaise
- 2 to 3 Tbsp. Sriracha chili sauce
- 1 to 2 Tbsp. lime juice
- 1 tsp. grated lime zest

1. Preheat air fryer to 400. Cut each avocado in half; remove pit and peel. Cut each half into thirds. Wrap 1 bacon slice around each avocado wedge. Working in batches if needed, place wedges in a single layer in fryer basket and cook until bacon is cooked through, 10-15 minutes.

2. Meanwhile, in a small bowl, stir together mayonnaise, sriracha sauce, lime juice and zest. Serve wedges with sauce.

1 wedge: 142 cal., 13g fat (3g sat. fat), 9mg chol., 274mg sod., 3g carb. (1g sugars, 2g fiber), 3g pro.

MAKEOVER MANICOTTI CREPES

—Christine Rukavena, Editor

Prep: 1½ hours + simmering • **Bake:** 35 min.
Makes: 10 servings

- 1 can (28 oz.) whole tomatoes, undrained
- 1½ cups water
- 1 can (8 oz.) tomato sauce
- 3 tsp. sugar
- 1 tsp. dried oregano
- ¼ tsp. celery salt

CREPES
- 2 large eggs
- 1 cup egg substitute
- 1¾ cups fat-free milk
- 1 tsp. canola oil
- 1½ cups all-purpose flour
- ¼ tsp. salt

FILLING
- 3 slices whole wheat bread, cubed
- ½ cup fat-free milk
- ¼ cup egg substitute
- 1 cup finely chopped green pepper
- 3 Tbsp. minced fresh parsley
- 2 garlic cloves, minced
- 1 tsp. salt
- 1 tsp. pepper
- 1 lb. lean ground beef (90% lean)
- ½ lb. Italian turkey sausage links, casings removed
- 1 cup shredded part-skim mozzarella cheese
- ¼ cup shredded Parmesan cheese

1. For sauce, place tomatoes in a blender; cover and process until smooth. Transfer to a large saucepan; add the water, tomato sauce, sugar, oregano and celery salt. Bring to a boil. Reduce the heat; gently simmer, uncovered, for 2 hours or until reduced to 4½ cups, stirring occasionally.

2. Meanwhile, for crepes, beat eggs, egg substitute, milk and oil in a bowl. Combine flour and salt; add egg mixture and stir until smooth. Cover and refrigerate for 1 hour.

3. For filling, in a large bowl, soak bread in milk for 5 minutes. Stir in the egg substitute, green pepper, parsley, garlic, salt and pepper. Crumble beef and sausage over mixture and mix well. Stir in mozzarella. Cover and refrigerate until assembling.

4. Coat an 8-in. nonstick skillet with cooking spray; heat. Stir crepe batter; pour 3 Tbsp. into center of skillet. Lift and tilt pan to coat

bottom evenly. Cook until top appears dry; turn and cook 15-20 seconds longer. Remove to a wire rack. Repeat with remaining batter, coating skillet with cooking spray as needed. When cool, stack crepes with waxed paper or paper towels in between.

5. Spread about ¼ cup filling down the center of each crepe; roll up and place in a 13x9-in. baking dish and an 11x7-in. baking dish coated with cooking spray. Spoon sauce over top; sprinkle with Parmesan cheese.

6. Cover and bake at 350° for 35-45 minutes or until a thermometer reads 160°

2 crepes: 319 cal., 10g fat (4g sat. fat), 91mg chol., 977mg sod., 30g carb. (8g sugars, 2g fiber), 26g pro. **Diabetic exchanges:** 3 medium-fat meat, 1½ starch, 1 vegetable.

DISHING WITH

Christine Rukavena
Editor

Looking for something special tonight? Try my light twist on traditional manicotti. You'll love the fresh aroma of green pepper and garlic as it bakes.

CHOCOLATE
BABKA

CHOCOLATE BABKA
—Lisa Kaminski, Associate Digital Editor

- -

Prep: 20 min. + chilling
Bake: 35 min. + cooling
Makes: 2 loaves (16 slices each)

4¼ to 4¾ cups all-purpose flour
½ cup sugar
2½ tsp. quick-rise yeast
¾ tsp. salt
⅔ cup butter
½ cup water
3 large eggs plus 1 large egg yolk, room temperature, beaten
2 Tbsp. grated orange zest

FILLING
½ cup butter, cubed
5 oz. dark chocolate chips
½ cup confectioners' sugar
⅓ cup baking cocoa
¼ tsp. salt

GLAZE
¼ cup sugar
¼ cup water

1. In a large bowl, mix 2 cups flour, sugar, yeast and salt. Cut in butter until crumbly. In a small saucepan, heat water to 120°-130°; stir into dry ingredients. Stir in eggs and yolk, orange zest and enough remaining flour to form a soft dough (dough will be sticky).

2. Turn dough onto a floured surface; knead until smooth and elastic, 6-8 minutes. Place in a greased bowl, turning once to grease the top. Cover dough and refrigerate 8 hours or overnight.

3. Turn out dough onto a lightly floured surface; divide in half. Roll each half into a 12x10-in. rectangle. For the filling, in a microwave, melt butter and chocolate chips; stir until smooth. Stir in confectioners' sugar, cocoa and salt. Spread filling to within ½ in. of edges. Roll up jelly-roll style, starting with a long side; pinch seam and ends to seal.

4. Using a sharp knife, cut each roll lengthwise in half; carefully turn each half cut side up. Loosely twist strips around each other, keeping cut surfaces facing up; pinch ends together to seal. Place in 2 greased 9x5-in. loaf pans, cut side up. Cover with kitchen towels; let rise in a warm place until almost doubled, about 1 hour. Preheat oven to 375°.

5. Bake until golden brown, 35-45 minutes, tenting with foil halfway through baking. Meanwhile, in a saucepan, combine sugar and water; bring to a boil. Reduce heat; simmer, uncovered, 10 minutes. Brush over warm babka. Cool for 10 minutes before removing from pans to wire racks.

1 slice: 181 cal., 9g fat (5g sat. fat), 41mg chol., 136mg sod., 23g carb. (10g sugars, 1g fiber), 3g pro.

DISHING WITH

Lisa Kaminnski
Associate Digital Editor

I love this chocolate babka. It's a rewarding recipe for taking the next step in your bread baking. Even if it's slightly imperfect going into the oven, it turns out gorgeous. Look at those swirls!

MAKEOVER CHEDDAR BISCUITS

These biscuits have a cheesy richness that everyone will love. I serve them with bowls of steaming chili or a hearty beef soup.
—Alicia Rooker, Recipe Editor/Tester

Takes: 30 min. • **Makes:** 15 biscuits

1	cup all-purpose flour
1	cup cake flour
1½	tsp. baking powder
¾	tsp. salt
½	tsp. garlic powder, divided
¼	tsp. baking soda
4	Tbsp. cold butter, divided
⅓	cup finely shredded cheddar cheese
1	cup buttermilk
½	tsp. dried parsley flakes

1. In a large bowl, combine the flours, baking powder, salt, ¼ tsp. garlic powder and baking soda. Cut in 3 Tbsp. butter until the mixture resembles coarse crumbs; add cheese. Stir in buttermilk just until moistened.
2. Drop by 2 tablespoonfuls 2 in. apart onto baking sheets coated with cooking spray. Bake at 425° until golden brown, 10-12 minutes. Melt remaining butter; stir in parsley and remaining garlic powder. Brush over biscuits. Serve warm.
1 biscuit: 106 cal., 4g fat (3g sat. fat), 11mg chol., 233mg sod., 14g carb. (1g sugars, 0 fiber), 3g pro.

BEST VANILLA BUTTERCREAM

With its powerfully decadent vanilla bean flavor and delightfully creamy texture, your family and friends will scrape every last bit of this frosting off their plates.
—Margaret Knoebel, Culinary Assistant

Prep: 30 min. + cooling • **Makes:** 5 cups

6	oz. white baking chips
¼	cup heavy whipping cream
1	Tbsp. vanilla bean paste
1	Tbsp. vanilla extract
6	large egg whites, room temperature
1½	cups sugar
½	tsp. cream of tartar
½	tsp. salt
2	cups unsalted butter, cubed

1. In a microwave, melt white baking chips with cream until smooth, stirring every 30 seconds. Stir in the vanilla bean paste and extract. Set aside to cool slightly. Meanwhile, in a heatproof bowl of a stand mixer, whisk egg whites, sugar, cream of tartar and salt until blended. Place over simmering water in a large saucepan over medium heat. Whisking constantly, heat mixture until a thermometer reads 160°, 8-10 minutes.
2. Remove from the heat. With whisk attachment of stand mixer, beat on high speed until cooled to 90°, about 7 minutes. Gradually beat in butter, a few tablespoons at a time, on medium speed until smooth. Beat in the cooled baking chip mixture until blended.
2 Tbsp.: 144 cal., 11g fat (7g sat. fat), 27mg chol., 43mg sod., 10g carb. (10g sugars, 0 fiber), 1g pro.

BEST VANILLA BUTTERCREAM

DISHING WITH

Josh Rink
Food Stylist

What makes this recipe so
unique is the slow overnight
fermentation of the dough. The
flour has time to hydrate and
relax, which makes the dough
so much easier to roll out.

THE BEST SAUSAGE PIZZAS
—Josh Rink, Food Stylist

Prep: 30 min. • **Bake:** 15 min.
Makes: 2 pizzas (8 slices each)

- 1 lb. bulk Italian sausage
- 1 batch Best Pizza Dough (recipe at right)
- 1 cup pizza sauce
- 4 cups shredded part-skim mozzarella cheese
- 1 medium red onion, sliced
- 1 medium green pepper, chopped
- 2 cups sliced fresh mushrooms
   Optional: Grated Parmesan cheese, crushed red pepper flakes and fresh oregano leaves

1. Divide dough in half. With greased fingers, pat each half onto an ungreased 12-in. pizza pan. Prick dough thoroughly with a fork. Bake at 400° until lightly browned, 10-12 minutes. Meanwhile, in a large skillet, cook the sausage over medium heat until no longer pink; drain.
2. Spread pizza sauce over crusts. Top with cheese, onion, green pepper, mushrooms and sausage. Bake at 400° until top is golden brown and cheese is bubbly, 12-15 minutes. If desired, top pizzas with grated Parmesan cheese, crushed red pepper flakes and fresh oregano leaves.
Freeze option: Wrap unbaked pizzas and freeze for up to 2 months. To use, unwrap and place on pizza pans; thaw in the refrigerator. Bake at 400° until crust is golden brown, 18-22 minutes.
1 slice: 344 cal., 20g fat (7g sat. fat), 41mg chol., 651mg sod., 26g carb. (2g sugars, 1g fiber), 15g pro.

TEST KITCHEN TIP
Too much sauce or cheese can add excess moisture to your pizza dough while baking. That means your crust will be soft and soggy instead of crisp. You should still be able to see dough after spreading on the sauce. And we recommend not using more than 2 cups of cheese.

THE BEST
PIZZA DOUGH

THE BEST PIZZA DOUGH
This dough is the key to an extraordinary homemade pizza. Using double zero flour—ultra refined flour—will take your crust to the next level. It can be hard to find, but you can usually score it at Italian grocery stores or online. If you're not able to find it, all-purpose flour works fine, too. Either way, you won't be disappointed with the results!
—Josh Rink, Food Stylist

Prep: 30 min. + chilling
Makes: 2 crusts (8 servings each)

- 1¼ cups warm water (110° to 115°)
- 2 tsp. sugar, divided
- 1 pkg. (¼ oz.) active dry yeast
- 3½ to 4 cups all-purpose or 00 flour
- 1 tsp. sea salt
- 1 tsp. each dried basil, oregano and marjoram, optional
- ⅓ cup vegetable or olive oil

1. In a small bowl, mix warm water and 1 tsp. sugar; add yeast and whisk until dissolved. Let stand until bubbles form on surface. In a large bowl, whisk 3 cups flour, salt, remaining 1 tsp. sugar and, if desired, dried herbs. Make a well in center; add yeast mixture and oil. Stir until smooth. Add enough remaining flour to form a soft dough.
2. Turn onto a floured surface; knead, adding more flour to surface as needed until no longer sticky and dough is smooth and elastic, 6-8 minutes. Place in a large greased bowl; turn once to grease top. Cover and let rise in a warm place for 30 minutes; transfer bowl to refrigerator and chill overnight. Allow dough to come to room temperature, about 30 minutes, before rolling.
1 piece: 144 cal., 5g fat (1g sat. fat), 0 chol., 121mg sod., 22g carb. (1g sugars, 1g fiber), 3g pro.

HOT SHRIMP DIP
PAGE 28

Snacks

We have our fair share of snack attacks! Here are some of our favorite ways to indulge a craving. These bite-sized appetizers and finger foods, including dips, sliders, meatballs and other tasty nibblers, always hit the spot.

FRESH SHRIMP
& AVOCADO NACHOS

FRESH SHRIMP & AVOCADO NACHOS

I'm a fan of shrimp, and my family loves nachos. When I combined those favorites and added fresh avocado, the result was a cool yet satisfying snack.
—Teri Rasey, Cadillac, MI

- -

Prep: 30 min. + chilling • **Makes:** 10 servings

- 4 plum tomatoes, chopped
- 3 tomatillos, husked and chopped
- 4 jalapeno peppers, seeded and finely chopped
- 1 small onion, chopped
- 2 garlic cloves, minced
- ¼ cup minced fresh cilantro
- 3 Tbsp. olive oil
- 2 Tbsp. seasoned rice vinegar
- 1 Tbsp. lime juice
- 1½ tsp. sea salt
- ½ tsp. dried oregano
- 1 lb. peeled and deveined cooked shrimp (31-40 per lb.), coarsely chopped

TOPPING
- 2 medium ripe avocados, peeled and pitted, divided
- ½ cup sour cream
- 2 Tbsp. lime juice
- 8 cups tortilla chips
- 1 cup shredded lettuce

1. In a large bowl, combine the first 11 ingredients. Cover and refrigerate until chilled, at least 30 minutes. Stir in shrimp.
2. For avocado cream, mash 1 avocado with sour cream and 1 Tbsp. lime juice until smooth. Cube remaining avocado and toss with remaining lime juice.
3. To serve, arrange chips on a large platter. Top with shrimp mixture, cubed avocado, lettuce and avocado cream; serve immediately.
1 serving: 264 cal., 16g fat (3g sat. fat), 72mg chol., 542mg sod., 20g carb. (3g sugars, 3g fiber), 12g pro.

TEST KITCHEN TIP
The tangy, smooth avocado cream also makes a tasty topping for tacos, burritos, quesadillas and even burgers.

SALTY DOG SANGRIA

SALTY DOG SANGRIA

Mix up grapefruit vodka, ginger ale, grapefruit juice, a little wine and simple syrup and what do you get? A perfectly refreshing and beautiful sipper fit for any holiday or special gathering.
—Becky Hardin, St. Peters, MO

- -

Prep: 30 min. + chilling
Makes: 16 servings (3 qt.)

- 1 cup sugar
- 1 cup water
- 2 bottles (750 ml each) rosé wine
- 2 cups ruby red grapefruit juice
- 1 can (12 oz.) ginger ale
- 1 cup ruby red grapefruit-flavored vodka
- Grapefruit slices
- Coarse sea salt and grated grapefruit zest

1. In a small saucepan, bring sugar and water to a boil. Reduce heat; simmer 10 minutes. Cool completely. Transfer to a large pitcher. Stir in the wine, juice, ginger ale, vodka and grapefruit slices. Refrigerate at least 2 hours.
2. Using water, moisten the rims of 16 wine glasses. Mix salt and grapefruit zest on a plate; hold each glass upside down and dip rim into salt mixture. Set aside. Discard remaining salt mixture on plate. Serve sangria in prepared glasses over ice.
¾ cup: 186 cal., 0 fat (0 sat. fat), 0 chol., 2mg sod., 24g carb. (15g sugars, 0 fiber), 0 pro.

SLIM BLOODY MARY DEVILED EGGS

When you're in the mood for some good finger food, try any one of these sinfully delicious variations on deviled eggs. They are a cinch to fill, and make a popular contribution to a potluck or brunch.
—*Taste of Home* Test Kitchen

Takes: 20 min. • **Makes:** 1 dozen

- 6 hard-boiled large eggs
- 3 Tbsp. reduced-fat mayonnaise
- 1 Tbsp. reduced-sodium tomato juice
- ¾ tsp. prepared horseradish
- ¼ tsp. hot pepper sauce
- ⅛ tsp. salt
- ⅛ tsp. pepper
  Crumbled cooked bacon, optional

1. Cut eggs in half lengthwise. Remove yolks; set aside egg whites and 4 yolks (discard remaining yolks or save for another use).
2. In a large bowl, mash reserved yolks. Stir in mayonnaise, tomato juice, horseradish, pepper sauce, salt and pepper. Stuff or pipe into egg whites. If desired, garnish with bacon. Chill until serving.

1 stuffed egg half: 39 cal., 3g fat (1g sat. fat), 70mg chol., 87mg sod., 1g carb. (0 sugars, 0 fiber), 3g pro.

CRANBERRY & BACON SWISS CHEESE DIP

CRANBERRY & BACON SWISS CHEESE DIP

This warm, rich and creamy Swiss cheese dip is guaranteed to please family and friends alike. Served with thin, crunchy slices of French bread, it makes the perfect appetizer—especially since you can prepare it ahead, put in the fridge, and then bake just before you want to serve it.
—Jeanne Holt, Mendota Heights, MN

Prep: 20 min. • **Bake:** 25 min. • **Makes:** 3 cups

- ⅔ cup mayonnaise
- ⅓ cup spreadable chive and onion cream cheese
- 1 Tbsp. stone-ground mustard
- ¼ tsp. garlic pepper blend
- 3 cups shredded Swiss cheese
- 1 pkg. (10 oz.) frozen chopped onions, thawed and patted dry
- 8 pieces ready-to-serve fully cooked bacon, chopped
- ½ cup sliced almonds, divided
- ⅓ cup dried cranberries, chopped
  Slices French bread baguette (¼ in. thick), toasted

1. Preheat oven to 325°. In a large bowl, combine the mayonnaise, cream cheese, mustard and garlic pepper blend. Add the Swiss cheese; mix well. Stir in onions, bacon, ¼ cup almonds and cranberries. Spread into a greased 3-cup baking dish. Sprinkle with the remaining ¼ cup almonds. Place on a baking sheet.
2. Bake, uncovered, until bubbly, 25-30 minutes. Serve warm with baguette slices.

¼ cup: 266 cal., 22g fat (8g sat. fat), 30mg chol., 222mg sod., 8g carb. (5g sugars, 1g fiber), 10g pro.

LAYERED HUMMUS DIP

My love for Greece inspired this fast-to-fix Mediterranean dip. It's great for parties and is a delicious way to include garden-fresh veggies on your menu.

—Cheryl Snavely, Hagerstown, MD

Takes: 15 min. • **Makes:** 12 servings

- 1 carton (10 oz.) hummus
- ¼ cup finely chopped red onion
- ½ cup Greek olives, chopped
- 2 medium tomatoes, seeded and chopped
- 1 large English cucumber, chopped
- 1 cup crumbled feta cheese
  Baked pita chips

Spread hummus into a shallow 10-in. round dish. Layer with onion, olives, tomatoes, cucumber and cheese. Refrigerate until serving. Serve with pita chips.

1 serving: 88 cal., 5g fat (2g sat. fat), 5mg chol., 275mg sod., 6g carb. (1g sugars, 2g fiber), 4g pro.

> "I love this dip and always have the ingredients on hand. It's my go-to snack or dinner when my kids and husband are busy, and I have the house to myself."
>
> —RAEANN THOMPSON, SENIOR ART DIRECTOR

FRIED CHICKEN & PULLED PORK CORNBREAD POPPERS

These fun little apps are an instant conversation starter wherever they're served. We love them on game day, but they'd be a hit at brunch, too.

—Crystal Schlueter, Northglenn, CO

Takes: 25 min. • **Makes:** 2 dozen

- 2 oz. frozen popcorn chicken
- 1 pkg. (8½ oz.) cornbread/muffin mix
- 4 seeded jalapeno peppers or pickled jalapeno peppers, cut into 6 slices each
- ¼ cup refrigerated fully cooked barbecued pulled pork
- ½ cup maple syrup or honey
- 1 tsp. Sriracha chili sauce, optional

1. Preheat oven to 400°. Bake popcorn chicken according to package directions. When cool enough to handle, cut chicken into 12 pieces.

2. Meanwhile, prepare cornbread mix according to package directions. Place a jalapeno slice in each of 24 foil-lined mini muffin cups. Fill each cup with 1 Tbsp. batter. Gently press a piece of popcorn chicken into the centers of half the cups. Spoon 1 tsp. pulled pork into the centers of remaining cups.

3. Bake until poppers are golden brown, about 12 minutes. Serve with maple syrup; if desired, whisk chili sauce into syrup.

1 mini muffin: 74 cal., 2g fat (1g sat. fat), 10mg chol., 120mg sod., 13g carb. (7g sugars, 1g fiber), 2g pro.

LAYERED HUMMUS DIP

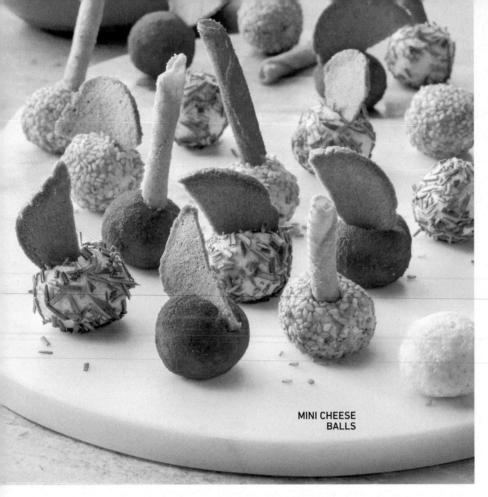

MINI CHEESE
BALLS

HOT SHRIMP DIP

I came across a similar recipe that called for crawfish, and it sounded delicious. We don't have a lot of crawfish available in my area and I'm a big fan of shrimp, so I used that instead. It's become a family favorite and I can guarantee there will be no leftovers!
—Jill Burwell, Renton, WA

- -

Takes: 25 min. • **Makes:** 4 cups

½ cup butter, cubed
8 green onions, thinly sliced
1 small green pepper, finely chopped
1 lb. peeled and deveined cooked shrimp (61-70 per lb.)
1 jar (4 oz.) diced pimientos, drained
2 garlic cloves, minced
2 tsp. Creole seasoning
1 pkg. (8 oz.) cream cheese, cubed
    Chopped fresh parsley
    French bread baguette slices or assorted crackers

In a Dutch oven, melt butter over medium heat. Add green onions and green pepper; cook and stir until tender, 3-4 minutes. Add the shrimp, pimientos, garlic and Creole seasoning. Cook and stir until heated through. Stir in cream cheese until melted; sprinkle with parsley. Serve with baguette slices or crackers.
¼ cup: 136 cal., 11g fat (7g sat. fat), 73mg chol., 217mg sod., 2g carb. (1g sugars, 0 fiber), 7g pro.

MINI CHEESE BALLS

These mini cheese balls are the perfect quick appetizer for any party. For even more flavor, roll them in toasted sesame seeds, fresh rosemary and/or paprika.
—Judy Spivey, Ennice, NC

- -

Prep: 30 min. + chilling
Makes: 36 cheese balls

1 pkg. (8 oz.) cream cheese, softened
2 cups shredded sharp cheddar cheese
    Optional toppings: Toasted sesame seeds, minced fresh rosemary and paprika
    Optional garnishes: Halved rye crisps and rolled tortilla chips

In a large bowl, combine cheeses. Shape into 36 balls; roll balls in toppings as desired. Cover and refrigerate balls for 8 hours or overnight. To serve, if desired, press a rye crisp or rolled corn chip into the top of each cheese ball.
1 cheese ball: 47 cal., 4g fat (2g sat. fat), 13mg chol., 61mg sod., 1g carb. (0 sugars, 0 fiber), 2g pro.

BEER DIP

Ranch dressing mix and beer flavor this fast dip packed with shredded cheese. Once you start eating it, you can't stop!
—Michelle Long, New Castle, CO

- -

Takes: 5 min. • **Makes:** 3½ cups

2 pkg. (8 oz. each) cream cheese, softened
⅓ cup beer or nonalcoholic beer
1 envelope ranch salad dressing mix
2 cups shredded cheddar cheese
    Pretzels

In a large bowl, beat the cream cheese, beer and dressing mix until smooth. Stir in cheddar cheese. Serve with pretzels.
2 Tbsp.: 89 cal., 8g fat (5g sat. fat), 26mg chol., 177mg sod., 1g carb. (0 sugars, 0 fiber), 3g pro.

TEST KITCHEN TIP
This dip has a little heat from the Creole seasoning—a blend of pepper, garlic powder, onion powder and dried herbs—but if you want to make it even spicier, add your favorite hot sauce and a little bit of acidity with a squeeze of fresh lemon juice.

HOT
SHRIMP DIP

CASHEW CHEESE

Spread this vegan cashew cheese on your favorite crackers or a toasted bagel, or serve it with fresh vegetables. It also makes a delicious, out-of-the-ordinary sandwich spread. Even non-vegans love it!
—*Taste of Home* Test Kitchen

- -

Prep: 1 hour + chilling • **Makes:** ¾ cup

- 1 cup raw cashews
- ⅓ cup water
- 2 Tbsp. nutritional yeast
- 2 tsp. lemon juice
- ½ tsp. salt
- ⅛ tsp. garlic powder

Place cashews in a small bowl. Add enough warm water to cover completely. Soak cashews for 1-2 hours; drain and discard water. Add cashews and the remaining ingredients to food processor. Cover and process until smooth, 1-2 minutes, scraping down sides occasionally. Transfer to serving dish. Cover and refrigerate for at least 1 hour before serving.

1 Tbsp.: 56 cal., 4g fat (1g sat. fat), 0 chol., 101mg sod., 3g carb. (1g sugars, 0 fiber), 2g pro. **Diabetic exchanges:** 1 fat.

ASK SARAH

WHAT IS CASHEW CHEESE?

Cashew cheese is a non-dairy, vegan substitute for cheese. It is typically made of blended cashews, nutritional yeast, water and a blend of seasonings. You can use cashew cheese for vegan mac and cheese, as a cheese spread for crackers or even as a substitute for cheesy vegetable soup.

CASHEW CHEESE

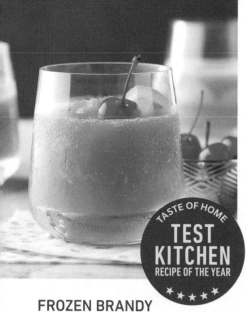

id="2" details="An image of a frozen brandy old-fashioned cocktail in a glass with a cherry on top, set on a light-colored surface with other glasses in the background. A round badge in the bottom right of the image reads 'TASTE OF HOME TEST KITCHEN RECIPE OF THE YEAR' with five stars below.">

TASTE OF HOME

TEST KITCHEN
RECIPE OF THE YEAR
★ ★ ★ ★ ★

FROZEN BRANDY OLD-FASHIONEDS

Both sides of my family are Midwestern, so our strong brandy tradition is evident in the slush we make for the holidays and in the Wisconsin old-fashioned cocktails we enjoy year-round. I decided to combine those recipes into something completely new. This goes very quickly at gatherings!
—Stephanie Vaughan, Madison, WI

Prep: 15 min. + freezing
Makes: 12 servings (about 2½ qt. slush mix)

- 6 cups water
- 1 cup sugar
- 2 cups brandy
- 1 can (12 oz.) frozen orange juice concentrate, thawed
- ¼ cup maraschino cherry juice
- ¼ cup bitters

EACH SERVING
- ¼ cup lemon-lime soda, chilled
  Optional: Maraschino cherries and orange wedges

1. In a large saucepan, bring water and sugar to a boil. Cook and stir until the sugar is dissolved; cool completely. Stir in brandy, orange juice concentrate, juice and bitters. Pour into a 3-qt. freezer container. Freeze overnight or until set.
2. For each serving, scoop ¾ cup slush into a rocks glass. Pour lemon-lime soda into the glass; serve with fruit as desired.
1 serving: 246 cal., 0 fat (0 sat. fat), 0 chol., 9mg sod., 38g carb. (32g sugars, 0 fiber), 1g pro.

FRIED LEMON-PEPPER WINGS

These lemon-pepper wings are perfect for game day. Try these out if you've been stuck in a chicken wing rut. Add grated lemon zest to the butter mixture if you want a more pronounced lemon flavor.
—*Taste of Home* Test Kitchen

Prep: 20 min. • **Cook:** 10 min./batch
Makes: 2 dozen

- 2½ lbs. chicken wings
- ½ cup all-purpose flour
- 2 tsp. salt
- ¼ tsp. pepper
  Oil for deep-fat frying
- 2 Tbsp. butter, melted
- 1½ tsp. lemon-pepper seasoning
- 2 Tbsp. minced fresh parsley

1. Cut wings into 3 sections; discard wing tip sections. In a large bowl, combine flour, salt and pepper. Add wings, a few at a time, and toss to coat.
2. In an electric skillet or deep fryer, heat oil to 375°. Fry wings, a few at a time, until no longer pink, 3-4 minutes on each side. Drain on paper towels. In a large bowl, combine butter and lemon-pepper seasoning. Add wings; toss to coat. Sprinkle with parsley. Serve immediately.
1 piece: 107 cal., 9g fat (2g sat. fat), 18mg chol., 92mg sod., 1g carb. (0 sugars, 0 fiber), 5g pro.

FRIED LEMON-PEPPER WINGS

id="1" details="A black-and-white photograph of fried lemon-pepper chicken wings piled in a black wire basket lined with a checkered cloth napkin. A white dish with herb garnish is partially visible in the top right corner.">

CHILLED PEA SOUP SHOOTERS

Enjoy pea soup in a whole new way! The garnish is curried crab, which will catch everyone by surprise.
—*Taste of Home* Test Kitchen

Prep: 20 min. + chilling • **Makes:** 2 dozen

- 1 pkg. (16 oz.) frozen peas, thawed
- 1 cup chicken broth
- ¼ cup minced fresh mint
- 1 Tbsp. lime juice
- 1 tsp. ground cumin
- ¼ tsp. salt
- 1½ cups plain yogurt

CURRIED CRAB

- 2 Tbsp. minced fresh mint
- 4 tsp. lime juice
- 4 tsp. canola oil
- 2 tsp. red curry paste
- ⅛ tsp. salt
- 1 cup lump crabmeat, drained

1. Place the peas, broth, mint, lime juice, cumin and salt in a blender. Cover and process until smooth. Add yogurt; process until blended. Refrigerate for at least 1 hour.
2. Meanwhile, in a small bowl, whisk the mint, lime juice, oil, curry paste and salt. Add crabmeat; toss gently to coat. Chill until serving.
3. To serve, pour soup into shot glasses; garnish with crab mixture.
1 serving: 40 cal., 1g fat (0 sat. fat), 20mg chol., 216mg sod., 4g carb. (2g sugars, 1g fiber), 3g pro. **Diabetic exchanges:** ½ starch.

MUSHROOM & OLIVE BRUSCHETTA

MUSHROOM & OLIVE BRUSCHETTA

I tried this delicious bruschetta toast at a party and knew I had to make it myself. I couldn't find the person who brought the dish, so I duplicated the recipe on my own. The original was made on an English muffin, but party rye or baguette slices work, too.
—Lynne German, Buford, GA

Prep: 15 min. • **Bake:** 10 min.
Makes: 4 dozen

- 1½ cups finely shredded cheddar cheese
- ½ cup canned mushroom stems and pieces, drained and chopped
- ½ cup chopped green onions
- ½ cup chopped pitted green olives
- ½ cup chopped ripe olives
- ½ cup mayonnaise
- ¼ tsp. curry powder
- 2 French bread baguettes (10½ oz. each), cut into ½-in. slices
  Julienned green onions, optional

1. Preheat oven to 400°. In a large bowl, combine the first 7 ingredients. Cut each baguette into 24 slices; place on ungreased baking sheets. Bake 5 minutes, or until bread is lightly toasted.
2. Top with cheese mixture. Bake until the cheese is melted, 4-5 minutes. If desired, top with julienned green onions.
Freeze option: Cover and freeze unbaked topped baguette slices on a parchment-lined baking sheet until firm. Transfer to a freezer container; return to freezer. To use, bake baguette slices on ungreased baking sheets in a preheated 400° oven until heated through, 8-10 minutes.
1 appetizer: 66 cal., 3g fat (1g sat. fat), 4mg chol., 161mg sod., 7g carb. (0 sugars, 0 fiber), 2g pro.

ORANGE-FENNEL SALSA

I love salsa! Enjoy this citrus variation with tortilla chips or serve as a garnish with your favorite meat. Its sweet and tangy flavor profile goes well with ham, pork and poultry
—Nancy Heishman, Las Vegas, NV

- -

Prep: 20 min. + chilling • **Makes:** 3 cups

- 3 large navel oranges
- 1 medium fennel bulb, finely chopped plus 1 Tbsp. chopped fennel fronds
- ½ cup finely chopped red onion
- ⅓ cup minced fresh cilantro
- 1 jalapeno pepper, seeded and finely chopped
- 4 large fresh basil leaves, finely chopped
- 2 tsp. rice vinegar
- 2 tsp. olive oil
- ¼ tsp. garlic salt

1. Cut a thin slice from the top and bottom of each orange; stand orange upright on a cutting board. With a knife, cut off peel and outer membrane from orange. Working over a bowl to catch the juices, cut along the membrane of each segment to remove fruit. Finely chop the oranges; add to bowl with reserved juices.
2. Add remaining ingredients; toss to coat. Refrigerate, covered, until serving.
½ cup: 77 cal., 2g fat (0 sat. fat), 0 chol., 130mg sod., 16g carb. (11g sugars, 4g fiber), 2g pro.

ORANGE-FENNEL SALSA

CRUDITE DIP

To bring out this dip's tangy flavor, chill it before serving. This will allow the flavors time to blend.
—*Taste of Home* Test Kitchen

- -

Prep: 5 min. + chilling • **Makes:** 1½ cups

- 1 cup sour cream
- ½ cup mayonnaise
- 2 green onions, finely chopped
- 1 Tbsp. lemon juice
- 1 Tbsp. minced fresh parsley
- 1 tsp. dill weed
- 1 garlic clove, minced
- ½ tsp. seasoned salt
- ⅛ tsp. pepper
  Assorted fresh vegetables

Combine the first 9 ingredients; mix well. Cover and refrigerate at least 2 hours. If desired, sprinkle with additional parsley. Serve with vegetables.
2 Tbsp.: 102 cal., 11g fat (3g sat. fat), 5mg chol., 117mg sod., 1g carb. (1g sugars, 0 fiber), 1g pro.

TEST KITCHEN TIP

Crudites are traditional French appetizers—raw, crisp veggies paired with a dipping sauce like this tangy, sour cream-based dip. Crudites are a simple and speedy appetizer for small and large groups alike.

BANH MI SKEWERS

I love banh mi sandwiches but wanted to make them a little easier to serve for a party. These skewers are a fun twist. For simple prep on the day of the party, make the meatballs in advance and freeze them.
—Elisabeth Larsen, Pleasant Grove, UT

Prep: 45 min. + chilling • **Cook:** 10 min./batch
Makes: 12 servings

- 1   cup white vinegar or rice vinegar
- ¼   cup sugar
- ½   tsp. salt
- 1   English cucumber, thinly sliced
- 2   medium carrots, thinly sliced
- 4   radishes, thinly sliced
- 1   cup mayonnaise
- 1   Tbsp. Sriracha chili sauce
- 2   Tbsp. minced fresh cilantro
- 2   green onions, thinly sliced
- 1   Tbsp. soy sauce
- 1   garlic clove, minced
- ¼   tsp. cayenne pepper
- 1½ lbs. ground pork
- 2   Tbsp. canola oil
- 1   French bread baguette
      (10½ oz.), cut into 24 slices

1. In a large bowl, combine vinegar, sugar and salt; whisk until sugar is dissolved. Add the cucumber, carrots and radishes; let stand until serving. Combine mayonnaise and chili sauce; refrigerate until serving.
2. In another large bowl, combine cilantro, green onions, soy sauce, garlic and cayenne. Add pork; mix lightly but thoroughly. Shape into 36 balls.
3. In a large skillet, heat oil over medium heat. Cook meatballs in batches until cooked through, turning occasionally.
4. Drain vegetable mixture. On 12 metal or wooden skewers, alternately thread the vegetables, meatballs and baguette slices. Serve with Sriracha mayonnaise.
1 skewer with about 1 Tbsp. sauce: 336 cal., 24g fat (5g sat. fat), 39mg chol., 416mg sod., 16g carb. (2g sugars, 1g fiber), 13g pro.

TOMATO
FRITTERS

TOMATO FRITTERS

A friend gave me the basic recipe for these fritters, then I tweaked it for my family's tastes. It's one of our favorite snacks in the summer. We love them right after they've been fried, when they're still hot and crispy.
—Pam Halter, Bridgeton, NJ

Prep: 15 min. • **Cook:** 5 min./batch
Makes: about 2½ dozen

- 1   cup all-purpose flour
- 1   tsp. baking powder
- ½   tsp. salt
       Dash dried basil
       Dash dried oregano
       Dash pepper
- 1   large tomato, finely chopped
- ½   cup chopped onion
- ½   cup shredded Parmesan cheese
- 1   jalapeno pepper, seeded
       and finely chopped
- 1   garlic clove, minced
- 1   to 6 Tbsp. water, optional
       Oil for deep-fat frying

1. In a large bowl, whisk flour, baking powder, salt, basil, oregano and pepper. Gently stir in tomato, onion, cheese, jalapeno and garlic just until moistened. If the batter seems thick, add water 1 Tbsp. at a time to thin it slightly until it loosens up and mixes easily.
2. In a cast-iron or other heavy skillet, heat oil to 375°. Drop the batter by rounded tablespoonfuls, a few at a time, into hot oil. Fry until golden brown, about 1½ minutes per side. Drain on paper towels.
1 fritter: 40 cal., 2g fat (0 sat. fat), 1mg chol., 79mg sod., 4g carb. (0 sugars, 0 fiber), 1g pro.

TEST KITCHEN TIP
The water in this recipe is optional. It will depend on how ripe and juicy your tomatoes are. Fry 1 fritter as a test. If the middle is still undercooked when the exterior is golden brown, add some water to the batter to loosen it and make a slightly thinner fritter.

EASY PUPPY CHOW

This simple version of everyone's favorite sweet-salty snack mix uses a whole box of cereal, so there's less measuring. And there's enough to feed a hungry crowd.
—*Taste of Home* Test Kitchen

Takes: 15 min. • **Makes:** 13 cups

- 1   box (12 oz.) Corn Chex
- 2   cups semisweet chocolate chips
- ¾   cup creamy peanut butter
- ⅓   cup butter, cubed
- 3   cups confectioners' sugar

1. Pour cereal into a very large bowl. In a large microwave-safe bowl, combine the chocolate chips, peanut butter and butter. Microwave on high 30 seconds. Stir gently. Continue microwaving on high, stirring every 30 seconds, until melted and blended. Pour over cereal; gently stir to coat.

2. In batches, place confectioners' sugar in a gallon-sized bag, add cereal mixture and shake until well coated. Spread cereal out on a baking sheet. Let stand until set. Store in airtight containers.

½ cup: 229 cal., 10g fat (5g sat. fat), 6mg chol., 146mg sod., 35g carb. (23g sugars, 2g fiber), 3g pro.

MAPLE PULLED PORK BUNS

MAPLE PULLED PORK BUNS

Maple syrup is my sweet secret to these irresistible buns. Slow-cooking the flavor-packed pork couldn't be easier, and the buns are quick to roll up. We love them for parties—they serve a packed house.
—Rashanda Cobbins, Food Editor

Prep: 25 min. + rising • **Cook:** 5½ hours
Makes: 16 servings

- 1   boneless pork shoulder butt roast (2½ lbs.)
- 1½ tsp. ground mustard
- 1   tsp. salt
- ½   tsp. cayenne pepper
- ½   tsp. ground ginger
- 1   cup thinly sliced onion
- 2   garlic cloves, peeled
- 1   cup maple syrup, divided
- ½   cup water
- 3   Tbsp. cider vinegar
- 2   loaves (1 lb. each) frozen bread dough, thawed
- 1   cup barbecue sauce
- 1   cup shredded pepper jack cheese
      Chopped green onions and crushed red pepper flakes

1. Season pork with mustard, salt, cayenne pepper and ginger; place in a 4-qt. slow cooker. Top with onion and garlic; pour in ½ cup maple syrup, water and cider vinegar. Cook, covered, on low 5-7 hours or until meat is tender. Shred meat with 2 forks; discard cooking liquid and vegetables.

2. On a lightly floured surface, roll 1 loaf of dough into a 16x10-in. rectangle. Combine barbecue sauce with remaining syrup; brush ¼ cup sauce mixture to within ½ in. of dough edges. Top with half of pork. Roll up jelly-roll style, starting with a long side; pinch seam to seal. Cut crosswise into 8 slices. Place in a 9-in. pie plate, cut side down. Repeat with remaining dough and additional pie plate. Cover with kitchen towels; let rise in a warm place until dough doubles, about 1 hour. Reserve remaining sauce mixture. Preheat oven to 400°.

3. Bake until golden brown, about 20 minutes. Sprinkle with cheese and bake until melted, 5-10 minutes longer. Serve with reserved sauce mixture; sprinkle with green onions and red pepper flakes.

1 roll: 358 cal., 12g fat (4g sat. fat), 50mg chol., 727mg sod., 41g carb. (14g sugars, 2g fiber), 20g pro.

CHICKEN PICCATA MEATBALLS

The classic chicken piccata entree is my favorite dish, but I wanted another way to enjoy all the same flavors. These chicken piccata meatballs are the perfect solution, whether served alone or with a sauce like marinara or Buffalo. Serve over buttered noodles for a main dish or stick toothpicks in them for appetizers.
—Dawn Collins, Rowley, MA

Prep: 20 min. • **Cook:** 25 min.
Makes: 2 dozen

- ½   cup dry bread crumbs
- ⅓   cup grated Parmesan cheese
- 1   large egg, lightly beaten
- 1   tsp. garlic powder
- ¼   tsp. salt
- ⅛   tsp. pepper
- 1   lb. ground chicken
- 2   Tbsp. canola oil, divided
- 2   garlic cloves, minced
- ⅓   cup chicken broth
- ¼   cup white wine
- 1   jar (3½ oz.) capers, drained
- 1   Tbsp. lemon juice
- 2   Tbsp. butter
      Shredded Parmesan cheese
      and lemon wedges

1. In a large bowl, combine the first 6 ingredients. Add chicken; mix lightly but thoroughly. With wet hands, shape into 1-in. balls.
2. In a large skillet, heat 1 Tbsp. oil over medium heat. Brown meatballs in batches; drain. Remove and keep warm. In the same skillet, heat remaining 1 Tbsp. oil over medium heat. Add garlic; cook 1 minute.
3. Add broth and wine to pan; increase heat to medium-high. Cook 1 minute, stirring to loosen browned bits from the pan. Add the capers and lemon juice; bring to a boil. Add meatballs. Reduce heat; simmer, uncovered, until the meatballs are cooked through, 5-7 minutes, stirring occasionally. Remove from heat; stir in the butter until melted. Sprinkle with Parmesan cheese and serve with lemon wedges.
1 meatball: 63 cal., 4g fat (1g sat. fat), 24mg chol., 193mg sod., 2g carb. (0 sugars, 0 fiber), 4g pro.

TASTE OF HOME
TEST KITCHEN
RECIPE OF THE YEAR
★ ★ ★ ★ ★

CHICKEN PICCATA MEATBALLS

CHICKEN FRIES

Kid-friendly and quick, these crunchy oven-baked chicken fries are coated with a mixture of crushed potato chips, panko bread crumbs and Parmesan cheese. Dip them in ranch dressing, barbecue sauce or honey-mustard.
—Nick Iverson, Denver, CO

Prep: 20 min. • **Bake:** 15 min.
Makes: 4 servings

- 2   large eggs, lightly beaten
- ½   tsp. salt
- ½   tsp. garlic powder
- ¼   to ½ tsp. cayenne pepper
- 2   cups finely crushed ridged potato chips
- 1   cup panko bread crumbs
- ½   cup grated Parmesan cheese
- 2   boneless skinless chicken breasts (6 oz. each), cut into ¼-in.-thick strips

Preheat oven to 400°. In a shallow bowl, whisk eggs, salt, garlic powder and cayenne. In a separate shallow bowl, combine chips, bread crumbs and cheese. Dip chicken in egg mixture, then in potato chip mixture, patting to help coating adhere. Transfer to a greased wire rack in a foil-lined rimmed baking sheet. Bake until golden brown, 12-15 minutes.
1 serving: 376 cal., 17g fat (6g sat. fat), 149mg chol., 761mg sod., 27g carb. (1g sugars, 2g fiber), 27g pro.

ROASTED BRUSSELS SPROUTS WITH SRIRACHA AIOLI

This dish constantly surprises you—it's crispy, easy to eat, totally shareable and yet it's a vegetable! This recipe is also gluten-free, dairy-free and paleo, and it can be vegan if you use vegan mayo.
—Molly Winsten, Brookline, MA

Prep: 20 min. • **Cook:** 20 min.
Makes: 8 servings

- 1 lb. fresh Brussels sprouts, trimmed and halved
- 2 Tbsp. olive oil
- 2 to 4 tsp. Sriracha chili sauce, divided
- ½ tsp. salt, divided
- ½ tsp. pepper, divided
- ½ cup mayonnaise
- 2 tsp. lime juice
- 1 Tbsp. lemon juice

1. Preheat oven to 425°. Place Brussels sprouts on a rimmed baking sheet. Drizzle with oil and 1 tsp. chili sauce; sprinkle with ¼ tsp. salt and ¼ tsp. pepper. Toss to coat. Roast until crispy, about 20-25 minutes.
2. Meanwhile, mix mayonnaise, lime juice, and the remaining 1-3 tsp. chili sauce, ¼ tsp. salt and ¼ tsp. pepper. Drizzle lemon juice over Brussels sprouts before serving with the aioli.
4 halves with 1 Tbsp. sauce: 146 cal., 14g fat (2g sat. fat), 1mg chol., 310mg sod., 6g carb. (2g sugars, 2g fiber), 2g pro.

CHEESY CARAMELIZED ONION SKILLET BREAD

While this app is perfect for a football game or informal party, it actually came about because I have two sons who are always hungry. I need time to get dinner on the table after coming home from work. They love the skillet bread for the flavor; I love it because it keeps them in the kitchen to chat while I prepare the rest of dinner! If you'd like, you can use homemade biscuits instead of prepared.
—Mary Leverette, Columbia, SC

Prep: 45 min. • **Bake:** 20 min.
Makes: 8 servings

- 2 tsp. caraway seeds
- 1 Tbsp. olive oil
- 1 large onion, chopped
- ¼ tsp. salt
- 1 cup shredded sharp cheddar cheese
- ½ cup butter, melted
- 1 tube (16.3 oz.) large refrigerated buttermilk biscuits
- 1 Tbsp. minced fresh thyme, optional

1. Preheat oven to 350°. In a 10-in. cast-iron or other ovenproof skillet, toast caraway seeds until fragrant, about 1 minute. Remove and set aside.
2. In the same skillet, heat oil over medium heat. Add onion; cook and stir until softened, 5-6 minutes. Reduce heat to medium-low; cook until deep golden brown, 30-40 minutes, stirring occasionally. Stir in salt; remove from the heat and cool slightly.
3. Sprinkle cheese over onions in skillet. Place melted butter and caraway seeds in a shallow bowl. Cut each biscuit into fourths. Dip biscuit pieces in butter mixture; place in a single layer over onion mixture in skillet.
4. Bake until puffed and golden brown, 20-25 minutes. Cool in skillet 5 minutes before inverting onto a serving plate. If desired, sprinkle with thyme. Serve warm.
1 serving: 352 cal., 25g fat (13g sat. fat), 45mg chol., 874mg sod., 27g carb. (4g sugars, 1g fiber), 7g pro.

TOASTED RAVIOLI

While visiting a friend in St. Louis, I ordered toasted ravioli, a local specialty, at almost every restaurant we tried. When I got home, I had replicate the hot, crispy bites. This recipe comes pretty close.
—Cristina Carrera, Kenosha, WI

Prep: 15 min. • **Cook:** 20 min.
Makes: about 1½ dozen

- 1 cup seasoned bread crumbs
- ¼ cup shredded Parmesan cheese
- 2 tsp. dried basil
- 1 cup all-purpose flour
- 2 large eggs, lightly beaten
- 1 pkg. (9 oz.) frozen beef ravioli, thawed
  Oil for deep-fat frying
  Fresh minced basil and additional shredded Parmesan cheese, optional
- 1 cup marinara sauce

1. In a shallow bowl, mix bread crumbs, Parmesan cheese and basil. Place flour and eggs in separate shallow bowls. Dip ravioli in flour to coat both sides; shake off excess. Dip in egg, then in crumb mixture, patting to help coating adhere.
2. In a deep cast-iron or electric skillet, heat ½ in. of oil to 375°. Fry ravioli, a few at a time, until golden brown, 1-2 minutes on each side. Drain on paper towels. If desired, immediately sprinkle with basil and cheese. Serve warm with marinara sauce.
1 piece: 73 cal., 5g fat (1g sat. fat), 6mg chol., 117mg sod., 6g carb. (1g sugars, 1g fiber), 2g pro.

"We host big pasta bar family dinners, and these quick and easy fried ravioli bites make delicious hot appetizers. You can make them in the air fryer, too, if you want to eliminate the oil for a healthier version."

—AMY GLANDER, EDITOR

TOASTED
RAVIOLI

BANG BANG SHRIMP CAKE SLIDERS

My family loves these shrimp sliders. The bang bang slaw dressing and shrimp cake patties can be made ahead. When ready to serve, toss the cabbage slaw and sear the shrimp cakes, then assemble and enjoy.
—Kim Banick, Turner, OR

- -

Prep: 30 min. + chilling • **Cook:** 10 min./batch
Makes: 12 sliders

- 1 lb. uncooked shrimp (41-50 per lb.), peeled and deveined
- 1 large egg, lightly beaten
- ½ cup finely chopped sweet red pepper
- 6 green onions, chopped and divided
- 1 Tbsp. minced fresh gingerroot
- ¼ tsp. salt
- 1 cup panko bread crumbs
- ¼ cup mayonnaise
- 1 Tbsp. Sriracha chili sauce
- 1 Tbsp. sweet chili sauce
- 5 cups shredded Chinese or napa cabbage
- 12 mini buns or dinner rolls
- 3 Tbsp. canola oil
  Additional Sriracha chili sauce, optional

1. Place shrimp in a food processor; pulse until chopped. In a large bowl, combine the egg, red pepper, 4 green onions, ginger and salt. Add the shrimp and bread crumbs; mix gently. Shape into twelve ½-in.-thick patties. Refrigerate 20 minutes.
2. Meanwhile, in a large bowl, combine mayonnaise and the chili sauces; stir in the cabbage and remaining green onions. Place buns on a baking sheet, cut sides up. Broil buns 3-4 in. from heat until golden brown, 2-3 minutes.
3. In a large cast-iron or other heavy skillet, heat oil over medium heat. Add shrimp cakes in batches; cook until golden brown on each side, 4-5 minutes. Serve on toasted buns with slaw; secure with toothpicks. If desired, serve with additional chili sauce.
1 slider: 210 cal., 10g fat (1g sat. fat), 63mg chol., 321mg sod., 20g carb. (3g sugars, 1g fiber), 11g pro.

BANG BANG SHRIMP CAKE SLIDERS

BLT BITES

These hors d'oeuvres may be mini, but their bacon and tomato flavor is full size. I serve them at parties, brunches and picnics, and they're always a hit.
—Kellie Remmen, Detroit Lakes, MN

Prep: 25 min. + chilling
Makes: 16-20 appetizers

- 16 to 20 cherry tomatoes
- 1 lb. sliced bacon, cooked and crumbled
- ½ cup mayonnaise
- ⅓ cup chopped green onions
- 3 Tbsp. grated Parmesan cheese
- 2 Tbsp. snipped fresh parsley

1. Cut a thin slice off each tomato top. Scoop out and discard pulp. Invert the tomatoes on a paper towel to drain.
2. In a small bowl, combine the remaining ingredients. Spoon into cherry tomatoes. Refrigerate for several hours.
1 stuffed tomato: 113 cal., 10g fat (3g sat. fat), 11mg chol., 206mg sod., 1g carb. (1g sugars, 0 fiber), 3g pro.

BAKED ASPARAGUS DIP

Since I'm from Wisconsin, I thought it was only natural to whip up a vegetable and cheese dip—two foods my state produces in abundance.
—Sandra Baratka, Phillips, WI

Takes: 30 min. • **Makes:** about 2 cups

- 1 lb. diced cooked fresh asparagus, drained
- 1 cup grated Parmesan cheese
- 1 cup mayonnaise
  Baked pita chips

In a large bowl, combine the asparagus, cheese and mayonnaise. Place in a 6-in. cast-iron skillet or 2-cup ovenproof bowl. Bake at 375° until heated through, about 20 minutes. Serve warm with pita chips.
2 Tbsp.: 120 cal., 11g fat (2g sat. fat), 5mg chol., 162mg sod., 2g carb. (1g sugars, 0 fiber), 2g pro.

MEATBALLS WITH CHIMICHURRI SAUCE

Serve some of this South American herb sauce featuring fresh cilantro and parsley on the side. You'll want plenty for extra dipping.
—Amy Chase, Vanderhoof, BC

Takes: 30 min.
Makes: about 20 (⅔ cup sauce)

- 1 pkg. (22 oz.) frozen fully cooked Angus beef meatballs
- 3 garlic cloves, peeled
- 1 cup packed Italian flat leaf parsley
- ¼ cup packed fresh cilantro leaves
- 1 tsp. salt
- ¼ tsp. coarsely ground pepper
- 2 Tbsp. red wine vinegar
- ½ cup extra virgin olive oil

1. Prepare beef meatballs according to package directions.
2. Meanwhile, place garlic in a small food processor; pulse until chopped. Add parsley, cilantro, salt and pepper; pulse until finely chopped. Add vinegar. While processing, gradually add oil in a steady stream.
3. In a large bowl, toss meatballs with a little more than half of the chimichurri sauce. Transfer to a platter. Serve with remaining sauce for dipping.
1 meatball with about 2 tsp. sauce: 130 cal., 12g fat (4g sat. fat), 17mg chol., 318mg sod., 2g carb. (0 sugars, 0 fiber), 4g pro.

BAKED ASPARAGUS DIP

LOADED HUEVOS RANCHEROS
WITH ROASTED POBLANO PEPPERS
PAGE 58

Breakfasts

Jump start your day with our favorite breakfast recipes. Whether you're craving something savory or a little sweet, we've got you covered with this nourishing round-up of fluffy golden waffles, comforting egg bakes and other rise-and-shine specialties.

CHILES RELLENOS BREAKFAST BAKE

We love anything with a Southwestern flavor, so I turned classic chiles rellenos into a breakfast casserole. My family became fans in an instant.
—Joan Hallford, North Richland Hills, TX

Prep: 10 min. • **Bake:** 35 min. + standing
Makes: 15 servings

- 1 pkg. (20 oz.) refrigerated shredded hash brown potatoes
- 1 can (27 to 28 oz.) whole green chiles
- 1 cup chunky salsa
- 1 lb. bulk pork sausage or fresh chorizo, cooked, drained and crumbled
- 2 cups shredded Mexican cheese blend
- 6 large eggs
- ½ cup 2% milk
- ¼ tsp. ground cumin
  Salt and pepper to taste
  Optional ingredients: Warm flour tortillas (8 in.), sour cream and salsa

1. Preheat oven to 350°. In a greased 13x9-in. baking dish, layer half the potatoes; all the chiles, opened flat; all the salsa; half the sausage; and half the cheese. Cover with remaining potatoes, sausage and cheese.
2. Beat eggs and milk; add cumin, salt and pepper. Pour over potato mixture.
3. Bake, uncovered, until eggs are set in center, 35-40 minutes. Let stand 15 minutes. If desired, serve with warm tortillas, sour cream and additional salsa.
1 piece: 210 cal., 13g fat (5g sat. fat), 105mg chol., 440mg sod., 11g carb. (3g sugars, 1g fiber), 10g pro.

TEST KITCHEN TIP
To give this breakfast casserole a little more heat, use chorizo instead of bulk pork sausage. Chorizo is a coarsely ground fresh or smoked pork sausage that has Mexican, Spanish and Portuguese origins. Traditionally flavored with paprika or chili powder, which gives it a reddish color, chorizo is often used in egg dishes, soups, casseroles and a variety of Mexican dishes.

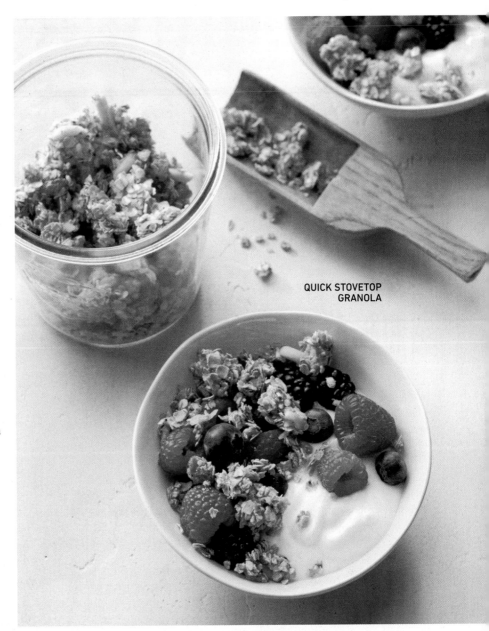

QUICK STOVETOP GRANOLA

QUICK STOVETOP GRANOLA

The fiber-rich oats in this granola will quell your cravings with just a small serving. Sprinkle some over yogurt for a wholesome breakfast or keep some handy in a small airtight container for moments when your tummy starts to grumble.
—*Taste of Home* Test Kitchen

Takes: 15 min. • **Makes:** 3 cups

- 2 cups quick-cooking oats
- 2 Tbsp. brown sugar
- 2 Tbsp. honey
- 1 Tbsp. butter
- ¼ cup slivered almonds
- 2 Tbsp. golden raisins
- 2 Tbsp. sweetened shredded coconut

1. In a large nonstick skillet, toast oats over medium heat until golden brown. Remove and set aside. In the same skillet, cook and stir the brown sugar, honey and butter over medium-low heat until bubbly, 1-2 minutes.
2. Stir in the almonds, raisins, coconut and oats until coated. Cool. Store granola in an airtight container.
¼ cup: 102 cal., 3g fat (1g sat. fat), 3mg chol., 14mg sod., 16g carb. (6g sugars, 2g fiber), 3g pro. **Diabetic exchanges:** 1 starch, ½ fat.

STICKY CINNAMON-SUGAR MONKEY BREAD

You can do all the prep work for this monkey bread the night before. I prepare the dough pieces and put all the sauce ingredients in the pan so it's ready for the morning. If you want a little crunch, sprinkle chopped nuts in with the dough pieces before pouring the sauce on and baking.
—Diana Kunselman, Rimersburg, PA

Prep: 20 min. + rising • **Bake:** 20 min.
Makes: 16 servings

- 2 loaves (1 lb. each) frozen bread dough, thawed
- 1 cup packed brown sugar
- ¾ cup butter, cubed
- 1 pkg. (3 oz.) cook-and-serve vanilla pudding mix
- 2 Tbsp. 2% milk
- 2 tsp. ground cinnamon

1. Cut dough into 1-in. pieces; place in a greased 13x9-in. baking dish. In a large saucepan, combine remaining ingredients; bring to a boil. Cook and stir 1 minute; remove from heat. Pour over dough pieces.
2. Cover loosely with parchment or nonstick foil; let the dough rise in a warm place until almost doubled, about 45 minutes. Preheat oven to 350°. Bake, uncovered, until golden brown, 20-25 minutes. Immediately invert onto a serving plate.
1 serving: 247 cal., 9g fat (4g sat. fat), 18mg chol., 339mg sod., 36g carb. (16g sugars, 2g fiber), 5g pro.

SALMON & ARTICHOKE
QUICHE SQUARES

SALMON & ARTICHOKE QUICHE SQUARES

Salmon, goat cheese and artichoke hearts make this quiche feel a little fancy and taste extra delicious. Baked in an 11x7-inch dish, it comes together in a snap and makes enough to serve a hungry brunch crowd.
—Jeanne Holt, Mendota Heights, MN

Prep: 15 min. • **Bake:** 40 min. + cooling
Makes: 15 servings

- 1 tube (8 oz.) refrigerated crescent rolls
- ⅔ cup shredded Parmesan cheese, divided
- ½ cup crumbled goat cheese
- 1 cup thinly sliced smoked salmon fillets
- 1 cup water-packed artichoke hearts, drained
- ¼ cup chopped green onion (green portion only)
- 2 Tbsp. finely chopped fresh dill
- ¼ tsp. pepper
- 5 large eggs
- 1 cup heavy whipping cream

1. Preheat oven to 350°. Unroll dough into a long rectangle; place in ungreased 11x7-in. baking dish. Press the dough over bottom and up sides of dish, pressing perforations to seal.
2. Sprinkle with ⅓ cup Parmesan cheese. Top with goat cheese, salmon and artichoke hearts. Sprinkle with onion, chopped dill and pepper. Whisk eggs and cream; pour over salmon mixture. Sprinkle with remaining Parmesan cheese.
3. Bake until a knife inserted in the center comes out clean, 40-45 minutes (loosely cover with foil if edges are getting too dark). Cool 20 minutes. Cut into squares.
1 square: 179 cal., 13g fat (7g sat. fat), 89mg chol., 330mg sod., 8g carb. (2g sugars, 0 fiber), 8g pro.

CINNAMON BLUEBERRY FRENCH TOAST

This breakfast can be prepped ahead, which makes it convenient for entertaining. It's a go-to recipe for birthdays or holidays. You can also make it without the blueberries.
—Angela Lively, Conroe, TX

Prep: 15 min. + chilling • **Cook:** 3 hours
Makes: 6 servings

- 3 large eggs
- 2 cups 2% milk
- ¼ cup sugar
- 1 tsp. ground cinnamon
- 1 tsp. vanilla extract
- ¼ tsp. salt
- 9 cups cubed French bread (about 9 oz.)
- 1 cup fresh or frozen blueberries, thawed
  Maple syrup

1. Whisk together the first 6 ingredients. Place half of the bread in a greased 5-qt. slow cooker; top with ½ cup blueberries and half the milk mixture. Repeat layers. Refrigerate, covered, 4 hours or overnight.
2. Cook, covered, on low 3-4 hours or until a knife inserted in the center comes out clean. Serve warm with syrup.
1 cup: 265 cal., 6g fat (2g sat. fat), 100mg chol., 430mg sod., 42g carb. (18g sugars, 2g fiber), 11g pro.

TEST KITCHEN TIP

Swap whole wheat for white French bread to increase fiber. If you can't find it, cube 100% whole wheat buns.

EVERYTHING BREAKFAST SLIDERS

These tasty sliders combine your favorite morning foods into one tasty package.
—Rashanda Cobbins, Food Editor

Prep: 30 min. • **Bake:** 15 min.
Makes: 8 servings

- 8 large eggs
- ¼ cup 2% milk
- 2 green onions, thinly sliced
- ¼ tsp. pepper
- 8 Tbsp. spreadable chive and onion cream cheese
- 8 miniature bagels, split
- 8 slices cheddar cheese, halved
- 8 slices Canadian bacon
- 8 cooked bacon strips, halved

GLAZE

- 2 Tbsp. butter, melted
- 1½ tsp. maple syrup
- ⅛ tsp. garlic powder
- 2 Tbsp. everything seasoning blend

1. Preheat oven to 375°. Heat a large nonstick skillet over medium heat. In a large bowl, whisk eggs, milk, green onions and pepper until blended; pour into skillet. Cook and stir until eggs are thickened and no liquid egg remains; remove from heat.
2. Spread the cream cheese over bagel bottoms; place in a greased 13x9-in. baking dish. Layer each with a half-slice of cheese and Canadian bacon. Spoon scrambled eggs over top. Layer with remaining halved cheese slices, bacon and bagel tops. Stir together butter, maple syrup and garlic powder; brush over bagel tops. Sprinkle with everything seasoning blend.
3. Bake until tops are golden brown and cheese is melted, 12-15 minutes.
1 slider: 415 cal., 26g fat (13g sat. fat), 253mg chol., 1070mg sod., 18g carb. (4g sugars, 1g fiber), 24g pro.

CINNAMON BLUEBERRY FRENCH TOAST

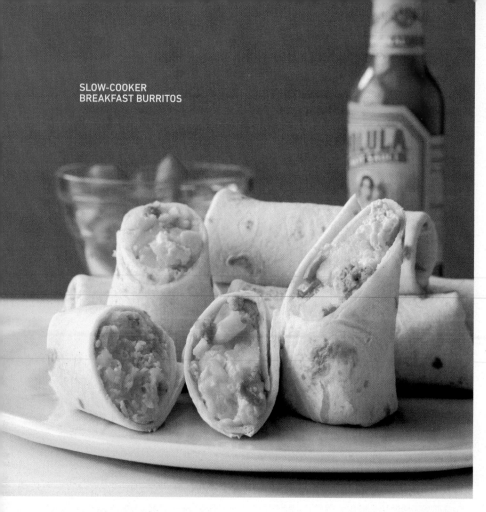

SLOW-COOKER
BREAKFAST BURRITOS

EASY MORNING WAFFLES

The touch of cinnamon in these waffles takes them beyond any store-bought kind.
—*Taste of Home* Test Kitchen

Prep: 20 min. • **Cook:** 5 min./batch
Makes: 14 waffles (1 cup syrup)

- 2 cups all-purpose flour
- 1 Tbsp. brown sugar
- 2 tsp. baking powder
- ½ tsp. salt
- ½ tsp. ground cinnamon
- 3 large eggs, separated, room temperature
- 2 cups 2% milk
- ¼ cup canola oil
- ¾ tsp. vanilla extract

SYRUP
- ½ cup butter, cubed
- ½ cup honey
- 1 tsp. ground cinnamon

1. In a large bowl, combine the flour, brown sugar, baking powder, salt and cinnamon. In a small bowl, whisk the egg yolks, milk, oil and vanilla; stir into dry ingredients just until moistened. In a small bowl, beat egg whites until stiff peaks form; fold into batter.
2. Bake waffles in a preheated waffle maker according to manufacturer's directions until golden brown.
3. In a microwave, melt the butter, honey and cinnamon; stir until smooth. Serve waffles with syrup.

2 waffles: 464 cal., 25g fat (10g sat. fat), 130mg chol., 442mg sod., 53g carb. (26g sugars, 1g fiber), 9g pro.

SLOW-COOKER BREAKFAST BURRITOS

Prep these tasty, hearty burritos the night before for a quick breakfast in the morning, or let them cook while you are away on a weekend afternoon for an easy supper.
—Anna Miller, Churdan, IA

Prep: 25 min. • **Cook:** 3¾ hours + standing
Makes: 12 servings

- 1 pkg. (12 oz.) uncooked breakfast sausage links
- 1 pkg. (28 oz.) frozen O'Brien potatoes, thawed
- 2 cups shredded sharp cheddar cheese
- 12 large eggs
- ½ cup 2% milk
- ¼ tsp. seasoned salt
- ⅛ tsp. pepper
- 12 flour tortillas (8 in.)
  Optional toppings: Salsa, sliced jalapenos, chopped tomatoes, sliced green onions and cubed avocado

1. Remove sausage from casings. In a large skillet, cook sausage over medium heat until no longer pink, 8-10 minutes, breaking into crumbles; drain.
2. In a greased 4- or 5-qt. slow cooker, layer potatoes, sausage and cheese. In a large bowl, whisk eggs, milk, seasoned salt and pepper until blended; pour over top.
3. Cook, covered, on low 3¾-4¼ hours or until the eggs are set and a thermometer inserted in egg mixture reads 160°. Uncover and let stand 10 minutes. Serve in tortillas with toppings of your choice.

1 burrito: 382 cal., 21g fat (9g sat. fat), 221mg chol., 711mg sod., 29g carb. (2g sugars, 3g fiber), 18g pro.

ASK SARAH

CAN I FREEZE WAFFLES?

You bet! Arrange waffles in a single layer on sheet pans. Freeze until frozen. Transfer waffles to a freezer container. Freeze for up to 2 months.

EASY MORNING
WAFFLES

EASY CHEESY CAULIFLOWER
BREAKFAST CASSEROLE

EASY CHEESY CAULIFLOWER BREAKFAST CASSEROLE

I love finding new ways to add veggies to my everyday meals. This twist on a breakfast favorite swaps in riced cauliflower for the usual hash browns. This makes it not only keto-friendly, but also a crowd-pleasing addition to the brunch rotation.
—Robyn Warren, Lakeway, AR

- -

Prep: 30 min. • **Bake:** 40 min. + standing
Makes: 12 servings

1	lb. bacon strips, chopped
1	cup chopped sweet onion
½	large sweet red pepper, chopped
½	large green pepper, chopped
9	large eggs, lightly beaten
1½	cups whole-milk ricotta cheese
4	cups frozen riced cauliflower, thawed
2	cups shredded cheddar cheese
1	cup shredded Swiss cheese
½	tsp. pepper
¼	tsp. salt

1. Preheat oven to 350°. In a large skillet, cook bacon over medium heat until crisp, stirring occasionally. Remove with a slotted spoon; drain on paper towels. Discard the drippings, reserving 1 Tbsp. in pan.
2. Add onion and chopped peppers to drippings; cook and stir over medium-high heat until tender, 6-8 minutes. In a large bowl, whisk eggs and ricotta. Stir in riced cauliflower, shredded cheeses, bacon, onion mixture, pepper and salt. Pour into a greased 13x9-in. baking dish. Bake, uncovered, until a knife inserted near the center comes out clean, 40-45 minutes. Let stand 10 minutes before serving.

Freeze option: Cool the baked casserole completely; cover and freeze. To use, partially thaw in refrigerator overnight. Remove from the refrigerator 30 minutes before baking. Preheat oven to 350°. Bake as directed, increasing time as necessary for casserole to heat through and for a thermometer inserted in center to read 165°.

1 piece: 307 cal., 22g fat (11g sat. fat), 194mg chol., 534mg sod., 7g carb. (4g sugars, 2g fiber), 21g pro.

MAKEOVER HASH & EGGS

A diner classic goes home-style in this better-than-ever version that delivers fresh flavors with a healthy dose of fiber.
—*Taste of Home* Test Kitchen

Takes: 30 min. • **Makes:** 4 servings

- 1 large onion, chopped
- 1 Tbsp. canola oil, divided
- 6 medium red potatoes (about 1½ lbs.), cut into ½-in. cubes
- ¼ cup water
- 3 pkg. (2 oz. each) thinly sliced deli corned beef, coarsely chopped
- ¼ tsp. pepper
- 4 large eggs
  Additional pepper, optional

1. In a large nonstick skillet, saute onion in 2 tsp. oil until tender. Stir in potatoes and water. Bring to a boil. Reduce heat; cover and simmer for 15-20 minutes or until potatoes are tender. Stir in corned beef and pepper; heat through.
2. Meanwhile, in a large nonstick skillet, fry the eggs in remaining oil as desired. Season with additional pepper if desired. Serve with corned beef hash.
1 egg with 1 cup hash: 301 cal., 12g fat (3g sat. fat), 239mg chol., 652mg sod., 31g carb. (4g sugars, 4g fiber), 18g pro. **Diabetic exchanges:** 2 starch, 2 medium-fat meat, ½ fat.

BERRY RICOTTA PUFF PANCAKE

This slightly sweet berry pancake is filled with berries and has a custardy texture that puffs up beautifully when baked. It makes an easy yet impressive breakfast.
—Jessi Smith, Fort Myers, FL

Prep: 20 min. • **Bake:** 25 min.
Makes: 8 slices

- 3 Tbsp. butter
- 5 large eggs, room temperature
- 1½ cups reduced-fat ricotta cheese
- ½ cup fat-free milk
- 1½ tsp. vanilla extract
- ½ tsp. grated lemon zest
- ¾ cup all-purpose flour
- ¼ cup sugar
- ½ tsp. baking powder
- ½ tsp. salt
- ½ cup sliced fresh strawberries
- ½ cup fresh raspberries
- ½ cup fresh blueberries
  Confectioners' sugar

1. Preheat oven to 400°. Place butter in a 12-in. cast-iron or other ovenproof skillet. Place in oven until butter is melted, 4-5 minutes; carefully swirl to coat evenly.
2. Meanwhile, in a blender, process eggs, ricotta, milk, vanilla and lemon zest until blended. Add flour, sugar, baking powder and salt; process until blended. Pour into hot skillet. Top with berries.
3. Bake until pancake is puffed and sides are golden brown and crisp, 25-30 minutes. Remove from oven; serve immediately with confectioners' sugar.
1 slice: 287 cal., 13g fat (6g sat. fat), 186mg chol., 406mg sod., 29g carb. (15g sugars, 2g fiber), 13g pro.

BERRY RICOTTA PUFF PANCAKE

**ROASTED
VEGETABLE STRATA**

COCONUT-MACADAMIA SHEET-PAN PANCAKES

These tropical pancakes are great for when you want to serve a group without standing over the stove. To make them even more fun, swap the usual butter and maple syrup topping for pineapple-flavored ice cream.
—Trisha Kruse, Eagle, ID

Prep: 15 min. + standing • **Bake:** 15 min.
Makes: 10 servings

- 3½ cups complete buttermilk pancake mix
- ½ cup sweetened shredded coconut
- 2 cups 2% milk
- 1 Tbsp. coconut oil or butter, softened
- ½ cup macadamia nuts, coarsely chopped
- 2 medium bananas, sliced
  Butter and maple syrup

1. Preheat oven to 425°. In a large bowl, combine pancake mix and coconut. Stir in milk just until dry ingredients are moistened; let stand 10 minutes. Meanwhile, line a 15x10x1-in. baking pan with parchment; grease parchment with coconut oil.
2. Spread batter into prepared pan; sprinkle with macadamia nuts. Bake until puffy and golden brown, 15-20 minutes. Cool in pan on a wire rack 5 minutes. Holding on to the parchment, lift pancake from pan. Cut into individual servings. Top with bananas; serve with butter and syrup.
1 piece: 288 cal., 11g fat (4g sat. fat), 4mg chol., 642mg sod., 44g carb. (13g sugars, 2g fiber), 7g pro.

> "We loved this easy recipe. What a great take on a morning staple. I even cut the pancake into individual servings and stashed them in the freezer for quick breakfasts on busy days."

—MARK HAGEN, EXECUTIVE EDITOR

ROASTED VEGETABLE STRATA

We have an abundance of zucchini in the fall, and this is the perfect dish for putting it to good use. Cheesy and rich, the warm, classic breakfast dish is sure to please!
—Colleen Doucette, Truro, NS

Prep: 55 min. + chilling • **Bake:** 40 min.
Makes: 8 servings

- 3 large zucchini, halved lengthwise and cut into ¾-in. slices
- 1 each medium red, yellow and orange peppers, cut into 1-in. pieces
- 2 Tbsp. olive oil
- 1 tsp. dried oregano
- ½ tsp. salt
- ½ tsp. pepper
- ½ tsp. dried basil
- 1 medium tomato, chopped
- 1 loaf (1 lb.) unsliced crusty Italian bread
- ½ cup shredded sharp cheddar cheese
- ½ cup shredded Asiago cheese
- 6 large eggs
- 2 cups fat-free milk

1. Preheat oven to 400°. Toss zucchini and peppers with oil and seasonings; transfer to a 15x10x1-in. pan. Roast until tender, 25-30 minutes, stirring once. Stir in the chopped tomato; cool slightly.
2. Trim ends from bread; cut bread into 1-in. slices. In a greased 13x9-in. baking dish, layer half of each of the following: bread, roasted vegetables and cheeses. Repeat the layers. Whisk together eggs and milk; pour evenly over top. Refrigerate, covered, for 6 hours or overnight.
3. Preheat oven to 375°. Remove casserole from refrigerator while oven heats. Bake, uncovered, until top is golden brown, 40-50 minutes. Let stand 5-10 minutes before cutting.
Freeze option: Cover and freeze unbaked casserole. To use, partially thaw in the refrigerator overnight. Remove from the refrigerator 30 minutes before baking. Preheat oven to 375°. Bake casserole as directed, increasing time as necessary to heat through and for a thermometer inserted in center to read 165°.
1 piece: 349 cal., 14g fat (5g sat. fat), 154mg chol., 642mg sod., 40g carb. (9g sugars, 4g fiber), 17g pro. **Diabetic exchanges:** 2 starch, 1 medium-fat meat, 1 vegetable, 1 fat.

COCONUT-MACADAMIA
SHEET-PAN PANCAKES

COASTAL CAROLINA MUFFIN-TIN FRITTATAS

Incorporating the flavors of a low country South Carolina crab boil, these delicious frittatas are easy to make and fun to eat. If you have leftover cooked potatoes (roasted or boiled), dice them up and use them in place of the refrigerated shredded potatoes in this recipe.
—Shannon Kohn, Summerville, SC

- -

Prep: 30 min. • **Bake:** 30 min.
Makes: 1 dozen

- ½ cup mayonnaise
- 1 Tbsp. lemon juice
- 2 tsp. sugar
- 1 tsp. seafood seasoning
- 2 cups refrigerated shredded hash brown potatoes
- 1½ cups chopped smoked sausage
- 1 can (8 oz.) jumbo lump crabmeat, drained
- ¼ cup chopped roasted sweet red peppers
- 7 large eggs
- ¾ cup heavy whipping cream
- 1 Tbsp. Louisiana-style hot sauce
- ½ tsp. salt
- 12 bacon strips, cooked and crumbled
- ¼ cup thinly sliced green onions

1. Preheat oven to 350°. In a small bowl, combine mayonnaise, lemon juice, sugar and seafood seasoning. Refrigerate until serving.
2. Meanwhile, in a large bowl, combine potatoes, sausage, crab and red peppers. Divide among 12 greased jumbo muffin cups. In another large bowl, whisk the eggs, cream, hot sauce and salt. Pour over potato mixture. Top with bacon.
3. Bake until a knife inserted in center comes out clean, 30-35 minutes. Serve with sauce and green onions.
1 frittata: 292 cal., 23g fat (8g sat. fat), 164mg chol., 768mg sod., 7g carb. (2g sugars, 1g fiber), 13g pro.

TEST KITCHEN TIP
Lump crabmeat is worth the splurge in these handheld frittatas because the flavor really shines through.

BLUEBERRY CORNMEAL PANCAKES

Blueberry cornmeal pancakes are one of my family's favorite breakfast staples. No time to make them from scratch? No problem! My grandmother's standby of store-bought cornbread mix makes quick work of the job.
—Carolyn Eskew, Dayton, OH

- -

Takes: 30 min. • **Makes:** 10 corncakes

- 1 pkg. (8½ oz.) cornbread/muffin mix
- 1 cup fresh or frozen blueberries
- ⅓ cup canned white or shoepeg corn
  Maple syrup

In a large bowl, prepare muffin mix according to package directions. Gently stir in the blueberries and corn. Lightly grease a griddle; warm over medium heat. Pour batter by ¼ cupfuls onto griddle; flatten slightly. Cook until bottoms are golden brown. Turn; cook until second sides are golden brown. Serve with syrup.
2 cakes: 251 cal., 7g fat (2g sat. fat), 39mg chol., 454mg sod., 41g carb. (14g sugars, 4g fiber), 6g pro.

COASTAL CAROLINA MUFFIN-TIN FRITTATAS

AIR-FRYER HAM & EGG POCKETS

Convenient refrigerated crescent roll dough makes these savory breakfast pockets a snap to prepare.

—*Taste of Home* Test Kitchen

Takes: 25 min. • Makes: 2 servings

- 1 large egg
- 2 tsp. 2% milk
- 2 tsp. butter
- 1 oz. thinly sliced deli ham, chopped
- 2 Tbsp. shredded cheddar cheese
- 1 tube (4 oz.) refrigerated crescent rolls

1. Preheat air fryer to 300°. In a small bowl, combine egg and milk. In a small skillet, heat butter until hot. Add the egg mixture; cook and stir over medium heat until the eggs are completely set. Remove from the heat. Fold in ham and cheese.
2. Separate the dough into 2 rectangles. Seal perforations; spoon half the filling down the center of each rectangle. Fold dough over filling; pinch to seal. Place in a single layer on greased tray in air-fryer basket. Cook until golden brown, 8-10 minutes.
1 serving: 326 cal., 20g fat (5g sat. fat), 118mg chol., 735mg sod., 25g carb. (6g sugars, 0 fiber), 12g pro.

BANANA BLUEBERRY OATMEAL BAKE

BANANA BLUEBERRY OATMEAL BAKE

When my brother, sister and I were young, Mom would bake this cinnamon-scented oatmeal before she drove us to school. Whenever I make it for my family, I have lots of happy memories.
—Vincent Taylor, Houston, TX

Prep: 15 min. • Bake: 30 min. + standing
Makes: 4 servings

- 1½ cups unsweetened almond milk or 2% milk
- ⅓ cup honey
- 1 tsp. vanilla extract
- ½ tsp. ground cinnamon
- ⅛ tsp. salt
- 1¼ cups old-fashioned oats
- 2 medium bananas, sliced
- 1 cup fresh or frozen blueberries

TOPPING
- ¼ cup packed brown sugar
- 2 Tbsp. all-purpose flour
- 2 Tbsp. butter, softened
- ½ cup chopped pecans

1. Preheat oven to 350°. In a bowl, whisk the first 5 ingredients until blended. Stir in oats.
2. Arrange banana slices in a single layer in a greased 9-in. square baking pan; sprinkle with blueberries. Pour oatmeal mixture over top, spreading evenly. Bake until oatmeal is set, 25-30 minutes. Remove from oven. Preheat broiler.
3. For topping, in a small bowl, mix brown sugar, flour and butter with a fork until crumbly; stir in chopped pecans. Sprinkle over oatmeal. Broil 7-8 in. from heat until lightly browned, 2-3 minutes. Let stand for 10 minutes before serving.
1 cup: 483 cal., 19g fat (5g sat. fat), 15mg chol., 193mg sod., 78g carb. (49g sugars, 7g fiber), 6g pro.

GREEK SALAD-INSPIRED QUICHE

GREEK SALAD-INSPIRED QUICHE

I use my trusty cast-iron skillet to create this family-sized Greek quiche for a flavor-filled breakfast. The quiche is meatless, but you can serve it with a side of sausage or bacon if you have meat lovers in the family. It also makes a great dinner entree with pita bread and a green salad.
—Donna Ryan, Topsfield, MA

Prep: 20 min. • **Bake:** 20 min. + standing
Makes: 6 servings

- 1 Tbsp. olive oil
- 1 cup cherry tomatoes, halved
- ⅔ cup finely chopped green pepper
- ½ cup thinly sliced red onion
- ⅔ cup chopped fresh spinach
- 2 garlic cloves, minced
- 1 cup crumbled feta cheese
- ½ cup pitted Greek olives, sliced
- 6 large eggs
- 1 cup 2% milk
- 1 Tbsp. minced fresh oregano
   or 1 tsp. dried oregano
- ½ tsp. salt
- ⅛ to ¾ tsp. crushed red pepper flakes

1. In a 9-in. cast-iron or other ovenproof skillet, heat oil over medium-high heat. Add tomatoes, green peppers and onion; cook and stir until the vegetables are tender, 6-7 minutes; drain. Add spinach and garlic; cook and stir until spinach is wilted, 1-2 minutes. Remove from heat and stir in feta and olives.
2. In a large bowl, whisk eggs, milk, oregano, salt and pepper flakes until blended. Pour over vegetables.
3. Bake until a knife inserted in the center comes out clean, 20-25 minutes. Let stand 10 minutes before serving.

1 piece: 354 cal., 22g fat (9g sat. fat), 175mg chol., 778mg sod., 25g carb. (5g sugars, 2g fiber), 12g pro.

TEST KITCHEN TIP

To determine if an egg is still fresh, drop it into a glass of water. If the egg floats, it has gone bad and should be discarded. Bad eggs also often smell like sulfur, so it's not too tricky to tell when they're rotten.

BERRY SMOOTHIE BOWL

BERRY SMOOTHIE BOWL

We turned one of our favorite smoothies into a smoothie bowl and topped it with even more fresh fruit and a few toasted almonds for a little crunch.
—*Taste of Home* Test Kitchen

Takes: 5 min. • **Makes:** 2 servings

- 1 cup fat-free milk
- 1 cup frozen unsweetened strawberries
- ½ cup frozen unsweetened raspberries
- 3 Tbsp. sugar
- 1 cup ice cubes
   Optional: Sliced fresh strawberries, fresh raspberries, chia seeds, fresh pumpkin seeds, unsweetened shredded coconut and sliced almonds

Place the milk, berries and sugar in a blender; cover and process until smooth. Add ice cubes; cover and process until smooth. Divide mixture between 2 serving bowls. Add optional toppings as desired.

1½ cups: 155 cal., 0 fat (0 sat. fat), 2mg chol., 54mg sod., 35g carb. (30g sugars, 2g fiber), 5g pro.

FETA ASPARAGUS FRITTATA

Asparagus and feta cheese come together to make this frittata extra special. It is perfect for a lazy Sunday or to serve with a tossed salad for a light lunch.
—Mildred Sherrer, Fort Worth, TX

- -

Takes: 30 min. • **Makes:** 2 servings

12	fresh asparagus spears, trimmed
6	large eggs
2	Tbsp. heavy whipping cream
	Dash salt
	Dash pepper
1	Tbsp. olive oil
2	green onions, chopped
1	garlic clove, minced
½	cup crumbled feta cheese

1. Preheat oven to 350°. Place ½ in. of water and asparagus in a large skillet; bring to a boil. Cook, covered, until the asparagus is crisp-tender, 3-5 minutes; drain. Cool slightly.

2. In a bowl, whisk together eggs, cream, salt and pepper. Chop 2 asparagus spears. In an 8-in. cast-iron or other ovenproof skillet, heat oil over medium heat until hot. Saute green onions, garlic and chopped asparagus 1 minute. Stir in egg mixture; cook, covered, over medium heat until eggs are nearly set, 3-5 minutes. Top with whole asparagus spears and cheese.

3. Bake until the eggs are completely set, 7-9 minutes.

½ frittata: 425 cal., 31g fat (12g sat. fat), 590mg chol., 1231mg sod., 8g carb. (3g sugars, 3g fiber), 27g pro.

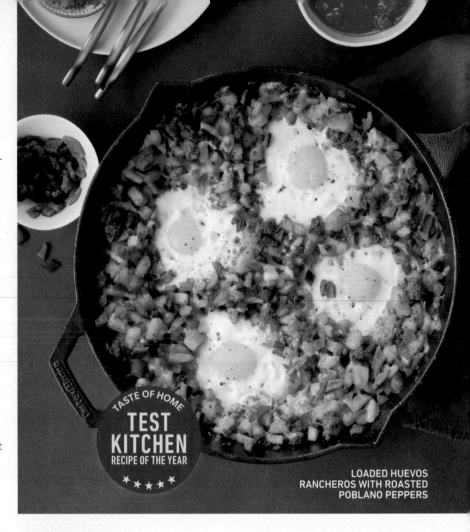

LOADED HUEVOS
RANCHEROS WITH ROASTED
POBLANO PEPPERS

LOADED HUEVOS RANCHEROS WITH ROASTED POBLANO PEPPERS

Try my unique but tasty version of huevos rancheros. It's similar to a cowboy hash, as the O'Brien potatoes take the place of the corn tortillas.
—Joan Hallford, North Richland Hills, TX

- -

Prep: 15 min. + standing • **Cook:** 20 min.
Makes: 4 servings

1	poblano pepper
½	lb. fresh chorizo or bulk spicy pork sausage
4	cups frozen O'Brien potatoes, thawed
½	cup shredded pepper jack cheese
1	tsp. smoked paprika
½	tsp. kosher salt
½	tsp. garlic powder
½	tsp. pepper
4	large eggs
	Salsa, sour cream and minced fresh cilantro

1. Place poblano pepper in a 12-in. cast-iron or other ovenproof skillet. Broil 4 in. from heat until skins blister, rotating with tongs until all sides are blistered and blackened, about 5 minutes. Immediately place pepper in a small bowl; let peppers stand, covered, 20 minutes.

2. Peel off and discard charred skin from pepper. Remove stems and seeds. Finely chop pepper; set aside.

3. In the same skillet, cook the chorizo or bulk pork sausage over medium heat until cooked through, 6-8 minutes, breaking into crumbles; drain. Add potatoes; cook and stir until potatoes are tender, 8-10 minutes. Stir in cheese, smoked paprika, kosher salt, garlic powder and pepper.

4. With the back of a spoon, make 4 wells in potato mixture. Break an egg in each well. Cook, covered, on medium-low until egg whites are completely set and yolks begin to thicken but are not hard, 5-7 minutes. Serve with reserved roasted pepper, salsa, sour cream and cilantro.

1 serving: 426 cal., 26g fat (10g sat. fat), 251mg chol., 1114mg sod., 20g carb. (2g sugars, 3g fiber), 24g pro.

CARAMEL-SCOTCH CREAM CHEESE COFFEE CAKE

I came up with this cream cheese coffee cake recipe so I could make a delicious brunch treat using refrigerated pastry for the base. Serve it cold so all the cozy filling stays with each slice.
—Sherry Little, Sherwood, AR

Prep: 25 min. • **Bake:** 20 min. + chilling
Makes: 8 servings

- 1 tube (12 oz.) large refrigerated buttery crescent rolls
- 1 carton (7½ oz.) spreadable brown sugar and cinnamon cream cheese
- ⅓ cup butterscotch-caramel ice cream topping
- ½ cup chopped pecans
- ⅓ cup packed brown sugar
- ¼ cup all-purpose flour
- 2 Tbsp. cold butter
- 1 large egg, beaten

1. Preheat oven to 375°. Unroll crescent dough into long rectangle; place on a parchment-lined baking sheet. Press perforations to seal. Spread cream cheese down center third of rectangle. Drizzle with ice cream topping; sprinkle with pecans. Combine brown sugar and flour; cut in butter until crumbly. Sprinkle half the mixture over pecans.

2. On each long side of dough, cut 8 strips at an angle, about 2 in. into the center. Fold 1 strip from each side over filling and pinch ends together; repeat. Brush with beaten egg. Sprinkle with the remaining brown sugar mixture.

3. Bake until deep golden brown, 18-22 minutes. Cool 5 minutes before removing from pan to a wire rack. Refrigerate coffee cake until cold.

1 slice: 381 cal., 19g fat (8g sat. fat), 16mg chol., 472mg sod., 47g carb. (25g sugars, 2g fiber), 5g pro.

PEANUT BUTTER & JELLY OVERNIGHT OATS

This breakfast dish gives everyone's favorite sandwich a healthy twist. Switch to crunchy peanut butter and sprinkle some chopped peanuts over the top of the oatmeal if you like the extra crunch.
—*Taste of Home* Test Kitchen

Prep: 10 min. + chilling • **Makes:** 4 servings

- ¼ cup creamy peanut butter
- 2 Tbsp. honey
- 1½ cups 2% milk
- 1⅓ cups old-fashioned oats
- ¼ cup strawberry jelly

1. In a small bowl, beat peanut butter and honey until smooth. Gradually add the milk until smooth. Add oats and mix to combine. Refrigerate, covered, overnight.

2. Whisk the jelly slightly and swirl 1 Tbsp. into each serving.

1 serving: 323 cal., 12g fat (3g sat. fat), 7mg chol., 112mg sod., 48g carb. (27g sugars, 3g fiber), 10g pro.

DID YOU KNOW?
If you want to make a big batch of overnight oats, just stick to the above ratio, increasing the amounts as much as you'd like. Store each serving in an individual container for easy grab-and-go eatin'.

CARAMEL-SCOTCH CREAM CHEESE COFFEE CAKE

THE BEST
QUICHE LORRAINE

THE BEST QUICHE LORRAINE

Nestled in a buttery, rustic crust, this quiche is filled with sweet onions, bacon bits and cheese. It's the perfect addition to brunch.
—Shannon Norris, Senior Food Stylist

- -

Prep: 1 hour. • **Bake:** 1¼ hours + standing
Makes: 8 servings

Pastry for single-crust pie
(9 in. deep-dish)
1   pkg. (12 oz.) thick-sliced bacon strips, coarsely chopped
3   large sweet onions, chopped
1   Tbsp. minced fresh thyme
½   tsp. coarsely ground pepper
⅛   tsp. ground nutmeg
1½ cups shredded Gruyere cheese
½   cup grated Parmesan cheese
8   large eggs, room temperature
2   cups whole milk
1   cup heavy whipping cream

1. On a lightly floured surface, roll dough to a 14-in. circle. Transfer to a 9-in. springform pan; press firmly against bottom and sides. Refrigerate while preparing filling.
2. In a large skillet, cook bacon over medium heat until crisp, stirring occasionally. Remove with a slotted spoon; drain on paper towels. Discard drippings, reserving 1 Tbsp. in pan. Add onions to drippings; cook and stir over medium heat until caramelized, 20-25 minutes. Stir in thyme, pepper and nutmeg; remove from the heat. Cool slightly. Stir in cheeses and reserved bacon; spoon into crust. Preheat oven to 350°. In a large bowl, whisk eggs, milk, and cream until blended; pour over top. Place springform pan on a rimmed baking sheet.
3. Bake on a lower oven rack until a knife inserted near the center comes out clean, 75-85 minutes. Cool on a wire rack for 15 minutes. Loosen sides from pan with a knife. Remove rim from pan.
1 piece: 609 cal., 44g fat (24g sat. fat), 295mg chol., 789mg sod., 29g carb. (11g sugars, 2g fiber), 24g pro.
Pastry for single-crust deep-dish pie (9 in.): Combine 1½ cups all-purpose flour and ¼ tsp. salt; cut in ⅔ cup cold butter until crumbly. Gradually add 3-6 Tbsp. ice water, tossing with a fork until the dough holds together when pressed. Wrap and refrigerate 1 hour.

APPLE BUTTER BISCUIT BREAKFAST BAKE

My grandmother created this recipe to use up the leftovers from Christmas Eve dinner. By combining the leftover ham and biscuits with her homemade apple butter, milk and eggs, she could serve up a warm, delicious breakfast and still have lots of time to spend with her grandkids.
—Mary Leverette, Columbia, SC

Prep: 30 min. + chilling
Bake: 50 min. + standing • **Makes:** 12 servings

- 10 leftover biscuits (3-in. diameter)
- ¾ cup apple butter
- 2 cups shredded sharp cheddar cheese
- 1½ cups cubed fully cooked ham
- ¼ cup minced fresh parsley
- 6 large eggs
- 2½ cups 2% milk
- 1 tsp. salt
- ½ tsp. pepper
- ¼ tsp. ground mustard

1. Cut biscuits crosswise in half. Spread apple butter over cut sides of biscuits. Replace tops. Cut each biscuit into quarters; arrange in a single layer in a greased 13x9-in. baking dish. Top with cheese, ham and parsley.
2. In a large bowl, whisk eggs, milk, salt, pepper and mustard. Pour over biscuits. Cover and refrigerate overnight.
3. Preheat oven to 325°. Remove strata from refrigerator while oven heats. Bake, uncovered, until top is puffed and edges are golden brown, 50-60 minutes. Let stand 10 minutes before cutting.
1 piece: 331 cal., 15g fat (7g sat. fat), 126mg chol., 976mg sod., 31g carb. (12g sugars, 1g fiber), 16g pro.

APPLE CINNAMON OVERNIGHT OATS

Many folks love this oatmeal cold, but I like to heat it up a little since I'm not a big fan of eating it right out of the fridge. Add a handful of nuts for crunch, flavor and extra health benefits.
—Sarah Farmer, Executive Culinary Director

Prep: 5 min. + chilling • **Makes:** 1 serving

- ½ cup old-fashioned oats
- ½ medium Gala or Honeycrisp apple, chopped
- 1 Tbsp. raisins
- 1 cup 2% milk
- ¼ tsp. ground cinnamon
  Dash salt
  Toasted chopped nuts, optional

In a small container or Mason jar, combine all ingredients. Seal; refrigerate overnight.
1½ cups: 349 cal., 8g fat (4g sat. fat), 20mg chol., 263mg sod., 59g carb. (28g sugars, 7g fiber), 14g pro.

"This easy, no-cook method for making homemade oats is a lifesaver on busy days. I like to add sliced banana or blueberries on top for extra nutrients."

—JAZMIN DELGADO, GRAPHIC DESIGNER

APPLE CINNAMON OVERNIGHT OATS

GREEN ONION ROLLS
PAGE 67

Breads, Biscuits & More

We all love bread, rolls and other baked beauties straight from the oven. From easy quick breads to more complex loaves, the *Taste of Home* Test Kitchen has dozens of recipes perfect for beginner and seasoned bread-makers alike. Rely on these foolproof recipes and tips for classic bakes that will complement any meal.

HONEY-SQUASH
DINNER ROLLS

HONEY-SQUASH ROLLS

Squash gives a rich color to these fluffy rolls. Any variety of squash works well.
—Marcia Whitney, Gainesville, FL

- -

Prep: 40 min. + rising • **Bake:** 20 min.
Makes: 2 dozen

- 2 pkg. (¼ oz. each) active dry yeast
- 2 tsp. salt
- ¼ tsp. ground nutmeg
- 6 to 6½ cups all-purpose flour
- 1¼ cups 2% milk
- ½ cup butter, cubed
- ½ cup honey
- 1 pkg. (12 oz.) frozen mashed winter squash, thawed (about 1⅓ cups)
- 1 large egg, lightly beaten
  Poppy seeds, salted pumpkin seeds or pepitas, or sesame seeds

1. In a large bowl, mix yeast, salt, nutmeg and 3 cups flour. In a small saucepan, heat milk, butter and honey to 120°-130°. Add to the dry ingredients; beat on medium speed for 2 minutes. Add the squash; beat on high 2 minutes. Stir in enough remaining flour to form a soft dough (dough will be sticky).
2. Turn dough onto a floured surface; knead until smooth and elastic, 6-8 minutes. Place in a greased bowl, turning once to grease the top. Cover and let rise in a warm place until doubled, about 1 hour.
3. Punch down dough. Turn onto a lightly floured surface; divide and shape into 24 balls. Divide balls between 2 greased 9-in. cast-iron skillets or round baking pans. Cover with kitchen towels; let rise in a warm place until doubled, about 45 minutes.
4. Preheat oven to 375°. Brush tops with beaten egg; sprinkle with seeds. Bake until dark golden brown, 20-25 minutes. Cover loosely with foil during the last 5-7 minutes if needed to prevent overbrowning. Remove from pans to wire racks; serve warm.
1 roll: 186 cal., 5g fat (3g sat. fat), 19mg chol., 238mg sod., 32g carb. (6g sugars, 1g fiber), 4g pro. **Diabetic exchanges:** 2 starch, 1 fat.

MOIST IRISH SODA BREAD

I'm allergic to yeast, so I appreciate recipes that don't call for that ingredient, such as quick breads, biscuits and this soda bread. This tender loaf dotted with raisins is my favorite way to enjoy toast for breakfast.
—Carol Fritz, Fulton, IL

- -

Prep: 20 min. • **Bake:** 40 min.
Makes: 1 loaf (16 slices)

- 4 cups all-purpose flour
- 1 Tbsp. sugar
- 1½ tsp. baking soda
- 1 tsp. baking powder
- ½ tsp. salt
- ¼ cup cold butter
- 1 cup golden raisins
- 1¾ cups buttermilk

1. In a large bowl, combine the flour, sugar, baking soda, baking powder and salt. Cut in butter until the mixture resembles coarse crumbs. Add raisins. Stir in buttermilk just until moistened. Turn onto a lightly floured surface; gently knead 6-8 times.
2. Place on an ungreased baking sheet; pat into a 7-in. round loaf. Using a sharp knife, cut a 1-in. cross about ¼ in. deep on top of the loaf. Bake at 375° for 40-45 minutes or until golden brown. Cool on a wire rack.
1 slice: 181 cal., 3g fat (2g sat. fat), 9mg chol., 265mg sod., 33g carb. (0 sugars, 1g fiber), 4g pro. **Diabetic exchanges:** 1½ starch, ½ fruit, ½ fat.

"I've made this a couple times and it's really good bread. Simple recipe, too. I've made it with and without the raisins and it works well either way. I think I prefer it with the raisins. Spread with some butter, this bread was simply divine."

—ARIELLE JARDINE, GRAPHIC DESIGNER

DOWN EAST BLUEBERRY BUCKLE

This buckle won a contest at my daughter's college. They shipped us four lobsters, but the real prize was seeing the smile on our daughter's face.
—Dianne van der Veen, Plymouth, MA

- -

Prep: 15 min. • **Bake:** 30 min.
Makes: 9 servings

- 2 cups all-purpose flour
- ¾ cup sugar
- 2½ tsp. baking powder
- ¼ tsp. salt
- 1 large egg, room temperature
- ¾ cup 2% milk
- ¼ cup butter, melted
- 2 cups fresh or frozen blueberries
  TOPPING
- ½ cup sugar
- ⅓ cup all-purpose flour
- ½ tsp. ground cinnamon
- ¼ cup butter, softened

1. Preheat oven to 375°. In a large bowl, whisk flour, sugar, baking powder and salt. In another bowl, whisk egg, milk and melted butter until blended. Add to flour mixture; stir just until moistened. Fold in blueberries. Transfer mixture to a greased 9-in. square baking pan.
2. For topping, in a small bowl, mix sugar, flour and cinnamon. Using a fork, stir in softened butter until mixture is crumbly. Sprinkle over batter.
3. Bake until a toothpick inserted in the center comes out clean (do not overbake), 30-35 minutes. Cool in pan on a wire rack. Serve warm or at room temperature.
1 piece: 354 cal., 12g fat (7g sat. fat), 49mg chol., 277mg sod., 59g carb. (32g sugars, 2g fiber), 5g pro.

GRANOLA BLUEBERRY MUFFINS

I wanted to put a new spin on muffins, so I mixed in some granola. I brought a batch to work the next morning—success. The granola I used contained lots of nuts, pumpkin seeds and shredded coconut.
—Megan Weiss, Menomonie, WI

Prep: 20 min. • **Bake:** 15 min.
Makes: 1 dozen

- 1½ cups whole wheat flour
- ½ cup all-purpose flour
- ¼ cup packed brown sugar
- 2 tsp. baking powder
- ½ tsp. salt
- ½ tsp. baking soda
- 1 cup granola without raisins, divided
- 1 large egg, room temperature
- 1 cup buttermilk
- ¼ cup canola oil
- 2 Tbsp. orange juice
- 1 Tbsp. lemon juice
- 1 cup fresh or frozen unsweetened blueberries

1. Preheat oven to 400°. In a small bowl, whisk flours, brown sugar, baking powder, salt and baking soda. Stir in ½ cup granola. In another bowl, whisk egg, buttermilk, oil and juices until blended. Add to flour mixture; stir just until moistened. Fold in blueberries.

2. Fill 12 greased muffin cups three-fourths full; sprinkle remaining granola over batter. Bake 12-15 minutes or until a toothpick inserted in center comes out clean. Cool 5 minutes before removing from pan to a wire rack.

Freeze option: Freeze cooled muffins in freezer containers. To use, thaw at room temperature or, if desired, microwave each muffin on high for 20-30 seconds or until heated through.

1 muffin: 188 cal., 7g fat (1g sat. fat), 18mg chol., 251mg sod., 28g carb. (8g sugars, 4g fiber), 6g pro. **Diabetic exchanges:** 2 starch, 1 fat.

I LIKE TO EAT APPLES & BANANAS BREAD

I LIKE TO EAT APPLES & BANANAS BREAD

My children love to bake (and eat) all kinds of homemade banana bread. They make this all by themselves, with just a little help from me to put it in the oven.
—Kristin Metcalf, Charlton, MA

Prep: 20 min. • **Bake:** 50 min. + cooling
Makes: 1 loaf (16 slices)

- 1½ cups mashed ripe bananas (4-5 medium)
- 1½ cups chopped peeled apples (2 medium)
- ½ cup sugar
- ½ cup packed brown sugar
- 2 Tbsp. water
- 2 Tbsp. butter, melted
- 1½ cups all-purpose flour
- 1 tsp. baking soda
- 1 tsp. baking powder
- ¼ tsp. salt
- 1 cup sweetened shredded coconut
- ½ cup caramel sundae syrup
- ¼ tsp. sea salt

1. Preheat oven to 350°. Combine bananas, apples, sugars and water. Stir in melted the butter. In another bowl, whisk flour, baking soda, baking powder and salt. Stir into the banana mixture. Transfer to a greased and floured 9x5-in. loaf pan.

2. Bake until a toothpick inserted in center comes out clean, 50-60 minutes. Cool in pan 10 minutes before removing to a wire rack to cool completely.

3. Meanwhile, toast the coconut, stirring occasionally, in a shallow pan at 350° until golden brown, 4-6 minutes. Cool slightly. Mix coconut with caramel syrup and sea salt; spread over loaf.

1 slice: 187 cal., 4g fat (3g sat. fat), 4mg chol., 232mg sod., 38g carb. (25g sugars, 1g fiber), 2g pro.

GREEN ONION ROLLS

Better double the batch—these savory, elegant rolls will disappear fast!
—Jane Kroeger, Key Largo, FL

- -

Prep: 30 min. + rising • **Bake:** 20 min.
Makes: 1 dozen

- 1   Tbsp. butter
- 1½ cups chopped green onions
- ½   tsp. pepper
- ¾   tsp. garlic salt, optional
- 1   loaf (1 lb.) frozen bread dough, thawed
- ½   cup shredded part-skim mozzarella cheese
- ⅓   cup grated Parmesan cheese

1. Preheat oven to 375°. In a large skillet, heat butter over medium-high heat; saute green onions until tender. Stir in pepper and, if desired, garlic salt. Remove from heat.
2. On a lightly floured surface, roll dough into a 12x8-in. rectangle. Spread with onion mixture. Sprinkle with cheeses.
3. Roll up jelly-roll style, starting with a long side; pinch seam to seal. Cut into 12 slices; place in greased muffin cups. Cover; let rolls rise in a warm place until doubled, about 30 minutes. Preheat oven to 375°.
4. Bake until the rolls are golden brown, 18-20 minutes. Remove from pan to a wire rack. Serve warm.
1 roll: 142 cal., 4g fat (1g sat. fat), 7mg chol., 415mg sod., 20g carb. (2g sugars, 2g fiber), 6g pro.

SWEET ITALIAN HOLIDAY BREAD

This is authentic ciambellotto, a sweet loaf my great-grandmother used to bake in Italy. I still use her traditional recipe—the only update I made was for modern appliances.
—Denise Perrin, Vancouver, WA

- -

Prep: 15 min. • **Bake:** 45 min.
Makes: 1 loaf (20 slices)

- 4   cups all-purpose flour
- 1   cup sugar
- 2   Tbsp. grated orange zest
- 3   tsp. baking powder
- 3   large eggs, room temperature
- ½   cup 2% milk
- ½   cup olive oil
- 1   large egg yolk, lightly beaten
- 1   Tbsp. coarse sugar

1. Preheat oven to 350°. In a large bowl, whisk flour, sugar, orange zest and baking powder. In another bowl, whisk eggs, milk and oil until blended. Add to flour mixture; stir just until moistened.
2. Shape into a 6-in. round loaf on a greased baking sheet. Brush top with egg yolk; sprinkle with coarse sugar. Bake until a toothpick inserted in center comes out clean, 45-50 minutes. Cover top loosely with foil during the last 10 minutes if needed to prevent overbrowning. Remove from pan to a wire rack; serve warm.
1 slice: 197 cal., 7g fat (1g sat. fat), 38mg chol., 87mg sod., 30g carb. (11g sugars, 1g fiber), 4g pro.

GREEN ONION ROLLS

GRANDMA'S
ONION SQUARES

EASY CAST-IRON PEACH BISCUIT ROLLS

I used to love going to the local coffee shop and enjoying fresh peach cinnamon rolls, but being a busy mom of three, I don't have the time anymore. To re-create it at home, I developed this no-yeast recipe that is quick and easy to make!
—Heather Karow, Burnett, WI

- -

Prep: 25 min. • **Bake:** 25 min. + cooling
Makes: 1 dozen

- 1 cup packed brown sugar
- ¼ cup butter, softened
- 3 tsp. ground cinnamon

DOUGH

- 2 cups all-purpose flour
- 2 Tbsp. sugar
- 1 Tbsp. baking powder
- 1 tsp. salt
- 3 Tbsp. butter
- ¾ cup 2% milk
- 1 can (15 oz.) sliced peaches in juice, undrained
- 1 cup confectioners' sugar

1. Preheat oven to 350°. In a small bowl, mix brown sugar, butter and cinnamon until crumbly. Reserve half for topping. Sprinkle remaining crumb mixture onto bottom of a 10-in. cast-iron or other ovenproof skillet.
2. For dough, in a large bowl, mix flour, sugar, baking powder and salt. Cut in butter until crumbly. Add milk; stir to form a soft dough (dough will be sticky). Roll into an 18x12-in. rectangle. Sprinkle reserved topping to within ½ in. of edges.
3. Drain peaches, reserving 2 Tbsp. juice for glaze. Chop peaches; place over topping. Roll up jelly-roll style, starting with a long side; pinch seam to seal. Cut into 12 slices. Place in prepared skillet, cut side down.
4. Bake until lightly browned, 25-30 minutes. Cool on a wire rack 10 minutes. For glaze, combine confectioners' sugar and 1-2 Tbsp. of the reserved peach juice to reach desired consistency. Drizzle over warm rolls.
1 roll: 279 cal., 7g fat (4g sat. fat), 19mg chol., 746mg sod., 52g carb. (35g sugars, 1g fiber), 3g pro.

GRANDMA'S ONION SQUARES

My grandma brought this recipe with her when she emigrated from Italy as a young wife and mother. It is still a family favorite.
—Janet Eddy, Stockton, CA

- -

Prep: 40 min. • **Bake:** 35 min.
Makes: 9 servings

- 2 Tbsp. olive oil
- 2 cups sliced onions
- 1 tsp. salt, divided
- ¼ tsp. pepper
- 2 cups all-purpose flour
- 3 tsp. baking powder
- 5 Tbsp. shortening
- ⅔ cup 2% milk
- 1 large egg, room temperature
- ¾ cup sour cream

1. Preheat oven to 400°. In a large skillet, heat oil over medium heat. Add onions; cook and stir until softened, 8-10 minutes. Reduce heat to medium-low; cook until deep golden brown, 30-40 minutes, stirring occasionally. Stir in ½ tsp. salt and the pepper.
2. Meanwhile, in a large bowl, combine flour, baking powder and remaining ½ tsp. salt. Cut in shortening until mixture resembles coarse crumbs. Stir in the milk just until moistened. Press into a greased 9-in. square baking pan; top with onions.
3. Combine egg and sour cream; spread over the onion layer. Bake until golden brown, 35-40 minutes. Cut into squares. Serve warm.
1 piece: 256 cal., 15g fat (5g sat. fat), 27mg chol., 447mg sod., 25g carb. (3g sugars, 1g fiber), 5g pro.

EASY CAST-IRON
PEACH BISCUIT ROLLS

LEMON RICOTTA FRITTERS

These lemony fritters are golden brown outside, soft and cakelike inside.
—Tina Mirilovich, Johstown, PA

Takes: 30 min. • **Makes:** about 2 dozen

1	cup all-purpose flour
2	tsp. baking powder
1½	tsp. grated lemon zest
	Pinch salt
3	large eggs, room temperature
1	cup whole-milk ricotta cheese
3	Tbsp. sugar
½	tsp. lemon extract
	Oil for deep-fat frying
	Confectioners' sugar
	Honey or strawberry jam

1. In a large bowl, whisk flour, baking powder, lemon zest and salt. In another bowl, whisk eggs, cheese, sugar and extract. Add to dry ingredients, stirring just until moistened.
2. In a deep cast-iron skillet or deep-fat fryer, heat the oil to 375°. Drop batter by tablespoonfuls, several at a time, into hot oil. Fry 2-3 minutes or until golden brown. Drain on paper towels. Dust with confectioners' sugar. Serve warm with honey or jam.

1 fritter: 60 cal., 3g fat (1g sat. fat), 24mg chol., 58mg sod., 5g carb. (2g sugars, 0 fiber), 2g pro.

ASK SARAH

IS THERE A SUBSTITUTE FOR BAKING POWDER?

Absolutely! If you're out of baking powder, follow this simple formula using baking soda and lemon juice. Use ¼ tsp. baking soda for each 1 tsp. baking powder and add ½ tsp. lemon juice to the recipe's wet ingredients. The acid in the juice will create the reaction your goodies need to puff up.

LEMON RICOTTA FRITTERS

LEMON POPOVERS WITH PECAN HONEY BUTTER

I received this recipe from my mom many years ago. We love the delicate lemon flavor with the pecan honey butter. The popovers are a nice addition to any dinner but they're especially delicious at breakfast with fruit.
—Joan Hallford, North Richland Hills, TX

Prep: 10 min. • **Bake:** 25 min.
Makes: 6 servings

  2 **large eggs, room temperature**
  1 **cup 2% milk**
  1 **cup all-purpose flour**
  ½ **tsp. salt**
  5 **Tbsp. finely chopped toasted pecans, divided**
  ¾ **tsp. grated lemon zest**
  2 **tsp. lemon juice**
  6 **Tbsp. butter, softened**
  6 **Tbsp. honey**

1. Preheat oven to 450°. In a large bowl, whisk eggs and milk until blended. Whisk in the flour and salt until smooth (do not overbeat). Stir in 3 Tbsp. pecans, lemon zest and lemon juice.
2. Generously grease a 6-cup popover pan with nonstick spray; fill cups half full with batter. Bake 15 minutes. Reduce oven setting to 350° (do not open oven door). Bake until deep golden brown, 10-15 minutes longer (do not underbake).
3. Meanwhile, combine butter, honey and remaining 2 Tbsp. pecans. Immediately remove popovers from pan to a wire rack. Pierce side of each popover with a sharp knife to let steam escape. Serve immediately with pecan honey butter.
1 popover with about 2 Tbsp. honey butter: 325 cal., 18g fat (9g sat. fat), 96mg chol., 332mg sod., 36g carb. (20g sugars, 1g fiber), 6g pro.

CRUSTY HOMEMADE BREAD

Homemade bread makes an average day extraordinary. Enjoy this recipe as written, or stir in a few favorites like cheese, garlic, herbs or dried fruits.
—Megumi Garcia, Milwaukee, WI

Prep: 20 min. + rising • **Bake:** 50 min.
Makes: 1 loaf (16 slices)

  1½ **tsp. active dry yeast**
  1¾ **cups warm water (110° to 115°)**
  3½ **cups plus 1 Tbsp. all-purpose flour, divided**
  2 **tsp. salt**
  1 **Tbsp. cornmeal or additional flour**

1. In a large bowl, dissolve yeast in warm water. Using a rubber spatula, stir in 3½ cups flour and salt to form a soft, sticky dough. Do not knead. Cover and let rise at room temperature 1 hour.
2. Stir down dough (dough will be sticky). Turn onto a floured surface; with floured hands pat into a 9-in. square. Fold square into thirds, forming a 9x3-in. rectangle. Fold rectangle into thirds, forming a 3-in. square. Place in a large greased bowl, turning once to grease the top. Cover and let rise at room temperature until almost doubled, 1 hour.
3. Punch down dough and repeat folding process. Return dough to bowl; refrigerate, covered, overnight.

4. Grease the bottom of a disposable foil roasting pan with sides at least 4 in. high; dust pan with cornmeal. Turn dough onto a floured surface. Knead gently 6-8 times; shape into a 6-in. round loaf. Place into prepared pan; dust the top with remaining 1 Tbsp. flour. Cover pan and let rise at room temperature until dough expands to a 7½-in. loaf, about 1¼ hours.
5. Preheat oven to 500°. Using a sharp knife, make a slash (¼ in. deep) across top of loaf. Cover pan tightly with foil. Bake on lowest oven rack 25 minutes.
6. Reduce oven setting to 450°. Remove foil; bake bread until deep golden brown, 25-30 minutes. Remove loaf to a wire rack to cool.
1 slice: 105 cal., 0 fat (0 sat. fat), 0 chol., 296mg sod., 22g carb. (0 sugars, 1g fiber), 3g pro.

"We love that this super easy bread makes beginner bakers look like pros. My college student son makes this every week."

—CATHERINE WARD, PREP KITCHEN MANAGER

CRUSTY HOMEMADE BREAD

SIMPLE BISCUITS

It's super easy to whip up a batch of these buttery biscuits to serve with breakfast or dinner. The dough is easy to work with, so there's no need to roll with a rolling pin; just pat it to the ideal thickness.
—*Taste of Home* Test Kitchen

Takes: 25 min. • **Makes:** 15 biscuits

    2   cups all-purpose flour
    3   tsp. baking powder
    1   tsp. salt
    ⅓   cup cold butter, cubed
    ⅔   cup 2% milk

1. Preheat oven to 450°. In a large bowl, whisk flour, baking powder and salt. Cut in butter until mixture resembles coarse crumbs. Add milk; stir just until moistened.
2. Turn onto a lightly floured surface; knead gently 8-10 times. Pat the dough to ½-in. thickness. Cut with a 2½-in. biscuit cutter.
3. Place 1 in. apart on an ungreased baking sheet. Bake until biscuits are golden brown, 10-15 minutes. Serve warm.
1 biscuit: 153 cal., 7g fat (4g sat. fat), 18mg chol., 437mg sod., 20g carb. (1g sugars, 1g fiber), 3g pro.

BEST-EVER CRESCENT ROLLS

My daughter and I have cranked out dozens of homemade crescent rolls over the years. I cut the dough into pie-shaped wedges; she rolls them up. It's a team effort, but we love the results!
—Irene Yeh, Birmingham, AL

Prep: 40 min. + chilling • **Bake:** 10 min./batch
Makes: 32 rolls

    3¾ to 4¼ cups all-purpose flour
    2   pkg. (¼ oz. each) active dry yeast
    1   tsp. salt
    1   cup 2% milk
    ½   cup butter, cubed
    ¼   cup honey
    3   large egg yolks, room temperature
    2   Tbsp. butter, melted

1. Combine 1½ cups flour, yeast and salt. In a small saucepan, heat milk, cubed butter and honey to 120°-130°. Add to dry ingredients; beat on medium speed 2 minutes. Add egg yolks; beat on high 2 minutes. Stir in enough remaining flour to form a soft dough (dough will be sticky).
2. Turn dough onto a floured surface; knead until smooth and elastic, 6-8 minutes. Place in a greased bowl, turning once to grease the top. Cover and let rise in a warm place until doubled, about 45 minutes.

3. Punch down dough. Cover and refrigerate overnight.
4. To bake, turn dough onto a lightly floured surface; divide in half. Roll each portion into a 14-in. circle; cut each circle into 16 wedges. Lightly brush wedges with melted butter. Roll up from wide ends, pinching pointed ends to seal. Place 2 in. apart on parchment-lined baking sheets, point side down. Cover with lightly greased plastic wrap; let rise in a warm place until doubled, about 45 minutes.
5. Preheat oven to 375°. Bake until golden brown, 9-11 minutes. Remove from pans to wire racks; serve warm.
Freeze option: Immediately after shaping, freeze rolls on parchment-lined baking sheets until firm. Transfer to a freezer container. Freeze up to 4 weeks. To use, let rise; bake as directed, increasing rise time to 2½-3 hours.
Note: To make filled rolls, brush dough circles with butter. Sprinkle half the filling over each circle of dough; shape and bake as directed.
1 unfilled roll: 104 cal., 4g fat (3g sat. fat), 28mg chol., 107mg sod., 14g carb. (3g sugars, 1g fiber), 2g pro.
Chive Crescents: ⅔ cup minced fresh chives.
Orange-Pecan Crescents: Toss 1 cup finely chopped pecans with ⅓ cup sugar and 4 tsp. grated orange zest.
Cranberry-Thyme Crescents: Toss 1 cup finely chopped dried cranberries, ⅔ cup finely chopped walnuts and 2 tsp. minced fresh thyme leaves.

BEST-EVER
CRESCENT ROLLS

JALAPENO BUTTERMILK CORNBREAD

CHEESE-FILLED GARLIC ROLLS

I added mozzarella cheese to change up plain old dinner rolls one night. Now my family requests them at every gathering. I don't mind, even in a time crunch.
—Rosalie Fittery, Philadelphia, PA

Prep: 20 min. + rising • **Bake:** 15 min.
Makes: 2 dozen

- 1 loaf (1 lb.) frozen bread dough, thawed
- 24 cubes part-skim mozzarella cheese (¾ in. each, about 10 oz.)
- 3 Tbsp. butter, melted
- 2 tsp. minced fresh parsley
- 1 garlic clove, minced
- ½ tsp. Italian seasoning
- ½ tsp. crushed red pepper flakes
- 2 Tbsp. grated Parmigiano-Reggiano cheese

1. Divide the dough into 24 portions. Shape each portion around a cheese cube to cover completely; pinch to seal. Place each roll in a greased muffin cup, seam side down. Cover with kitchen towels; let rise in a warm place until doubled, about 30 minutes. Preheat oven to 350°.
2. In a small bowl, mix butter, parsley, garlic, Italian seasoning and pepper flakes. Brush over rolls; sprinkle with cheese. Bake until golden brown, 15-18 minutes.
3. Cool 5 minutes before removing from pans. Serve warm.
1 roll: 103 cal., 5g fat (2g sat. fat), 12mg chol., 205mg sod., 10g carb. (1g sugars, 1g fiber), 5g pro.

JALAPENO BUTTERMILK CORNBREAD

If you're from the South, you know a good cornbread recipe is a must. Here's a lighter version of my mom's traditional cornbread.
—Debi Mitchell, Flower Mound, TX

- 1 cup self-rising flour
- 1 cup yellow cornmeal
- 1 cup buttermilk
- ¼ cup egg substitute
- 3 Tbsp. canola oil, divided
- 2 Tbsp. honey
- 1 Tbsp. reduced-fat mayonnaise
- ¼ cup fresh or frozen corn, thawed
- 3 Tbsp. shredded reduced-fat cheddar cheese
- 3 Tbsp. finely chopped sweet red pepper
- ½ to 1 jalapeno pepper, seeded and finely chopped

1. Preheat oven to 425°. In a large bowl, whisk flour and cornmeal. In another bowl, whisk buttermilk, egg substitute, 2 Tbsp. oil, honey and mayonnaise. Pour remaining oil into an 8-in. cast-iron or other ovenproof skillet; place skillet in oven 4 minutes.
2. Meanwhile, add buttermilk mixture to flour mixture; stir just until moistened. Fold in corn, cheese and peppers.
3. Carefully tilt and rotate skillet to coat bottom with oil; add batter. Bake until a toothpick inserted in center comes out clean, 20-25 minutes. Serve warm.
1 wedge: 180 cal., 4g fat (1g sat. fat), 4mg chol., 261mg sod., 32g carb. (6g sugars, 2g fiber), 6g pro. **Diabetic exchanges:** 2 starch, 1 fat.

CAST-IRON CHOCOLATE
CHIP BANANA BREAD

CAST-IRON CHOCOLATE CHIP BANANA BREAD

I love this cast-iron banana bread because it cooks evenly every time. The end result is so moist and delicious!
—Ashley Hudd, Holton, MI

- -

Prep: 20 min. • **Bake:** 25 min. + cooling
Makes: 10 servings

- ¼   cup butter, softened
- 1   cup sugar
- 1   large egg, room temperature
- 3   medium ripe bananas, mashed (about 1¼ cups)
- 1   tsp. vanilla extract
- 2   cups all-purpose flour
- 1   tsp. baking soda
- ½   tsp. salt
- 1   cup semisweet chocolate chips, divided
      Dried banana chips, optional

1. Preheat oven to 350°. In a large bowl, beat butter and sugar until crumbly. Beat in egg, bananas and vanilla. In another bowl, whisk flour, baking soda and salt; gradually beat into the banana mixture. Stir in ½ cup of the chocolate chips.

2. Transfer to a greased 10-in. cast-iron or other ovenproof skillet; sprinkle batter with remaining ½ cup chocolate chips. If desired, top with banana chips. Bake until a toothpick inserted in the center comes out clean, 25-30 minutes. Cool in pan on a wire rack.

1 slice: 330 cal., 10g fat (6g sat. fat), 31mg chol., 290mg sod., 58g carb. (34g sugars, 3g fiber), 4g pro.

TEST KITCHEN TIP

Homemade bread, due to its lack of preservatives, only lasts 3-5 days at room temperature. To maximize that time, place bread in a plastic bag and seal shut to trap in moisture. Make sure there's no condensation in the bag. Or, better yet, opt for a bread box, which creates the perfect humid yet breathable environment. To freeze bread, let it cool, then wrap in plastic wrap followed by a layer of foil. Loaves will last up to 6 months before they lose flavor and texture.

APPLE QUINOA SPOON BREAD

My cousin is a strict vegetarian, so creating satisfying veggie dishes is my annual holiday challenge. This spoon bread can act as a side, but the addition of hearty, healthy quinoa and vegetables makes it a well-rounded winter casserole. This can be an amazing Thanksgiving side dish, or a main vegetarian meal with a seasonal salad.
—Christine Wendland, Browns Mills, NJ

- -

Prep: 25 min. • **Bake:** 25 min.
Makes: 9 servings

- ⅔   cup water
- ⅓   cup quinoa, rinsed
- 1   Tbsp. canola oil
- 1   small apple, peeled and diced
- 1   small onion, finely chopped
- 1   small parsnip, peeled and diced
- ½   tsp. celery seed
- 1¼ tsp. salt, divided
- 1   Tbsp. minced fresh sage
- ¾   cup yellow cornmeal
- ¼   cup all-purpose flour
- 1   Tbsp. sugar
- 1   tsp. baking powder
- 1   large egg, room temperature
- 1½ cups 2% milk, divided

1. Preheat oven to 375°. In a small saucepan, bring water to a boil. Add quinoa. Reduce heat; simmer, covered, until the liquid is absorbed, 12-15 minutes. Fluff with a fork; cool slightly.

2. Meanwhile, in a large skillet, heat oil over medium heat; saute apple, onion and parsnip with celery seed and ½ tsp. of the salt until softened, 4-5 minutes. Remove from heat; stir in sage.

3. In a large bowl, whisk together cornmeal, flour, sugar, baking powder and remaining ¾ tsp. salt. In another bowl, whisk together egg and 1 cup milk. Add to the cornmeal mixture, stirring just until moistened. Fold in quinoa and apple mixture.

4. Transfer to a greased 8-in. square baking dish. Pour remaining milk over top.

5. Bake, uncovered, until edges are golden brown, 25-30 minutes. Let stand 5 minutes before serving.

1 serving: 153 cal., 4g fat (1g sat. fat), 24mg chol., 412mg sod., 26g carb. (6g sugars, 2g fiber), 5g pro. **Diabetic exchanges:** 1½ starch, 1 fat.

HAM & GREEN ONION BISCUITS

I started with my grandmother's biscuits and added a bit of my personality. When I make these biscuits with my kids, it feels as if she's with us.
—Amy Chase, Vanderhoof, BC

- -

Prep: 20 min. • **Bake:** 10 min.
Makes: about 1 dozen

- 2   cups all-purpose flour
- 3   tsp. baking powder
- 1   tsp. sugar
- ¼   tsp. garlic salt
      Dash pepper
- 6   Tbsp. cold butter, cubed
- 1   cup finely chopped fully cooked ham
- 2   green onions, chopped
- ¾   cup 2% milk

1. Preheat oven to 450°. In a large bowl, whisk the first 5 ingredients. Cut in butter until mixture resembles coarse crumbs. Stir in ham and green onions. Add milk; stir just until moistened.

2. Turn dough onto a lightly floured surface; knead gently 8-10 times. Pat or roll dough to ½-in. thickness; cut with a floured 2½-in. biscuit cutter. Place biscuits 2 in. apart on an ungreased baking sheet. Bake 10-12 minutes or until golden brown. Serve warm.

1 biscuit: 151 cal., 7g fat (4g sat. fat), 23mg chol., 315mg sod., 17g carb. (1g sugars, 1g fiber), 5g pro.

PESTO PINWHEEL BUNS

An easy spinach-basil pesto gives delectable flavor to these rolls.
—*Taste of Home* Test Kitchen

Prep: 30 min. + rising • **Bake:** 25 min.
Makes: 1 dozen

1 pkg. (¼ oz.) active dry yeast
3 Tbsp. warm water (110° to 115°)
½ cup warm 2% milk (110° to 115°)
2 Tbsp. butter, softened
1 large egg, room temperature
1 Tbsp. sugar
¾ tsp. salt
2¼ to 2¾ cups all-purpose flour
PESTO
1 cup fresh baby spinach
1 cup fresh basil leaves
2 garlic cloves
¼ cup walnut halves, toasted
¼ cup grated Parmesan cheese
⅛ tsp. pepper
¼ cup olive oil

1. In a large bowl, dissolve yeast in warm water. Add the milk, butter, egg, sugar, salt and 1½ cups flour. Beat until smooth. Stir in enough of the remaining flour to form a firm dough.
2. Turn onto a lightly floured surface; knead until smooth and elastic, 6-8 minutes. Place in a greased bowl, turning once to grease the top. Cover and let rise in a warm place until doubled, about 1 hour.
3. Meanwhile, place the babyspinach, basil, garlic, walnuts, cheese and pepper in a food processor; cover and process until blended. While processing, gradually add olive oil in a steady stream. Set aside.
4. Punch dough down. Turn onto a lightly floured surface. Roll dough into a 12x10-in. rectangle. Spread pesto to within ½ in. of edges. Roll up jelly-roll style, starting with a long side; pinch seam to seal. Cut into 12 rolls.
5. Place the rolls cut side up in a greased 13x9-in. baking pan. Cover and let rise until doubled, about 40 minutes.
6. Bake rolls at 350° until golden brown, 25-30 minutes. Remove from pan to a wire rack. Serve warm. Refrigerate leftovers.
1 bun: 181 cal., 9g fat (3g sat. fat), 25mg chol., 200mg sod., 20g carb. (2g sugars, 1g fiber), 5g pro.

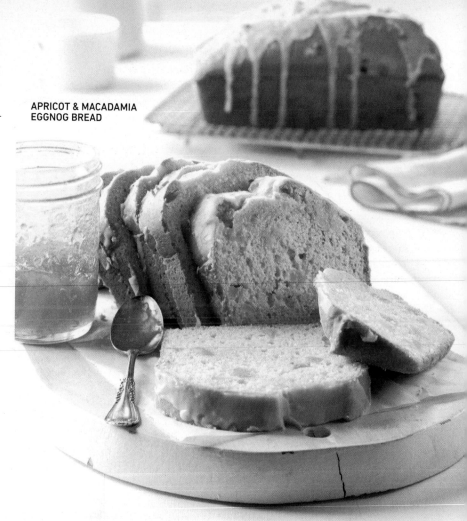

APRICOT & MACADAMIA EGGNOG BREAD

APRICOT & MACADAMIA EGGNOG BREAD

Holidays and nut breads are made for each other. My spiced quick bread has three of the ingredients I can't resist—eggnog, apricots and macadamia nuts.
—Nancy Heishman, Las Vegas, NV

Prep: 20 min. • **Bake:** 50 min. + cooling
Makes: 2 loaves (12 slices each)

4¾ cups all-purpose flour
¾ cup sugar
2 Tbsp. baking powder
½ tsp. salt
1 tsp. ground cinnamon
1 tsp. ground nutmeg
2 large eggs, room temperature
2½ cups eggnog
½ cup canola oil
1 Tbsp. grated orange zest
¼ cup orange juice
¾ cup chopped dried apricots
¾ cup chopped macadamia nuts

GLAZE
¾ cup confectioners' sugar
1 to 2 Tbsp. eggnog

1. Preheat oven to 350°. In a large bowl, whisk the first 6 ingredients. In another bowl, whisk eggs, 2½ cups eggnog, oil, orange zest and orange juice until blended. Add the liquid ingredients to the flour mixture; stir just until moistened. Fold in chopped apricots and macadamia nuts.
2. Transfer to 2 greased 9x5-in. loaf pans. Bake 50-60 minutes or until a toothpick inserted in center comes out clean. Cool in pans 10 minutes before removing to wire racks to cool completely.
3. For glaze, in a bowl, mix confectioners' sugar and enough eggnog to reach drizzling consistency. Spoon over loaves.
Freeze option: Securely wrap cooled loaves in plastic wrap and foil, then freeze. To use, thaw at room temperature.
1 slice: 242 cal., 10g fat (2g sat. fat), 32mg chol., 186mg sod., 35g carb. (15g sugars, 1g fiber), 5g pro.

SOCCA

Socca is a traditional flatbread from Nice, France. It's common to see it cooked on grills as street food, served chopped in a paper cone and sprinkled with salt, pepper or other delicious toppings. Bonus: It's gluten-free.
—*Taste of Home* Test Kitchen

- -

Prep: 5 min. + standing • **Cook:** 5 minutes
Makes: 6 servings

- 1 cup chickpea flour
- 1 cup water
- 2 Tbsp. extra virgin olive oil, divided
- ¾ tsp. salt
  Optional toppings: Za'atar seasoning, sea salt flakes, coarsely ground pepper and additional extra virgin olive oil

1. In a small bowl, whisk chickpea flour, water, 1 Tbsp. oil and salt until smooth. Let stand 30 minutes.
2. Meanwhile, preheat broiler. Place a 10-in. cast-iron skillet in oven until hot, about 5 minutes. Add remaining 1 Tbsp. oil to the pan; swirl to coat. Pour batter into the hot pan and tilt to coat evenly.
3. Broil 6 in. from heat until edges are crisp and browned and center just begins to brown, 5-7 minutes. Cut into wedges. If desired, top with optional ingredients.

1 wedge: 113 cal., 6g fat (1g sat. fat), 0 chol., 298mg sod., 12g carb. (2g sugars, 3g fiber), 4g pro. **Diabetic exchanges:** 1 fat, ½ starch.

SOCCA

CHEDDAR CORN DOG MUFFINS

I wanted a change from typical hot dogs in a bun, so I made corn dog muffins. I added jalapenos to this kid-friendly recipe...and that won my husband over, too.
—Becky Tarala, Palm Coast, FL

- -

Takes: 25 min. • **Makes:** 9 muffins

- 1 pkg. (8½ oz.) cornbread/muffin mix
- ⅔ cup 2% milk
- 1 large egg, lightly beaten, room temperature
- 5 turkey hot dogs, sliced
- ½ cup shredded sharp cheddar cheese
- 2 Tbsp. finely chopped pickled jalapeno, optional

1. Preheat oven to 400°. Line 9 muffin cups with foil liners or grease 9 nonstick muffin cups.
2. In a small bowl, combine the muffin mix, milk and egg; stir in hot dogs, cheese and, if desired, jalapeno. Fill prepared muffin cups three-fourths full.
3. Bake until a toothpick inserted in center comes out clean, 14-18 minutes. Cool for 5 minutes before removing from pan to a wire rack. Serve warm. Refrigerate leftovers.
Freeze option: Freeze cooled muffins in freezer containers. To use, microwave each muffin on high until heated through, 30-60 seconds.

1 muffin: 216 cal., 10g fat (4g sat. fat), 46mg chol., 619mg sod., 23g carb. (7g sugars, 2g fiber), 8g pro.

MEATBALL ALPHABET
SOUP, PAGE 91

Soups, Salads & Sandwiches

Soup's on! And grab a big plate for a salad or sandwich, too. The fun, hearty and creative flavor combinations in these recipes shake up dull lunch and dinnertime routines. Whether you enjoy a fresh mix of greens as a light lunch on a warm day or hot, hearty soup and sub to fortify your family on chilly night, you'll agree this is comfort food at its finest.

YUMMY CORN
CHIP SALAD

YUMMY CORN CHIP SALAD

Corn chips give crunch and unexpected flavor to this potluck-favorite salad. Bacon adds a hint of smokiness while cranberries bring a touch of sweetness. It's the perfect picnic companion!
—Nora Friesen, Aberdeen, MS

- -

Takes: 25 min. • **Makes:** 12 servings

- ¾ cup canola oil
- ¼ cup cider vinegar
- ¼ cup mayonnaise
- 2 Tbsp. yellow mustard
- ½ tsp. salt
- ¾ cup sugar
- ½ small onion
- ¾ tsp. poppy seeds

SALAD

- 2 bunches leaf lettuce, chopped (about 20 cups)
- 1 pkg. (9¼ oz.) corn chips
- 8 bacon strips, cooked and crumbled
- 1 cup shredded part-skim mozzarella cheese
- 1 cup dried cranberries

1. For dressing, place first 7 ingredients in a blender. Cover; process until smooth. Stir in poppy seeds.
2. Place salad ingredients in a large bowl; toss with dressing. Serve immediately.
1⅓ cups: 436 cal., 30g fat (4g sat. fat), 12mg chol., 456mg sod., 38g carb. (24g sugars, 2g fiber), 7g pro.

DUTCH-OVEN BARBECUED PORK SANDWICHES

TEST KITCHEN TIP

If you don't want to stand over the stovetop to fry bacon or want to cook a large amount at once, try the easy oven-bake method. Line a 15x10x1-in. sheet pan with aluminum foil. Arrange bacon in a single layer and bake at 400° to desired doneness, which will take 16-25 minutes. Remove bacon to paper towels. With this simple method, there's no need turn the bacon while cooking, and all the strips of bacon will bake up evenly. And because the grease collects on the foil, cleanup is a breeze.

THAT GOOD SALAD

When a friend shared this recipe, it had a fancy French name. Our children can never remember it, so they say, "Mom, please make *that good salad.*" Now our friends and neighbors request it for potluck dinners.
—Betty Lamb, Orem, UT

- -

Takes: 20 min.
Makes: 14 servings

- ¾ cup canola oil
- ¼ cup lemon juice
- 2 garlic cloves, minced
- ½ tsp. salt
- ½ tsp. pepper
- 2 bunches (1 lb. each) romaine, torn
- 2 cups chopped tomatoes
- 1 cup shredded Swiss cheese
- ⅔ cup slivered almonds, toasted, optional
- ½ cup grated Parmesan cheese
- 8 bacon strips, cooked and crumbled
- 1 cup Caesar salad croutons

1. In a jar with a tight-fitting lid, combine the oil, lemon juice, garlic, salt and pepper; cover and shake well. Chill in the refrigerator.
2. In a large serving bowl, toss the romaine, tomatoes, Swiss cheese, almonds if desired, Parmesan cheese and bacon.
3. Shake dressing; pour over salad and toss. Add croutons and serve immediately.
1 cup: 193 cal., 17g fat (4g sat. fat), 13mg chol., 257mg sod., 5g carb. (1g sugars, 1g fiber), 6g pro.

DUTCH-OVEN BARBECUED PORK SANDWICHES

These fabulous pulled pork sandwiches have a sweet, tangy flavor. If you want a smokier taste, add a little liquid smoke to the pulled pork before returning the meat to the Dutch oven.
—*Taste of Home* Test Kitchen

- -

Prep: 15 min. • **Cook:** 4 hours
Makes: 8 servings

- 1 can (8 oz.) tomato sauce
- 1 large onion, chopped
- 1 cup barbecue sauce
- 3 tsp. chili powder
- 1 tsp. ground cumin
- ½ tsp. ground cinnamon
- 1 boneless pork sirloin roast (2 lbs.)
- 8 seeded hamburger bun, split

1. In a Dutch oven, combine the first 6 ingredients; add the pork. Spoon some of the sauce over pork. Bring to a boil; reduce heat and simmer, covered, until meat is tender, 3-4 hours.
2. Remove meat; shred with 2 forks. Return to pan and heat through. Spoon ½ cup onto each bun.
1 sandwich: 357 cal., 9g fat (3g sat. fat), 68mg chol., 771mg sod., 40g carb. (16g sugars, 2g fiber), 28g pro.

MARINATED TENDERLOIN & AVOCADO ON BAGUETTE TOASTS

There's never any waste with tenderloin (and leftovers are rare). You can dress it up by substituting baguette toppings and having fun with it.
—Bonnie Hawkins, Elkhorn, WI

- -

Prep: 20 min. • **Cook:** 15 min. + marinating
Makes: 2 servings

- 2 **beef tenderloin steaks (1 in. thick and 4 oz. each)**
- 1 **Tbsp. olive oil**
- 1 **Tbsp. canola oil**
- 1 **Tbsp. red wine vinegar**
- ½ **tsp. salt**
- ½ **tsp. Dijon mustard**
- 4 **slices red onion, separated into rings**
- 8 **slices French bread baguette (½ in. thick), toasted**
- ½ **medium ripe avocado, peeled and sliced**
- 1 **Tbsp. minced fresh parsley**

1. Heat a large nonstick skillet over medium heat until hot. Place steaks in skillet; cook until meat reaches desired doneness (for medium-rare, a thermometer should read 135°; medium, 140°; medium-well, 145°), 5-7 minutes per side. Let stand 10 minutes; cut into thin slices.
2. In a small bowl, combine oils, vinegar, salt and mustard. Add onion and steak; turn to coat. Refrigerate overnight.
3. Drain beef, discarding the marinade. Layer toasts with beef, onion and avocado; sprinkle with parsley.
1 serving: 432 cal., 26g fat (5g sat. fat), 49mg chol., 817mg sod., 22g carb. (1g sugars, 3g fiber), 29g pro.

KALE CAESAR SALAD

I love Caesar salads, so I created this blend of kale and romaine lettuces with a creamy homemade Caesar dressing. It's perfect paired with grilled chicken or steak for a light weeknight meal.
—Rashanda Cobbins, Food Editor

- -

Takes: 15 min. • **Makes:** 8 servings

- 4 **cups chopped fresh kale**
- 4 **cups torn romaine**
- 1 **cup Caesar salad croutons**
- ½ **cup shredded Parmesan cheese**
- ½ **cup mayonnaise**
- 2 **Tbsp. lemon juice**
- 1 **Tbsp. Worcestershire sauce**
- 2 **tsp. Dijon mustard**
- 2 **tsp. anchovy paste**
- 1 **garlic clove, minced**
- ¼ **tsp. salt**
- ¼ **tsp. pepper**

In a large salad bowl, toss the chopped kale, lettuce, croutons and cheese. For dressing, combine remaining ingredients in a small bowl; pour over the salad and toss to coat. Serve immediately.
1 cup: 148 cal., 13g fat (3g sat. fat), 10mg chol., 417mg sod., 6g carb. (1g sugars, 1g fiber), 3g pro. **Diabetic exchanges:** 2½ fat, 1 vegetable.

DID YOU KNOW?
Anchovies are fish related to herring and are usually purchased canned in oil or packed in salt. Anchovy paste is made from cured anchovies ground into a paste. It's usually sold in a tube in the canned seafood section.

KALE CAESAR SALAD

**DILLY CHICKPEA
SALAD SANDWICHES**

THE ULTIMATE CHICKEN NOODLE SOUP

My first Wisconsin winter was so cold, all I wanted to eat was soup. This recipe is in heavy rotation at our house from November to April.
—Gina Nistico, Denver, CO

- -

Prep: 15 min. • **Cook:** 45 min. + standing
Makes: 10 servings (about 3½ qt.)

2½ lbs. bone-in chicken thighs
½ tsp. salt
½ tsp. pepper
1 Tbsp. canola oil
1 large onion, chopped
1 garlic clove, minced
10 cups chicken broth
4 celery ribs, chopped
4 medium carrots, chopped
2 bay leaves
1 tsp. minced fresh thyme
   or ¼ tsp. dried thyme
3 cups uncooked kluski or other
   egg noodles (about 8 oz.)
1 Tbsp. chopped fresh parsley
1 Tbsp. lemon juice
   Optional: Additional salt and pepper

1. Pat chicken dry with paper towels; sprinkle with salt and pepper. In a 6-qt. stockpot, heat oil over medium-high heat. Add chicken in batches, skin side down; cook until dark golden brown, 3-4 minutes. Remove chicken from pan; remove and discard skin. Discard drippings, reserving 2 Tbsp..
2. Add onion to drippings; cook and stir over medium-high heat until tender, 4-5 minutes. Add garlic; cook 1 minute longer. Add broth, stirring to loosen browned bits from pan. Bring to a boil. Return chicken to pan. Add celery, carrots, bay leaves and fresh thyme. Reduce heat; simmer, covered, until chicken is tender, 25-30 minutes.
3. Transfer chicken to a plate. Remove soup from heat. Add noodles; let stand, covered, until noodles are tender, 20-22 minutes.
4. Meanwhile, when chicken is cool enough to handle, remove meat from bones; discard bones. Shred meat into bite-sized pieces. Return meat to stockpot. Stir in chopped parsley and lemon juice. If desired, adjust seasoning with additional salt and pepper. Discard the bay leaves.
1⅓ cups: 239 cal., 12g fat (3g sat. fat), 68mg chol., 1176mg sod., 14g carb. (3g sugars, 2g fiber), 18g pro.

DILLY CHICKPEA SALAD SANDWICHES

This chickpea salad is flavorful and contains less fat and cholesterol than chicken salad. These make delightful picnic sandwiches.
—Deanna Wolfe, Muskegon, MI

- -

Takes: 15 min. • **Makes:** 6 servings

1 can (15 oz.) chickpeas or
   garbanzo beans, rinsed and drained
½ cup finely chopped onion
½ cup finely chopped celery
½ cup reduced-fat mayonnaise
   or vegan mayonnaise
3 Tbsp. honey mustard
   or Dijon mustard
2 Tbsp. snipped fresh dill
1 Tbsp. red wine vinegar
¼ tsp. salt
¼ tsp. paprika
¼ tsp. pepper
12 slices multigrain bread
   Optional: Romaine leaves, tomato
   slices, dill pickle slices and sweet red
   pepper rings

Place garbanzo beans in a large bowl; mash to desired consistency. Stir in onion, celery, mayonnaise, mustard, dill, vinegar, salt, paprika and pepper. Spread over each of 6 bread slices; layer with toppings of your choice and remaining bread.
1 sandwich: 295 cal., 11g fat (2g sat. fat), 7mg chol., 586mg sod., 41g carb. (9g sugars, 7g fiber), 10g pro.

ROASTED BEET SALAD
WITH ORANGE VINAIGRETTE

BEST ITALIAN SAUSAGE SANDWICHES

Need a different type of sandwich? The rich tomato sauce simmers all afternoon in the slow cooker, ready to top freshly grilled Italian sausages. It's a great combination with lots of crowd appeal!
—*Taste of Home* Test Kitchen

Prep: 10 min. • **Cook:** 4 hours
Makes: 10 servings

- 2 jars (24 oz. each) pasta sauce
- 2 medium green peppers, cut into strips
- 2 medium onions, thinly sliced
- ½ tsp. garlic powder
- ½ tsp. fennel seed, crushed
- 2 pkg. (20 oz. each) Italian turkey sausage links
- 10 hoagie buns, split

1. In a 3-qt. slow cooker, combine the first 5 ingredients. Cook, covered, on low for about 4 hours or until vegetables are tender.
2. Grill the sausages according to package directions. Serve on buns with sauce.

Freeze option: Freeze cooled sauce in freezer containers. To use, partially thaw in refrigerator overnight. Heat through in a saucepan, stirring occasionally; add water if necessary.

1 sandwich: 454 cal., 15g fat (3g sat. fat), 68mg chol., 1716mg sod., 52g carb. (17g sugars, 4g fiber), 29g pro.

ROASTED BEET SALAD WITH ORANGE VINAIGRETTE

I fill my salad bowl with beets, oranges and baby spinach. Beet are good for you and colorful, too. This fresh medley makes an appealing side for any occasion.
—Nancy Heishman, Las Vegas, NV

Prep: 25 min. • **Bake:** 50 min. + cooling
Makes: 12 servings

- 3 medium fresh beets (about 1 lb.)
- 3 Tbsp. olive oil
- 1 tsp. grated orange zest
- 2 Tbsp. orange juice
- 1 Tbsp. white wine vinegar
- 2 tsp. honey
- 1 tsp. Dijon mustard
- ½ tsp. salt
- ¼ tsp. pepper
- 3 Tbsp. minced fresh tarragon, divided
- 1 pkg. (6 oz.) fresh baby spinach
- 4 cups torn mixed salad greens
- 2 medium navel oranges, peeled and sectioned
- 4 oz. crumbled goat cheese
- ½ cup chopped walnuts, toasted

1. Preheat oven to 425°. Scrub beets and trim tops to 1 in. Wrap in foil; place on a baking sheet. Bake 50-60 minutes or until tender. Remove foil; cool completely. Peel beets and cut into wedges.
2. In a small bowl, whisk oil, orange zest, orange juice, vinegar, honey, mustard, salt and pepper until blended; stir in 1 Tbsp. tarragon. In a large bowl, combine spinach, salad greens and remaining tarragon. Drizzle with vinaigrette and toss gently to coat.
3. Transfer to a platter or divide among 12 salad plates. Top with orange sections and beets; sprinkle with cheese and walnuts. Serve immediately.

1 cup: 125 cal., 9g fat (2g sat. fat), 12mg chol., 195mg sod., 10g carb. (6g sugars, 2g fiber), 4g pro. **Diabetic exchanges:** 2 vegetable, 2 fat.

ASK SARAH

WHAT IS FENNEL SEED?

Fennel seed is the fruit of the vegetable of the same name. It has a slightly sweet and licorice-like flavor, similar to anise. It is frequently used in baked goods, sausage, pork and seafood dishes, and cuisines from around the world.

BEST ITALIAN
SAUSAGE SANDWICHES

QUICK HAM & BEAN SOUP

If you like ham and bean soup but don't want to spend hours in the kitchen, this version is the one for you. It's delicious and takes just 30 minutes from start to finish.
—*Taste of Home* Test Kitchen

- -

Takes: 30 min. • **Makes:** 7 servings

   2   medium carrots, sliced
   2   celery ribs, chopped
   ½   cup chopped onion
   2   Tbsp. butter
   4   cans (15½ oz. each) great
        northern beans, rinsed and drained
   4   cups chicken broth
   2   cups cubed fully cooked ham
   1   tsp. chili powder
   ½   tsp. minced garlic
   ¼   tsp. pepper
   1   bay leaf

In a large saucepan, saute the carrots, celery and onion in butter until tender. Stir in the remaining ingredients. Bring mixture to a boil. Reduce heat; cook for 15 minutes or until heated through. Discard bay leaf.

1 cup: 168 cal., 7g fat (3g sat. fat), 30mg chol., 1242mg sod., 14g carb. (3g sugars, 4g fiber), 12g pro.

TEST KITCHEN TIP

Bay leaves are sold whole, and may be fresh or dried. Their savory, spicy and aromatic flavor makes them ideal for enhancing the flavor of soups, stews, meats, casseroles and other dishes. You can find fresh bay leaves with other herbs in the produce section of most supermarkets. Alhough they're nontoxic, bay leaves are not meant to be eaten, so be sure to remove them before serving. To preserve leftover bay leaves, rinse and pat them dry, freeze quickly in a single layer, then store in a freezer container.

QUICK HAM &
BEAN SOUP

EASY SLOW-COOKER POTATO SOUP

This hearty slow-cooker potato soup tastes just like a loaded baked potato. Pop in the ingredients before heading to work in the morning for a quick and easy supper.
—*Taste of Home* Test Kitchen

Prep: 10 min. • **Cook:** 6 hours
Makes: 8 servings

- 1   carton (32 oz.) chicken broth
- 1   pkg. (30 oz.) frozen shredded hash brown potatoes, thawed
- 1   small onion, finely chopped
- 2   garlic cloves, minced
- ¼   tsp. pepper
- 1   pkg. (8 oz.) cream cheese, softened and cubed
- 1   cup half-and-half cream
- 1   cup shredded cheddar cheese
       Optional: crumbled cooked bacon and chopped green onions

1. In a 4- or 5-qt. slow cooker, combine broth, potatoes, onion, garlic and pepper. Cook, covered, on low 6-8 hours or until vegetables are tender.
2. Mash potatoes to desired consistency. Whisk in cream cheese until melted. Stir in half-and-half. Cook, covered, until heated through, 5-10 minutes longer. Serve with cheese and, if desired, crumbled bacon and green onions.
1 cup: 294 cal., 18g fat (10g sat. fat), 60mg chol., 711mg sod., 24g carb. (4g sugars, 1g fiber), 9g pro.

GRILLED CHEESE & AVOCADO SANDWICH

Who doesn't love a grilled cheese sandwich? This grown-up version kicks it up a notch with avocado, five kinds of cheese and extra-crispy bread.
—Josh Rink, Food Stylist

Takes: 25 min. • **Makes:** 4 servings

- 6   Tbsp. butter, softened, divided
- 8   slices sourdough bread
- ½   cup shredded sharp white cheddar cheese
- ½   cup shredded Monterey Jack cheese
- ½   cup shredded Gruyere cheese
- 3   Tbsp. mayonnaise
- 3   Tbsp. finely shredded Manchego or Parmesan cheese
- ⅛   tsp. onion powder
- 4   oz. Brie cheese, rind removed, sliced
- 2   medium ripe avocado, peeled and sliced

1. Spread 3 Tbsp. butter on 1 side of each slice of bread. Place bread, butter side down, in a large cast-iron skillet or on an electric griddle over medium-low heat until golden brown, 2-3 minutes; remove. In a small bowl, combine cheddar, Monterey Jack and Gruyere. In another bowl, mix together remaining 3 Tbsp. butter, mayonnaise, Manchego cheese and onion powder.
2. To assemble sandwiches, top toasted side of 4 bread slices with sliced Brie; add avocado slices. Sprinkle cheddar cheese mixture evenly over avocado slices. Top with remaining bread slices, toasted side facing inward. Spread the butter-mayonnaise mixture on the outsides of each sandwich. Place in same skillet and cook until golden brown and cheese is melted, 5-6 minutes on each side. Serve immediately.
1 sandwich: 773 cal., 60g fat (28g sat. fat), 122mg chol., 1023mg sod., 36g carb. (3g sugars, 6g fiber), 26g pro.

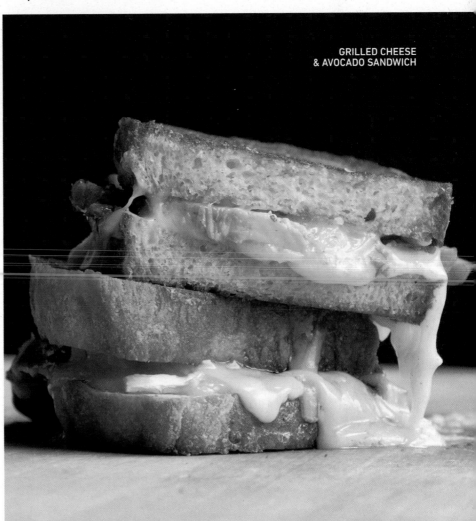

GRILLED CHEESE & AVOCADO SANDWICH

CRUNCHY LEMON-PESTO
GARDEN SALAD

TURKEY WAFFLEWICHES

Who knew lunch could be so fun? You'll see smiles around the table when you serve this decadent waffle-inspired sandwich.
—*Taste of Home* Test Kitchen

- -

Takes: 15 min. • **Makes:** 4 servings

- 3 oz. cream cheese, softened
- ¼ cup whole-berry cranberry sauce
- 1 Tbsp. maple pancake syrup
- ¼ tsp. pepper
- 8 slices white bread
- ¾ lb. sliced deli turkey
- 2 Tbsp. butter, softened

1. In a small bowl, beat the cream cheese, cranberry sauce, syrup and pepper until combined. Spread over 4 slices of bread; top with turkey and remaining bread. Spread butter over both sides of sandwiches.
2. Bake in a preheated waffle iron or indoor grill according to manufacturer's directions until golden brown, 2-3 minutes.
1 sandwich: 407 cal., 17g fat (8g sat. fat), 67mg chol., 1179mg sod., 41g carb. (10g sugars, 2g fiber), 23g pro.

TEST KITCHEN TIP
Deli meat is typically lean, like the turkey used in these sandwiches, but it's also high in sodium. Switch to low-sodium lunch meat or leftover cooked turkey or chicken to keep your salt intake in check.

CRUNCHY LEMON-PESTO GARDEN SALAD

I use fresh vegetables straight from the garden to prepare this salad. If I pick the squash and cucumbers early enough, their skins are so tender they don't need to be removed. This salad is adaptable—any fresh veggie from the garden can be swapped in with delicious results!
—Carmell Childs, Orangeville, UT

- -

Takes: 25 min. • **Makes:** 6 servings

- 5 Tbsp. prepared pesto
- 1 Tbsp. lemon juice
- 2 tsp. grated lemon zest
- 1½ tsp. Dijon mustard
- ¼ tsp. garlic salt
- ¼ tsp. pepper
- 2½ cups thinly sliced yellow summer squash
- 1¾ cups thinly sliced mini cucumbers
- ¾ cup fresh peas
- ½ cup shredded Parmesan cheese
- ¼ cup thinly sliced green onions
- 5 thick-sliced bacon strips, cooked and crumbled

In a small bowl, whisk together the first 6 ingredients until blended. In a large salad bowl, combine squash, cucumbers, peas, Parmesan and green onions. Pour dressing over salad; toss to coat. Top with crumbled bacon to serve.
¾ cup: 159 cal., 11g fat (3g sat. fat), 13mg chol., 586mg sod., 8g carb. (4g sugars, 2g fiber), 8g pro. **Diabetic exchanges:** 2 fat, 1 vegetable.

SPICY PERUVIAN POTATO SOUP

This robust Peruvian soup (known there as *locro de papa*) has the comfort of potatoes and the warming spiciness of chiles. Light enough for a simple lunch, it's also satisfying served as a main dish for dinner.
—*Taste of Home* Test Kitchen

- -

Prep: 35 min. • **Cook:** 4 hours
Makes: 8 servings (2 qt.)

- 1 Tbsp. olive oil
- 1 medium onion, chopped
- 1 medium sweet red pepper, cut into 1-in. pieces
- 3 garlic cloves, minced
- 1 carton (32 oz.) chicken stock
- 2 large Yukon Gold potatoes, peeled and cut into 1-in. cubes
- 1 can (4 oz.) chopped green chiles
- ½ cup minced fresh cilantro, divided
- ½ to 1 serrano pepper, seeded and finely chopped
- 2 tsp. ground cumin
- 1 tsp. dried oregano
- ¼ tsp. salt
- ¼ tsp. pepper
- 1 fully cooked Spanish chorizo link (3 oz.), chopped
  Optional toppings: Sour cream and cubed avocado

1. In a large skillet, heat oil over medium-high heat. Add onion and sweet pepper; cook and stir until crisp-tender, 6-8 minutes. Add the garlic; cook 1 minute longer. Transfer to a 4- or 5-qt. slow cooker. Add the chicken stock, potatoes, chiles, ¼ cup cilantro, serrano pepper and seasonings. Cook, covered, on low 4-6 hours, until potatoes are tender.
2. Remove soup from heat; cool slightly. Process in batches in a blender until smooth. Return to slow cooker. Stir in chorizo and remaining ¼ cup cilantro; heat through. If desired, serve with sour cream and avocado.
1 cup: 153 cal., 5g fat (1g sat. fat), 7mg chol., 472mg sod., 23g carb. (3g sugars, 2g fiber), 6g pro. **Diabetic exchanges:** 1½ starch, 1 fat.

HEALTHY GAZPACHO FOR 2

Nutritious vegetables are the basis of this tasty chilled soup. We recommend using spicy V-8 juice for a more kicked-up version.
—*Taste of Home* Test Kitchen

- -

Prep: 20 min. + chilling • **Makes:** 2 servings

- 2 medium tomatoes, seeded and chopped
- ½ small green pepper, chopped
- ⅓ cup chopped peeled cucumber
- ⅓ cup chopped red onion
- 1⅓ cups reduced-sodium tomato juice
- ¼ tsp. dried oregano
- ¼ tsp. dried basil
- ⅛ tsp. salt
- 1 small garlic clove, minced
  Dash pepper
  Dash hot pepper sauce
- 1 Tbsp. minced chives
  Chopped sweet yellow pepper, optional

1. In a large bowl, combine the tomatoes, green pepper, cucumber and onion. In another bowl, combine the tomato juice, oregano, basil, salt, garlic, pepper and pepper sauce; pour over vegetables.
2. Cover and refrigerate for at least 4 hours or overnight. Just before serving, sprinkle with chives and, if desired, yellow pepper.
1½ cups: 81 cal., 0 fat (0 sat. fat), 0 chol., 252mg sod., 17g carb. (11g sugars, 4g fiber), 3g pro. **Diabetic exchanges:** 1 starch.

SPICY PERUVIAN
POTATO SOUP

MEATBALL
ALPHABET SOUP

MEATBALL ALPHABET SOUP

Bite-sized meatballs made from ground turkey perk up this fun alphabet soup. A variety of vegetables are mixed in a rich tomato broth seasoned with herbs.
—*Taste of Home* Test Kitchen

Prep: 20 min. • **Cook:** 35 min.
Makes: 9 servings (about 3½ qt.)

- 1 **large egg, lightly beaten**
- 2 **Tbsp. quick-cooking oats**
- 2 **Tbsp. grated Parmesan cheese**
- ¼ **tsp. garlic powder**
- ¼ **tsp. Italian seasoning**
- ½ **lb. lean ground turkey**
- 1 **cup chopped onion**
- 1 **cup chopped celery**
- 1 **cup chopped carrots**
- 1 **cup diced peeled potatoes**
- 1 **Tbsp. olive oil**
- 2 **garlic cloves, minced**
- 4 **cans (14½ oz. each) reduced-sodium chicken broth**
- 1 **can (28 oz.) diced tomatoes, undrained**
- 1 **can (6 oz.) tomato paste**
- ¼ **cup minced fresh parsley**
- 1 **tsp. dried basil**
- 1 **tsp. dried thyme**
- ¾ **cup uncooked alphabet pasta**

1. In a bowl, combine the first 5 ingredients. Crumble turkey over mixture and mix well. Shape into ½-in. balls. In a nonstick skillet, brown the meatballs in small batches over medium heat until no longer pink. Remove from the heat; set aside.

2. In a large saucepan or Dutch oven, saute the onion, celery, carrots and potatoes in oil for 5 minutes or until crisp-tender. Add the garlic; saute 1 minute longer. Add the broth, tomatoes, tomato paste, parsley, basil and thyme; bring to a boil. Add pasta; cook for 5-6 minutes. Reduce heat; add meatballs. Simmer, uncovered, for 15-20 minutes or until vegetables are tender.

1½ cups: 192 cal., 5g fat (1g sat. fat), 39mg chol., 742mg sod., 26g carb. (8g sugars, 4g fiber), 13g pro.

MICHIGAN CHERRY SALAD

MICHIGAN CHERRY SALAD

This salad brings to mind what I love about my home state: apple picking with my kids, buying greens at the farmers market and tasting cherries while on vacation.
—Jennifer Gilbert, Brighton, MI

Takes: 15 min. • **Makes:** 8 servings

- 7 **oz. fresh baby spinach (about 9 cups)**
- 3 **oz. spring mix salad greens (about 5 cups)**
- 1 **large apple, chopped**
- ½ **cup coarsely chopped pecans, toasted**
- ½ **cup dried cherries**
- ¼ **cup crumbled Gorgonzola cheese**

DRESSING

- ¼ **cup fresh raspberries**
- ¼ **cup red wine vinegar**
- 3 **Tbsp. cider vinegar**
- 3 **Tbsp. cherry preserves**
- 1 **Tbsp. sugar**
- 2 **Tbsp. olive oil**

1. In a large salad bowl, combine the first 6 ingredients.

2. Place raspberries, vinegars, cherry preserves and sugar in a blender. While processing, gradually add oil in a steady stream. Drizzle over salad; toss to coat.

1½ cups: 172 cal., 10g fat (2g sat. fat), 3mg chol., 78mg sod., 21g carb. (16g sugars, 3g fiber), 3g pro. **Diabetic exchanges:** 2 vegetable, 2 fat, 1 starch.

KOHLRABI, CUCUMBER & TOMATO SALAD

This chilled, refreshing salad is wonderful on hot days. It has a nice crunch and a delicious balance of sweet and spicy flavors.
—Kristina Segarra, Yonkers, NY

- -

Prep: 30 min. + chilling • **Makes:** 6 servings

- 2   **Tbsp. olive oil**
- 1   **medium red onion, finely chopped**
- 2   **pickled hot cherry peppers, seeded and finely chopped**
- 2   **garlic cloves, minced**
- 2   **Tbsp. cider vinegar**
- 1   **tsp. salt**
- 1   **kohlrabi, peeled and cut into ½-in. pieces**
- 2   **large yellow tomatoes, seeded and chopped**
- 2   **mini cucumbers, cut into ½-in. pieces**
- 2   **Tbsp. minced fresh cilantro**

1. In a small skillet, heat oil over medium-high heat. Add onion; cook and stir 2-3 minutes or until crisp-tender. Add peppers and garlic; cook 2 minutes longer. Stir in vinegar and salt; remove from heat.

2. In a large bowl, combine the kohlrabi, tomatoes and cucumbers. Pour in onion mixture; gently toss to coat. Chill for 1 hour. Sprinkle with cilantro before serving.

¾ cup: 59 cal., 4g fat (1g sat. fat), 0 chol., 372mg sod., 6g carb. (2g sugars, 2g fiber), 2g pro. **Diabetic exchanges:** 1 vegetable, ½ fat.

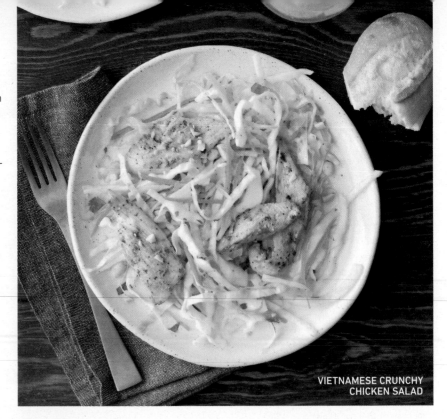

VIETNAMESE CRUNCHY CHICKEN SALAD

VIETNAMESE CRUNCHY CHICKEN SALAD

When I lived in Cleveland, I frequently dined at a stellar Vietnamese restaurant. This chicken salad quickly became my favorite. Because I had it so often, I figured out the components and flavors and created my own easy-to-make version.
—Erin Schillo, Northfield, OH

- -

Prep: 30 min. + marinating • **Cook:** 10 min.
Makes: 4 servings

- 3   **Tbsp. olive oil**
- 2   **Tbsp. lime juice**
- 1   **Tbsp. minced fresh cilantro**
- 1½ **tsp. grated lime zest**
- ½   **tsp. salt**
- ½   **tsp. pepper**
- ¼   **tsp. cayenne pepper**
- 1   **lb. boneless skinless chicken breasts, cut into thin strips**

DRESSING
- ½   **cup olive oil**
- ¼   **cup lime juice**
- 2   **Tbsp. rice vinegar**
- 2   **Tbsp. sugar**
- 1   **Tbsp. grated lime zest**
- ¾   **tsp. salt**
- ½   **tsp. crushed red pepper flakes**
- ¼   **tsp. pepper**

SALAD
- 5   **cups thinly sliced cabbage (about 1 lb.)**
- 1   **cup minced fresh cilantro**
- 1   **cup julienned carrots**
- 1   **cup salted peanuts, coarsely chopped**

1. In a large bowl, mix the first 7 ingredients; add chicken and toss to coat. Refrigerate, covered, 30 minutes. In a small bowl, whisk dressing ingredients.

2. In a large skillet over medium-high heat, stir-fry half the chicken mixture until no longer pink, 4-5 minutes. Remove from pan; repeat with remaining chicken. Cool slightly.

3. In a large bowl, combine the cabbage, minced cilantro, carrots and chicken; toss to combine. Add chopped peanuts and dressing; toss to coat. Serve immediately.

2 cups: 743 cal., 59g fat (9g sat. fat), 63mg chol., 1068mg sod., 25g carb. (12g sugars, 7g fiber), 35g pro.

"This recipe is an old standby. I never add the chicken to mine and serve it as a side dish instead. The peanuts and cilantro make this fresh and flavorful!"

—STEPHANIE MARCHESE, VISUAL PRODUCTION EXECUTIVE DIRECTOR

EASY BUTTERNUT SQUASH SOUP

When the weather turns cold, get cozy with a bowl of this butternut squash soup. The cream adds richness, but if you're looking to cut calories, it can be omitted.
—*Taste of Home* Test Kitchen

Takes: 30 min. • **Makes:** 9 servings

- 1 Tbsp. olive oil
- 1 large onion, chopped
- 3 garlic cloves, minced
- 1 medium butternut squash (3 lbs.), peeled and cubed
- 4 cups vegetable broth
- ¾ tsp. salt
- ¼ tsp. pepper
- ½ cup heavy whipping cream
    Optional: Additional heavy whipping cream and crispy sage leaves

1. In a large saucepan, heat oil over medium heat. Add onion; cook and stir until tender. Add garlic; cook 1 minute longer.
2. Stir in squash, broth, salt and pepper; bring to a boil. Reduce the heat; simmer, covered, 10-15 minutes or until squash is tender. Puree soup using an immersion blender. Or, cool slightly and puree soup in batches in a blender; return to pan. Add cream; cook and stir until heated through. If desired, garnish with additional heavy whipping cream and crispy sage.
1 cup: 157 cal., 7g fat (4g sat. fat), 17mg chol., 483mg sod., 23g carb. (6g sugars, 6g fiber), 3g pro.

MELON-BERRY SALAD

The best way to cool down on a warm day is to serve up a chilled fruit salad—the best of summer's bounty! The dressing gives this salad a creamy and rich texture, and the coconut milk makes it even more decadent. This can be served at breakfast or brunch, or as dessert. Wait until just before serving to garnish the salad. Otherwise the toasted coconut will get soggy.
—Carrie Hirsch, Hilton Head Island, SC

Takes: 20 min. • **Makes:** 12 servings

- 1 cup fat-free vanilla Greek yogurt
- ½ cup coconut milk
- ½ cup orange juice
- 4 cups cubed cantaloupe (½ in.)
- 4 cups cubed watermelon (½ in.)
- 2 medium navel oranges, sectioned
- 1 cup fresh raspberries
- 1 cup fresh blueberries
- ½ cup sweetened shredded coconut, toasted

1. For dressing, whisk together the yogurt, coconut milk and orange juice. Refrigerate until serving.
2. To serve, place fruit in a large bowl; toss gently with dressing. Sprinkle with coconut.
¾ cup: 105 cal., 3g fat (3g sat. fat), 0 chol., 30mg sod., 19g carb. (16g sugars, 2g fiber), 3g pro. **Diabetic exchanges:** 1 fruit, ½ fat.

EASY BUTTERNUT SQUASH SOUP

HASSELBACK
TOMATO CLUBS

CHIPOTLE SWEET POTATO SALAD

I love the velvety taste and texture of sweet potatoes. A friend served sweet potatoes cooked with peppers and they tasted delicious together. I took those flavors and developed them into this creamy, smoky potato salad.
—Carolyn Eskew, Dayton, OH

- -

Prep: 20 min. • **Bake:** 25 min. + cooling
Makes: 9 servings

- 3 lbs. sweet potatoes, peeled and cut into ¾-in. pieces (about 7 cups)
- ¼ cup finely chopped sweet onion
- ¼ cup finely chopped celery
- ¼ cup finely chopped seeded fresh poblano pepper
- 1 jalapeno pepper, seeded and finely chopped
- 1 cup mayonnaise
- 2 Tbsp. lime juice
- ½ to 1 tsp. ground chipotle pepper
- ½ tsp. salt
- ¼ tsp. pepper
  Minced fresh cilantro

1. Preheat oven to 425°. Place the sweet potatoes in a parchment-lined 15x10x1-in. baking pan; cover tightly with foil. Roast until tender, 25-30 minutes. Cool. Transfer to a large bowl.
2. Add onion, celery, poblano and jalapeno. Combine mayonnaise, lime juice, chipotle pepper, salt and pepper; pour over potato mixture and toss gently to coat. Refrigerate, covered, until serving. Sprinkle with cilantro.
¾ cup: 322 cal., 18g fat (3g sat. fat), 2mg chol., 278mg sod., 38g carb. (16g sugars, 5g fiber), 3g pro.

TEST KITCHEN TIP

If you're going to chill this salad for more than a couple of hours before serving, stir in just half of the dressing mixture. Add the rest right before serving for a nice, creamy texture.

HASSELBACK TOMATO CLUBS

This no-fuss, no-bread riff on a classic is perfect during tomato season. Make it for lunch or pair it with your favorite pasta salad for a light dinner.
—*Taste of Home* Test Kitchen

- -

Takes: 15 min. • **Makes:** 2 servings

- 4 plum tomatoes
- 2 slices slices Swiss cheese, quartered
- 4 slices cooked bacon strips, halved
- 4 slices deli turkey
- 4 Bibb lettuce leaves
- ½ medium ripe avocado, peeled and cut into 8 slices
  Cracked pepper

Cut 4 crosswise slices in each tomato, leaving them intact at the bottom. Fill each slice with cheese, bacon, turkey, lettuce and avocado. Sprinkle with pepper.
2 stuffed tomatoes: 272 cal., 17g fat (5g sat. fat), 48mg chol., 803mg sod., 9g carb. (3g sugars, 4g fiber), 21g pro.

TURKEY PITAS WITH CREAMY SLAW

Pack these tasty pockets for school, work or a weekend picnic—or just eat them at home. Toss in a few slices of red pepper for extra color and crunch.
—*Taste of Home* Test Kitchen

- -

Takes: 10 min. • **Makes:** 4 servings

- 3 cups coleslaw mix
- ¼ cup golden raisins
- 3 Tbsp. chopped red onion
- ⅓ cup reduced-fat mayonnaise
- 3 Tbsp. mango chutney
- 8 pita pocket halves
- ½ lb. sliced deli turkey
- 8 ready-to-serve fully cooked bacon strips, warmed
- 1 medium cucumber, thinly sliced

In a large bowl, combine coleslaw mix, raisins and onion. Add mayonnaise and chutney; toss to coat. Line pita pocket halves with turkey, bacon and cucumber slices; fill with coleslaw mixture.
2 filled pita halves: 427 cal., 12g fat (2g sat. fat), 27mg chol., 1257mg sod., 57g carb. (18g sugars, 3g fiber), 21g pro.

CHIPOTLE SWEET
POTATO SALAD

SWISS CHARD BEAN SOUP

SWISS CHARD BEAN SOUP

This hearty soup combines nutritious Swiss chard with other garden favorites. Its light broth is surprisingly rich in flavor, and the grated Parmesan packs an additional punch.
—*Taste of Home* Test Kitchen

Prep: 25 min. • **Cook:** 30 min.
Makes: 10 servings (2½ qt.)

- 1 medium carrot, coarsely chopped
- 1 small zucchini, coarsely chopped
- 1 small yellow summer squash, coarsely chopped
- 1 small red onion, chopped
- 2 Tbsp. olive oil
- 2 garlic cloves, minced
- 3 cans (14½ oz. each) reduced-sodium chicken broth
- 4 cups chopped Swiss chard
- 1 can (15½ oz.) great northern beans, rinsed and drained
- 1 can (14½ oz.) diced tomatoes, undrained
- 1 tsp. dried thyme
- ½ tsp. salt
- ½ tsp. dried oregano
- ¼ tsp. pepper
- ¼ cup grated Parmesan cheese

1. In a Dutch oven , saute carrot, zucchini, yellow squash and onion in oil until tender. Add garlic; saute 1 minute longer. Add the chicken broth, Swiss chard, beans, tomatoes, thyme, salt, oregano and pepper.
2. Bring to a boil. Reduce heat; simmer, uncovered, for 15 minutes or until chard is tender. Just before serving, sprinkle with Parmesan cheese.
1 cup: 94 cal., 4g fat (1g sat. fat), 2mg chol., 452mg sod., 12g carb. (3g sugars, 4g fiber), 5g pro.

PRESSURE-COOKER CHILI CON CARNE

Although pressure cookers can't replace every tool in the kitchen, they sure are coming close. Chili con carne is one of our favorite dishes to make in them. This cooks up fast but tastes like it simmered all day!
—*Taste of Home* Test Kitchen

Takes: 30 min. • **Makes:** 7 cups

- 1   can (16 oz.) pinto beans, rinsed and drained
- 1   can (14½ oz.) Mexican diced tomatoes, undrained
- 1   can (8 oz.) tomato sauce
- 1   medium green pepper, chopped
- 1   medium onion, chopped
- 1   cup beef broth
- 1   jalapeno pepper, seeded and minced
- 2   Tbsp. chili powder
- ¼   tsp. salt
- ¼   tsp. pepper
- 1½ lbs. lean ground beef (90% lean)
     Optional: Sour cream and sliced jalapeno

1. Combine the first 10 ingredients in a 6-qt. electric pressure cooker. Crumble ground beef over top; stir to combine. Lock lid; close pressure-release valve. Adjust to pressure-cook on high for 5 minutes.

2. Allow the pressure to naturally release for 10 minutes, then quick-release any remaining pressure. Stir chili. If desired, serve with sour cream and additional jalapenos.

1 cup: 248 cal., 9g fat (3g sat. fat), 61mg chol., 687mg sod., 18g carb. (5g sugars, 5g fiber), 24g pro. **Diabetic exchanges:** 3 lean meat, 1 starch.

PEAR & POMEGRANATE SALAD

Pomegranate and Boursin cheese add zip to this cool salad of Bosc pears over lettuce. Look for the 5.2-ounce Boursin, which is more firm than the spreadable version.
—Erika Monroe-Williams, Scottsdale, AZ

Takes: 25 min. • **Makes:** 4 servings

- ¼   cup apple juice
- 2   Tbsp. canola oil
- 1   Tbsp. cider vinegar
- 1   Tbsp. white balsamic vinegar or white wine vinegar
- ⅛   tsp. onion powder
- ⅛   tsp. coarsely ground pepper
     Dash salt
- 3   medium Bosc pears
- 1   head Boston or Bibb lettuce (about 6 oz.), torn
- 1   cup pomegranate seeds
- 1   cup coarsely chopped pecans, toasted
- ¾   cup crumbled Boursin garlic and fine herbs cheese (half of a 5.2-oz. pkg.) or garlic and herb feta cheese

1. In a blender, combine first 7 ingredients. Cut 1 pear lengthwise in half; peel, core and coarsely chop 1 pear half. Add chopped pear to blender; cover and process until blended. Cut remaining pears and pear half lengthwise into ¼-in. slices.

2. Arrange lettuce on 4 plates. Top with pears, pomegranate seeds and pecans; sprinkle with cheese. Drizzle with dressing; serve immediately.

1 serving: 388 cal., 29g fat (4g sat. fat), 6mg chol., 74mg sod., 34g carb. (23g sugars, 7g fiber), 4g pro.

TEST KITCHEN TIPS
- Do not buy spreadable cheese for this recipe, which needs a cheese with firmer texture.
- To toast pecans for the salad, bake in a shallow pan in a 350° oven for 5-10 minutes or cook in a skillet over low heat until lightly browned, stirring occasionally.

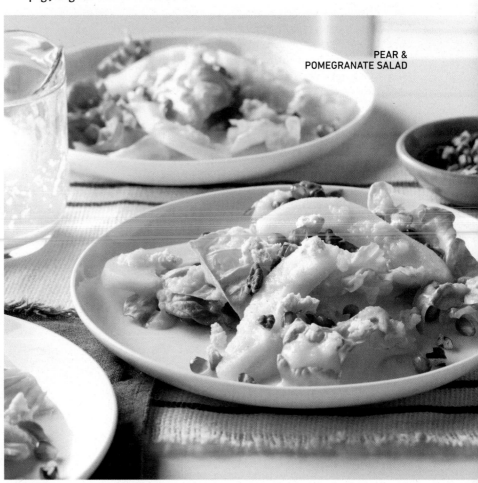

PEAR & POMEGRANATE SALAD

SWEET CLUB SANDWICH

I first tasted this delicious layered loaf at a potluck at work. It seems fancy with its raspberry jam surprise, yet it's convenient because it can be assembled ahead of time and then warmed just before serving.
—Joanne Klopfenstein, North Liberty, IN

Prep: 20 min. + cooling • **Bake:** 10 min.
Makes: 8 servings

- 2 tubes (8 oz. each) refrigerated crescent rolls
- 2 Tbsp. butter
- 4 Tbsp. honey, divided
- 6 oz. thinly sliced deli turkey
- 6 oz. sliced Muenster or Monterey Jack cheese
- 6 oz. thinly sliced deli ham
- ⅓ cup raspberry preserves
- 1 Tbsp. sesame seeds

1. Unroll each tube of crescent roll dough into 2 rectangles. Place 4 dough portions 2 in. apart on ungreased baking sheets; press perforations to seal.
2. In a small bowl, combine the butter and 2 Tbsp. honey. Brush over dough. Bake at 375° for 10-12 minutes or until lightly browned. Cool on pans for 15 minutes.
3. Carefully transfer 1 crust to a greased 15x10x1-in. baking pan. Layer with turkey, second crust, cheese and ham. Add third crust; spread with preserves.
4. Top with remaining crust; spread with remaining honey. Sprinkle with sesame seeds. Bake, uncovered, at 375° until crust is golden brown and loaf is heated through, 10-15 minutes. Carefully cut into slices.
1 slice: 343 cal., 18g fat (8g sat. fat), 49mg chol., 938mg sod., 30g carb. (19g sugars, 0 fiber), 15g pro.

> "I remember my mom making this *Taste of Home* recipe when I was in high school. It's very unique and tasty. I like the play of sweet and savory flavors."
>
> —MARK NEUFANG, CULINARY ASSISTANT

MIXED GREENS WITH ORANGE-GINGER VINAIGRETTE

Zingy vinaigrette starts with orange juice, ginger and a flick of cayenne. Just whisk, toss with greens and top the salad your way.
—Joy Zacharia, Clearwater, FL

Takes: 20 min. • **Makes:** 8 servings

- ¼ cup orange juice
- ¼ cup canola oil
- 2 Tbsp. white vinegar
- 2 Tbsp. honey
- 2 tsp. grated fresh gingerroot
- ½ tsp. salt
- ¼ tsp. cayenne pepper

SALAD
- 12 cups torn mixed salad greens
- 2 medium navel oranges, peeled and sliced crosswise
- 1 cup thinly sliced red onion

In a small bowl, whisk the first 7 ingredients until blended. In a large bowl, toss salad greens with ¼ cup vinaigrette; transfer to a serving dish. Top with orange slicess and onion. Serve salad immediately with the remaining vinaigrette.
1½ cups: 119 cal., 7g fat (1g sat. fat), 0 chol., 202mg sod., 15g carb. (9g sugars, 3g fiber), 2g pro. **Diabetic exchanges:** 1½ fat, 1 vegetable, ½ starch.

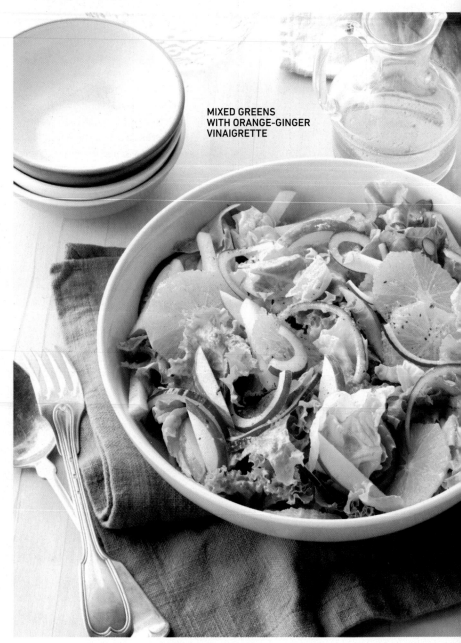

MIXED GREENS WITH ORANGE-GINGER VINAIGRETTE

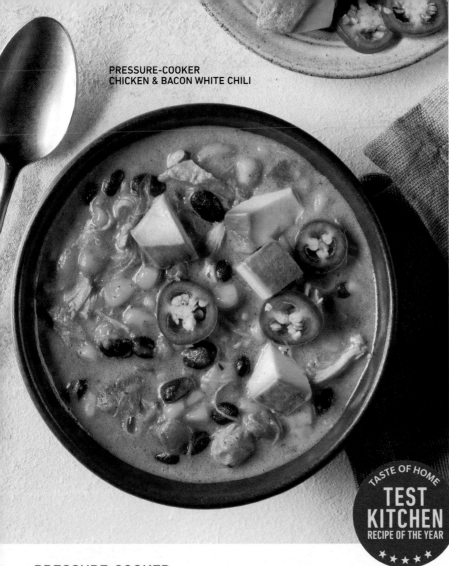

PRESSURE-COOKER
CHICKEN & BACON WHITE CHILI

SHAVED FENNEL SALAD

This salad tastes even more impressive than
it looks. It's got an incredible crunch thanks
to the cucumbers, radishes and apples, and
the finish of fennel fronds adds just the
faintest hint of licorice flavor.
—William Milton III, Clemson, SC

- -

Takes: 15 min. • **Makes:** 8 servings

1	large fennel bulb, fronds reserved
1	English cucumber
1	medium Honeycrisp apple
2	Tbsp. extra virgin olive oil
½	tsp. kosher salt
¼	tsp. coarsely ground pepper
2	radishes, thinly sliced

With a mandoline or vegetable peeler, cut
the fennel, cucumber and apple into very
thin slices. Transfer to a large bowl; toss with
olive oil, salt and pepper. Top with radishes
and reserved fennel fronds to serve.
¾ cup: 55 cal., 4g fat (1g sat. fat), 0 chol.,
138mg sod., 6g carb. (4g sugars, 2g fiber),
1g pro.

TEST KITCHEN TIP

It's easy to modify this recipe
based on your taste and what
you have on hand. You can add
more or less fennel and apple.
And try adding a squeeze of
lemon. The bit of acid would
complement the dressing.

PRESSURE-COOKER CHICKEN & BACON WHITE CHILI

I made a creative twist on my favorite white
chicken chili and used my pressure cooker,
which made it quick and easy. I serve it with
avocado, cilantro and onions.
—Teri Rasey, Cadillac, MI

- -

Prep: 10 min. • **Cook:** 15 min.
Makes: 16 servings (4 qt.)

½	lb. bacon strips, coarsely chopped
6	boneless skinless chicken thighs
1	pkg. (20 oz.) frozen corn
2	cans (15 oz. each) white kidney or cannellini beans, rinsed and drained
2	cans (15 oz. each) black beans, rinsed and drained
2	cans (11 oz. each) diced tomatoes and green chiles
1	can (4 oz.) chopped green chiles
1	cup reduced-sodium chicken broth
1	Tbsp. chili powder
1	tsp. ground cumin
1	tsp. onion powder
1	tsp. minced garlic
1	envelope (1 oz.) ranch salad dressing mix
12	oz. cream cheese
2	cups shredded cheddar cheese
	Optional: Cubed avocado and sliced jalapeno

1. Select saute or browning setting on a 6-qt.
electric pressure cooker; adjust for medium
heat. Cook bacon until crisp, 5-6 minutes;
remove bacon and reserve. Brown chicken
in bacon drippings until lightly browned, 5-6
minutes. Return bacon to pan; top with corn
and next 11 ingredients in the order listed.
2. Lock lid; close pressure-release valve.
Adjust to pressure-cook on high for 15
minutes. Let pressure release naturally for
10 minutes; quick-release any remaining
pressure. Stir in cheese until melted. If
desired, serve with avocado and jalapeno.
1 cup: 387 cal., 21g fat (10g sat. fat), 73mg
chol., 1033mg sod., 29g carb. (2g sugars,
6g fiber), 20g pro.

TASTE OF HOME
TEST
KITCHEN
RECIPE OF THE YEAR
★ ★ ★ ★ ★

**PESTO CORN SALAD
WITH SHRIMP, PAGE 113**

Fish, Seafood & Meatless

Whether you enjoy an occasional meatless meal, follow a vegetarian diet or just want to take your dinner seaside for a night, these hearty fish, seafood and vegetarian dishes are so good, you'll forget all about meat.

SPANISH-STYLE
PAELLA

SPANISH-STYLE PAELLA

If you enjoy cooking and eating ethnic foods, you'll love this hearty rice dish. It's brimming with shrimp and veggies. Omit the chorizo and chicken and use vegetable broth if you want to make it meatless.
—*Taste of Home* Test Kitchen

Prep: 10 min. • **Cook:** 35 min.
Makes: 8 servings

½   lb. Spanish chorizo links, sliced
½   lb. boneless skinless chicken breasts, cubed
1   Tbsp. olive oil
1   garlic clove, minced
1   cup uncooked short grain rice
1   cup chopped onion
1½ cups chicken broth
1   can (14½ oz.) stewed tomatoes, undrained
½   tsp. paprika
¼   tsp. ground cayenne pepper
¼   tsp. salt
10 strands saffron, crushed or ⅛ tsp. ground saffron
½   lb. uncooked medium shrimp, peeled and deveined
½   cup sweet red pepper strips
½   cup green pepper strips
½   cup frozen peas
    Optional: Minced fresh parsley and lemon wedges

1. In a large saucepan or skillet over medium-high heat, cook the sausage and chicken in oil for 5 minutes or until sausage is lightly browned and chicken is no longer pink, stirring frequently. Add garlic; cook 1 minute longer. Drain if necessary.
2. Stir in rice and onion. Cook until onion is tender and rice is lightly browned, stirring frequently. Add the chicken broth, tomatoes, paprika, cayenne, salt and saffron. Bring to a boil. Reduce heat to low; cover and cook for 10 minutes.
3. Stir in the shrimp, peppers and peas. Cover and cook 10 minutes longer or until rice is tender, shrimp turn pink and liquid is absorbed. Top with fresh parsley and lemon wedges, if desired.
1 cup: 237 cal., 7g fat (2g sat. fat), 62mg chol., 543mg sod., 27g carb. (5g sugars, 2g fiber), 16g pro.

LEMON-BASIL GRILLED SHRIMP & COUSCOUS

The basil and lemon flavors in this grilled shrimp dish are a perfect complement to each other. Make sure to use fresh basil and fresh lemon juice and zest—you will notice the difference!
—Trisha Kruse, Eagle, ID

Takes: 30 min. • **Makes:** 6 servings

1½ cups uncooked pearl (Israeli) couscous
⅓   cup lemon juice
¼   cup olive oil
2   Tbsp. Dijon mustard
3   garlic cloves, minced
½   tsp. salt
¼   tsp. pepper
½   cup minced fresh basil, divided
2   lbs. uncooked large shrimp, peeled and deveined
2   tsp. grated lemon zest

1. Cook couscous according to package directions; remove from heat. Meanwhile, in a large bowl, whisk lemon juice, olive oil, Dijon mustard, garlic, salt and pepper until blended; stir in ¼ cup fresh basil. Stir ¼ cup dressing into cooked couscous; reserve remaining dressing.
2. Thread the shrimp onto metal or soaked wooden skewers. Grill shrimp, covered, on an oiled grill rack over medium-high heat until pink, 2-3 minutes on each side.
3. Remove shrimp from skewers; toss with reserved dressing. Serve with couscous. Sprinkle with the lemon zest and remaining minced basil.
8 shrimp with ½ cup couscous: 363 cal., 12g fat (2g sat. fat), 184mg chol., 497mg sod., 34g carb. (0 sugars, 0 fiber), 29g pro.

DID YOU KNOW?

Couscous is a commercially produced grain product usually made from semolina and shaped into tiny beads, with origins in the Middle East and North Africa. Found in the rice or pasta section of the grocery store, it is available in regular or quick-cooking forms. Use as a side dish and in salads as you would rice or pasta.

ARTICHOKE COD WITH SUN-DRIED TOMATOES

Cod is a great break from really rich dishes around the holidays. I like to serve it over a bed of greens, pasta or quinoa. A squeeze of lemon gives it another layer of freshness.
—Hiroko Miles, El Dorado Hills, CA

Takes: 30 min. • **Makes:** 6 servings

1   can (14 oz.) quartered water-packed artichoke hearts, drained
½   cup julienned soft sun-dried tomatoes (not packed in oil)
2   green onions, chopped
3   Tbsp. olive oil
1   garlic clove, minced
6   cod fillets (6 oz. each)
1   tsp. salt
½   tsp. pepper
    Optional: Salad greens and lemon wedges

1. Preheat oven to 400°. In a small bowl, combine the first 5 ingredients; toss well to combine.
2. Sprinkle both sides of cod fillets with salt and pepper; place in a 13x9-in. baking dish coated with cooking spray. Top with the artichoke mixture.
3. Bake, uncovered, 15-20 minutes or until the fish just begins to flake easily with a fork. If desired, serve over salad greens with lemon wedges.
1 fillet with ⅓ cup artichoke mixture: 231 cal., 8g fat (1g sat. fat), 65mg chol., 665mg sod., 9g carb. (3g sugars, 2g fiber), 29g pro.
Diabetic exchanges: 4 lean meat, 1½ fat, 1 vegetable.

BLACK BEAN BURGERS WITH CHIPOTLE SLAW

We like to eat meatless at least one day a week, so I always keep cans of various beans in the pantry for quick meals like this one.
—Deborah Biggs, Omaha, NE

Prep: 25 min. + chilling • **Cook:** 10 min.
Makes: 4 servings

- 1   **can (15 oz.) black beans, rinsed and drained**
- 6   **Tbsp. panko bread crumbs**
- ¼   **cup finely chopped onion**
- ¼   **cup finely chopped sweet red pepper**
- ¼   **cup minced fresh cilantro**
- 2   **large egg whites, lightly beaten**
- 1   **garlic clove, minced**
- ¼   **tsp. salt**
- 2   **Tbsp. red wine vinegar**
- 1   **Tbsp. plus 4 tsp. olive oil, divided**
- 1   **Tbsp. minced chipotle pepper in adobo sauce**
- 1½ **tsp. sugar**
- 2¼ **cups coleslaw mix**
- 2   **green onions, chopped**
- 4   **whole wheat hamburger buns, split**

1. In a large bowl, mash beans. Add the panko, onion, red pepper, cilantro, egg whites, garlic and salt; mix well. Shape bean mixture into 4 patties; refrigerate patties for 30 minutes.
2. Meanwhile, in a small bowl, whisk the vinegar, 1 Tbsp. oil, chipotle pepper and sugar; stir in coleslaw mix and onions. Chill until serving.
3. In a large nonstick skillet, cook burgers in remaining oil over medium heat until a thermometer reads 160°, 3-5 minutes on each side. Serve on buns with slaw.
1 burger: 327 cal., 10g fat (1g sat. fat), 0 chol., 635mg sod., 48g carb. (9g sugars, 9g fiber), 12g pro. **Diabetic exchanges:** 3 starch, 1½ fat, 1 lean meat.

QUINOA & BLACK BEAN-STUFFED PEPPERS

If you're thinking about a meatless meal, give these no-fuss peppers a try. They come together with just a few ingredients and put a tasty spin on a low-fat dinner!
—Cindy Reams, Philipsburg, PA

Takes: 30 min. • **Makes:** 4 servings

- 1½ **cups water**
- 1   **cup quinoa, rinsed**
- 4   **large green peppers**
- 1   **jar (16 oz.) chunky salsa, divided**
- 1   **can (15 oz.) black beans, rinsed and drained**
- ½   **cup reduced-fat ricotta cheese**
- ½   **cup shredded Monterey Jack cheese, divided**

1. Preheat oven to 400°. In a small saucepan, bring water to a boil. Add quinoa. Reduce heat; simmer, covered, until the water is absorbed, 10-12 minutes.
2. Meanwhile, cut and discard tops from peppers; remove seeds. Place in a greased 8-in. square baking dish, cut side down. Microwave, uncovered, on high until peppers are crisp-tender, 3-4 minutes. Turn peppers cut side up.
3. Reserve ⅓ cup salsa; add remaining salsa to quinoa. Stir in beans, ricotta cheese and ¼ cup Monterey Jack cheese. Spoon mixture into peppers; sprinkle with the remaining cheese. Bake, uncovered, until the filling is heated through, 10-15 minutes. Top with the reserved salsa.
1 stuffed pepper: 393 cal., 8g fat (4g sat. fat), 20mg chol., 774mg sod., 59g carb. (10g sugars, 10g fiber), 18g pro.

CLASSIC CRAB BOIL

Dig in to Dungeness crab boiled in a special mix of spices.
—Matthew Hass, Ellison Bay, WI

Prep: 10 min. • **Cook:** 30 min.
Makes: 2 servings

- 2   **Tbsp. mustard seed**
- 2   **Tbsp. celery seed**
- 1   **Tbsp. dill seed**
- 1   **Tbsp. coriander seeds**
- 1   **Tbsp. whole allspice**
- ½   **tsp. whole cloves**
- 4   **bay leaves**
- 8   **qt. water**
- ¼   **cup salt**
- ¼   **cup lemon juice**
- 1   **tsp. cayenne pepper**
- 2   **whole live Dungeness crab (2 lbs. each)**
     Melted butter and lemon wedges

1. Place first 7 ingredients on a double thickness of cheesecloth. Gather corners of cloth to enclose seasonings; tie securely with string.
2. In a large stockpot, bring water, salt, lemon juice, cayenne and spice bag to a boil. Using tongs, add crab to stockpot; return to a boil. Reduce heat; simmer, covered, until shells turn bright red, about 15 minutes.
3. Using tongs, remove crab from pot. Run under cold water or plunge into ice water. Serve with melted butter and lemon wedges.
1 crab: 245 cal., 3g fat (0 sat. fat), 169mg chol., 956mg sod., 2g carb. (0 sugars, 0 fiber), 50g pro.

QUINOA & BLACK BEAN-STUFFED PEPPERS

VEGETARIAN FARRO SKILLET

Farro is a type of wheat that was popular in ancient Rome. A good source of fiber, it includes more protein than most grains, making it a smart choice for meatless meals.
—*Taste of Home* Test Kitchen

Prep: 20 min. • **Cook:** 30 min.
Makes: 4 servings

- 1 Tbsp. canola oil
- 1 medium onion, chopped
- 1 medium sweet red pepper, chopped
- 3 garlic cloves, minced
- 1 can (14½ oz.) vegetable broth
- 1 can (14½ oz.) diced tomatoes
- 1 can (15 oz.) garbanzo beans or chickpeas, rinsed and drained
- 1 small zucchini, halved and cut into ½-in. slices
- 1 cup farro, rinsed
- 1 cup frozen corn
- ¾ tsp. ground cumin
- ¼ tsp. salt
- ¼ tsp. pepper
  Chopped fresh cilantro

Heat oil in a large skillet over medium-high heat. Add onion and pepper; cook and stir until tender, 2-3 minutes. Add garlic; cook 1 minute longer. Stir in broth, tomatoes, beans, zucchini, farro, corn, cumin, salt and pepper. Bring to a boil. Reduce the heat; cover and simmer until the farro is tender, 25-30 minutes. Sprinkle with cilantro.

1½ cups: 416 cal., 8g fat (0 sat. fat), 0 chol., 757mg sod., 73g carb. (10g sugars, 15g fiber), 14g pro.

ASIAN SALMON TACOS

ASIAN SALMON TACOS

This Asian/Mexican fusion dish is ready in minutes—perfect for an on-the-run meal! If the salmon begins to stick in the skillet, just add 2-3 tablespoons of water and continue cooking.
—Marisa Raponi, Vaughan, ON

Takes: 20 min. • **Makes:** 4 servings

- 1 lb. salmon fillet, skin removed, cut into 1-in. cubes
- 2 Tbsp. hoisin sauce
- 1 Tbsp. olive oil
  Shredded lettuce
- 8 corn tortillas (6 in.), warmed
- 1½ tsp. black sesame seeds
  Mango salsa, optional

1. Toss salmon with hoisin sauce. In a large nonstick skillet, heat oil over medium-high heat. Cook salmon until it begins to flake easily with a fork, 3-5 minutes, turning gently to brown all sides.
2. Serve salmon and lettuce in tortillas; sprinkle with sesame seeds. If desired, top with salsa.

2 tacos: 335 cal., 16g fat (3g sat. fat), 57mg chol., 208mg sod., 25g carb. (3g sugars, 3g fiber), 22g pro. **Diabetic exchanges:** 3 lean meat, 2 starch, 1 fat.

DID YOU KNOW?

Hoisin sauce is used as a sauce, glaze and condiment in both Chinese and Vietnamese cuisines. It is sweet and salty in taste, but the flavor can vary between brands, so feel free to adjust the amount used to suit your personal preference.

**LINGUINE WITH
BROCCOLI RABE & PEPPERS**

SEARED SCALLOPS WITH CITRUS HERB SAUCE

Be sure to pat the scallops with a paper towel to remove any excess moisture. This will help create perfectly browned and flavorful scallops.

—April Lane, Greeneville, TN

- -

Takes: 20 min. • **Makes:** 2 servings

¾	lb. sea scallops
¼	tsp. salt
¼	tsp. pepper
⅛	tsp. paprika
3	Tbsp. butter, divided
1	garlic clove, minced
2	Tbsp. dry sherry or chicken broth
1	Tbsp. lemon juice
⅛	tsp. minced fresh oregano
⅛	tsp. minced fresh tarragon

1. Pat scallops dry with paper towels; sprinkle with salt, pepper and paprika. In a large skillet, heat 2 Tbsp. butter over medium-high heat. Add scallops; sear for 1-2 minutes on each side or until golden brown and firm. Remove from the skillet; keep warm.
2. Wipe skillet clean if necessary. Saute garlic in remaining butter until tender; stir in the sherry. Cook until the liquid is almost evaporated; stir in the remaining ingredients. Serve with scallops.

3 scallops with 1½ tsp. sauce: 314 cal., 18g fat (11g sat. fat), 101mg chol., 691mg sod., 6g carb. (0 sugars, 0 fiber), 29g pro.

ASK SARAH

HOW DO I STORE FRESH HERBS?

Storing fresh herbs in water can extend their freshness by weeks. Simply place herbs in a jar of water. Cover the jar with a plastic bag and cinch the bottom with a rubber band. Replace water every few days.

LINGUINE WITH BROCCOLI RABE & PEPPERS

Broccoli rabe is one of my favorite veggies, and this recipe makes using it a snap, since it cooks right with the pasta. Before you know it, dinner is served!

—Gilda Lester, Millsboro, DE

- -

Takes: 25 min. • **Makes:** 6 servings

1	lb. broccoli rabe
1	pkg. (16 oz.) linguine
3	Tbsp. olive oil
2	anchovy fillets, finely chopped, optional
3	garlic cloves, minced
½	cup sliced roasted sweet red peppers
½	cup pitted Greek olives, halved
½	tsp. crushed red pepper flakes
¼	tsp. pepper
⅛	tsp. salt
½	cup grated Romano cheese

1. Cut ½ in. off ends of broccoli rabe; trim woody stems. Cut stems and leaves into 2-in. pieces. Cook linguine according to package directions, adding broccoli rabe during the last 5 minutes of cooking. Drain, reserving ½ cup pasta water.
2. Meanwhile, in a large skillet, heat oil over medium-high heat. Add anchovies and garlic; cook and stir 1 minute. Stir in red peppers, olives, pepper flakes, pepper and salt.
3. Add linguine and broccoli rabe to skillet; toss to combine, adding reserved pasta water as desired to moisten. Serve with Romano cheese.

1¼ cups: 429 cal., 15g fat (4g sat. fat), 2mg chol., 487mg sod., 60g carb. (4g sugars, 5g fiber), 17g pro.

SEARED SCALLOPS
WITH CITRUS HERB SAUCE

KIMCHI FRIED RICE

Forget ordinary fried rice! Kimchi fried rice is just as easy, but it packs a flavorful punch. You can freeze this for up to three months. When reheating, add a little extra soy sauce so it doesn't dry out.
—*Taste of Home* Test Kitchen

Takes: 20 min. • **Makes:** 4 cups

- 2　Tbsp. canola oil, divided
- 1　small onion, chopped
- 1　cup kimchi, coarsely chopped
- ½　cup matchstick carrots
- ¼　cup kimchi juice
- 1　garlic cloves, minced
- 1　tsp. minced fresh gingerroot
- 3　cups leftover short grain rice
- 2　green onions, thinly sliced
- 3　tsp. soy sauce
- 1　tsp. sesame oil
- 4　large eggs
  　Optional toppings: Sliced nori, green onions and black sesame seeds

1. In large skillet, heat 1 Tbsp. canola oil over medium-high heat. Add onion; cook and stir until tender, 2-4 minutes. Add the kimchi, carrots, kimchi juice, garlic and ginger; cook 2 minutes longer. Add rice, green onions, soy sauce and sesame oil; heat through, stirring frequently.
2. In another large skillet, heat remaining 1 Tbsp. canola oil over medium-high heat. Break eggs, 1 at a time, into pan; reduce heat to low. Cook to desired doneness, turning after whites are set if desired. Serve over rice. If desired, sprinkle with with nori, green onions and sesame seeds.
1 cup fried rice with 1 egg: 331 cal., 14g fat (2g sat. fat), 186mg chol., 546mg sod., 41g carb. (4g sugars, 2g fiber), 11g pro.

TEST KITCHEN TIP
Black sesame seeds have a slightly nuttier flavor than white ones. If you don't have them, you can use toasted white sesame seeds instead.

KIMCHI FRIED RICE

CHICKPEA POTPIES

My family loves potpies, and with this recipe, no one even misses the meat. It's that tasty.
—Annette Woofenden, Middleboro, MA

- -

Prep: 15 min. • **Bake:** 25 min.
Makes: 4 servings

- 1 small onion, chopped
- 6 Tbsp. butter
- 2 garlic cloves, minced
- 6 Tbsp. all-purpose flour
- ½ tsp. salt
- ¼ tsp. pepper
- 3 cups vegetable broth
- 2 cups frozen mixed vegetables, thawed
- 1 can (15 oz.) chickpeas or garbanzo beans, rinsed and drained
- 1¼ cups frozen cubed hash brown potatoes
- ¼ cup heavy whipping cream
- ¾ tsp. Italian seasoning
- 1 sheet refrigerated pie crust

1. Saute onion in butter in a large saucepan until tender. Add the garlic; cook 1 minute longer. Stir in the flour, salt and pepper until blended. Gradually add vegetable broth; bring to a boil. Cook and stir for 2 minutes or until thickened.
2. Stir in vegetables, chickpeas, potatoes, cream and Italian seasoning. Divide mixture among 4 ungreased 10-oz. ramekins.
3. Unroll pie crust; divide into 4 portions. Roll out each portion to fit ramekins; place crust over filling. Trim, seal and flute edges. Cut slits in crust. Place the ramekins on a baking sheet.
4. Bake at 400° for 25-30 minutes or until crust is golden brown.
1 potpie: 680 cal., 39g fat (20g sat. fat), 76mg chol., 1518mg sod., 72g carb. (10g sugars, 9g fiber), 11g pro.

DAD'S FAMOUS STUFFIES

The third of July is almost as important as the Fourth in my family. We make these stuffies on the third every year, and it's an event in and of itself!
—Karen Barros, Bristol, RI

- -

Prep: 1¼ hours • **Bake:** 20 min.
Makes: 10 servings

- 20 fresh large quahog clams (about 10 lbs.)
- 1 lb. hot chourico or linguica (smoked Portuguese sausage) or fully cooked Spanish chorizo
- 1 large onion, chopped (about 2 cups)
- 3 tsp. seafood seasoning
- 1 pkg. (14 oz.) herb stuffing cubes
- 1 cup water
  Lemon wedges, optional
  Hot pepper sauce, optional

1. Add 2 in. of water to a stockpot. Add clams and chourico; bring to a boil. Cover; steam until clams open, 15-20 minutes.
2. Remove the clams and sausage from pot, reserving 2 cups cooking liquid; cool slightly. Discard any unopened clams.
3. Preheat oven to 350°. Remove clam meat from shells. Separate shells; reserve 30 half-shells for stuffing. Place clam meat in a food processor; process until finely chopped. Transfer to a large bowl.
4. Remove the casings from sausage; cut sausage into 1½-in. pieces. Place in a food processor; process until finely chopped. Add the sausage, chopped onion and seafood seasoning to chopped clams. Stir in stuffing cubes. Add reserved cooking liquid and enough water to reach desired moistness, about 1 cup.
5. Spoon the clam mixture into reserved shells. Place in 15x10x1-in. baking pans. Bake until heated through, 15-20 minutes. Preheat broiler.
6. Broil clams 4-6 in. from heat 4-5 minutes or until golden brown. If desired, serve with lemon wedges and pepper sauce.
Freeze option: Cover and freeze unbaked stuffed clams in a 15x10x1-in. baking pan until firm. Transfer to freezer containers; return to freezer. To use, place 3 stuffed clams on a microwave-safe plate. Cover with paper towel; microwave on high 3-4 minutes.
Note: Find hot chourico at *michaelsprovision.com* and *gasparssausage.com*.
3 stuffed clams: 296 cal., 11g fat (3g sat. fat), 71mg chol., 1188mg sod., 34g carb. (3g sugars, 2g fiber), 18g pro.

DAD'S FAMOUS STUFFIES

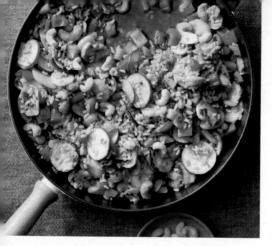

VEGGIE-CASHEW STIR-FRY

Getting my meat-loving husband and two sons to eat more veggies was a struggle until I whipped up this stir-fry one night. I was shocked when they cleaned their plates and asked for seconds.
—Abbey Hoffman, Ashland, OH

- -

Prep: 20 min. • **Cook:** 15 min.
Makes: 4 servings

- ¼ cup reduced-sodium soy sauce
- ¼ cup water
- 2 Tbsp. brown sugar
- 2 Tbsp. lemon juice
- 2 Tbsp. olive oil
- 1 garlic clove, minced
- 2 cups sliced fresh mushrooms
- 1 cup coarsely chopped fresh baby carrots
- 1 small zucchini, cut into ¼-in. slices
- 1 small sweet red pepper, coarsely chopped
- 1 small green pepper, coarsely chopped
- 4 green onions, sliced
- 2 cups cooked brown rice
- 1 can (8 oz.) sliced water chestnuts, drained
- ½ cup honey-roasted cashews

1. In a small bowl, mix soy sauce, water, brown sugar and lemon juice until smooth; set aside.

2. In a large skillet, heat oil over medium-high heat. Stir-fry garlic for 1 minute. Add the vegetables; cook until vegetables are crisp-tender, 6-8 minutes.

3. Stir the soy sauce mixture and add to pan. Bring to a boil. Add rice and water chestnuts; heat through. Top with cashews.

1½ cups: 385 cal., 16g fat (3g sat. fat), 0 chol., 671mg sod., 56g carb. (15g sugars, 6g fiber), 9g pro.

SURF & TURF

For an intimate dinner with close friends, serve this stunning dinner of tenderloin steaks and lobster tail. Your guests will think they are dining at a fine restaurant.
—*Taste of Home* Test Kitchen

- -

Prep: 25 min. + chilling • **Bake:** 15 min.
Makes: 4 servings

- 2 garlic cloves, minced
- 2 tsp. plus 2 Tbsp. olive oil, divided
- ¼ cup minced fresh parsley
- 3 Tbsp. chopped green onions
- 2 Tbsp. minced fresh thyme
- 2 tsp. grated lemon zest
- ½ tsp. salt
- ¼ tsp. pepper
- ⅛ tsp. cayenne pepper
- ½ cup butter, softened
- 1 cup soft bread crumbs
- ¼ cup butter, melted
- 4 lobster tails (8 to 10 oz. each)
- 4 beef tenderloin steaks (4 oz. each)
- 4 tsp. coarsely ground pepper

1. In a small skillet, saute garlic in 2 tsp. oil until tender; remove from the heat. In a small bowl, combine the parsley, green onions, thyme, lemon zest, salt, pepper, cayenne pepper and reserved garlic. Set aside ½ cup for crumb topping.

2. Add softened butter to remaining herb mixture; mix well. Shape into a 1-in.-thick log; wrap and refrigerate for 30 minutes or until firm.

3. For crumb topping, combine the bread crumbs, melted butter and reserved herb mixture; set aside.

4. Split lobster tails in half lengthwise. With cut side up and using scissors, cut along the edge of shell to loosen the cartilage covering the tail meat from the shell; remove and discard cartilage.

5. Place lobster tails on a baking sheet; top with reserved crumb topping. Bake lobster, uncovered, at 375° until meat is firm and opaque and crumbs are golden brown, 15-20 minutes.

6. Meanwhile, sprinkle steaks with coarse pepper. In a large skillet over medium heat, cook the steaks in remaining oil until meat reaches desired doneness, 4-5 minutes on each side (for medium-rare, a thermometer should read 135°; medium, 140°; medium-well, 145°).

7. Unwrap herb butter; cut four ¼-in. slices from log. Place 1 slice on each steak. Serve with lobster. Rewrap remaining herb butter; refrigerate for 1 week or freeze for up to 3 months.

1 serving: 793 cal., 52g fat (26g sat. fat), 355mg chol., 1289mg sod., 10g carb. (1g sugars, 1g fiber), 69g pro.

SURF & TURF

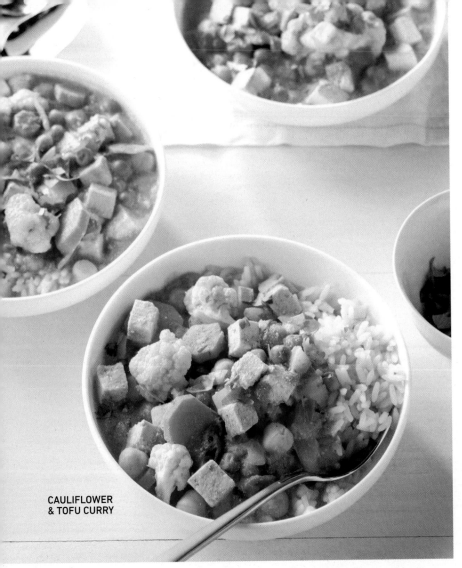

CAULIFLOWER & TOFU CURRY

MUFFIN-TIN LASAGNAS

This is a super fun way to serve lasagna and a great way to surprise everyone at the table. Easy and quick, these little cups can be made with whatever ingredients your family likes best.
—Sally Kilkenny, Granger, IA

Takes: 30 min. • **Makes:** 1 dozen

- 1 large egg, lightly beaten
- 1 carton (15 oz.) part-skim ricotta cheese
- 2 cups shredded Italian cheese blend, divided
- 1 Tbsp. olive oil
- 24 wonton wrappers
- 1 jar (24 oz.) garden-style pasta sauce
  Minced fresh parsley, optional

1. Preheat oven to 375°. In a bowl, mix beaten egg, ricotta cheese and 1¼ cups Italian cheese blend.
2. Generously grease 12 muffin cups with oil; line each with a wonton wrapper. Fill each with 1 Tbsp. of the ricotta mixture and 1½ Tbsp. pasta sauce. Top each with a second wrapper, rotating corners and pressing down centers. Repeat ricotta and sauce layers. Sprinkle with remaining cheese.
3. Bake until cheese melts, 20-25 minutes. If desired, sprinkle with parsley.
2 mini lasagnas: 414 cal., 19g fat (9g sat. fat), 83mg chol., 970mg sod., 36g carb. (8g sugars, 2g fiber), 22g pro.

CAULIFLOWER & TOFU CURRY

Cauliflower, garbanzo beans and tofu are subtle on their own, but together they make an awesome base for curry. We have this recipe weekly because one of us is always craving it.
—Patrick McGilvray, Cincinnati, OH

Takes: 30 min. • **Makes:** 6 servings

- 1 Tbsp. olive oil
- 2 medium carrots, sliced
- 1 medium onion, chopped
- 3 tsp. curry powder
- ¼ tsp. salt
- ¼ tsp. pepper
- 1 small head cauliflower, broken into florets (about 3 cups)
- 1 can (14½ oz.) fire-roasted crushed tomatoes
- 1 pkg. (14 oz.) extra-firm tofu, drained and cut into ½-in. cubes
- 1 cup vegetable broth
- 1 can (15 oz.) garbanzo beans or chickpeas, rinsed and drained
- 1 can (13.66 oz.) coconut milk
- 1 cup frozen peas
  Hot cooked rice
  Chopped fresh cilantro

1. In a 6-qt. stockpot, heat oil over medium-high heat. Add carrots and onion; cook and stir until onion is tender, 4-5 minutes. Stir in seasonings.
2. Add cauliflower, tomatoes, tofu and broth; bring to a boil. Reduce heat; simmer, covered, 10 minutes. Stir in garbanzo beans, coconut milk and peas; return to a boil. Reduce heat to medium; cook, uncovered, stirring occasionally, until curry is slightly thickened and the cauliflower is tender, 5-7 minutes.
3. Serve with rice. Sprinkle with cilantro.
1⅓ cups: 338 cal., 21g fat (13g sat. fat), 0 chol., 528mg sod., 29g carb. (9g sugars, 7g fiber), 13g pro.

PESTO CORN SALAD
WITH SHRIMP

PESTO CORN SALAD WITH SHRIMP

This recipe showcases the beautiful bounty of summer with its fresh corn, tomatoes and delicious basil. Prevent browning by spritzing salad with lemon juice.
—Deena Bowen, Chico, CA

Takes: 30 min. • **Makes:** 4 servings

- 4 medium ears sweet corn, husked
- ½ cup packed fresh basil leaves
- ¼ cup olive oil
- ½ tsp. salt, divided
- 1½ cups cherry tomatoes, halved
- ⅛ tsp. pepper
- 1 medium ripe avocado, peeled and chopped
- 1 lb. uncooked shrimp (31-40 per lb.), peeled and deveined

1. In a pot of boiling water, cook corn until tender, about 5 minutes. Drain; cool slightly. Meanwhile, in a food processor, pulse basil, oil and ¼ tsp. salt until blended.

2. Cut corn from cob and place in a bowl. Stir in tomatoes, pepper and remaining salt. Add avocado and 2 Tbsp. basil mixture; toss gently to combine.

3. Thread shrimp onto metal or soaked wooden skewers; brush with remaining basil mixture. Grill, covered, over medium heat until shrimp turn pink, 2-4 minutes per side. Remove shrimp from skewers; serve with corn mixture.

1 serving: 371 cal., 22g fat (3g sat. fat), 138mg chol., 450mg sod., 25g carb. (8g sugars, 5g fiber), 23g pro.

> "Delicious flavors and texture make this salad a summertime favorite at my house."
>
> —CATHERINE WARD, PREP KITCHEN MANAGER

MAKEOVER
MEATLESS LASAGNA

MAKEOVER MEATLESS LASAGNA

If you've never tried tofu before, this is the best way to give it a try. It blends with all the other ingredients, adding protein without the fat and calories of ground beef.
—Mary Lou Moeller, Wooster, OH

Prep: 30 min. • **Bake:** 45 min. + standing
Makes: 12 servings

- 10 uncooked whole wheat lasagna noodles
- 1½ cups sliced fresh mushrooms
- ¼ cup chopped onion
- 2 garlic cloves, minced
- 1 can (14½ oz.) Italian diced tomatoes, undrained
- 1 can (12 oz.) tomato paste
- 1 pkg. (14 oz.) firm tofu, drained and cubed
- 2 large eggs, lightly beaten
- 3 cups 2% cottage cheese
- ½ cup grated Parmesan cheese
- ½ cup packed fresh parsley leaves
- ½ tsp. pepper
- 2 cups shredded part-skim mozzarella cheese, divided

1. Preheat oven to 375°. Cook the noodles according to package directions for al dente. Meanwhile, in a large saucepan, cook the mushrooms and onion over medium heat until tender. Add garlic; cook 1 minute. Add tomatoes and tomato paste; cook and stir until heated through.

2. Pulse cubed tofu in a food processor until smooth. Add the next 5 ingredients; pulse until combined. Drain noodles.

3. Place 5 noodles into a 13x9-in. baking dish coated with cooking spray, overlapping as needed. Layer with half the tofu mixture, half the sauce and half the mozzarella. Top with remaining noodles, tofu mixture and sauce.

4. Bake, covered, 35 minutes. Sprinkle with remaining mozzarella. Bake, uncovered, until cheese is melted, 10-15 minutes. Let stand 10 minutes before serving.

1 piece: 258 cal., 9g fat (4g sat. fat), 48mg chol., 498mg sod., 26g carb. (9g sugars, 3g fiber), 19g pro. **Diabetic exchanges:** 2 medium-fat meat, 1½ starch.

GRILLED SALMON WITH CHORIZO-OLIVE SAUCE

Every one of the ingredients in this recipe brings a ton of flavor. Both the chorizo and salmon cook in a hurry, and garlic and citrus go beautifully with them.
—Charlene Chambers, Ormond Beach, FL

- -

Takes: 25 min. • **Makes:** 4 servings

3   links (3 to 4 oz. each) fresh chorizo
4   green onions, chopped
2   garlic cloves, minced
1   can (14½ oz.) diced
    tomatoes, drained
¼   cup chopped pitted green olives
½   tsp. grated orange zest
¼   tsp. salt
¼   tsp. pepper
4   salmon fillets (6 oz. each)

1. Remove chorizo from casings. In a large ovenproof skillet on a stove or grill, cook and stir chorizo, green onions and garlic over medium-high heat until cooked through, 4-6 minutes, breaking chorizo into crumbles; drain.
2. Reduce heat to medium. Add tomatoes, olives and orange zest; stir to combine. Sprinkle salt and pepper over salmon.
3. On a greased grill rack, grill salmon, covered, over medium heat until fish just begins to flake easily with a fork, 3-4 minutes per side. Top with chorizo mixture.

1 salmon fillet with ½ cup sauce: 545 cal., 36g fat (10g sat. fat), 142mg chol., 1355mg sod., 7g carb. (4g sugars, 2g fiber), 43g pro.

FRESH CORN &
TOMATO FETTUCCINI

FRESH CORN & TOMATO FETTUCCINI

This recipe combines delicious whole wheat pasta with the best of fresh garden produce. It's tossed with heart-healthy olive oil, and a little feta cheese gives it bite.
—Angela Spengler, Niceville, FL

- -

Takes: 30 min. • **Makes:** 4 servings

8   oz. uncooked whole
    wheat fettuccine
2   medium ears sweet corn, husked
2   tsp. plus 2 Tbsp. olive oil, divided
½   cup chopped sweet red pepper
4   green onions, chopped
2   medium tomatoes, chopped
½   tsp. salt
½   tsp. pepper
1   cup crumbled feta cheese
2   Tbsp. minced fresh parsley

1. In a Dutch oven, cook the fettuccine according to package directions, adding corn during the last 8 minutes of cooking.
2. Meanwhile, in a small skillet, heat 2 tsp. oil over medium-high heat. Add red pepper and green onions; cook and stir until tender.
3. Drain pasta and corn; transfer pasta to a large bowl. Cool corn slightly; cut corn from cobs and add to pasta. Add tomatoes, salt, pepper, remaining oil and pepper mixture; toss to combine. Sprinkle with feta cheese and parsley.

2 cups: 422 cal., 15g fat (4g sat. fat), 15mg chol., 580mg sod., 56g carb. (6g sugars, 10g fiber), 17g pro.

TOMATO-GARLIC LENTIL BOWLS

An Ethiopian recipe inspired this feel-good dinner that's tangy, creamy and packed with hearty comfort.
—Rachael Cushing, Portland, OR

- -

Takes: 30 min. • **Makes:** 6 servings

- 1 Tbsp. olive oil
- 2 medium onions, chopped
- 4 garlic cloves, minced
- 2 cups dried brown lentils, rinsed
- 1 tsp. salt
- ½ tsp. ground ginger
- ½ tsp. paprika
- ¼ tsp. pepper
- 3 cups water
- ¼ cup lemon juice
- 3 Tbsp. tomato paste
- ¾ cup fat-free plain Greek yogurt
  Optional: Chopped tomatoes and minced fresh cilantro

1. In a large saucepan, heat the olive oil over medium-high heat; saute onions 2 minutes. Add the garlic; cook 1 minute. Stir in lentils, seasonings and water; bring to a boil. Reduce heat; simmer, covered, until the lentils are tender, 25-30 minutes.

2. Stir in lemon juice and tomato paste; heat through. Serve with yogurt and, if desired, tomatoes and cilantro.

¾ cup: 294 cal., 3g fat (0 sat. fat), 0 chol., 419mg sod., 49g carb. (5g sugars, 8g fiber), 21g pro. **Diabetic exchanges:** 3 starch, 2 lean meat, ½ fat.

> "My whole family likes these. I make a double recipe on Sunday and eat it for lunches throughout the week. The yogurt, tomatoes and cilantro on top are a must!"
>
> —ELLIE MARTIN CLIFFE, EXECUTIVE DIGITAL EDITOR

TUNA CAKES WITH MUSTARD MAYO

These patties take the cake! The recipe starts off simple with canned tuna. If you'd like, add more kick to the creamy mustard-mayo sauce with prepared horseradish.
—*Taste of Home* Test Kitchen

- -

Takes: 30 min. • **Makes:** 4 servings

- 2 large eggs, beaten
- 3 Tbsp. minced fresh parsley, divided
- ½ tsp. seafood seasoning
- 2 cans (5 oz. each) light water-packed tuna, drained and flaked
- ½ cup seasoned bread crumbs
- ½ cup shredded carrot
- 2 Tbsp. butter, divided
- 1 pkg. (12 oz.) frozen peas
- ¼ tsp. pepper
- ⅓ cup mayonnaise
- 1 Tbsp. Dijon mustard
- 1 tsp. 2% milk

1. In a large bowl, combine the eggs, 2 Tbsp. parsley and seafood seasoning. Stir in the tuna, bread crumbs and carrot. Shape into 8 patties.

2. In a large skillet, brown patties in 1 Tbsp. butter for 3-4 minutes on each side or until golden brown.

3. Meanwhile, microwave peas according to package directions. Stir in the pepper and remaining butter and parsley. Combine the mayonnaise, mustard and milk. Serve with tuna cakes and peas.

2 tuna cakes with ½ cup peas and 4 tsp. sauce: 433 cal., 25g fat (7g sat. fat), 149mg chol., 910mg sod., 24g carb. (6g sugars, 5g fiber), 28g pro.

TOMATO-GARLIC
LENTIL BOWLS

VEGAN MAC & CHEESE

Buttery cashews and nutritional yeast create a rich, savory sauce in this vegan rendition of good ol' mac and cheese.
—*Taste of Home* Test Kitchen

Prep: 20 min. + standing • **Cook:** 10 min.
Makes: 6 servings

- 2 **cups raw cashews**
- 16 **oz. uncooked elbow macaroni**
- 1½ **cups water**
- ⅓ **cup nutritional yeast**
- 2 **tsp. lemon juice**
- 2 **tsp. salt**
- 2 **tsp. onion powder**
- 1½ **tsp. paprika**
- 1 **tsp. pepper**
- ⅛ **tsp. cayenne pepper**

1. Rinse cashews in cold water. Place in a large bowl; add water to cover by 3 in. Cover and let stand overnight.
2. Cook macaroni according to package directions. Drain and rinse the cashews, discarding liquid. Transfer nuts to a food processor. Add 1½ cups water, nutritional yeast, lemon juice and seasonings; cover and process until pureed, 3-4 minutes, scraping down sides as needed.
3. Drain macaroni; return to pan. Stir in the cashew mixture. Cook and stir over medium-low heat until heated through. Sprinkle with additional paprika if desired.
1⅔ cups: 497 cal., 18g fat (3g sat. fat), 0 chol., 803mg sod., 67g carb. (5g sugars, 5g fiber), 18g pro.

BEST EVER VEGGIE BURGER

My delicious new take on the classic veggie burger dishes out smoky-savory flavor complete with cumin, smoked paprika, fennel seed and hints of sun-dried tomato.
—Sarah Tramonte,
Associate Culinary Producer

Prep: 30 min. • **Cook:** 10 min.
Makes: 4 servings

- 1 **cup canned black beans, rinsed and drained**
- 1 **cup chopped walnuts**
- 1½ **tsp. ground cumin**
- ½ **tsp. ground fennel seed**
- ¼ **tsp. smoked paprika**
- 1 **Tbsp. oil from sun-dried tomatoes**
- ¼ **cup shredded carrot**
- 1 **large shallot, minced**
- 2 **Tbsp. oil-packed sun-dried tomatoes, chopped**
- 1 **garlic clove, minced**
- ¼ **cup old-fashioned oats**
- 1 **Tbsp. chia seeds**
- 2 **tsp. reduced-sodium soy sauce**
- ½ **tsp. garlic salt**
- 1 **Tbsp. olive oil**
  Optional: Barbecue sauce, toasted hamburger buns, sriracha mayo, lettuce, red onion and tomato

1. Preheat oven to 325°. Spread the beans evenly on a parchment-lined rimmed baking pan. Bake until beans split open, 6-8 minutes.
2. Meanwhile, in a large dry nonstick skillet over medium heat, cook and stir walnuts, cumin, fennel and smoked paprika until fragrant, 2-3 minutes. Remove from pan and cool. In the same skillet skillet, heat oil from sun-dried tomatoes over medium heat. Add carrot, shallot and sun-dried tomatoes; cook and stir until tender, about 5 minutes. Add garlic; cook 1 minute longer. Remove from the heat; cool slightly.
3. Transfer the carrot mixture to a food processor. Add beans, walnut mixture, oats, chia seeds, soy sauce and garlic salt. Pulse until combined. Shape into four 4-in. patties.
4. In the same skillet over medium heat, cook patties in olive oil until browned, 3-4 minutes on each side. If desired, baste with barbecue sauce and serve on buns with toppings of your choice.
1 burger: 357 cal., 28g fat (3g sat. fat), 0 chol., 479mg sod., 22g carb. (2g sugars, 7g fiber), 9g pro.

CRUNCHY CHILI CILANTRO LIME ROASTED SHRIMP

This shrimp recipe is dairy-free and comes together in about half an hour. The secret is in the bright, flavor-packed sauce. Serve over salad greens, store-bought coleslaw or cauliflower rice.
—Julie Peterson, Crofton, MD

Takes: 30 min. • **Makes:** 8 servings

- 2 **lbs. uncooked shrimp (26-30 per lb.), peeled and deveined**
- 4 **garlic cloves, minced**
- 1 **tsp. paprika**
- 1 **tsp. ground ancho chili pepper**
- 1 **tsp. ground cumin**
- ½ **tsp. salt**
- ¼ **tsp. pepper**
- 1 **medium lime**
- 1 **cup crushed tortilla chips**
- ¼ **cup chopped fresh cilantro**
- ¼ **cup olive oil**
- 1 **cup cherry tomatoes, halved**
- 1 **medium ripe avocado, peeled and cubed**

1. Preheat oven to 425°. Place the first 7 ingredients in a greased 15x10x1-in. pan. Finely grate zest from lime. Cut the lime crosswise in half; squeeze juice. Add zest and juice to shrimp mixture; toss to coat.
2. In a small bowl, combine crushed tortilla chips, cilantro and oil; sprinkle over shrimp mixture. Bake until the shrimp turn pink, 12-15 minutes. Top with tomatoes and avocado. If desired, serve with additional lime wedges and cilantro.
1 serving: 230 cal., 13g fat (2g sat. fat), 138mg chol., 315mg sod., 10g carb. (1g sugars, 2g fiber), 20g pro. **Diabetic exchanges:** 3 lean meat, 1½ fat, ½ starch.

TEST KITCHEN TIP

Unless you live along the coast, most shrimp are frozen when they arrive at your local store. So, if you are not cooking them that night, just buy them frozen and thaw them the day before.

CRUNCHY CHILI
CILANTRO LIME
ROASTED SHRIMP

BLACK BEAN & SWEET POTATO RICE BOWLS

With three hungry boys in my house, dinners need to be quick and filling, and it helps to get in some veggies, too. This is a favorite because it's hearty and fun to tweak with different ingredients.
—Kim Van Dunk, Caldwell, NJ

- -

Takes: 30 min. • **Makes:** 4 servings

- ¾ cup uncooked long grain rice
- ¼ tsp. garlic salt
- 1½ cups water
- 3 Tbsp. olive oil, divided
- 1 large sweet potato, peeled and diced
- 1 medium red onion, finely chopped
- 4 cups chopped fresh kale
  (tough stems removed)
- 1 can (15 oz.) black beans,
  rinsed and drained
- 2 Tbsp. sweet chili sauce
  Lime wedges, optional
  Additional sweet chili sauce,
  optional

1. Place rice, garlic salt and water in a large saucepan; bring to a boil. Reduce the heat; simmer, covered, until water is absorbed and rice is tender, 15-20 minutes. Remove from heat; let stand 5 minutes.
2. Meanwhile, in a large skillet, heat 2 Tbsp. olive oil over medium-high heat; saute sweet potato 8 minutes. Add onion; cook and stir until potato is tender, 4-6 minutes. Add kale; cook and stir until tender, 3-5 minutes. Stir in beans; heat through.
3. Gently stir 2 Tbsp. chili sauce and the remaining olive oil into rice; add to potato mixture. If desired, serve with lime wedges and additional chili sauce.

2 cups: 435 cal., 11g fat (2g sat. fat), 0 chol., 405mg sod., 74g carb. (15g sugars, 8g fiber), 10g pro.

TEST KITCHEN TIP
Sweet potato + kale + black beans = nearly ⅓ of the daily value for fiber per serving!

BLACK BEAN & SWEET POTATO RICE BOWLS

CRAB-TOPPED TOMATO SLICES

When we're camping, my wife and I top large beefsteak tomatoes with spicy chunks of crabmeat. Then we warm this summer treat over the fire.
—Thomas Faglon, Somerset, NJ

Takes: 30 min. • **Makes:** 4 servings

- 1 carton (8 oz.) mascarpone cheese
- 2 Tbsp. finely chopped sweet red pepper
- 1½ tsp. grated lemon zest
- 2 Tbsp. lemon juice
- 1 tsp. seafood seasoning
- 1 tsp. hot pepper sauce
- ½ tsp. salt
- ¼ tsp. freshly ground pepper
- 2 cans (6 oz. each) lump crabmeat, drained
- 8 slices tomato (½ in. thick) Minced chives

1. Preheat oven to 375°. In a large bowl, combine the first 8 ingredients; gently stir in crabmeat.
2. Place tomato slices on a foil-lined baking sheet; top with the crab mixture. Bake until heated through, 12-15 minutes. Sprinkle with minced chives.
1 serving: 325 cal., 27g fat (14g sat. fat), 153mg chol., 980mg sod., 3g carb. (1g sugars, 1g fiber), 20g pro.

AIR-FRYER CRUMB-TOPPED SOLE

Looking for a low-carb supper that's ready in a flash? These buttery sole fillets are covered with a rich sauce and topped with toasty bread crumbs. They're super speedy thanks to your air fryer.
—*Taste of Home* Test Kitchen

Prep: 10 min. • **Cook:** 10 min./batch
Makes: 4 servings

- 3 Tbsp. reduced-fat mayonnaise
- 3 Tbsp. grated Parmesan cheese, divided
- 2 tsp. mustard seed
- ¼ tsp. pepper
- 4 sole fillets (6 oz. each)
- 1 cup soft bread crumbs
- 1 green onion, finely chopped
- ½ tsp. ground mustard
- 2 tsp. butter, melted
  Cooking spray

1. Preheat air fryer to 375°. Combine the mayonnaise, 2 Tbsp. cheese, mustard seed and pepper; spread over tops of fillets.
2. Place fish in a single layer on greased tray in air-fryer basket. Cook until fish flakes easily with a fork, 3-5 minutes.
3. Meanwhile, in a small bowl, combine bread crumbs, onion, ground mustard and remaining 1 Tbsp. cheese; stir in butter. Spoon over fillets, patting gently to adhere; spritz topping with cooking spray. Cook until golden brown, 2-3 minutes longer. If desired, sprinkle with additional green onions.
1 fillet: 233 cal., 11g fat (3g sat. fat), 89mg chol., 714mg sod., 8g carb. (1g sugars, 1g fiber), 24g pro.

AIR-FRYER CRUMB-TOPPED SOLE

BASIL-LEMON CRAB LINGUINE

I love using fresh herbs to punch up pasta dishes. This linguine looks and tastes like a meal from a five-star restaurant.
—Tonya Burkhard, Palm Coast, FL

Takes: 25 min. • **Makes:** 4 servings

- 1 pkg. (9 oz.) refrigerated linguine
- ⅓ cup butter, cubed
- 1 jalapeno pepper, seeded and finely chopped
- 1 garlic clove, minced
- 1 tsp. grated lemon zest
- 3 Tbsp. lemon juice
- 2 cans (6 oz. each) lump crabmeat, drained
- ¼ cup loosely packed basil leaves, thinly sliced
- ½ tsp. sea salt
- ¼ tsp. freshly ground pepper

1. Cook linguine according to the package directions. Meanwhile, in a large skillet, heat butter over medium heat. Add jalapeno and garlic; cook and stir for 1-2 minutes or until tender. Stir in lemon zest and juice. Add crab; heat through, stirring gently.
2. Drain linguine; add to skillet. Sprinkle with basil, salt and pepper; toss to combine.
1¼ cups: 392 cal., 18g fat (11g sat. fat), 161mg chol., 856mg sod., 35g carb. (1g sugars, 2g fiber), 23g pro.

GULF COAST JAMBALAYA RICE

As the stew of the South, jambalaya is a definite staple. For ages, home cooks have been making their own renditions of the traditional recipe. This slow-cooked version is my personal favorite.
—Judy Batson, Tampa, FL

Prep: 20 min. • **Cook:** 3¼ hours
Makes: 8 servings

- 1 lb. boneless skinless chicken breasts, cut into 1-in. cubes
- 1 lb. smoked kielbasa, cut into ¼-in. slices
- 2 cups chicken stock
- 1 large green pepper, chopped
- 1 cup chopped sweet onion
- 2 celery ribs, chopped
- 2 garlic cloves, minced
- 2 tsp. Creole seasoning
- 1 tsp. seafood seasoning
- 1 tsp. pepper
- 1 lb. uncooked medium shrimp, peeled and deveined
- 2 cups uncooked instant rice

1. Place the first 10 ingredients in a 5-qt. slow cooker. Cook, covered, on low for 3-4 hours, until chicken is tender.
2. Stir in shrimp and rice. Cook, covered, 15-20 minutes longer, until shrimp turn pink and rice is tender.
1⅓ cups: 395 cal., 18g fat (6g sat. fat), 138mg chol., 861mg sod., 25g carb. (3g sugars, 1g fiber), 31g pro.

BASIL-LEMON CRAB LINGUINE

FARMERS MARKET
ENCHILADAS

WHITE BEANS & BOW TIES

When we have fresh veggies, we toss them with pasta shapes like penne or bow ties. What a tasty way to enjoy a meatless meal!
—Angela Buchanan, Longmont, CO

Takes: 25 min. • **Makes:** 4 servings

- 2½ cups uncooked whole wheat bow tie pasta (about 6 oz.)
- 1 Tbsp. olive oil
- 1 medium zucchini, sliced
- 2 garlic cloves, minced
- 2 large tomatoes, chopped (about 2½ cups)
- 1 can (15 oz.) cannellini beans, rinsed and drained
- 1 can (2¼ oz.) sliced ripe olives, drained
- ¾ tsp. freshly ground pepper
- ½ cup crumbled feta cheese

1. Cook pasta according to the package directions. Drain, reserving ½ cup of the pasta water.
2. Meanwhile, in a large skillet, heat oil over medium-high heat; saute the zucchini until crisp-tender, 2-4 minutes. Add garlic; cook and stir 30 seconds. Stir in tomatoes, beans, olives and pepper; bring to a boil. Reduce heat; simmer, uncovered, until tomatoes are softened, 3-5 minutes, stirring occasionally.
3. Stir in pasta and enough pasta water to moisten as desired. Stir in cheese.
1½ cups: 348 cal., 9g fat (2g sat. fat), 8mg chol., 394mg sod., 52g carb. (4g sugars, 11g fiber), 15g pro.

FARMERS MARKET ENCHILADAS

These vegetarian enchiladas incorporate garden favorites in a quick weeknight meal. Feel free to substitute whatever veggies you find at the farm stand or harvest from your own backyard patch—summer squash, eggplant and corn all taste great here, too.
—Elisabeth Larsen, Pleasant Grove, UT

Prep: 20 min. • **Bake:** 45 min.
Makes: 7 servings

- 3 medium zucchini, quartered lengthwise and sliced
- 1 poblano pepper, seeded and chopped
- 8 oz. sliced fresh mushrooms
- 8 oz. cherry tomatoes
- 1 Tbsp. olive oil
- 1 tsp. ground cumin
- ½ tsp. salt
- ¼ tsp. cayenne pepper
- 2 cups shredded Monterey Jack cheese
- 1 cup crumbled queso fresco or feta cheese, divided
- ½ cup minced fresh cilantro, divided
- 2 Tbsp. lime juice
- 14 corn tortillas (6 in.), warmed
- 1 can (15 oz.) enchilada sauce

1. Preheat oven to 400°. In a large bowl, combine zucchini, poblano, mushrooms and tomatoes; drizzle with oil and sprinkle with cumin, salt and cayenne. Toss to coat. Divide vegetable mixture between 2 lightly greased 15x10x1-in. baking pans. Roast 15 minutes; rotate baking pans top to bottom. Roast an additional 10 minutes or until vegetables are tender. Return to bowl and cool slightly.
2. Stir in Monterey Jack cheese, ½ cup queso fresco, ¼ cup cilantro and lime juice. Place a scant ½ cup vegetable mixture off center on each tortilla. Roll up and place in a greased 13x9-in. baking dish, seam side down. Top with enchilada sauce; sprinkle with remaining queso fresco.
3. Bake, uncovered, until enchiladas are heated through and cheese is melted, about 20 minutes. Top with remaining cilantro.
2 enchiladas: 346 cal., 17g fat (9g sat. fat), 40mg chol., 780mg sod., 33g carb. (5g sugars, 5g fiber), 18g pro.

BUFFALO CHICKEN
ENCHILADAS, PAGE 128

Beef, Chicken & Pork

Bored with your usual repertoire of beef, chicken and pork recipes? These irresistible meaty entrees make it easier than ever to transform weekday regulars into must-have dinner favorites. From comforting classics you know and love to bold new flavors in global specialties, these are guaranteed to become your greatest hits!

MISO BUTTER
ROASTED CHICKEN

MISO BUTTER ROASTED CHICKEN

I love this recipe because the prep work is done in the beginning. You can spatchcock the chicken yourself or purchase a bird that is already spatchcocked at a grocery store or butcher's shop. The only work left to do is to chop the veggies!
—Stefanie Schaldenbrand, Los Angeles, CA

Prep: 25 min. • **Bake:** 1½ hours + standing
Makes: 6 servings

- 1 lb. medium fresh mushrooms
- 1 lb. baby red potatoes
- 1 lb. fresh Brussels sprouts, halved
- 6 garlic cloves, minced
- 1 Tbsp. olive oil
- 1½ tsp. minced fresh thyme
  or ½ tsp. dried thyme
- ½ tsp. salt
- ½ tsp. pepper
- 1 roasting chicken (5 to 6 lbs.)
- ¼ cup butter, softened
- ¼ cup white miso paste

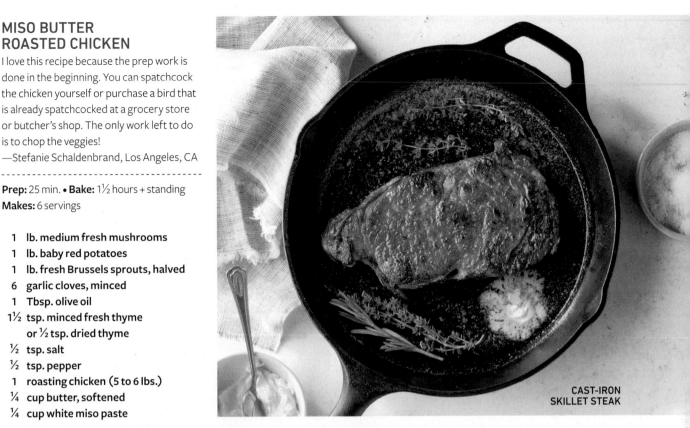

CAST-IRON SKILLET STEAK

1. Preheat oven to 425°. Mix mushrooms, potatoes, Brussels sprouts and garlic; drizzle with olive oil. Sprinkle with the thyme, salt and pepper; toss to coat. Place in a shallow roasting pan.
2. Place chicken on a work surface, breast side down and tail end facing you. Using kitchen shears, cut along each side of the backbone; remove and save for making gravy. Turn chicken over so breast side is up; flatten by pressing down firmly on the breastbone until it cracks. Place chicken on a rack over vegetables. Twist and tuck wings under to secure in place. Combine butter and miso paste; spread over skin (mixture will be thick).
3. Roast until a thermometer inserted in the thickest part of the thigh reads 170°-175°, 1½-1¾ hours, covering chicken loosely with aluminum foil after 45 minutes of cooking. (Miso mixture on chicken will appear very dark while roasting.)
4. Remove chicken from oven; tent with foil. Let stand for 15 minutes before carving. If desired, skim fat and thicken pan drippings for gravy. Serve with chicken. If desired, top with additional fresh thyme.
1 serving: 653 cal., 37g fat (13g sat. fat), 170mg chol., 912mg sod., 25g carb. (3g sugars, 4g fiber), 54g pro.

CAST-IRON SKILLET STEAK

If you have never cooked steak at home before, it can be a little intimidating. That's why I came up with this simple steak recipe that's so easy, you could make it any day of the week.
—James Schend, Deputy Editor, Culinary

Prep: 5 min. + standing • **Cook:** 5 min.
Makes: 2 servings

- 3 tsp. kosher salt, divided
- 1 beef New York strip or ribeye steak (1 lb.), 1 in. thick

1. Remove steak from refrigerator and sprinkle with 2 tsp. salt; let stand for 45-60 minutes.
2. Preheat a cast-iron skillet over high heat until extremely hot, 4-5 minutes. Sprinkle remaining 1 tsp. salt in bottom of skillet; pat beef dry with paper towels. Place steak in skillet and cook until it is easily moved, 1-2 minutes; flip, placing steak in a different section of the skillet. Cook for 30 seconds and then begin moving steak, occasionally pressing slightly to ensure the steak has even contact with skillet.
3. Continue turning and flipping until steak is cooked to desired degree of doneness (for medium-rare, a thermometer should read

135°; medium, 140°; medium-well, 145°), 1-2 minutes.
6 oz. cooked beef: 494 cal., 36g fat (15g sat. fat), 134mg chol., 2983mg sod., 0 carb. (0 sugars, 0 fiber), 40g pro.

ASK SARAH

HOW DO I CHOOSE THE BEST STEAK AT THE STORE?

Steak should be evenly marbled with creamy white fat. Look for pieces with a bright, cherry red color. Avoid meat with gray or brown patches or cuts that look dried out. Packages shouldn't have any holes, tears or excessive liquid. If they do, it might indicate improper handling and storage.

SLOW-COOKER MONGOLIAN BEEF

This dish uses inexpensive ingredients to offer big flavor in a small amount of time. The slow cooker makes easy work of it as well—easier than getting takeout!
—*Taste of Home* Test Kitchen

Prep: 10 min. • **Cook:** 4¼ hours
Makes: 4 servings

- ¾ cup reduced-sodium chicken broth
- 2 Tbsp. reduced-sodium soy sauce
- 1 Tbsp. hoisin sauce
- 2 tsp. minced fresh gingerroot
- 2 tsp. sesame oil
- 1 tsp. minced garlic
- ½ tsp. salt
- ¼ tsp. crushed red pepper flakes
- 1 lb. beef flank steak, cut into thin strips
- 2 Tbsp. cornstarch
- 2 Tbsp. water
- 2 cups hot cooked rice
- 5 green onions, cut into 1-in. pieces
  Sesame seeds, optional

1. In a 4- or 5-qt. slow cooker, combine first 8 ingredients. Add beef and toss to coat. Cook, covered, on low 4-5 hours, until meat is tender.

2. In a small bowl, mix cornstarch and water until smooth; gradually stir into beef. Cook, covered, on high until sauce is thickened, 15-30 minutes. Serve over hot cooked rice. Sprinkle with green onions and, if desired, sesame seeds.

1 serving: 329 cal., 11g fat (4g sat. fat), 54mg chol., 530mg sod., 30g carb. (2g sugars, 1g fiber), 26g pro.

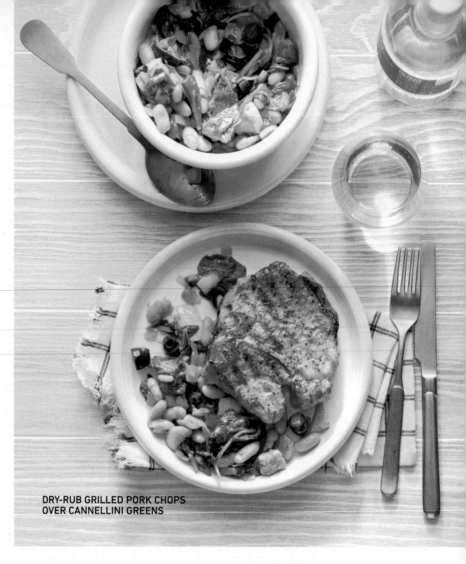

DRY-RUB GRILLED PORK CHOPS OVER CANNELLINI GREENS

DRY-RUB GRILLED PORK CHOPS OVER CANNELLINI GREENS

My family was not a huge fan of pork until I made this recipe. Feel free to incorporate your favorite herbs into the dry rub. You can use the rub on boneless skinless chicken breast or other meats, too.
—Michael Cirlincione, Stockton, NJ

Prep: 20 min. • **Cook:** 25 min + standing
Makes: 4 servings

- 1 Tbsp. olive oil
- 1 medium onion, chopped
- 2 garlic cloves, minced
- 1 can (15 oz.) cannellini beans, rinsed and drained
- 1 cup water-packed artichoke hearts, drained and chopped
- ¾ cup pitted Greek olives, chopped
- ¼ cup dry white wine or chicken broth
- ¼ cup chicken broth
- ¼ tsp. salt
- ¼ tsp. smoked paprika
- ¼ tsp. pepper
- 4 bone-in pork loin chops (8 oz. each)
- 2 tsp. Greek seasoning or seasoning of your choice
- 5 oz. fresh baby spinach (about 6 cups)

1. In a large skillet, heat oil over medium-high heat. Add onion; cook and stir until tender, 4-5 minutes. Add the garlic; cook 1 minute longer. Stir in beans, artichokes, olives, wine, broth, salt. paprika and pepper. Bring to a boil; reduce heat. Simmer until the liquid is almost evaporated, 12-15 minutes.

2. Meanwhile, sprinkle chops with Greek seasoning. Grill over medium heat until a thermometer reads 145°, 6-8 minutes on each side. Let pork chops stand 5 minutes before serving.

3. Stir spinach into bean mixture; cook and stir until wilted, 2-3 minutes. Serve with pork.

1 serving: 530 cal., 29g fat (8g sat. fat), 111mg chol., 1345mg sod., 22g carb. (1g sugars, 6g fiber), 42g pro.

EASY CHICKEN PESTO STUFFED PEPPERS

On busy weeknights, I don't want to spend more than 30 minutes preparing dinner, nor do I want to wash a towering pile of dishes. This recipe delivers without having to sacrifice flavor!
—Olivia Cruz, Greenville, SC

- -

Takes: 25 min. • **Makes:** 4 servings

4	medium sweet yellow or orange peppers
1½	cups shredded rotisserie chicken
1½	cups cooked brown rice
1	cup prepared pesto
½	cup shredded Havarti cheese
	Fresh basil leaves, optional

1. Cut peppers lengthwise in half; remove stems and seeds. Place peppers on a baking sheet, skin side up. Broil 4 in. from heat until skins blister, about 5 minutes. Reduce oven temperature to 350°.

2. Meanwhile, in a large bowl, combine chicken, rice and pesto. When cool enough to handle, fill peppers with chicken mixture; return to baking sheet. Bake until heated through, about 5 minutes. Sprinkle with shredded cheese; bake until cheese is melted, 3-5 minutes. If desired, sprinkle with basil.

2 stuffed pepper halves: 521 cal., 31g fat (7g sat. fat), 62mg chol., 865mg sod., 33g carb. (7g sugars, 5g fiber), 25g pro.

WEEKNIGHT GOULASH

With this recipe, you can put in a full day's work, run some errands and still get dinner on the table in no time. Make it extra special by serving the meat sauce over spaetzle.
—Cyndy Gerken, Naples, FL

- -

Prep: 25 min. • **Cook:** 8½ hours
Makes: 2 servings

1	lb. beef stew meat
1	Tbsp. olive oil
1	cup beef broth
1	small onion, chopped
¼	cup ketchup
1	Tbsp. Worcestershire sauce
1½	tsp. brown sugar
1½	tsp. paprika
¼	tsp. ground mustard
1	Tbsp. all-purpose flour
2	Tbsp. water
	Hot cooked egg noodles or spaetzle

1. In a large skillet, brown beef in oil; drain. Transfer to a 1½-qt. slow cooker. Combine the broth, onion, ketchup, Worcestershire sauce, brown sugar, paprika and mustard. Pour over beef. Cover and cook on low for 8-10 hours, until meat is tender.

2. In a small bowl, combine flour and water until smooth. Gradually stir into the beef mixture. Cover and cook on high until thickened, about 30 minutes longer. Serve with noodles.

1 cup: 478 cal., 23g fat (7g sat. fat), 141mg chol., 1005mg sod., 20g carb. (14g sugars, 1g fiber), 45g pro.

EASY CHICKEN PESTO STUFFED PEPPERS

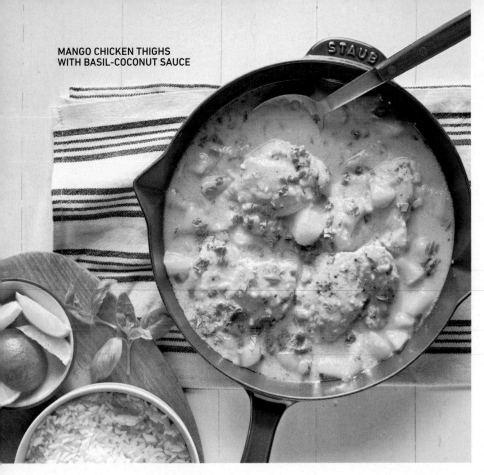

MANGO CHICKEN THIGHS
WITH BASIL-COCONUT SAUCE

BUFFALO CHICKEN ENCHILADAS

Chicken wing lovers, meet your new favorite meal! These enchiladas, filled with tender rotisserie chicken and lots of cheese—and, of course, Buffalo sauce—will be the most craveable, easy and delicious dish you've ever tasted. The entire family will ask for them again and again.
—Becky Hardin, St. Peters, MO

Prep: 15 min. • **Bake:** 25 min.
Makes: 10 servings

- 3 cups shredded rotisserie chicken
- 2 cups shredded cheddar cheese, divided
- 1 can (10 oz.) diced tomatoes and green chiles, drained
- 1 can (10 oz.) enchilada sauce
- ½ cup Buffalo wing sauce
- 1 can (10½ oz.) condensed cream of celery soup, undiluted
- 4 oz. reduced-fat cream cheese, cubed
- ½ cup blue cheese salad dressing
- 10 flour tortillas (8 in.)
- ⅓ cup crumbled blue cheese
  Optional: Chopped tomatoes, sliced celery, shredded lettuce, sliced green onions, minced fresh cilantro and additional cheddar cheese

1. Preheat oven to 350°. In a large bowl, combine chicken, 1¾ cups shredded cheese, diced tomatoes and green chiles, enchilada sauce and wing sauce. In a small saucepan, heat the soup, cream cheese, dressing and remaining ¼ cup shredded cheese over low heat until cheeses are melted, 5-10 minutes. Remove from heat.
2. Place ½ cup chicken mixture off center on each tortilla. Roll up and place in a greased 13x9-in. baking dish, seam side down. Top with sauce.
3. Bake, uncovered, until the enchiladas are heated through and cheese is melted, 25-30 minutes. Sprinkle with blue cheese and additional toppings of your choice.
1 enchilada: 472 cal., 26g fat (10g sat. fat), 76mg chol., 1387mg sod., 34g carb. (2g sugars, 3g fiber), 25g pro.

MANGO CHICKEN THIGHS WITH BASIL-COCONUT SAUCE

This recipe brings the restaurant to my home kitchen. And it's easy, too! The meal comes together quickly and fills my kitchen with wonderful aromas. If there are any leftovers, they are just as good reheated the next day.
—Kathi Jones-DelMonte, Rochester, NY

Prep: 20 min. • **Cook:** 30 min.
Makes: 4 servings

- 4 boneless skinless chicken thighs (about 1 lb.)
- ½ tsp. salt
- ¼ tsp. pepper
- 1 Tbsp. olive oil
- 3 garlic cloves, minced
- 1 Tbsp. minced fresh gingerroot
- 1 can (13.66 oz.) coconut milk
- 1 medium mango, peeled and chopped
- 4 green onions, sliced
- ½ cup thinly sliced fresh basil, divided
- ¼ cup miso paste
- 2 tsp. Sriracha chili sauce
- 2 cups cooked jasmine rice
- 2 medium limes, quartered

1. Sprinkle chicken with salt and pepper. In a large skillet, heat oil over medium heat. Brown chicken on both sides. Add garlic and ginger; cook 1 minute longer.
2. Stir in coconut milk, mango, green onions, ¼ cup basil, miso paste and chili sauce. Cook and stir until sauce is slightly reduced and a thermometer inserted in chicken reads 170°, about 20 minutes. Sprinkle with remaining ¼ cup basil. Serve with rice and limes.
1 serving: 552 cal., 28g fat (18g sat. fat), 76mg chol., 1209mg sod., 46g carb. (17g sugars, 4g fiber), 28g pro.

TEST KITCHEN TIP

Choose plump mangoes with a sweet, fruity fragrance. Avoid those that are bruised or very soft. Ripe mangoes have green-yellow skin with a pronounced red blush; unripened ones are firm and green with just a hint of red. To ripen a mango, let it stand at room temperature and out of sunlight. Then refrigerate the ripened mango until ready to use.

BUFFALO CHICKEN
ENCHILADAS

TASTE OF HOME
TEST
KITCHEN
RECIPE OF THE YEAR
★★★★

LARB
GAI

LARB GAI

Larb gai is a Thai dish made with ground chicken, chiles, mint and basil. Serve it as an appetizer in lettuce cups or as a main dish.
—*Taste of Home* Test Kitchen

Takes: 30 minutes • **Makes:** 4 servings

- 1 lb. ground chicken
- 2 Tbsp. canola oil
- 2 green or red fresh chiles, seeded and chopped
- 2 shallots, thinly sliced
- 2 garlic cloves, minced
- 2 Tbsp. lime juice
- 3 Tbsp. fish sauce
- 1 Tbsp. sweet chili sauce
- 2 tsp. brown sugar
- 1 to 2 tsp. Sriracha chili sauce
- ¼ cup fresh cilantro leaves
- 2 Tbsp. minced fresh mint
  Hot cooked sticky rice
  Boston lettuce leaves, optional

In a large skillet cook chicken over medium heat until no longer pink, 8-10 minutes, breaking into crumbles; drain. In the same skillet, heat oil over medium heat. Add the shallots and chiles; cook and stir until tender, 3-4 minutes. Add the garlic; cook 1 minute longer. Stir in the cooked chicken, lime juice, fish sauce, chili sauce, brown sugar and Sriracha. Cook and stir until heated through. Stir in mint and cilantro. Serve with rice and, if desired, lettuce leaves.

½ cup: 262 cal., 16g fat (3g sat. fat), 75mg chol., 1211mg sod., 10g carb. (6g sugars, 0 fiber), 20g pro.

TEST KITCHEN TIP

Also known as "sweet rice" or glutinous rice (even though it's gluten-free), sticky rice is a staple in many traditional Thai dishes. To make sticky rice, rinse 2 cups uncooked sweet rice and place in a 3-qt. microwave-safe dish. Cover with water; let rice stand for 1 hour. Drain rice and return to dish; add 2 cups water. Microwave, covered, on high until rice is tender, 8-12 minutes, stirring every 3 minutes. Let rice stand 10 minutes.

EPIPHANY HAM

I wanted to cook a ham but didn't have the ingredients for my usual glaze recipe, so I made substitutions. You can experiment, too. Instead of black cherry soda, try another flavor, or use sweet and sour sauce in place of duck sauce.
—Edith Griffith, Havre de Grace, MD

- -

Prep: 10 min. • **Bake:** 3 hours
Makes: 12 servings

- 1 **fully cooked bone-in ham (8 to 10 lbs.; not spiral cut)**
- 1 **can (12 oz.) black cherry soda**
- 2 **tsp. Chinese five-spice powder**
- ⅔ **cup duck sauce**

1. Preheat oven to 350°. Place ham on a rack in a baking pan or dish; pour soda over ham. Sprinkle with five-spice powder. Cover with aluminum foil; bake 30 minutes.
2. Remove foil and discard. Baste with duck sauce; return to oven and bake, uncovered, until a thermometer reads 140°, about 2½ hours, basting again halfway through.
6 oz. cooked ham: 303 cal., 8g fat (3g sat. fat), 133mg chol., 1659mg sod., 13g carb. (9g sugars, 0 fiber), 45g pro.

SHEET-PAN HONEY MUSTARD CHICKEN

This chicken dish is an easy gluten-free, low-carb meal ideal for busy weekdays. The chicken is tender, juicy and so delicious! It's now on the list of our favorite meals. You can substitute any low-carb vegetable for the green beans.
—Denise Browning, San Antonio, TX

- -

Prep: 20 min. • **Bake:** 45 min.
Makes: 6 servings

- 6 **bone-in chicken thighs (about 2¼ lbs.)**
- ¾ **tsp. salt, divided**
- ½ **tsp. pepper, divided**
- 2 **medium lemons**
- ⅓ **cup olive oil**
- ⅓ **cup honey**
- 3 **Tbsp. Dijon mustard**
- 4 **garlic cloves, minced**
- 1 **tsp. paprika**
- ½ **cup water**
- ½ **lb. fresh green beans, trimmed**
- 6 **miniature sweet peppers, sliced into rings**
- ¼ **cup pomegranate seeds, optional**

1. Preheat oven to 425°. Place chicken in a greased 15x10x1-in. baking pan. Sprinkle with ½ tsp. salt and ¼ tsp. pepper. Thinly slice 1 lemon; place over chicken. Cut remaining lemon crosswise in half; squeeze juice into a small bowl. Whisk in oil, honey, mustard, garlic and paprika. Pour half the mixture over chicken; reserve remaining sauce for beans. Pour water into pan. Bake 25 minutes.
2. Meanwhile, combine the beans, sweet peppers, remaining sauce, ¼ tsp. salt and ¼ tsp. pepper; toss to coat. Arrange the vegetables around chicken in pan. Bake until a thermometer inserted in chicken reads 170°-175° and the beans are tender, 15-20 minutes. If desired, sprinkle with pomegranate seeds.
1 serving: 419 cal., 26g fat (6g sat. fat), 81mg chol., 548mg sod., 22g carb. (17g sugars, 2g fiber), 24g pro.

TASTE OF HOME
TEST KITCHEN
RECIPE OF THE YEAR
★ ★ ★ ★

SHEET-PAN HONEY MUSTARD CHICKEN

ASIAN CHICKEN THIGHS

A thick, tangy sauce coats golden brown chicken. Serve the thighs over long grain rice or with ramen noodle slaw.
—Dave Farrington, Midwest City, OK

Prep: 15 min. • **Cook:** 50 min.
Makes: 5 servings

- 5 tsp. olive oil
- 5 bone-in chicken thighs (about 1¾ lbs.), skin removed
- ⅓ cup water
- ¼ cup packed brown sugar
- 2 Tbsp. orange juice
- 2 Tbsp. reduced-sodium soy sauce
- 2 Tbsp. ketchup
- 1 Tbsp. white vinegar
- 4 garlic cloves, minced
- ½ tsp. crushed red pepper flakes
- ¼ tsp. Chinese five-spice powder
- 2 tsp. cornstarch
- 2 Tbsp. cold water
  Sliced green onions
  Hot cooked rice, optional

1. In a large skillet, heat oil over medium heat. Add chicken; cook until golden brown, 8-10 minutes on each side. In a small bowl, whisk water, brown sugar, orange juice, soy sauce, ketchup, white vinegar, minced garlic, red pepper flakes and five-spice powder. Pour over chicken. Bring to a boil. Reduce heat; simmer, uncovered, until the chicken thighs are tender, 30-35 minutes, turning chicken occasionally.

2. In a small bowl, mix cornstarch and cold water until smooth; stir into pan. Bring to a boil; cook and stir until sauce is thickened, about 1 minute. Sprinkle with green onions. If desired, serve with rice.

Freeze option: Cool chicken. Freeze in freezer containers. To use, partially thaw in refrigerator overnight. Heat slowly in a covered skillet until a thermometer inserted in chicken reads 165°, stirring occasionally and adding a little water if necessary.

1 chicken thigh: 292 cal., 14g fat (3g sat. fat), 87mg chol., 396mg sod., 15g carb. (13g sugars, 0 fiber), 25g pro. **Diabetic exchanges:** 3 lean meat, 1 starch, 1 fat.

> "What I love about this recipe is that it's super easy and customizable, and the chicken thighs are so tender. Even if you don't have all of the seasoning ingredients, it will still taste good. It's so flavorful."
>
> —RACHEL WILKE,
> SENIOR SOCIA MEDIA EDITOR/DESIGNER

HAM & SWISS BAKED PENNE

As a kid I loved to eat the hot ham and Swiss sandwiches from a local restaurant. With its melty, gooey goodness, this bake makes me think of them.
—Ally Billhorn, Wilton, IA

Takes: 30 min. • **Makes:** 6 servings

- 2⅓ cups uncooked penne pasta
- 3 Tbsp. butter
- 3 Tbsp. all-purpose flour
- 2 cups 2% milk
- 1 cup half-and-half cream
- 1½ cups shredded Swiss cheese
- ½ cup shredded Colby cheese
- 2 cups cubed fully cooked ham

TOPPING
- ¼ cup seasoned bread crumbs
- ¼ cup grated Parmesan cheese
- 2 Tbsp. butter, melted

1. Preheat oven to 375°. Cook the pasta according to the package directions for al dente; drain.

2. Meanwhile, in a large saucepan, melt butter over medium heat. Stir in flour until smooth; gradually whisk in milk and cream. Bring mixture to a boil, stirring constantly; cook and stir until thickened, 1-2 minutes. Gradually stir in the Swiss and Colby cheeses until melted. Add ham and drained pasta; toss to coat.

3. Transfer to a greased 11x7-in. baking dish. In a small bowl, mix the topping ingredients; sprinkle over pasta. Bake, uncovered, until bubbly, 15-20 minutes.

1 cup: 559 cal., 30g fat (18g sat. fat), 116mg chol., 905mg sod., 41g carb. (7g sugars, 2g fiber), 31g pro.

ASIAN CHICKEN THIGHS

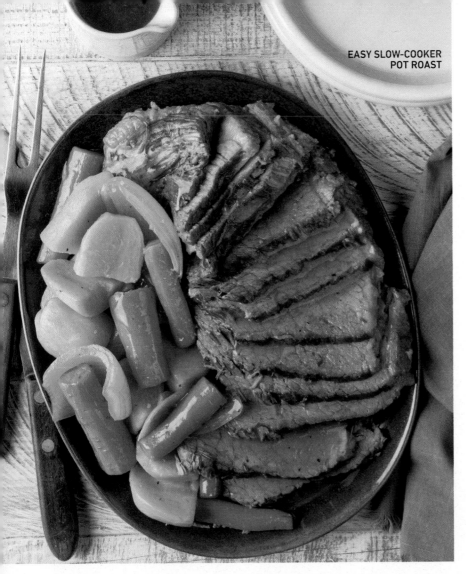

EASY SLOW-COOKER
POT ROAST

GREEK CHICKEN & RICE

Here's a fresh take on comfort food! This dish is my go-to on busy weeknights and when unexpected company stops by. Toss in chopped spinach to boost the nutrition.
—Savannah Lay, Baker City, OR

Takes: 30 min. • **Makes:** 4 servings

- 1 **lb. boneless skinless chicken breasts, cut into 1-in. cubes**
- ¼ **tsp. garlic powder**
- ¼ **tsp. pepper**
- 2 **tsp. olive oil**
- 1 **jar (12 oz.) marinated quartered artichoke hearts, drained and chopped**
- 1 **jar (12 oz.) roasted sweet red peppers, drained and chopped**
- ⅓ **cup oil-packed sun-dried tomatoes, chopped**
- ⅓ **cup Greek olives, sliced**
- 1 **pkg. (8.8 oz.) ready-to-serve brown rice**
- 1 **Tbsp. minced fresh parsley**

1. Sprinkle chicken with garlic powder and pepper. In a large skillet, heat oil over medium heat. Add chicken; cook and stir until no longer pink, 8-10 minutes. Stir in the artichokes, roasted peppers, tomatoes and Greek olives. Cook and stir until heated through, 3-5 minutes.
2. Meanwhile, prepare rice according to package directions. Serve with chicken. Sprinkle with parsley.
1¼ cups: 436 cal., 21g fat (4g sat. fat), 63mg chol., 1008mg sod., 29g carb. (3g sugars, 7g fiber), 26g pro.

EASY SLOW-COOKER POT ROAST

I love pot roast. First of all, it's delicious. Second, it's easy! I can't describe the feeling of walking into my house after a long day at work and smelling this dish that has been simmering in the slow cooker all day. There's nothing better.
—James Schend, Deputy Editor, Culinary

Prep: 10 min. • **Cook:** 12 hours
Makes: 10 servings

- 1 **boneless beef rump or chuck roast (3 to 3½ lbs.)**
- 1 **Tbsp. canola oil**
- 6 **medium carrots, cut into thirds**
- 6 **medium potatoes, peeled and quartered**
- 1 **large onion, quartered**
- 3 **tsp. Montreal steak seasoning**
- 1 **carton (32 oz.) beef broth**
- 3 **Tbsp. cornstarch**
- 3 **Tbsp. water**

1. In a large skillet over medium heat, brown roast in oil on all sides. Place the carrots, potatoes and onion in a 6-qt. slow cooker. Place roast on top of vegetables; sprinkle with steak seasoning. Add beef broth. Cook, covered, on low 10-12 hours, until beef and vegetables are tender.
2. Remove roast and vegetables from slow cooker; keep warm.
3. Transfer cooking juices to a saucepan; skim fat. Bring juices to a boil. In a small bowl, mix the cornstarch and water until smooth; stir into juices. Return to a boil, stirring constantly; cook and stir until thickened, 1-2 minutes. Serve with roast and vegetables.
1 serving: 354 cal., 15g fat (5g sat. fat), 88mg chol., 696mg sod., 24g carb. (4g sugars, 3g fiber), 30g pro. **Diabetic exchanges:** 4 lean meat, 1½ starch, ½ fat.

POMEGRANATE SHORT RIBS

I like drizzling the pomegranate molasses sauce on top of simple roasted vegetables. It's a bit tangy and a bit sweet, and adds a nice depth of flavor to sweet and savory dishes alike. Pomegranate molasses can be found in specialty food stores or online.
—Shannon Sarna, South Orange, NJ

- -

Prep: 25 min. + chilling • **Cook:** 6 hours
Makes: 8 servings

- 1 tsp. salt
- ½ tsp. ground cinnamon
- ½ tsp. pepper
- ¼ tsp. ground coriander
  Dash crushed red pepper flakes
- 8 bone-in beef short ribs (about 4 lbs.)
- 2 Tbsp. safflower oil
- 1 medium onion, chopped
- 3 garlic cloves, minced
- 1 Tbsp. tomato paste
- 1½ cups chicken or beef stock
- 1½ cups dry red wine or pomegranate juice
- 3 Tbsp. soy sauce, optional
- ⅓ cup pomegranate molasses
  Minced fresh parsley and pomegranate seeds

1. Combine the first 5 ingredients; rub over ribs. Refrigerate, covered, at least 2 hours. In a large skillet, heat oil over medium heat. Brown ribs on all sides in batches. Transfer to a 5-qt. slow cooker. Discard drippings, reserving 2 Tbsp. Add onion to drippings; cook and stir over medium-high heat until tender, 8-10 minutes. Add garlic and tomato paste; cook 1 minute longer.
2. Add red wine to the pan; increase heat to medium-high. Cook 10 minutes until slightly thickened, stirring to loosen browned bits from pan. Transfer to slow cooker. Add the stock, molasses and, if desired, soy sauce, making sure the ribs are fully submerged in liquid. Cook, covered, on low for 6-8 hours, until ribs are tender. Serve ribs with parsley and pomegranate seeds.

1 short rib: 267 cal., 14g fat (5g sat. fat), 55mg chol., 428mg sod., 11g carb. (7g sugars, 0 fiber), 19g pro.

**ONE-POT
SALSA CHICKEN**

ONE-POT SALSA CHICKEN

This skillet recipe is a colorful and healthy main dish that can be on the table in just over an hour. The subtle, sweet-spicy flavor is a nice surprise.
—Ann Sheehy, Lawrence, MA

- -

Prep: 20 min. • **Cook:** 45 min.
Makes: 6 servings

- 2 Tbsp. canola oil
- 2 lbs. boneless skinless chicken thighs, cut into 1-in. pieces
- 1 tsp. pepper
- ½ tsp. salt
- 2 medium sweet potatoes, peeled and cubed
- 1 jar (16 oz.) medium salsa
- 2 medium nectarines, peeled and chopped
- 2 Tbsp. Tajin seasoning
- 1 cup uncooked instant brown rice
- 1 cup water
- ¼ cup minced fresh parsley
  Minced fresh chives

1. In a Dutch oven, heat the canola oil over medium-high heat. Sprinkle chicken with pepper and salt. Brown in batches; return all to pan. Add potatoes, salsa, nectarines and seasoning. Bring to a boil; reduce heat. Cover and simmer until potatoes are almost tender, about 15 minutes.
2. Stir in brown rice and water; bring to a boil. Reduce heat. Cover and simmer until the potatoes are tender, about 10 minutes. Stir in the minced parsley. Serve in bowls; sprinkle with chives.

1⅔ cups: 432 cal., 16g fat (3g sat. fat), 101mg chol., 1254mg sod., 39g carb. (13g sugars, 4g fiber), 31g pro.

TEST KITCHEN TIP
Tajin seasoning is a unique blend of lime, chile peppers and sea salt. Look for it in the spice aisle.

CURRY COCONUT CHICKEN

My husband and I love this yummy dish. It's a breeze to prepare in the slow cooker, and it tastes just like a meal you'd have at your favorite Indian or Thai restaurant.
—Andi Kauffman, Beavercreek, OR

- -

Prep: 20 min. • **Cook:** 4 hours
Makes: 2 servings

- 1   medium potato, peeled and cubed
- ¼   cup chopped onion
- 2   boneless skinless chicken breast halves (4 oz. each)
- ½   cup light coconut milk
- 2   tsp. curry powder
- 1   garlic clove, minced
- ½   tsp. reduced-sodium chicken bouillon granules
- ⅛   tsp. salt
- ⅛   tsp. pepper
- 1   cup hot cooked rice
- 1   green onion, thinly sliced
      Optional: Raisins, shredded coconut and chopped unsalted peanuts

1. Place potatoes and onion in a 1½- or 2-qt. slow cooker. In a large skillet coated with cooking spray, brown chicken on both sides. Trasfer to slow cooker.

2. In a small bowl, combine the coconut milk, curry, garlic, bouillon, salt and pepper; pour over chicken. Cover and cook on low 4-5 hours, until meat is tender.

3. Serve chicken and sauce with rice; sprinkle with green onions. If desired, garnish with raisins, coconut and peanuts.

1 serving: 353 cal., 7g fat (4g sat. fat), 63mg chol., 266mg sod., 42g carb. (3g sugars, 3g fiber), 27g pro.

ONE-POT BACON CHEESEBURGER PASTA

ONE-POT BACON CHEESEBURGER PASTA

When the weather's too chilly to grill burgers, I whip up a big pot of this cheesy pasta. Believe it or not, it tastes just like a bacon cheeseburger, and it's much easier for my young children to enjoy. It's great paired with Tater Tots or french fries.
—Carly Terrell, Granbury, TX

- -

Prep: 15 min. • **Cook:** 35 min.
Makes: 12 servings

- 8   bacon strips, chopped
- 2   lbs. ground beef
- ½   large red onion, chopped
- 12   oz. uncooked spiral pasta
- 4   cups chicken broth
- 2   cans (15 oz. each) crushed tomatoes
- 1   can (8 oz.) tomato sauce
- 1   cup water
- ¼   cup ketchup
- 3   Tbsp. prepared mustard
- 2   Tbsp. Worcestershire sauce
- ¼   tsp. salt
- ¼   tsp. pepper
- 2   cups shredded cheddar cheese, divided
- ⅓   cup chopped dill pickle
      Optional: Chopped tomatoes, shredded lettuce, sliced pickles and sliced red onion

1. In a 6-qt. stockpot, cook bacon over medium heat, stirring occasionally, until crisp, 6-8 minutes. Remove with a slotted spoon; drain bacon on paper towels. Discard drippings.

2. In the same pot, cook ground beef and onion over medium heat until meat is no longer pink, 6-8 minutes, breaking into crumbles; drain. Add next 10 ingredients; bring to a boil. Reduce heat; simmer, covered, until pasta is al dente, stirring occasionally, about 10 minutes.

3. Stir in 1 cup cheese, pickle and bacon; cook and stir until cheese is melted. Serve with the remaining cheese and, if desired, tomatoes, lettuce, pickles and red onions.

1⅓ cups: 390 cal., 18g fat (8g sat. fat), 73mg chol., 1023mg sod., 31g carb. (7g sugars, 3g fiber), 25g pro.

CHIPOTLE-ORANGE CHICKEN

Big on flavor and easy on the cook's time, this slow-cooker chicken recipe is a winner. The sweet-hot sauce gets its heat from the chipotle pepper. I serve this dish with a side of rice to use up every delectable drop of the sauce.

—Susan Hein, Burlington, WI

- -

Prep: 15 min. • **Cook:** 3 hours
Makes: 2 servings

- 2 boneless skinless chicken breast halves (6 oz. each)
- ⅛ tsp. salt
  Dash pepper
- ¼ cup chicken broth
- 3 Tbsp. orange marmalade
- 1½ tsp. canola oil
- 1½ tsp. balsamic vinegar
- 1½ tsp. minced chipotle pepper in adobo sauce
- 1½ tsp. honey
- ½ tsp. chili powder
- ⅛ tsp. garlic powder
- 2 tsp. cornstarch
- 1 Tbsp. cold water

1. Sprinkle chicken with salt and pepper. Transfer to a 1½-qt. slow cooker. In a small bowl, combine the broth, marmalade, oil, balsamic vinegar, chipotle pepper, honey, chili powder and garlic powder; pour over chicken. Cover and cook on low 3-4 hours, until a thermometer reads 165°.
2. Remove chicken to a serving platter and keep warm. Place the cooking juices in a small saucepan; bring to a boil. Combine the cornstarch and water until smooth. Gradually stir into pan. Bring to a boil; cook and stir until thickened, about 2 minutes. Serve with chicken.
Freeze option: Cool chicken mixture. Freeze in freezer containers. To use, partially thaw in refrigerator overnight. Heat through slowly in a covered skillet until a thermometer inserted in chicken reads 165°, stirring occasionally; add broth or water if necessary.
1 chicken breast half : 324 cal., 8g fat (1g sat. fat), 95mg chol., 414mg sod., 29g carb. (24g sugars, 1g fiber), 35g pro.

TRIPLE-CITRUS STEAKS WITH JICAMA & MANGO

I came up with this recipe several years ago. It's one of our all-time favorites. It's colorful and easy to make.

—Sherry Little, Sherwood, AR

- -

Prep: 30 min. + marinating • **Cook:** 15 min.
Makes: 4 servings

- 1 medium orange
- 1 medium lemon
- 1 medium lime
- 4 Tbsp. honey
- 1¼ tsp. salt, divided
- 4 beef flat iron steaks or top sirloin steaks (6 oz. each and ¾ in. thick)
- ½ cup water
- 1 cup julienned peeled jicama
- 1 medium mango, peeled and cubed

1. Cut orange, lemon and lime crosswise in half; squeeze juice from fruits. Stir in honey and salt. Pour ⅓ cup marinade into a bowl or shallow dish. Add steaks and turn to coat. Refrigerate at least 3 hours, turning once. Cover and refrigerate remaining marinade.
2. Drain steaks, discarding marinade. Heat a large skillet over medium heat. Cook steaks until meat reaches desired doneness (for medium-rare, a thermometer should read 135°; medium, 140°; medium-well, 145°), 6-8 minutes on each side. Remove steaks and keep warm.
3. Add water and the reserved marinade. Bring to a boil; cook until liquid is reduced to 3 Tbsp., 10-12 minutes. Add jicama and mango; heat through. Serve with steaks. If desired, garnish servings with orange, lemon or lime slices.
1 serving: 412 cal., 18g fat (7g sat. fat), 109mg chol., 609mg sod., 29g carb. (24g sugars, 3g fiber), 34g pro.

CHIPOTLE-ORANGE CHICKEN

CHICKEN POTPIE GALETTE WITH CHEDDAR-THYME CRUST

GARLICKY CHICKEN DINNER

Bone-in chicken brings comforting flavor, which is enhanced by herbs, lemon and hearty vegetables.
—Shannon Norris, Senior Food Stylist

- -

Prep: 25 min. • **Bake:** 45 min.
Makes: 8 servings

- 1¼ **lbs. small red potatoes, quartered**
- 4 **medium carrots, cut into ½-in. slices**
- 1 **medium red onion, cut into thin wedges**
- 1 **Tbsp. olive oil**
- 6 **garlic cloves, minced**
- 2 **tsp. minced fresh thyme, divided**
- 1½ **tsp. salt, divided**
- 1 **tsp. pepper, divided**
- 1 **tsp. paprika**
- 4 **chicken drumsticks**
- 4 **bone-in chicken thighs**
- 1 **small lemon, sliced**
- 1 **pkg. (5 oz.) fresh spinach**

1. Preheat oven to 425°. In a large bowl, combine potatoes, carrots, onion, oil, garlic, 1 tsp. thyme, ¾ tsp. salt and ½ tsp. pepper; toss to coat. Transfer to a 15x10x1-in. baking pan coated with cooking spray.

2. In a small bowl, mix paprika and remaining thyme, salt and pepper. Sprinkle chicken with paprika mixture; arrange over vegetables. Top chicken with lemon slices. Roast until a thermometer inserted in chicken reads 170°-175° and vegetables are just tender, 35-40 minutes.

3. Remove chicken to a serving platter; keep warm. Top vegetables with spinach. Roast until vegetables are tender and spinach is wilted, 8-10 minutes longer. Stir vegetables to combine; serve with chicken.

1 piece chicken with 1 cup vegetables: 264 cal., 12g fat (3g sat. fat), 64mg chol., 548mg sod., 18g carb. (3g sugars, 3g fiber), 21g pro.
Diabetic exchanges: 3 medium-fat meat, 1 starch, 1 vegetable, ½ fat.

"This recipe is perfection. I add a shallot with the onion, and sometimes play with the flavors by using garam masala."

—HAZEL WHEATON, EDITOR

CHICKEN POTPIE GALETTE WITH CHEDDAR-THYME CRUST

This gorgeous galette puts a fun open-faced spin on traditional chicken potpie. The rich filling and flaky cheddar-flecked crust make it taste so homey.
—Elisabeth Larsen, Pleasant Grove, UT

- -

Prep: 45 min. + chilling
Bake: 30 min. + cooling • **Makes:** 8 servings

- 1¼ **cups all-purpose flour**
- ½ **cup shredded sharp cheddar cheese**
- 2 **Tbsp. minced fresh thyme**
- ¼ **tsp. salt**
- ½ **cup cold butter, cubed**
- ¼ **cup ice water**

FILLING

- 3 **Tbsp. butter**
- 2 **large carrots, sliced**
- 1 **celery rib, diced**
- 1 **small onion, diced**
- 8 **oz. sliced fresh mushrooms**
- 3 **cups julienned Swiss chard**
- 3 **garlic cloves, minced**
- 1 **cup chicken broth**
- 3 **Tbsp. all-purpose flour**
- ½ **tsp. salt**
- ¼ **tsp. pepper**
- 2 **cups shredded cooked chicken**
- ½ **tsp. minced fresh oregano**
- 2 **Tbsp. minced fresh parsley**

1. Combine flour, cheese, thyme and salt; cut in butter until crumbly. Gradually add ice water, tossing with a fork until dough holds together when pressed. Shape into a disk; refrigerate 1 hour.

2. For filling, melt butter in a large saucepan over medium-high heat. Add carrots, celery and diced onion; cook and stir until slightly softened, 5-7 minutes. Add mushrooms; cook 3 minutes longer. Add Swiss chard and garlic; cook until chard is wilted, 2-3 minutes.

3. Whisk together chicken broth, flour, salt and pepper; slowly pour over vegetables, stirring constantly. Cook until thickened, 2-3 minutes. Stir in chicken and oregano.

4. Preheat oven to 400°. On a floured sheet of parchment, roll dough into a 12-in. circle. Transfer to a baking sheet. Spoon filling over crust to within 2 in. of edge. Fold crust edge over filling, pleating as you go, leaving center uncovered. Bake on a lower oven rack until crust is golden brown and filling is bubbly, 30-35 minutes. Cool for 15 minutes before slicing. Sprinkle with parsley.

1 piece: 342 cal., 21g fat (12g sat. fat), 81mg chol., 594mg sod., 22g carb. (2g sugars, 2g fiber), 16g pro.

GARLICKY
CHICKEN DINNER

BUFFALO CHICKEN STUFFED POBLANO PEPPERS

BUFFALO CHICKEN STUFFED POBLANO PEPPERS

I'm not a fan of green bell peppers, so I decided to create a filling that would go well with my favorite pepper—the poblano. After a few taste tests with my family, this stuffed poblano peppers recipe is now one of our favorites. I've also added black beans to the filling, used Cubanelle peppers, and served cilantro lime rice on the side.
—Lorri Stout, Gaithersburg, MD

Prep: 15 min. • **Bake:** 30 min.
Makes: 8 servings

- 4 **poblano peppers**
- 2 **Tbsp. butter**
- 4 **green onions, thinly sliced, divided**
- 3 **cups shredded cooked chicken breast**
- 1 **cup frozen corn (about 5 oz.), thawed**
- 4 **oz. cream cheese, cubed**
- ¾ **cup shredded Mexican cheese blend, divided**
- ½ **cup Buffalo wing sauce**
- ¼ **cup crumbled blue cheese**
- 1 **tsp. granulated garlic**

1. Preheat oven to 350°. Cut the peppers lengthwise in half; remove seeds. Place in a greased 15x10-in. baking pan. In a large skillet, heat butter over medium-high heat. Add 3 green onions; cook and stir until tender, about 5 minutes. Add chicken, corn, cream cheese, ½ cup shredded cheese, wing sauce, blue cheese and garlic; cook and stir until cheeses are melted.
2. Fill pepper halves with chicken mixture. Bake, covered, 25-30 minutes. Sprinkle with remaining ¼ cup shredded cheese and green onion; bake, uncovered, until the cheese is melted, about 5 minutes.
1 stuffed pepper half: 246 cal., 14g fat (8g sat. fat), 75mg chol., 668mg sod., 9g carb. (3g sugars, 2g fiber), 21g pro.

CONTEST-WINNING CHICKEN WILD RICE CASSEROLE

While this special dish is perfect for serving company, it's so good that I often make it for everyday meals. We enjoy it with rolls or French bread.
—Elizabeth Tokariuk, Lethbridge, AB

Prep: 20 min. • **Bake:** 30 min.
Makes: 8 servings

- 1   small onion, chopped
- ⅓   cup butter
- ⅓   cup all-purpose flour
- 1½ tsp. salt
- ½   tsp. pepper
- 1   can (14½ oz.) chicken broth
- 1   cup half-and-half cream
- 4   cups cubed cooked chicken
- 4   cups cooked wild rice
- 2   jars (4½ oz. each) sliced mushrooms, drained
- 1   jar (4 oz.) diced pimientos, drained
- 1   Tbsp. minced fresh parsley
- ⅓   cup slivered almonds

1. In a large saucepan, saute onion in butter until tender. Stir in the flour, salt and pepper until blended. Gradually stir in broth; bring to a boil. Boil and stir for 2 minutes or until thickened and bubbly. Stir in the cream, chicken, rice, mushrooms, pimientos and parsley; heat through.
2. Transfer to a greased 2½-qt. baking dish. Sprinkle with almonds. Bake, uncovered, at 350° for 30-35 minutes or until bubbly.
1 cup: 382 cal., 19g fat (8g sat. fat), 98mg chol., 878mg sod., 26g carb. (3g sugars, 3g fiber), 27g pro.

THAI SLOPPY JOE CHICKEN & WAFFLES

Sloppy joes, chicken and waffles, and Thai food are family favorites at our house. So I decided to combine all three to create one tasty dish. The slaw with peanut dressing adds crunch and flavor.
—Arlene Erlbach, Morton Grove, IL

Takes: 30 min. • **Makes:** 6 servings

- ¼   cup creamy peanut butter
- ½   cup minced fresh cilantro, divided
- 6   Tbsp. teriyaki sauce, divided
- 3   Tbsp. chili sauce, divided
- 2   Tbsp. lime juice
- 2   cups coleslaw mix
- 1   lb. ground chicken
- ⅓   cup canned coconut milk
- 1   tsp. ground ginger
- ¾   tsp. garlic powder
- 6   frozen waffles
      Sliced green onions, optional

1. Place the peanut butter, ¼ cup cilantro, 4 Tbsp. cup teriyaki sauce, 1 Tbsp. chili sauce and lime juice in a food processor; process until combined. Place coleslaw mix in a large bowl; add peanut butter mixture. Toss to coat; set aside.
2. In a large skillet, cook the chicken over medium heat until the meat is no longer pink, 6-8 minutes, breaking into crumbles; drain. Stir in coconut milk, ginger, garlic powder, remaining ¼ cup cilantro and 2 Tbsp. teriyaki sauce. Cook and stir until heated through.
3. Meanwhile, prepare waffles according to package directions. Top waffles with chicken mixture and coleslaw. If desired, sprinkle with green onions.
1 serving: 314 cal., 17g fat (5g sat. fat), 55mg chol., 1046mg sod., 24g carb. (7g sugars, 2g fiber), 18g pro.

THAI SLOPPY JOE
CHICKEN & WAFFLES

GRILLED BASIL CHICKEN & TOMATOES

Relax after work with a cold drink while this savory chicken marinates in an herby tomato blend. Let it soak for an hour, then toss it on the grill. It tastes just like summer.
—Laura Lunardi, West Chester, PA

- -

Prep: 15 min. + marinating • **Grill:** 10 min.
Makes: 4 servings

- ¾ cup balsamic vinegar
- ¼ cup tightly packed fresh basil leaves
- 2 Tbsp. olive oil
- 1 garlic clove, minced
- ½ tsp. salt
- 8 plum tomatoes
- 4 boneless skinless chicken breast halves (4 oz. each)

1. For marinade, place the first 5 ingredients in a blender. Cut 4 tomatoes into quarters and add to blender; cover and process until blended. Halve the remaining 4 tomatoes for grilling.

2. In a bowl, combine chicken and ⅔ cup marinade; refrigerate, covered, 1 hour, turning occasionally. Reserve remaining marinade for serving.

3. Place chicken on an oiled grill rack over medium heat; discard marinade remaining in the bowl. Grill chicken, covered, until a thermometer reads 165°, 4-6 minutes per side. Grill tomatoes, covered, over medium heat until lightly browned, 2-4 minutes per side. Serve chicken and tomatoes with reserved marinade.

1 serving: 177 cal., 5g fat (1g sat. fat), 63mg chol., 171mg sod., 8g carb. (7g sugars, 1g fiber), 24g pro. **Diabetic exchanges:** 3 lean meat, 1 vegetable, ½ fat.

OKTOBERFEST CASSEROLE

Folks love German-inspired dishes here in northeastern Ohio. This casserole is a mashup of three of my favorites: cheesy hash brown casserole; bratwursts and sauerkraut; and pretzels and beer cheese. It takes just minutes to prep and bakes all in one dish. It's sure to please everyone.
—Sarah Markley, Ashland, OH

- -

Prep: 15 min. • **Bake:** 1½ hours
Makes: 12 servings

- 2 cans (10½ oz. each) condensed cheddar cheese soup, undiluted
- 1 cup beer or chicken broth
- 1 cup sour cream
- 1 pkg. (32 oz.) frozen cubed hash brown potatoes, thawed
- 1 pkg. (14 oz.) fully cooked bratwurst links, chopped
- 1 can (14 oz.) sauerkraut, rinsed and well drained
- 2 cups shredded cheddar cheese
- 2 cups pretzel pieces

Preheat oven to 350°. In a large bowl, whisk soup, beer and sour cream until combined. Stir in the potatoes, sauerkraut, chopped bratwurst and cheese. Transfer to a greased 13x9-in. baking dish. Cover and bake for 45 minutes. Uncover; bake for 30 minutes. Top with pretzel pieces. Bake until bubbly and heated through, 12-15 minutes longer. Let stand 10 minutes before serving.

1 serving: 356 cal., 21g fat (10g sat. fat), 49mg chol., 884mg sod., 29g carb. (4g sugars, 3g fiber), 13g pro.

GRILLED BASIL
CHICKEN & TOMATOES

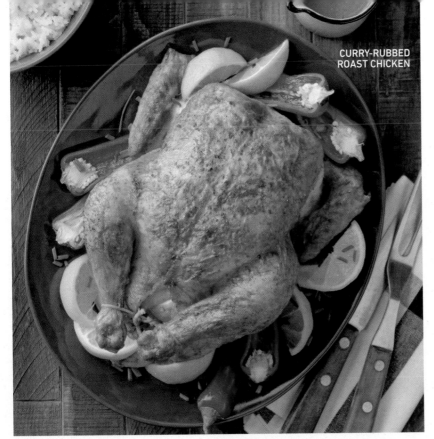

CURRY-RUBBED
ROAST CHICKEN

PORK & ASPARAGUS SHEET-PAN DINNER

When time is of the essence, it's nice to have a quick and easy meal idea in your back pocket. Not only is this delicious, but you can clean it up in a flash.
—Joan Hallford, North Richland Hills, TX

Prep: 20 min. • **Bake:** 20 min.
Makes: 4 servings

¼ cup olive oil, divided
3 cups diced new potatoes
3 cups cut fresh asparagus
   (1-in. pieces)
¼ tsp. salt
¼ tsp. pepper
1 large gala or Honeycrisp apple,
   peeled and cut into 1-in. wedges
2 tsp. brown sugar
1 tsp. ground cinnamon
¼ tsp. ground ginger
4 boneless pork loin chops
   (1 in. thick and about 6 oz. each)
2 tsp. Southwest seasoning

1. Preheat oven to 425°. Line a 15x10x1-in. baking pan with aluminum foil; brush with 2 tsp. olive oil.
2. In a large bowl, toss the potatoes with 1 Tbsp. olive oil. Place in 1 section of prepared baking pan. In same bowl, toss asparagus with 1 Tbsp. olive oil; place in another section of pan. Sprinkle salt and pepper over potatoes and asparagus.
3. In same bowl, toss apple with 1 tsp. olive oil. In a small bowl, mix the brown sugar, cinnamon and ginger; sprinkle over apples and toss to coat. Transfer to a different section of pan.
4. Brush pork chops with remaining 1 Tbsp. olive oil; sprinkle both sides with Southwest seasoning. Place chops in remaining section of pan. Bake until a thermometer inserted in pork reads 145° and potatoes and apples are tender, 20-25 minutes. Let stand 5 minutes before serving.
1 serving: 486 cal., 23g fat (5g sat. fat), 82mg chol., 447mg sod., 32g carb. (10g sugars, 5g fiber), 37g pro.

CURRY-RUBBED ROAST CHICKEN

There is just something so right about serving a savory roasted chicken to loved ones. This recipe is simple—yet it's packed with spicy showoff flavors suitable for any special occasion.
—Merry Graham, Newhall, CA

Prep: 20 min. • **Cook:** 1½ hours + standing
Makes: 6 servings

4   Tbsp. coconut oil, divided
2½   tsp. salt, divided
2   tsp. Madras curry powder
½   tsp. granulated garlic
1   roasting chicken (5 to 6 lbs.)
¼   tsp. pepper
1   cup chopped leeks (white
     portion only)
1   celery rib, coarsely chopped
3   green onions, chopped
1   medium lemon, quartered
1   cup reduced-sodium chicken broth
GRAVY
1   Tbsp. unsalted butter
1   Tbsp. all-purpose flour
1   cup reduced-sodium chicken broth
½   cup white wine
     Optional: Lemon slices, minced
     fresh parsley and minced chives

1. Preheat oven to 350°. Mix 2 Tbsp. coconut oil and 2 tsp. salt with curry powder and garlic. Carefully loosen skin from chicken breast and upper legs; rub coconut oil mixture under skin. Remove giblets from cavity; save for another use. Sprinkle cavity with pepper and remaining salt; rub inside and outside of chicken with remaining oil.
2. Combine leek, celery, green onions and lemon and toss lightly; loosely stuff cavity. Tuck wings under chicken; tie drumsticks together. Place breast side up on a rack in a shallow roasting pan.
3. Roast 45 minutes; add chicken broth to pan. Continue roasting until a thermometer reads 165° when inserted in the center of stuffing and at least 170° in the thigh, 45-60 minutes. (Cover loosely with foil if chicken browns too quickly.)
4. Pour juices from cavity into pan. Remove chicken to a platter; tent with foil. Let stand 15-20 minutes before removing stuffing.
5. For gravy, pour pan juices into a large saucepan; skim off fat. Bring juices to a boil over medium heat. Add butter and flour; cook and stir until slightly thickened. Add broth and wine; cook and stir until thickened, 2-3 minutes. Serve with chicken and, if desired, lemon slices, parsley and chives.
1 serving: 580 cal., 38g fat (17g sat. fat), 154mg chol., 1328mg sod., 6g carb. (2g sugars, 1g fiber), 49g pro.

SPICY PLUM PORK
MEATBALLS WITH BOK CHOY

SPICY PLUM PORK MEATBALLS WITH BOK CHOY

I'm a fan of sweet, salty and spicy flavors and trying to make healthier food choices. This is so satisfying, you won't miss any pasta or rice. If you don't care for spiralized zucchini, thin pasta noodles work, too.
—Susan Mason, Puyallup, WA

- -

Prep: 30 min. • **Cook:** 30 min.
Makes: 4 servings

- 1 jar (7 oz.) plum sauce
- ½ cup hoisin sauce
- 3 Tbsp. reduced-sodium soy sauce
- 2 Tbsp. rice vinegar
- 1 Tbsp. Sriracha chili sauce
- 1 large egg, lightly beaten
- 1½ cups panko bread crumbs, divided
- 1 lb. ground pork
- 4 Tbsp. olive oil, divided
- 2 medium zucchini, spiralized
- 1 lb. bok choy, trimmed and cut into 1-in. pieces
     Sesame seeds, optional

1. Whisk together the first 5 ingredients. Reserve 1¼ cups for sauce. Pour remaining mixture into a large bowl; add egg and ½ cup bread crumbs. Add the pork; mix lightly but thoroughly. Shape into 16 balls. Place the remaining 1 cup bread crumbs in a shallow bowl. Roll meatballs in bread crumbs to coat.
2. In a large skillet, heat 3 Tbsp. oil over medium heat. In batches, cook meatballs until cooked through, turning occasionally. Remove and keep warm. Heat remaining 1 Tbsp. oil in the same skillet. Add zucchini and bok choy; cook and stir over medium-high heat until crisp-tender, 6-8 minutes. Add the meatballs and reserved sauce; heat through. If desired, sprinkle with sesame seeds.
1 serving: 647 cal., 34g fat (9g sat. fat), 123mg chol., 1656mg sod., 55g carb. (16g sugars, 4g fiber), 29g pro.

TEST KITCHEN TIP
Our Test Kitchen's favorite way to make picture-perfect zucchini noodles is to use a spiralizer. But if you don't have one, you can also use a vegetable peeler, carefully carve with a knife, or shred with a box grater.

SPICE-CRUSTED STEAKS
WITH CHERRY SAUCE

SPICE-CRUSTED STEAKS WITH CHERRY SAUCE

If you are hosting meat lovers for dinner, these impressive cast-iron skillet steaks are guaranteed to please. They're perfect for a special occasion without too much fuss.
—*Taste of Home* Test Kitchen

- -

Prep: 20 min. + chilling • **Cook:** 45 min.
Makes: 4 servings

- ½ cup dried cherries
- ¼ cup port wine, warmed
- 3½ tsp. coarsely ground pepper
- 1 tsp. brown sugar
- ¾ tsp. garlic powder
- ¾ tsp. paprika
- ¾ tsp. ground coffee
- ½ tsp. kosher salt
- ¼ tsp. ground cinnamon
- ¼ tsp. ground cumin
- ⅛ tsp. ground mustard
- 4 beef tenderloin steaks (1¼ in. thick and 6 oz. each)
- 1 Tbsp. canola oil
- 1 large shallot, finely chopped
- 1 Tbsp. butter
- 1 cup reduced-sodium beef broth
- 1 tsp. minced fresh thyme
- ½ cup heavy whipping cream
     Crumbled blue cheese, optional

1. Preheat oven to 350°. In a small bowl, combine cherries and wine; set aside. In a shallow dish, combine the pepper, brown sugar, garlic powder, paprika, coffee, salt, cinnamon, cumin and mustard. Add 1 steak at a time and turn to coat. Cover and refrigerate for 30 minutes.
2. Place oil in a 10-in. cast-iron or other ovenproof skillet; tilt to coat bottom. Heat oil over medium-high heat; sear steaks, 2 minutes on each side. Bake, uncovered, until meat reaches desired doneness (for medium-rare, a thermometer should read 135°; medium, 140°; medium-well, 145°), about 15 minutes. Remove steaks from oven and keep warm.
3. Wipe skillet clean; saute shallot in butter until crisp-tender. Add broth and thyme. Bring to a boil; cook until liquid is reduced by half, about 8 minutes. Stir in the cream; bring to a boil. Cook until thickened, stirring occasionally, 8 minutes.
4. Stir in the reserved cherry mixture. Serve sauce over steaks. If desired, sprinkle with blue cheese.
1 steak with 3 Tbsp. sauce: 506 cal., 28g fat (13g sat. fat), 124mg chol., 381mg sod., 20g carb. (13g sugars, 1g fiber), 39g pro.

MEAT LOVER'S PIZZA RICE SKILLET

One night I needed a quick dinner, so I threw this together from what I had in the fridge and pantry. Add any other pizza toppings you desire. I often add black olive slices or mushrooms. My son calls it pizza rice.
—Teri Rasey, Cadillac, MI

- -

Takes: 25 min. • **Makes:** 6 servings

- 1   lb. bulk Italian sausage
- 1   can (14½ oz.) diced tomatoes with basil, oregano and garlic
- 1   can (15½ oz.) cannellini beans, rinsed and drained
- 1½ cups water
- 1½ cups uncooked instant rice
- ¼   cup grated Parmesan cheese
- ½   cup (2 oz.) sliced mini pepperoni
     Optional: Additional grated Parmesan cheese and chopped fresh basil

1. In a large skillet, cook the sausage over medium heat 5-7 minutes or until no longer pink, breaking into crumbles; drain. Return to skillet with next 4 ingredients. Bring to a boil; cover and remove from heat. Let stand for 5 minutes.

2. Fluff with a fork; stir in Parmesan cheese. Top with mini pepperoni and, if desired, additional Parmesan cheese and basil.

1¼ cups: 390 cal., 20g fat (6g sat. fat), 48mg chol., 906mg sod., 35g carb. (2g sugars, 4g fiber), 15g pro.

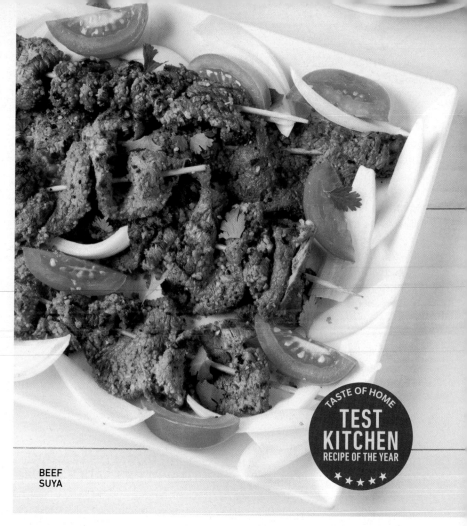

BEEF SUYA

TASTE OF HOME
TEST KITCHEN
RECIPE OF THE YEAR
★ ★ ★ ★ ★

BEEF SUYA

My Nigerian brother-in-law introduced me to beef suya, a spicy street food that is popular in western Africa. I was intrigued when I found out the spice rub is made from ground peanuts and a blend of different seasonings. After lots of experimenting, I came up with my own version.
—Elena Iorga, Helena, MT

- -

Prep: 30 min. + marinating • **Grill:** 15 min.
Makes: 8 servings

- 1   cup salted peanuts
- 1   Tbsp. paprika
- 2   tsp. onion powder
- 2   tsp. ground ginger
- 1   tsp. crushed red pepper flakes
- 1   tsp. garlic powder
- 1   beef tri-tip roast or beef top sirloin steak (2 lbs.), thinly sliced against the grain
- 2   Tbsp. canola oil
- 1   tsp. salt
- 1   medium onion, cut into wedges
- 1   large tomato, cut into wedges
     Fresh cilantro leaves

1. Place the peanuts in a food processor; process until finely chopped. Add paprika, onion powder, ginger, pepper flakes and garlic powder; pulse until combined.

2. Place beef in a large bowl or shallow dish. Drizzle with oil; sprinkle with salt. Toss to coat. Add the peanut mixture; turn to coat. Refrigerate, covered, for 2 hours. Drain beef, discarding marinade.

3. Thread beef slices onto metal or soaked wooden skewers. Grill beef, covered, over medium-high heat until the meat reaches desired doneness, 10-15 minutes, turning occasionally. Serve with onion, tomato and fresh cilantro.

1 kabob: 329 cal., 21g fat (5g sat. fat), 68mg chol., 405mg sod., 7g carb. (2g sugars, 3g fiber), 29g pro.

EGG ROLL NOODLE BOWL

We love Asian egg rolls, but they can be challenging to make. Simplify everything with this deconstructed egg roll made on the stovetop and served in a bowl.
—Courtney Stultz, Weir, KS

- -

Takes: 30 min. • **Makes:** 4 servings

- 1 Tbsp. sesame oil
- ½ lb. ground pork
- 1 Tbsp. soy sauce
- 1 garlic clove, minced
- 1 tsp. ground ginger
- ½ tsp. salt
- ¼ tsp. ground turmeric
- ¼ tsp. pepper
- 6 cups shredded cabbage (about 1 small head)
- 2 large carrots, shredded (about 2 cups)
- 4 oz. rice noodles
- 3 green onions, thinly sliced
  Additional soy sauce, optional

1. In a large cast-iron or other heavy skillet, heat oil over medium-high heat; cook and crumble pork until browned, 4-6 minutes. Stir in soy sauce, garlic and seasonings. Add cabbage and carrots; cook until tender, stirring occasionally, 4-6 minutes longer.
2. Cook rice noodles according to package directions; drain and immediately add to pork mixture, tossing to combine. Sprinkle with green onions. If desired, serve with additional soy sauce.

1½ cups: 302 cal., 12g fat (4g sat. fat), 38mg chol., 652mg sod., 33g carb. (2g sugars, 4g fiber), 14g pro. **Diabetic exchanges:** 2 medium-fat meat, 2 vegetable, 1½ starch, ½ fat.

> "I started making this during the COVID-19 quarantine. Now it's in my regular meal rotation. It's such an easy weeknight dinner—and it's healthy! I usually swap ground turkey for the pork, since I have that on hand more often."
>
> —EMILY PARULSKI, SENIOR DIGITAL EDITOR

SALSA STEAK GARLIC TOASTS

These open-faced steak sandwiches play up the popular combo of steak and garlic bread. The salsa, sour cream and garnish elevate it into quick, satisfying meal. Feel free to substitute chopped green onions or chives for the cilantro if desired.
—Arlene Erlbach, Morton Grove, IL

- -

Takes: 25 min. • **Makes:** 4 servings

- 4 slices frozen garlic Texas toast
- 1 Tbsp. olive oil
- 1 beef top sirloin steak (1 lb.), thinly sliced
- 1½ cups salsa
  Sour cream and chopped fresh cilantro

1. Prepare the garlic toast according to package directions.
2. Meanwhile, in a large skillet, heat oil over medium heat. Saute steak until no longer pink, 3-5 minutes; drain. Stir in salsa; cook and stir until heated through. Serve over toast. Top with sour cream and cilantro.

1 garlic toast with ¾ cup steak mixture: 375 cal., 16g fat (4g sat. fat), 52mg chol., 721mg sod., 27g carb. (5g sugars, 1g fiber), 29g pro.

EGG ROLL
NOODLE BOWL

SMOKY MACARONI & CHEESE
PAGE 154

SIDE DISHES

Discover the perfect accompaniment for your next meal. From speedy weeknight favorites to picnic and holiday crowd-pleasers, these side dishes rank among our most loved and most requested when we cook for our own families.

BACON MAC & CHEESE
CORNBREAD SKILLET

BACON MAC & CHEESE CORNBREAD SKILLET

My cast-iron skillet is a workhorse in my kitchen. I just love it for cooking and baking. And this cast-iron mac and cheese recipe can be served either as a main dish or as a smaller-portion side.

—Lisa Keys, Kennet Square, PA

- -

Prep: 35 min. • **Bake:** 30 min. + standing
Makes: 8 servings

- 1¾ cups uncooked elbow macaroni
- 8 bacon strips, chopped
- 1 cup shredded smoked Gouda or cheddar cheese
- 1 cup shredded pepper jack cheese
- 4 oz. cream cheese, cubed
- 6 large eggs, divided use
- 3 cups 2% milk, divided
- 4 green onions, chopped
- 1 tsp. kosher salt, divided
- ½ tsp. pepper, divided
- 1 pkg. (8½ oz.) cornbread/muffin mix
- ½ tsp. smoked paprika
  Additional green onions

1. Preheat oven to 400°. Cook macaroni according to package directions. Meanwhile, in a 12-in. cast-iron or other ovenproof skillet, cook chopped bacon over medium heat until crisp, stirring occasionally. Remove with a slotted spoon; drain on paper towels. Discard drippings, reserving 1 Tbsp. in pan.
2. Drain the macaroni; add macaroni to drippings. Stir in shredded cheeses and cream cheese; cook and stir over medium heat until cheese is melted, 2-3 minutes. Whisk 2 eggs, 1 cup milk, green onions, ½ tsp. kosher salt and ¼ tsp. pepper; pour the mixture into skillet. Cook and stir until slightly thickened, 3-4 minutes. Remove skillet from the heat.
3. Reserve ¼ cup bacon for topping; sprinkle the remaining bacon over macaroni. Place cornbread mix, paprika, remaining 4 eggs, 2 cups milk, ½ tsp. kosher salt and ¼ tsp. pepper in a blender; cover and process until smooth. Pour over bacon.
4. Bake until cornbread is puffed and golden brown, 30-35 minutes. Let stand 10 minutes before serving. Sprinkle with reserved ¼ cup bacon and additional green onions.
1 cup: 497 cal., 27g fat (13g sat. fat), 203mg chol., 978mg sod., 40g carb. (12g sugars, 3g fiber), 23g pro.

PERFECT
SUSHI RICE

PERFECT SUSHI RICE

Sushi rice can be used for more than just sushi. Use it to create a healthy rice bowl, tuck it into a lettuce wrap topped with grilled meat or use it as a base for your favorite stir-fry.

—*Taste of Home* Test Kitchen

- -

Prep: 40 min. + standing • **Cook:** 15 min.
Makes: 4 cups

- 2 cups sushi rice
- ¼ cup rice vinegar
- 2 Tbsp. sugar
- ½ tsp. salt

1. In large bowl, wash rice in several changes of cold water until water is clear. Transfer to a large saucepan; add 2 cups water. Let stand for 30 minutes.
2. Cover saucepan and bring to boil over high heat. Reduce heat to low; cook until water is absorbed and rice is tender, 15-20 minutes. Remove from the heat. Let stand, covered, for 10 minutes.
3. Meanwhile, in small bowl, combine the vinegar, sugar and salt, stirring until the sugar is dissolved.
4. Transfer rice to a shallow bowl; sprinkle with vinegar mixture. Set aside remaining vinegar mixture for assembly. With a wooden paddle or spoon, stir rice with a slicing motion until cooled. Cover with a damp cloth to keep moist. (The rice mixture may be made up to 6 hours ahead and stored at room temperature, covered, with a damp towel. Do not refrigerate.)
½ cup: 201 cal., 0 fat (0 sat. fat), 0 chol., 268mg sod., 45g carb. (6g sugars, 1g fiber), 3g pro.

> "Poke bowls are my new obsession. And a great bowl starts with a base of delicious rice."
>
> —CATHERINE WARD, PREP KITCHEN MANAGER

LOADED MASHED POTATO BITES

Put leftover mashed potatoes to good use! Turn them into yummy hot bites loaded with bacon, cheese and onions.
—Becky Hardin, St. Peters, MO

- -

Prep: 15 min. + chilling • **Cook:** 10 min.
Makes: 1½ dozen

- 3 cups mashed potatoes
- 1½ cups shredded sharp cheddar cheese
- ¾ cup crumbled cooked bacon
- ½ cup chopped green onions
- 2 oz. Colby-Monterey Jack cheese, cut into eighteen ½-in. cubes
- ½ cup panko bread crumbs
- ½ cup grated Parmesan cheese
- ½ tsp. salt
- ½ tsp. pepper
- 1 large egg, beaten
  Oil for deep-fat frying

1. In a large bowl, combine the potatoes, shredded cheese, bacon and green onions. Divide into eighteen ¼-cup portions. Shape each portion around a cheese cube to cover completely, forming a ball. Refrigerate, covered, at least 30 minutes.
2. In a shallow bowl, mix bread crumbs, Parmesan cheese, salt and pepper. Place egg in a separate shallow bowl. Dip potato balls in egg, then in crumb mixture, patting to help coating adhere.
3. In an electric skillet or a deep-fat fryer, heat oil to 375°. Fry potato balls, a few at a time, until golden brown, for 2 minutes. Drain on paper towels.
1 piece: 227 cal., 19g fat (5g sat. fat), 30mg chol., 420mg sod., 8g carb. (1g sugars, 1g fiber), 7g pro.

MOIST CORN SPOON BREAD

Enjoy this easy take on a Southern specialty by taking advantage of the convenience of your slow cooker. It's an excellent dish for Thanksgiving, Easter or any special feast.
—*Taste of Home* Test Kitchen

- -

Prep: 20 min. • **Cook:** 4 hours
Makes: 8 servings

- 1 pkg. (8 oz.) cream cheese, softened
- 2 Tbsp. sugar
- 2 large eggs, beaten
- 1 cup 2% milk
- 2 Tbsp. butter, melted
- ½ tsp. salt
- ¼ tsp. cayenne pepper
- ⅛ tsp. pepper
- 2 cups frozen corn
- 1 can (14¾ oz.) cream-style corn
- 1 cup yellow cornmeal
- 1 cup shredded Monterey Jack cheese
- 3 green onions, thinly sliced
  Optional: Coarsely ground pepper and thinly sliced green onions

1. In a large bowl, beat softened cream cheese and sugar until smooth. Gradually beat in eggs. Beat in the milk, butter, salt, cayenne and pepper until blended. Stir in remaining ingredients.
2. Pour into a greased 3-qt. slow cooker. Cover and cook on low for 4-5 hours, until a toothpick inserted in the center comes out clean. If desired, top with additional pepper and green onions.
1 serving: 350 cal., 18g fat (11g sat. fat), 54mg chol., 525mg sod., 38g carb. (8g sugars, 3g fiber), 12g pro.

MOIST CORN SPOON BREAD

HEIRLOOM TOMATO GALETTE WITH PECORINO

SPICED SWEET POTATO FRIES

A spicy homemade seasoning blend shakes up everyone's favorite finger food.
—*Taste of Home* Test Kitchen

Takes: 25 min. • **Makes:** 6 servings

- 1 pkg. (19 oz.) frozen french-fried sweet potatoes
- ½ tsp. garlic powder
- ½ tsp. curry powder
- ½ tsp. pepper
- ¼ tsp. chili powder
- ⅛ tsp. ground cinnamon
- ⅛ tsp. salt

Bake fries according to package directions. Meanwhile, in a small bowl, combine the remaining ingredients. Sprinkle over fries; toss to coat.
1 serving: 129 cal., 3g fat (1g sat. fat), 0 chol., 241mg sod., 24g carb. (10g sugars, 2g fiber), 0 pro.

> ### TEST KITCHEN TIP
> You can also make these fries using 2-3 large fresh sweet potatoes, peeled and cut into ¼-inch julienned strips (about 2¼ pounds).

HEIRLOOM TOMATO GALETTE WITH PECORINO

I found beautiful heirloom tomatoes and had to show them off. In this easy galette, the tomatoes are tangy and the crust is beyond buttery.
—Jessica Chang, Playa Vista, CA

Prep: 10 min. + chilling
Bake: 25 min. + cooling • **Makes:** 6 servings

- 1 cup all-purpose flour
- 1 tsp. baking powder
- ¾ tsp. kosher salt, divided
- ½ cup cold unsalted butter, cubed
- ½ cup sour cream
- 2 cups cherry tomatoes, halved
- 3 oz. pecorino Romano cheese, thinly sliced

1. Whisk flour, baking powder and ½ tsp. salt; cut in butter until mixture resembles coarse crumbs. Stir in the sour cream until dough forms a ball. Shape into a disk; cover and refrigerate until firm enough to roll, about 2 hours.
2. Meanwhile, place tomatoes in a colander; toss with remaining salt. Let tomatoes stand 15 minutes.

3. Preheat oven to 425°. On a floured sheet of parchment, roll dough into a 12-in. circle. Transfer to a baking sheet.
4. Place cheese slices over crust to within 2 in. of edge; arrange tomatoes over cheese. Fold crust edges over filling, pleating as you go and leaving center uncovered. Bake until crust is golden brown and cheese is bubbly, about 25 minutes. Cool for 10 minutes before slicing.
1 piece: 317 cal., 23g fat (15g sat. fat), 68mg chol., 559mg sod., 19g carb. (2g sugars, 1g fiber), 9g pro.

> "I love serving this to guests. The last time I made it, I didn't have pecorino Romano, so I used shredded Parmesan mixed with a little feta, and I put a smear of sour cream over the crust before adding the toppings."
>
> —HAZEL WHEATON, EDITOR

CRISPY FRIED ONION RINGS

SMOKY MACARONI & CHEESE

I found this recipe years ago in a magazine, and kept adding and taking away ingredients until I found the perfect combination. You can make it in the oven if you like, but grilling or smoking the dish is the real way to go.
—Stacey Dull, Gettysburg, OH

- -

Prep: 40 min. • **Grill:** 20 min. + standing
Makes: 2 casseroles (8 servings each)

- 6 cups small pasta shells
- 12 oz. Velveeta, cut into small cubes
- 2 cups shredded smoked cheddar cheese, divided
- 1 cup shredded cheddar cheese
- 1 cup 2% milk
- 4 large eggs, lightly beaten
- ¾ cup heavy whipping cream
- ⅔ cup half-and-half cream
- ½ cup shredded provolone cheese
- ½ cup shredded Colby-Monterey Jack cheese
- ½ cup shredded pepper jack cheese
- 1 tsp. salt
- ½ tsp. pepper
- ½ tsp. smoked paprika
- ½ tsp. liquid smoke, optional
  Dash cayenne pepper, optional
- 8 bacon strips, cooked and crumbled, optional

1. Preheat grill or smoker to 350°. Cook the pasta according to package directions for al dente. Drain and transfer to a large bowl. Stir in Velveeta, 1 cup smoked cheddar, cheddar cheese, milk, eggs, heavy cream, half-and-half, provolone, Colby-Monterey Jack, pepper jack, salt, pepper, paprika, and, if desired, liquid smoke and cayenne pepper.
2. Transfer to 2 greased 13x9-in. baking pans; sprinkle with remaining 1 cup smoked cheddar cheese. Place on grill or smoker rack. Grill or smoke, covered, until a thermometer reads at least 160°, 20-25 minutes, rotating pans partway through cooking. Do not overcook. Let stand for 10 minutes before serving; if desired, sprinkle with bacon.
1 cup: 403 cal., 23g fat (13g sat. fat), 117mg chol., 670mg sod., 30g carb. (4g sugars, 1g fiber), 18g pro.

CRISPY FRIED ONION RINGS

Enjoy these crispy rings on their own with dip or add them as a fun topper to burgers. They also give salads a little extra crunch.
—*Taste of Home* Test Kitchen

- -

Takes: 25 min. • **Makes:** 12 servings

- ½ cup all-purpose flour
- ½ cup water
- 1 large egg, lightly beaten
- 1 tsp. seasoned salt
- ½ tsp. baking powder
- 1 large onion, very thinly sliced
  Oil for deep-fat frying

In a shallow bowl, whisk first 5 ingredients. Separate onion slices into rings. Dip rings into batter. In a deep-fat fryer, heat 1 in. of oil to 375°. In batches, fry onion rings until golden brown, 1-1½ minutes on each side. Drain on paper towels. Serve immediately.
½ cup: 71 cal., 5g fat (0 sat. fat), 16mg chol., 153mg sod., 5g carb. (1g sugars, 0 fiber), 1g pro.
Baked Onion Rings: Preheat oven to 425°. Beat egg in a shallow bowl. In another shallow bowl, mix ⅔ cup dry bread crumbs, ½ tsp. seasoned salt and ¼ tsp. pepper. Dip onion rings into egg, then roll in crumb mixture. Place on a baking sheet coated with cooking spray. Bake 15-18 minutes or until golden brown, turning once.
Red Onion Rings: Substitute a red onion for the onion. With the flour mixture, whisk in ¼ tsp. cayenne.

ROASTED ASPARAGUS & LEEKS

No veggie says spring quite like asparagus. In this recipe, we combine pretty green spears with leeks. Crushed red pepper adds a bit of zest.
—*Taste of Home* Test Kitchen

- -

Prep: 15 min. • **Bake:** 20 min.
Makes: 12 servings

- 3 lbs. fresh asparagus, trimmed
- 12 medium leeks (white portion only), halved lengthwise
- 4½ tsp. olive oil
- 1½ tsp. dill weed
- ½ tsp. salt
- ½ tsp. crushed red pepper flakes
- ¼ tsp. pepper

1. Place the asparagus and halved leeks on an ungreased 15x10x1-in. baking pan. Combine the remaining ingredients; pour over the vegetables.
2. Bake at 400° for 20-25 minutes or until tender, stirring occasionally.
1 serving: 83 cal., 2g fat (0 sat. fat), 0 chol., 98mg sod., 15g carb. (4g sugars, 3g fiber), 3g pro. **Diabetic exchanges:** 2 vegetable, ½ fat.

SMOKY MACARONI
& CHEESE

BANANA-ORANGE SWEET POTATO BAKE

Welcome fall with this simple side dish. It's a pleasant change of pace from the traditional casserole with marshmallows, and it's quite popular at potlucks.
—Joan Hallford, North Richland Hills, TX

- -

Prep: 50 min. • **Bake:** 35 min.
Makes: 10 servings

5	medium sweet potatoes (about 3 lbs.), peeled and cubed
⅔	cup packed brown sugar
3	Tbsp. butter
¼	tsp. salt
¼	tsp. ground cloves
⅛	tsp. pepper
2	tsp. grated orange zest
⅓	cup orange juice
¼	cup orange liqueur, optional
3	medium ripe bananas, mashed
2	large eggs, lightly beaten

TOPPING

½	cup granola cereal
½	cup chopped pecans, toasted
¼	cup sweetened shredded coconut, toasted
2	Tbsp. brown sugar
¼	cup butter, melted

1. Preheat oven to 350°. Place the sweet potatoes in a large Dutch oven; add water to cover. Bring to a boil. Reduce heat; cook, covered, just until tender, 12-15 minutes. Drain; cool slightly. Return to pan; mash with brown sugar, butter, salt, cloves and pepper until smooth. Stir in orange zest, orange juice and, if desired, liqueur. Add bananas and eggs; mix well. Transfer to a greased 2-qt. baking dish.

2. For the topping, mix granola, pecans, coconut and brown sugar; sprinkle over sweet potatoes. Drizzle with melted butter. Bake, uncovered, until heated through, 35-45 minutes.

¾ cup: 355 cal., 15g fat (7g sat. fat), 59mg chol., 160mg sod., 54g carb. (33g sugars, 5g fiber), 5g pro.

BANANA-ORANGE
SWEET POTATO BAKE

AIR-FRYER CANDIED ACORN SQUASH SLICES

This acorn squash recipe was passed down to me from my grandma, who always served it at Thanksgiving. Now I make it in my air fryer whenever I'm feeling nostalgic.
—Rita Addicks, Weimar, TX

- -

Prep: 15 min. • **Cook:** 15 min./batch
Makes: 6 servings

2 medium acorn squash
⅔ cup packed brown sugar
½ cup butter, softened

1. Preheat air fryer to 350°. Cut squash in half lengthwise; remove and discard seeds. Cut each half crosswise into ½-in. slices; discard ends. In batches, arrange squash in a single layer on greased tray in air-fryer basket. Cook until squash is just tender, about 5 minutes per side.
2. Combine sugar and butter; spread over squash. Cook 3 minutes longer.
1 serving: 320 cal., 16g fat (10g sat. fat), 41mg chol., 135mg sod., 48g carb. (29g sugars, 3g fiber), 2g pro.

TEST KITCHEN TIP
If you don't have an air fryer, you can make this recipe in an oven.

VEGETABLE BARLEY SAUTE

Here's a wonderful side dish you can easily adjust to suit your tastes. You can use broccoli instead of green beans, sweet potato ribbons instead of carrots, and any type of nuts you prefer.
—*Taste of Home* Test Kitchen

- -

Takes: 30 min. • **Makes:** 4 servings

½ cup quick-cooking barley
⅓ cup water
3 Tbsp. reduced-sodium soy sauce
2 tsp. cornstarch
1 garlic clove, minced
1 Tbsp. canola oil
2 carrots, thinly sliced
1 cup cut fresh green beans (2-in. pieces)
2 green onions, sliced
½ cup unsalted cashews, optional

1. Prepare barley according to package directions. In a small bowl, combine the water, soy sauce and cornstarch until smooth; set aside.
2. In a large skillet or wok, saute garlic in oil for 15 seconds. Add carrots and beans; stir-fry for 2 minutes. Add onions; stir-fry 1 minute longer. Stir soy sauce mixture; stir into skillet. Bring to a boil; cook and stir until thickened, about 1 minute. Add barley; heat through. If desired, stir in cashews.
⅔ cup: 148 cal., 4g fat (1g sat. fat), 0 chol., 458mg sod., 24g carb. (3g sugars, 6g fiber), 5g pro. **Diabetic exchanges:** 1½ starch, 1 fat.

VEGETABLE BARLEY SAUTE

MASHED CAULIFLOWER

This side dish is lower in carbs than mashed potatoes but just as flavorful and satisfying. It makes an enticing addition to a holiday menu. Add chopped green onions for a festive garnish.
—Tina Martini, Sparks, NV

Takes: 25 min. • **Makes:** 2½ cups

- 1 medium head cauliflower, broken into florets
- ½ cup shredded Swiss cheese
- 1 Tbsp. butter
- ¾ tsp. salt
- ¼ tsp. pepper
- ⅛ tsp. garlic powder
- 2 to 3 Tbsp. 2% milk

1. In a large saucepan, bring 1 in. water to a boil. Add cauliflower; cook, covered, until very tender, 8-12 minutes. Drain.

2. Mash cauliflower, adding Swiss cheese, butter, seasonings and enough milk to reach desired consistency.

¾ cup: 160 cal., 10g fat (6g sat. fat), 28mg chol., 718mg sod., 11g carb. (4g sugars, 4g fiber), 9g pro.

> "I'm digging the mashed cauliflower trend. This is the simplest method I've come across. Being able to swap carb-heavy mashed potatoes for something lighter is a huge win."
>
> —EMILY PARULSKI, SENIOR DIGITAL EDITOR

GOLDEN BEET CURRY RISOTTO WITH CRISPY BEET GREENS

I was delighted to find golden beets at the farmers market and knew they'd be perfect in this risotto.
—Merry Graham, Newhall, CA

Prep: 30 min. • **Cook:** 50 min.
Makes: 6 servings

- 3 medium fresh golden beets and beet greens
- 3 Tbsp. melted coconut oil, divided
- ¾ tsp. sea salt, divided
- 5 cups reduced-sodium chicken broth
- 1 cup chopped leeks (white portion only)
- 1 tsp. curry powder
- 1 tsp. garlic salt
- 1 cup medium pearl barley
- ½ cup white wine or unsweetened apple juice
- 1 cup grated Manchego cheese
- 3 Tbsp. lemon juice (Meyer lemons preferred)
- 4 tsp. grated lemon zest, divided
- ¼ tsp. coarsely ground pepper
- ¼ cup chopped fresh parsley Lemon slices

1. Preheat oven to 350°. Wash and trim the beet greens, removing stems; dry with paper towels. Place the greens in a single layer on parchment-lined baking sheets. Brush with 1 Tbsp. coconut oil; sprinkle with ¼ tsp. sea salt. Bake until dry and crisp, 15-18 minutes. Set aside.

2. Meanwhile, peel and dice beets. In a large saucepan, bring chicken broth to a boil. Add beets. Reduce heat; simmer, covered, until beets are tender, 15-18 minutes. Remove beets with a slotted spoon. Keep broth hot.

3. In another large saucepan, heat remaining coconut oil over medium heat. Add the leeks; cook and stir 2-3 minutes. Add curry powder, garlic salt and remaining sea salt; cook, stirring, until the leeks are tender, 2-3 minutes. Increase heat to medium-high. Add pearl barley; stir constantly until lightly toasted, 2-3 minutes. Add wine; stir until liquid has evaporated.

4. Add enough broth, about 1 cup, to cover barley. Reduce heat to medium; cook and stir until the broth is absorbed. Add remaining broth, ½ cup at a time, cooking and stirring until broth is absorbed after each addition. Stir in beets with last addition of broth. Cook until barley is tender but firm to the bite and risotto is creamy, 25-30 minutes.

5. Remove from heat. Stir in cheese, lemon juice, 2½ tsp. grated lemon zest and pepper. Transfer to a serving dish. Sprinkle with parsley and remaining lemon zest. Serve with crispy beet greens and lemon slices.

⅔ cup: 314 cal., 14g fat (11g sat. fat), 19mg chol., 1238mg sod., 37g carb. (7g sugars, 8g fiber), 12g pro.

GOLDEN BEET CURRY RISOTTO WITH CRISPY BEET GREENS

MUSHROOM MARSALA WITH BARLEY

MUSHROOM MARSALA WITH BARLEY

This tasty recipe is a vegetarian mashup of chicken Marsala and mushroom barley soup. It's great as a main entree, but can also be served, with or without the barley, as a side dish.
—Arlene Erlbach, Morton Grove, IL

- -

Prep: 20 min. • **Cook:** 4¼ hours
Makes: 6 servings

- 1½ lbs. baby portobello mushrooms, cut into ¾-in. chunks
- 1 cup thinly sliced shallots
- 3 Tbsp. olive oil
- ½ tsp. minced fresh thyme
- ¾ cup Marsala wine, divided
- 3 Tbsp. reduced-fat sour cream
- 2 Tbsp. all-purpose flour
- 1½ tsp. grated lemon zest
- ¼ tsp. salt
- ¼ cup crumbled goat cheese
- ¼ cup minced fresh parsley
- 2½ cups cooked barley

1. In a 4- or 5-qt. slow cooker, combine mushrooms, shallots, olive oil and thyme. Add ¼ cup Marsala wine. Cook, covered, on low for about 4 hours, until vegetables are tender.
2. Stir in sour cream, flour, lemon zest, salt and remaining Marsala. Cook, covered, on low 15 minutes longer. Sprinkle with goat cheese and minced parsley. Serve with hot cooked barley.
¾ cup: 235 cal., 9g fat (2g sat. fat), 7mg chol., 139mg sod., 31g carb. (6g sugars, 5g fiber), 7g pro. **Diabetic exchanges:** 2 starch, 2 fat, 1 vegetable.

TEST KITCHEN TIP
Marsala is a wine fortified with alcohol. It's produced in the region surrounding the Italian city of Marsala, and its distinctive flavor is in many Italian dishes. You can use red or white wine, beer or broth in place of Marsala, but be aware that this can change the flavor.

BROWN RICE & VEGETABLES

This nutritious rice dish, full of big chunks of butternut squash and sweet potatoes, is a standout combination of sweet and savory flavors. It's a winner every Thanksgiving.
—*Taste of Home* Test Kitchen

- -

Prep: 20 min. • **Cook:** 5 hours
Makes: 12 servings

- 1 cup uncooked brown rice
- 1 medium butternut squash (about 3 lbs.), cubed
- 2 medium apples, coarsely chopped
- 1 medium sweet potato, peeled and cubed
- 1 medium onion, chopped
- 1 tsp. salt
- ½ tsp. pepper
- 1 can (14½ oz.) reduced-sodium chicken broth
- ½ cup raisins
- 1 Tbsp. minced fresh tarragon or 1 tsp. dried tarragon

1. Place rice in a greased 4- or 5-qt. slow cooker. In a large bowl, combine the squash, apples, sweet potato, onion, salt and pepper; add to slow cooker. Pour chicken broth over the vegetables.
2. Cover and cook on low 5-6 hours, until vegetables are tender. Stir in raisins and tarragon.
¾ cup: 148 cal., 1g fat (0 sat. fat), 0 chol., 303mg sod., 35g carb. (11g sugars, 5g fiber), 3g pro. **Diabetic exchanges:** 2 starch.

BROWN RICE WITH
ALMONDS & CRANBERRIES

BROWN RICE WITH ALMONDS & CRANBERRIES

I'm always looking to switch things up during the holiday season. This rice salad is just the ticket, as it's on the lighter side and uses ingredients I always have on hand.
—Joan Hallford, North Richland Hills, TX

Prep: 35 min. • **Bake:** 1¼ hours
Makes: 10 servings

- 3 cans (14½ oz. each) beef broth
- ¼ cup butter, cubed
- 1 large onion, chopped
- 1 cup uncooked long grain brown rice
- ½ cup bulgur
- ½ cup slivered almonds
- ½ cup dried cranberries
- ¾ cup minced fresh parsley, divided
- ¼ cup chopped green onions
- ¼ tsp. salt
- ¼ tsp. pepper

1. Preheat oven to 375°. In a large saucepan, bring broth to a simmer; reduce heat to low and keep hot. In a large skillet, heat butter over medium heat. Add onion; cook and stir until tender, 3-4 minutes. Add rice, bulgur and slivered almonds; cook and stir until the rice is lightly browned and has a nutty aroma, 2-3 minutes.

2. Transfer to a greased 13x9-in. baking dish. Stir in cranberries, ½ cup parsley, green onions, salt and pepper. Stir in hot broth. Bake, covered, 45 minutes. Uncover and continue to cook until liquid is absorbed and rice is tender, 30-35 minutes longer. Remove from oven and fluff with a fork. Cover; let stand 5-10 minutes. Sprinkle with remaining parsley before serving.

¾ cup: 207 cal., 8g fat (3g sat. fat), 12mg chol., 658mg sod., 29g carb. (7g sugars, 4g fiber), 5g pro. **Diabetic exchanges:** 2 starch, 1½ fat.

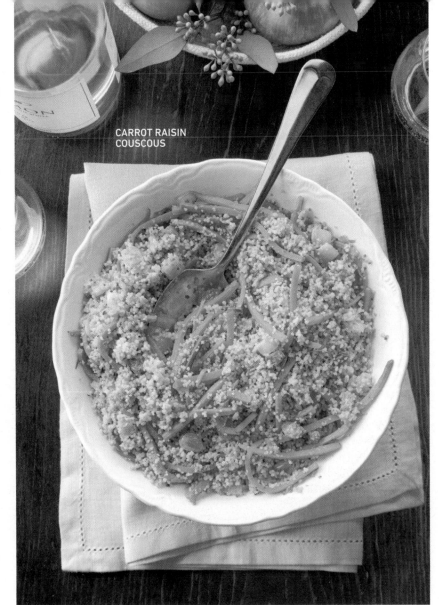

CARROT RAISIN COUSCOUS

CARROT RAISIN COUSCOUS

Golden raisins add a slightly sweet flavor to this unique side dish featuring couscous and julienned carrots. The recipe will brighten any holiday table.
—Jordan Sucher, Brooklyn, NY

Prep: 15 min. • **Cook:** 20 min.
Makes: 10 servings

- ⅓ cup port wine or chicken broth
- ⅓ cup golden raisins
- 1 medium onion, chopped
- 3 Tbsp. olive oil, divided
- 1 pkg. (10 oz.) couscous
- 2 cups chicken broth
- ¼ tsp. salt, divided
- ¼ tsp. pepper, divided
- 4 medium carrots, julienned
- 1 Tbsp. sugar
- 1 tsp. molasses

1. In a small saucepan, heat wine until hot. In a small bowl, soak raisins in wine for 5 minutes. Drain raisins, reserving wine.

2. In a large saucepan, saute onion in 1 Tbsp. oil until tender. Stir in couscous. Cook and stir until lightly browned. Stir in the broth, raisins and half the salt and pepper. Bring to a boil. Cover and remove from the heat. Let stand for 5 minutes; fluff with a fork.

3. In a small skillet, saute the carrots in remaining oil until crisp-tender. Combine sugar, molasses, reserved wine and the remaining salt and pepper. Stir into carrots; heat through.

4. In a large bowl, combine the couscous mixture and carrots; toss to combine.

¾ cup: 188 cal., 5g fat (1g sat. fat), 1mg chol., 277mg sod., 32g carb. (8g sugars, 2g fiber), 5g pro. **Diabetic exchanges:** 1½ starch, 1 vegetable, 1 fat.

POTATO & CHORIZO CASSEROLE

I love the smoky flavor chorizo gives this dish, but I've also made it with Italian sausage and substituted an Italian blend cheese for the Mexican cheese. Or you can use cream of mushroom soup and fresh mushrooms for a vegetarian option.
—Ana Beteta, Aberdeen, MD

Prep: 25 min. • **Bake:** 40 min.
Makes: 12 servings

- 8   oz. fresh chorizo or bulk spicy pork sausage
- 1   pkg. (32 oz.) frozen cubed hash brown potatoes, thawed
- 1   can (10½ oz.) condensed cream of chicken soup, undiluted
- 2   cups shredded Mexican cheese blend
- 1   pkg. (8 oz.) cream cheese, cubed
- 1   medium onion, chopped
- 1   small sweet red pepper, chopped
- 1   small green pepper, chopped
- ½   tsp. crushed red pepper flakes
- ¾   cup panko bread crumbs
     Chopped fresh parsley and cilantro

1. Preheat oven to 375°. In a small skillet, cook the chorizo over medium heat until cooked through, breaking into crumbles, 5-7 minutes; drain. Transfer to a large bowl. Stir in the hash browns, soup, cheeses, onion, peppers and pepper flakes. Transfer to a greased 13x9-in. baking dish. Sprinkle with panko.
2. Bake, uncovered, until golden brown and bubbly, 40-45 minutes. Sprinkle with parsley and cilantro before serving.
¾ cup: 316 cal., 20g fat (9g sat. fat), 54mg chol., 611mg sod., 22g carb. (3g sugars, 2g fiber), 12g pro.

BALSAMIC BRUSSELS SPROUTS

BALSAMIC BRUSSELS SPROUTS

These Brussels sprouts couldn't be easier to make—and you need only a few ingredients!
—Kallee Krong-McCreery, Escondido, CA

Takes: 15 min. • **Makes:** 4 servings

- 3   to 4 Tbsp. extra virgin olive oil
- 1   pkg. (16 oz.) frozen Brussels sprouts, thawed
- 2   Tbsp. balsamic vinegar
- 2   Tbsp. torn fresh basil leaves
- ½   to 1 tsp. flaky sea salt
- ½   tsp. coarsely ground pepper

In a large skillet, heat oil over medium-high heat. Add Brussels sprouts to skillet and cook until heated through, 5-7 minutes. Transfer to a serving bowl. Drizzle with vinegar; sprinkle with basil, salt and pepper.
⅔ cup: 145 cal., 11g fat (2g sat. fat), 0 chol., 252mg sod., 11g carb. (2g sugars, 4g fiber), 4g pro. **Diabetic exchanges:** 2 fat, 1 vegetable.

ROASTED RADISHES

Radishes aren't just for salads. This abundant springtime veggie makes a colorful side to any meal.
—*Taste of Home* Test Kitchen

Prep: 10 min. • **Bake:** 30 min.
Makes: 6 servings

- 2¼   lbs. radishes, trimmed and quartered (about 6 cups)
- 3   Tbsp. olive oil
- 1   Tbsp. minced fresh oregano or 1 tsp. dried oregano
- ¼   tsp. salt
- ⅛   tsp. pepper

1. Preheat oven to 425°. Toss radishes with remaining ingredients. Transfer to a greased 15x10x1-in. pan.
2. Roast until radishes are crisp-tender, about 30 minutes, stirring once.
⅔ cup: 88 cal., 7g fat (1g sat. fat), 0mg chol., 165mg sod., 6g carb. (3g sugars, 3g fiber), 1g pro. **Diabetic exchanges:** 1 vegetable, 1½ fat.

SHIITAKE & BUTTERNUT RISOTTO

I like to think of this recipe as a labor of love. The risotto takes a bit of extra attention, but once you take your first bite you'll know it was worth the effort.

—Stephanie Campbell, Elk Grove, CA

Prep: 25 min. • **Cook:** 25 min.
Makes: 2 servings

- 1 cup cubed peeled butternut squash
- 2 tsp. olive oil, divided
  Dash salt
- 1¼ cups reduced-sodium chicken broth
- ⅔ cup sliced fresh shiitake mushrooms
- 2 Tbsp. chopped onion
- 1 small garlic clove, minced
- ⅓ cup uncooked arborio rice
  Dash pepper
- ¼ cup white wine or ¼ cup additional reduced-sodium chicken broth
- ¼ cup grated Parmesan cheese
- 1 tsp. minced fresh sage

1. Place squash in a greased 9-in. square baking pan. Add 1 tsp. olive oil and salt; toss to coat.

2. Bake, uncovered, at 350° until tender, 25-30 minutes, stirring occasionally.

3. Meanwhile, in a small saucepan, heat the chicken broth and keep warm. In a small skillet, saute the mushrooms, onion and garlic in remaining 1 tsp. oil until tender, 3-4 minutes. Add rice and pepper; cook and stir for 2-3 minutes. Reduce the heat; stir in wine. Cook and stir until all the liquid is absorbed.

4. Add the heated broth, ¼ cup at a time, stirring constantly. Allow the liquid to absorb between additions. Cook just until risotto is creamy and the rice is almost tender, about 20 minutes. Stir in cheese until melted. Add squash and sage. Serve immediately.

¾ cup: 282 cal., 9g fat (3g sat. fat), 12mg chol., 567mg sod., 40g carb. (3g sugars, 3g fiber), 10g pro.

SPRING ONION PIMIENTO CHEESE GRITS

Grits were a breakfast staple when I was growing up. Even today, we still have them about three times a week. The trick with grits is the more you whisk, the creamier they'll be.

—Melissa Pelkey Hass, Waleska, GA

Prep: 15 min. • **Cook:** 20 min.
Makes: 16 servings

- 2 cups uncooked stone-ground yellow grits
- 1 pkg. (8 oz.) cream cheese, softened
- ½ cup mayonnaise
- 3 cups shredded Monterey Jack cheese
- 1 jar (4 oz.) diced pimientos, drained
- 3 green onions, diced
- 1 tsp. sugar
  Dash cayenne pepper
- ¼ cup butter, softened
  Salt and pepper to taste

1. Prepare grits according to the package directions. Keep warm.

2. Meanwhile, using a mixer, beat cream cheese. Add mayonnaise; continue beating until creamy. Add next 5 ingredients, mixing until well blended.

3. Stir butter and pimiento cheese mixture into the warm grits; season to taste. Mix well.

¾ cup: 281 cal., 20g fat (10g sat. fat), 41mg chol., 231mg sod., 19g carb. (1g sugars, 1g fiber), 8g pro.

SHIITAKE & BUTTERNUT RISOTTO

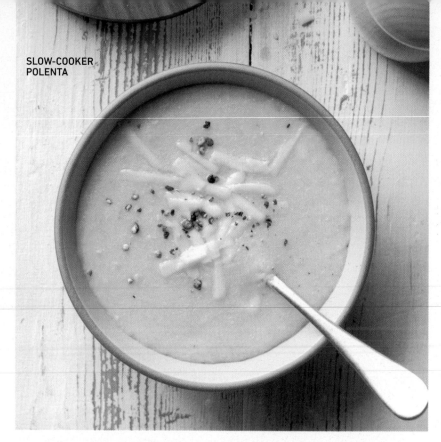

SLOW-COOKER
POLENTA

GRILLED MEDITERRANEAN ZUCCHINI SALAD

Looking for the perfect side dish? Try my grilled zucchini salad with Mediterranean dressing. I also add summer squash, when it's in season, for a variation, or crumbled goat cheese when I want creaminess.
—Rashanda Cobbins, Food Editor

Takes: 20 min. • **Makes:** 4 servings

  3   **medium zucchini, thinly sliced**
  ¼   **cup olive oil, divided**
  ¼   **tsp. salt**
  ¼   **tsp. pepper**
  ¼   **cup chopped red onion**
  3   **Tbsp. minced fresh mint**
  2   **Tbsp. minced fresh parsley**
  1   **medium lemon, juiced and zested**
  ⅓   **cup crumbled feta cheese**
  3   **Tbsp. pine nuts, toasted**

1. In a large bowl, combine zucchini and 2 Tbsp. olive oil. Add salt and pepper; toss to coat. Transfer to a grill wok or open grill basket; place on grill rack. Grill, covered, over medium-high heat until zucchini is crisp-tender, 5-10 minutes, turning occasionally.
2. Transfer zucchini to a serving bowl; sprinkle with remaining 2 Tbsp. olive oil and chopped red onion. When cooled slightly, sprinkle with mint, parsley, lemon juice and zest, and feta cheese. Stir gently. Sprinkle with pine nuts before serving.
1 cup: 220 cal., 20g fat (3g sat. fat), 5mg chol., 252mg sod., 8g carb. (4g sugars, 3g fiber), 5g pro.

TEST KITCHEN TIP
If you do not have a grill wok or basket, use a disposable foil pan. Poke holes in the bottom of the pan with a meat fork to allow liquid to drain.

SLOW-COOKER POLENTA

This Italian classic is so simple to make, you can now make it any night of the week.
—Elisabeth Matelski, Boston, MA

Prep: 10 min. • **Cook:** 6 hours
Makes: 12 servings

  13   **cups reduced-sodium chicken broth, divided**
  3   **cups cornmeal**
  1   **medium onion, finely chopped**
  3   **garlic cloves, minced**
  2   **bay leaves**
  2   **tsp. salt**
  1   **cup half-and-half cream**
  1   **cup shredded Parmesan cheese**
  ¼   **cup butter, cubed**
  1   **tsp. pepper**
       Additional shredded Parmesan cheese

In a 6-qt. slow cooker, combine 12 cups broth, cornmeal, onion, garlic, bay leaves and salt. Cook, covered, on low 6-8 hours, until the liquid is absorbed and polenta is creamy. Remove bay leaves. Stir in cream, cheese, butter, pepper and remaining broth. If desired, serve with additional cheese.
1 cup: 255 cal., 8g fat (5g sat. fat), 25mg chol., 1168mg sod., 34g carb. (3g sugars, 2g fiber), 9g pro.

QUICK CHEESY BROCCOLI

Topped with crumbs, this cheesy broccoli is a decadent side dish for any occasion. And it can be on the table in just 10 minutes!
—Joan Hallford, North Richland Hills, TX

Takes: 10 min. • **Makes:** 4 servings

  1   **pkg. (16 oz.) frozen broccoli florets**
  ⅓   **cup panko bread crumbs, toasted**
  ⅓   **cup extra-sharp shredded cheddar cheese**
  ½   **tsp. salt**
  ¼   **tsp. ground black pepper**
  ¼   **tsp. garlic powder**

Prepare broccoli according to the package directions; drain. Combine bread crumbs, cheese, salt, pepper and garlic powder; sprinkle over broccoli.
1 cup: 101 cal., 4g fat (2g sat. fat), 9mg chol., 109mg sod., 9g carb. (3g sugars, 3g fiber), 5g pro. **Diabetic exchanges:** 1 vegetable, ½ fat.

GRILLED MEDITERRANEAN
ZUCCHINI SALAD

EASY GRILLED CORN WITH CHIPOTLE-LIME BUTTER

Grilling corn in the husks is so easy. There's no need to remove the silk and tie the husk closed before grilling. Just soak, grill and add your favorite flavored butter.
—*Taste of Home* Test Kitchen

Prep: 5 min. + soaking • **Grill:** 25 min.
Makes: 8 servings

- 8 large ears sweet corn in husks
- ½ cup butter, softened
- 1½ tsp. grated lime zest
- 1 tsp. minced fresh cilantro
- ½ tsp. salt
- ½ tsp. ground chipotle pepper
  Coarse sea salt, optional

1. In a large stockpot, cover corn with cold water. Soak 30 minutes; drain. Grill corn, covered, over medium heat until tender, turning occasionally, 25-30 minutes.
2. Meanwhile, combine the remaining ingredients. Carefully peel back husks; discard silk. Spread the butter mixture over corn.

1 ear of corn with 2 Tbsp. butter: 225 cal., 13g fat (8g sat. fat), 31mg chol., 265mg sod., 27g carb. (9g sugars, 3g fiber), 5g pro.

ASK SARAH

HOW DO I PICK FRESH SWEET CORN?

Start by inspecting the husk. The freshest corn will have a husk that is bright green, wrapped tightly and slightly damp. Note the tassel, which is the fluff of silks at the top. It should be light brown or gold, and a little sticky. It should smell sweet with no signs of decay. Finally, give the corn a squeeze. It should feel firm, and the kernels should feel plump.

EASY GRILLED CORN WITH CHIPOTLE-LIME BUTTER

BACON & GARLIC SUGAR SNAP PEAS

This flavorful side dish calls for only four ingredients! Feel free to use fresh sugar snap peas if you'd like.
—Tami Kuehl, Loup City, NE

- -

Takes: 10 min. • **Makes:** 4 servings

- 2   bacon strips, coarsely chopped
- 1   pkg. (14 oz.) frozen sugar snap peas, thawed
- 1   shallot or small onion, thinly sliced
- 2   garlic cloves, thinly sliced

In a large skillet, cook chopped bacon over medium heat until crisp, stirring occasionally. Remove with a slotted spoon; drain on paper towels. Cook and stir peas in bacon drippings until heated through. Add shallot and garlic; cook 1 minute longer. Sprinkle with the reserved bacon.
½ cup: 126 cal., 6g fat (2g sat. fat), 9mg chol., 100mg sod., 13g carb. (5g sugars, 3g fiber), 5g pro. **Diabetic exchanges:** 1 starch, 1 fat.

BADGER STATE STUFFING

Your family will love the contrasting sweet, savory and slightly tart flavors in this twist on a Thanksgiving classic. Feel free to use your favorite beer or dried fruit to make the dish your own.
—Andrea Fetting, Franklin, WI

- -

Prep: 35 min. • **Bake:** 50 min. + standing
Makes: 8 cups

- ½   lb. bacon strips, diced
- ½   lb. sliced fresh mushrooms
- 1   medium onion, diced
- 1   cup chopped celery (about 3 stalks)
- 1   cup chopped carrot (about 4 medium carrots)
- 2   garlic cloves, minced
- 1   can (8 oz.) sauerkraut, rinsed and well drained
- ½   cup amber beer or chicken broth
- 5   cups cubed sourdough bread (½-in. cubes)
- 1   cup dried cherries or dried cranberries
- 1   large egg
- 1¼ cups chicken broth
- 3   Tbsp. minced fresh parsley
- 1   tsp. poultry seasoning
- ½   tsp. pepper

1. Preheat oven to 350°. In a large skillet, cook bacon over medium heat until crisp, stirring occasionally. Remove with a slotted spoon; drain on paper towels. Discard the drippings, reserving 3 Tbsp. in pan.
2. Add mushrooms, onion, celery and carrot to drippings; cook and stir over medium-high heat until tender, 8-10 minutes. Add garlic; cook 1 minute longer. Stir in sauerkraut and beer. Bring to a boil; cook, uncovered, until liquid is reduced by half.
3. In a large bowl, combine the bread cubes, cherries, bacon and sauerkraut mixture. In a small bowl, whisk egg, broth, parsley, poultry seasoning and pepper. Gradually stir into the bread mixture.
4. Transfer to a greased 2-qt. baking dish. Bake, covered, 20 minutes. Uncover; bake until lightly browned, 30-35 minutes longer. Let stand 10 minutes before serving.
1 cup: 271 cal., 11g fat (4g sat. fat), 39mg chol., 700mg sod., 35g carb. (18g sugars, 3g fiber), 9g pro.

BADGER STATE STUFFING

PEPPER JACK HASH BROWN CASSEROLE

I found myself in need of an impromptu potato dish, but I had no potatoes. Frozen hash browns and the plethora of cheeses I had in the freezer offered me the solution to my side-dish dilemma.
—Cyndy Gerken, Naples, FL

- -

Prep: 25 min. • **Bake:** 25 min.
Makes: 12 servings

- 1   pkg. (30 oz.) frozen shredded hash brown potatoes, thawed
- 1   can (10½ oz.) condensed cream of chicken soup, undiluted
- 2   cups shredded pepper jack cheese
- 1½ cups heavy whipping cream
- ½   cup butter, melted
- ½   cup sour cream
- ¼   cup shredded Parmesan cheese
- ½   tsp. salt
- ½   tsp. onion powder
- ¼   tsp. garlic powder
- ¼   tsp. pepper

TOPPING
- 1   cup crushed potato chips
- 5   bacon strips, cooked and crumbled
- ¾   cup shredded Parmesan cheese
- 1   tsp. paprika

1. Preheat oven to 350°. In a large bowl, combine the first 11 ingredients. Transfer to a greased 13x9-in. baking dish. For topping, combine potato chips, bacon and Parmesan; sprinkle over casserole. Top with paprika.
2. Bake, uncovered, until edges are bubbly and topping is golden brown, 25-30 minutes.
⅔ cup: 416 cal., 33g fat (19g sat. fat), 87mg chol., 682mg sod., 20g carb. (2g sugars, 2g fiber), 12g pro.

RUSTIC TOMATO PIE

Perk up your plate with this humble tomato pie. We like to use fresh-from-the-garden tomatoes and herbs, but store-bought produce will work in a pinch.
—*Taste of Home* Test Kitchen

- -

Prep: 15 min. **Bake:** 30 min.
Makes: 8 servings

-     Pastry for single-crust pie
- 1¾ lbs. mixed tomatoes, seeded and cut into ½-in. slices
- ¼   cup thinly sliced green onions
- ½   cup mayonnaise
- ½   cup shredded cheddar cheese
- 2   Tbsp. minced fresh basil
- ¼   tsp. salt
- ¼   tsp. pepper
- 2   bacon strips, cooked and crumbled
- 2   Tbsp. grated Parmesan cheese

1. Preheat oven to 400°. On a lightly floured surface, roll dough to a ⅛-in.-thick circle; transfer to a 9-in. pie plate. Trim crust to ½ in. beyond rim of plate.
2. Place half of the tomatoes and half of the onions in crust. Combine mayonnaise, cheddar cheese, fresh basil, salt and pepper; spread over tomatoes. Top with remaining onions and tomatoes. Fold crust edge over filling, pleating as you go and leaving an 8-in. opening in the center. Sprinkle with bacon and Parmesan cheese. Bake on a lower oven rack until until crust is golden and filling is bubbly, 30-35 minutes. Transfer pie to a wire rack to cool. If desired, sprinkle pie with additional basil.
1 piece: 325 cal., 25g fat (11g sat. fat), 41mg chol., 409mg sod., 19g carb. (3g sugars, 2g fiber), 6g pro.
Pastry for single-crust pie (9 in.) Combine 1¼ cups all-purpose flour and ¼ tsp. salt; cut in ½ cup cold butter until crumbly. Gradually add 3-5 Tbsp. ice water, tossing with a fork until dough holds together when pressed. Wrap and refrigerate 1 hour.

RUSTIC TOMATO PIE

SWEET & TANGY BEETS

Fresh beets are delicious when combined with aromatic spice and a hint of orange. These have the perfect balance of sweet and sour flavors.
—*Taste of Home* Test Kitchen

Prep: 15 min. • **Cook:** 7 hours
Makes: 6 servings

2	lbs. small fresh beets, peeled and halved
½	cup sugar
¼	cup packed brown sugar
2	Tbsp. cornstarch
½	tsp. salt
¼	cup orange juice
¼	cup cider vinegar
2	Tbsp. butter
1½	tsp. whole cloves

1. Place beets in a 3-qt. slow cooker. Mix sugars, cornstarch and salt. Stir in orange juice and cider vinegar. Pour over beets; dot with butter.
2. Place cloves on a double thickness of cheesecloth. Gather corners of cloth to enclose cloves; tie securely with string. Place bag in slow cooker. Cook, covered, on low 7-8 hours, until beets are tender. Discard spice bag.

¾ cup: 214 cal., 4g fat (2g sat. fat), 10mg chol., 344mg sod., 44g carb. (38g sugars, 3g fiber), 3g pro. **Diabetic exchanges:** 2 vegetable, 1½ starch, 1 fat.

SPICY CHUCK WAGON BEANS

Baked beans don't get any easier than this! Just open some cans, chop an onion, and add a dash (or two) of hot sauce. They'll simmer to perfection in minutes.
—James Schend, Deputy Editor, Culinary

Takes: 30 min.
Makes: 24 servings

1	Tbsp. canola oil
1	medium onion, chopped
2	cans (28 oz. each) baked beans
3	cans (15 oz. each) chili beans, undrained
2	cans (15 oz. each) black beans, rinsed and drained
2	pkg. (7 oz. each) frozen fully cooked breakfast sausage links, thawed and cut into ½-in. pieces
1	cup beer or reduced-sodium chicken broth
2	chipotle peppers in adobo sauce, minced
1	to 2 Tbsp. hot pepper sauce

In a Dutch oven, heat oil over medium-high heat; saute onion until tender, 3-5 minutes. Stir in remaining ingredients; bring to a boil. Reduce heat; simmer, uncovered, until beans are thickened and flavors are blended, about 15 minutes, stirring occasionally.

⅔ cup: 221 cal., 8g fat (3g sat. fat), 15mg chol., 663mg sod., 30g carb. (2g sugars, 8g fiber), 10g pro.

TEST KITCHEN TIP

This recipe can also be made in a greased 6-qt. slow cooker. Omitting the oil, combine all ingredients. Cook on low 6-8 hours until heated through.

SPICY CHUCK WAGON BEANS

SOFT GIANT PRETZELS
PAGE 183

Odds
& Ends

Is there anything better than homemade jam on biscuits or canned green beans you grew yourself? Our recipes for condiments, sauces, canned fruits and veggies, and other suprising snacks and treats will spruce up your meals.

SWEET HOOSIER DOG SAUCE

In our area of Indiana, we love sweet coney sauce on hot dogs. A drive-in restaurant in our town is famous for its version.
—Jill Thomas, Washington, IN

- -

Takes: 30 min. • **Makes:** 5 cups

- 2 lbs. ground beef
- 1 can (6 oz.) tomato paste
- 1 cup water
- 1 can (8 oz.) tomato sauce
- ½ cup sweet pickle relish
- ¼ cup dried minced onion
- 2 Tbsp. sugar
- 1 Tbsp. chili powder
- 2 tsp. Worcestershire sauce
- 1 tsp. salt
- 1 tsp. cider vinegar
- 1 tsp. yellow mustard
- ½ tsp. celery salt
- ¼ tsp. garlic powder
- ¼ tsp. onion powder
    Hot dogs and buns
    Optional: Diced onion, sliced pickles and shredded cheddar cheese

In a Dutch oven, cook beef over medium heat until no longer pink, 8-10 minutes, breaking into crumbles; drain. Stir in tomato paste; cook and stir 3 minutes. Stir in next 13 ingredients. Bring to a boil; reduce heat. Simmer sauce, uncovered, until thickened, 15-20 minutes, stirring occasionally. Serve sauce over hot dogs in buns. Add optional toppings as desired.

Freeze option: Freeze cooled sauce in freezer containers. To use, partially thaw in refrigerator overnight. Heat through in a covered saucepan, stirring gently; add water if necessary.

¼ cup: 111 cal., 5g fat (2g sat. fat), 28mg chol., 298mg sod., 7g carb. (4g sugars, 1g fiber), 9g pro.

TEST KITCHEN TIP

If you're grilling hot dogs or brats, be sure the grill grate is clean. It's not the most exciting task, but keeping those grates clean is essential. Extra residue can make food stick or absorb unwanted flavors. We recommend using a grill brush to keep grates spotless.

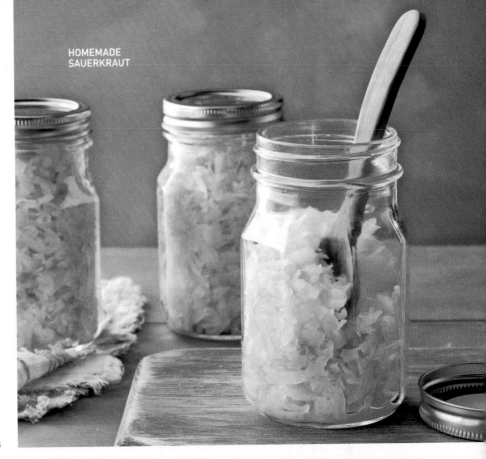

HOMEMADE SAUERKRAUT

HOMEMADE SAUERKRAUT

Put down that jar! You only need two simple ingredients to make fresh, zippy sauerkraut at home. Get those brats ready!
—Josh Rink, Food Stylist

- -

Prep: 45 min. + standing
Makes: 40 servings (about 10 cups)

- 6 lbs. cabbage (about 2 heads)
- 3 Tbsp. canning salt
    Optional: 2 peeled and thinly sliced Granny Smith apples, 2 thinly sliced sweet onions, 2 tsp. caraway seeds and 1 tsp. ground coriander

1. Quarter cabbages and remove cores; slice ⅛ in. thick. In an extra-large bowl, combine salt and cabbage. With clean hands, squeeze cabbage until it wilts and releases liquid, about 10 minutes. If desired, add optional ingredients.

2. Firmly pack cabbage mixture into 4-qt. fermenting crock or large glass container, removing as many air bubbles as possible. If cabbage mixture is not covered by 1-2 in. of liquid, make enough brine to cover by 1-2 in. To make brine, combine 4½ tsp. canning salt per 1 qt. of water in a saucepan; bring to a boil until salt is dissolved. Cool brine before adding to crock.

3. Place crock weight over cabbage; the weight should be submerged in the brine. Or, place an inverted dinner plate or glass pie plate over cabbage. The plate should be slightly smaller than the container opening, but large enough to cover most of the shredded cabbage mixture. Weigh down the plate with 2 or 3 sealed quart jars filled with water. If using a glass container with a lid, cover the opening loosely so that any gas produced by the fermenting cabbage can escape. Alternately, you can cover the opening with a clean, heavy towel. If using a crock, seal according to manufacturer's instructions.

4. Store crock, undisturbed, at 70°-75° for 3-4 weeks (bubbles will form and aroma will change). Cabbage must be kept submerged below the surface of the fermenting liquid throughout fermentation. Check the crock 2-3 times each week; skim and remove any scum that may form on top of the liquid. Fermentation is complete when the bubbling stops. Transfer the sauerkraut to individual containers. Cover and store in refrigerator for up to 3 months.

¼ cup: 11 cal., 0 fat (0 sat. fat), 0 chol., 344mg sod., 3g carb. (1g sugars, 1g fiber), 1g pro.

HOMEMADE EGGNOG

After just one taste, folks will know this homemade holiday treat came from the kitchen, not from the store.
—Pat Waymire, Yellow Springs, OH

Prep: 15 min. • **Cook:** 30 min. + chilling
Makes: 12 servings (3 qt.)

- 12 **large eggs**
- 1½ **cups sugar**
- ½ **tsp. salt**
- 8 **cups whole milk, divided**
- 2 **Tbsp. vanilla extract**
- 1 **tsp. ground nutmeg**
- 2 **cups heavy whipping cream**
  Additional nutmeg, optional

1. In a heavy saucepan, whisk together eggs, sugar and salt. Gradually add 4 cups whole milk; cook and stir over low heat until a thermometer reads 160°-170°, 30-35 minutes. Do not allow to boil. Immediately transfer to a large bowl.
2. Stir in vanilla, nutmeg and the remaining milk. Place bowl in an ice-water bath, stirring until the milk mixture is cool. (If mixture separates, process it in a blender until smooth.) Refrigerate, covered, until cold, at least 3 hours.
3. To serve, beat cream until soft peaks form. Whisk gently into cooled milk mixture. If desired, sprinkle with additional nutmeg before serving.
1 cup: 411 cal., 25g fat (14g sat. fat), 247mg chol., 251mg sod., 35g carb. (35g sugars, 0 fiber), 13g pro.

QUICK JALAPENO HUSH PUPPIES

QUICK JALAPENO HUSH PUPPIES

The crunchy exterior of these Southern-style snacks is a nice contrast to the moist cornbread. Jalapeno peppers and hot sauce add a hint of heat.
—*Taste of Home* Test Kitchen

Prep: 15 min. • **Cook:** 5 min./batch
Makes: 2½ dozen

- 1½ **cups yellow cornmeal**
- ½ **cup all-purpose flour**
- 1 **tsp. baking powder**
- 1 **tsp. salt**
- 2 **large eggs, lightly beaten**
- ¾ **cup 2% milk**
- 2 **jalapeno peppers, seeded and minced**
- ¼ **cup finely chopped onion**
- 1 **tsp. Louisiana-style hot sauce**
  Oil for deep-fat frying

1. In a large bowl, combine the cornmeal, flour, baking powder and salt. In another bowl, beat the eggs, milk, jalapenos, onion and hot sauce. Stir into dry ingredients just until combined.
2. In a cast-iron or other heavy skillet, heat oil to 375°. Drop tablespoonfuls of batter, a few at a time, into hot oil. Fry until golden brown on both sides. Drain on paper towels. Serve warm.
1 hush puppy: 56 cal., 3g fat (0 sat. fat), 14mg chol., 94mg sod., 7g carb. (0 sugars, 1g fiber), 1g pro.

DOG BISCUITS

If members of your family are of the furry, four-legged kind, treat them to these homemade biscuits. They're a cinch to make, and your canine pals will go crazy for the peanut butter flavor.
—Shannon Norris, Senior Food Stylist

Prep: 15 min. • **Bake:** 30 min. + cooling
Makes: 31 dog biscuits

- 2 **cups whole wheat flour**
- 1 **cup toasted wheat germ**
- ½ **tsp. ground cinnamon**
- ¾ **cup water**
- ¼ **cup creamy peanut butter**
- 1 **large egg, room temperature**
- 2 **Tbsp. canola oil**

1. Preheat oven to 350°. Combine flour, wheat germ and cinnamon. Stir in remaining ingredients. On a floured surface, roll dough to ¼-in. thickness. Cut with a 3-in. bone-shaped cookie cutter.
2. Place 2 in. apart on ungreased baking sheets. Bake until the bottoms are lightly browned (tops may crack), 30-35 minutes. Cool on a wire rack. Store biscuits in an airtight container.
1 dog biscuit: 61 cal., 3g fat (0 sat. fat), 7mg chol., 12mg sod., 8g carb. (0 sugars, 1g fiber), 3g pro.

PICKLED GREEN BEANS

This recipe preserves my green beans for months...that's if we don't eat them all first! I crank up the heat with cayenne pepper.
—Marisa McClellan, Philadelphia, PA

Prep: 20 min. • **Process:** 10 min.
Makes: 4 pints

- 1¾ lbs. fresh green beans, trimmed
- 1 tsp. cayenne pepper
- 4 garlic cloves, peeled
- 4 tsp. dill seed or 4 fresh dill heads
- 2½ cups water
- 2½ cups white vinegar
- ¼ cup canning salt

1. Pack beans into 4 hot 1-pint jars to within ½ in. of the top. Add cayenne, garlic and dill seed to jars.
2. In a large saucepan, bring water, vinegar and salt to a boil.
3. Carefully ladle hot liquid over the beans, leaving ½-in. headspace. Remove air bubbles and adjust headspace, if necessary, by adding hot mixture. Wipe rims. Center lids on jars; screw on bands until fingertip tight.
4. Place jars into canner with simmering water, ensuring that they are completely covered with water. Bring to a boil; process for 10 minutes. Remove jars and cool.
8 green beans: 9 cal., 0 fat (0 sat. fat), 0 chol., 83mg sod., 2g carb. (1g sugars, 1g fiber), 1g pro.

> "Last summer we grew a bumper crop of haricots verts, so I canned a lot of these addicting Pickled Green Beans. I love them so much I could almost eat an entire jar in one sitting!"
>
> —ELLIE MARTIN CLIFFE, EXECUTIVE DIGITAL EDITOR

HOMEMADE BUTTERFINGER BITES

Bent on using up a stash of leftover candy corn, I decided to experiment. Turns out, if you melt it, mix it with peanut butter and coat the balls with chocolate, you get a softer, denser version of a Butterfinger bite. Who knew? They're delicious!
—Melissa Hansen, Ellison Bay, WI

Prep: 30 min. + standing
Makes: about 4 dozen

- 1 cup candy corn
- ⅔ cup peanut butter
- 1 cup semisweet chocolate chips
- 1 tsp. coconut oil

1. Microwave candy corn on high for 30 seconds; stir. Cook in 15-second intervals until melted; stir until smooth. Add peanut butter; microwave mixture, stirring 3 times, until smooth, 45-60 seconds.
2. Gently shape teaspoonfuls of mixture into balls (if mixture becomes crumbly, reheat for 15-20 seconds). Place on waxed paper; let stand until set. In a microwave, melt the chocolate chips and oil; stir until smooth. Dip the balls in chocolate mixture, allowing excess to drip off. Place on waxed paper; let stand until set.
1 piece: 50 cal., 3g fat (1g sat. fat), 0 chol., 16mg sod., 6g carb. (6g sugars, 0 fiber), 1g pro.

PICKLED GREEN BEANS

THE BEST
MARINARA SAUCE

GIARDINIERA

Sweet and tangy, this Italian condiment is packed with peppers, cauliflower, carrots and other crisp-tender veggies. It's perfect to offer alongside pickles or olives on a relish tray.
—Alicia Rooker, Recipe Editor/Tester

- -

Prep: 1 hour • **Process:** 10 min./batch
Makes: 10 pints

- 6 cups white vinegar
- 3½ cups sugar
- 3 cups water
- 4½ tsp. canning salt
- 1 Tbsp. dried oregano
- 1 Tbsp. fennel seed
- 2 small heads cauliflower, broken into small florets (about 12 cups)
- 4 large carrots, sliced
- 4 celery ribs, cut into ½-in. slices
- 48 pearl onions, peeled and trimmed (about 1¼ lbs.)
- 4 large sweet red peppers, cut into ½-in. strips
- 4 serrano peppers, seeds removed and thinly sliced
- 10 bay leaves
- 20 whole peppercorns
- 10 garlic cloves, thinly sliced

1. In a large stockpot, combine vinegar, sugar, water, canning salt, oregano and fennel seed. Bring to a boil. Add cauliflower, carrots, celery and onions; return to a boil. Remove from heat; add peppers.
2. Carefully ladle hot mixture into 10 hot 1-pint jars, leaving ½- in. headspace. Add a bay leaf and 2 peppercorns to each jar; divide garlic slices among jars. Remove air bubbles and adjust headspace, if necessary, by adding more hot mixture. Wipe rims. Center lids on jars; screw on bands until fingertip tight.
3. Place jars into canner with simmering water, ensuring that they are completely covered with water. Bring to a boil; process for 10 minutes. Remove jars and cool.
¼ cup: 74 cal., 1g fat (0 sat. fat), 0 chol., 323mg sod., 16g carb. (15g sugars, 1g fiber), 1g pro.

THE BEST MARINARA SAUCE

I developed this recipe with a friend to make the most of a bumper crop of tomatoes. Now we like to make huge batches—we're talking 220 pounds of huge tomatoes—and then give jars along with a pound of pasta as gifts around the holidays. Knowing this sauce is made from the heart with the best possible ingredients makes me feel good about giving it to my family and friends.
—Shannon Norris, Senior Food Stylist

- -

Prep: 1 hour + simmering • **Process:** 40 min.
Makes: 9 cups

- 3 Tbsp. olive oil
- 1 cup chopped onion
- ⅓ cup minced garlic, divided
- 12 lbs. plum tomatoes, quartered
- 2 cups water
- 1¼ cups minced fresh basil, divided
- ¼ cup minced fresh oregano
- ¼ cup tomato paste
- 2 tsp. kosher salt
- 1 tsp. coarsely ground pepper
- ¼ cup plus 1½ tsp. lemon juice

1. In a stockpot, heat oil over medium heat. Add the onion; cook and stir until softened, 3-4 minutes. Add 2 Tbsp. minced garlic; cook 1 minute longer. Add tomatoes, water and ½ cup basil; bring to a boil. Reduce the heat; simmer, covered, until the tomatoes are completely broken down and soft, about 1 hour, stirring occasionally.
2. Press tomato mixture through a food mill into a large bowl; discard skins and seeds. Return tomato mixture to stockpot; add ½ cup of remaining basil, oregano and the remaining garlic. Bring to a boil. Reduce the heat; simmer, uncovered, until thickened, 3½-4 hours, stirring occasionally. Add the tomato paste and remaining ¼ cup of basil; season with salt and pepper.
3. Add 1 Tbsp. plus 1½ tsp. lemon juice to each of 3 hot 1½-pint jars. Ladle hot mixture into jars, leaving ½-in. headspace. Remove any air bubbles and adjust headspace, if necessary, by adding hot mixture. Wipe rims. Center lids on jars; screw on bands until fingertip tight.
4. Place jars into canner with simmering water, ensuring that they are completely covered with water. Bring to a boil; process for 40 minutes. Remove jars and cool.
¾ cup: 131 cal., 4g fat (1g sat. fat), 0 chol., 348mg sod., 22g carb. (13g sugars, 6g fiber), 5g pro. **Diabetic exchanges:** 1½ starch, 1 fat.

CANNED BLUEBERRY JAM

Summer doesn't feel complete without at least one berry-picking trip and a batch of homemade blueberry jam. Eat atop fresh scones or biscuits for maximum enjoyment!
—Marisa McClellan, Philadelphia, PA

- -

Prep: 35 min. • **Process:** 10 min./batch
Makes: 9 half-pints

- 8 cups fresh blueberries
- 6 cups sugar
- 3 Tbsp. lemon juice
- 2 tsp. ground cinnamon
- 2 tsp. grated lemon zest
- ½ tsp. ground nutmeg
- 2 pouches (3 oz. each) liquid fruit pectin

1. Place blueberries in a food processor; cover and process until blended. Transfer to a stockpot. Stir in the sugar, lemon juice, cinnamon, lemon zest and nutmeg. Bring to a full rolling boil over high heat, stirring constantly. Stir in pectin. Boil for 1 minute, stirring constantly.
2. Remove from the heat; skim off foam. Ladle hot mixture into hot sterilized half-pint jars, leaving ¼-in. headspace. Remove air bubbles; wipe rims and adjust lids. Process for 10 minutes in a boiling-water canner.
2 Tbsp.: 74 cal., 0 fat (0 sat. fat), 0 chol., 0 sod., 19g carb. (18g sugars, 0 fiber), 0 pro.

ASK SARAH

SHOULD I ADJUST PROCESSING TIME IF I LIVE AT A HIGHER ALTITUDE?

Yes, the air is thinner at higher altitudes, which causes water to boil at a lower temperature. Lower boiling temperatures are not as effective at killing bacteria. To compensate, increase the processing time or canner pressure.

CANNED BLUEBERRY JAM

OLD-FASHIONED ERMINE FROSTING

This old-timey frosting brings back fond memories of being in the kitchen with my grandmother. It was her go-to for cakes when she didn't have cornstarch or cream cheese on hand.
—Rashanda Cobbins, Food Editor

Prep: 10 min. • **Cook:** 10 min. + chilling
Makes: 5 cups

- ½ cup all-purpose flour
- 2½ cups whole milk
- 1¾ cups sugar
- ½ tsp. salt
- 1¾ cups butter, softened
- 1½ tsp. vanilla extract

1. In a small heavy saucepan, whisk flour and milk until smooth. Cook and stir over medium heat until thickened and bubbly, 5-7 minutes.

2. Remove from heat; stir in sugar and salt until dissolved; transfer to a small bowl. Press plastic wrap onto surface. Refrigerate until cold.

3. In a large mixing bowl, beat butter until light and fluffy, about 5 minutes. Gradually beat in cooled mixture. Beat in the vanilla. Switch to whisk attachment; continue beating on medium speed until frosting is stiff and fluffy. Frost cake immediately.

2 Tbsp.: 60 cal., 4g fat (3g sat. fat), 11mg chol., 50mg sod., 5g carb. (5g sugars, 0 fiber), 0 pro.

NASHVILLE BBQ SAUCE

Nashville barbecue sauce is vinegar-forward with smoky undertones. Use it liberally on your favorite grilled or smoked meats.
—*Taste of Home* Test Kitchen

Prep: 5 min. • **Cook:** 25 min.
Makes: 1½ cups

- 1½ cups ketchup
- ½ cup packed brown sugar
- ⅓ cup cider vinegar
- 2 Tbsp. Worcestershire sauce
- 2 Tbsp. liquid smoke, optional
- 2 Tbsp. molasses
- 1 tsp. salt
- 1 tsp. ground mustard
- 1 tsp. chili powder
- ½ tsp. paprika
- ½ tsp. pepper

In a large saucepan, combine all ingredients. Bring to a boil. Reduce the heat; simmer, uncovered, until slightly thickened and darkened in color, 20-25 minutes.

2 Tbsp.: 30 cal., 0 fat (0 sat. fat), 0 chol., 231mg sod., 8g carb. (7g sugars, 0 fiber), 0 pro.

OLD-FASHIONED ERMINE FROSTING

MINI ZUCCHINI PIZZAS

This simple snack recipe is the perfect, low-carb way to satisfy your pizza cravings.
—*Taste of Home* Test Kitchen

- -

Takes: 20 min. • **Makes:** about 2 dozen

- 1   large zucchini (about 11 oz.), cut diagonally into ¼-in. slices
- ⅛   tsp. salt
- ⅛   tsp. pepper
- ⅓   cup pizza sauce
- ¾   cup shredded part-skim mozzarella cheese
- ½   cup miniature pepperoni slices
  Minced fresh basil

1. Preheat broiler. Arrange the zucchini in a single layer on a greased baking sheet. Broil 3-4 in. from heat just until crisp-tender, 1-2 minutes per side.

2. Sprinkle zucchini with salt and pepper; top with sauce, cheese and pepperoni. Broil until the cheese is melted, about 1 minute. Sprinkle with basil.

1 appetizer: 29 cal., 2g fat (1g sat. fat), 5mg chol., 108mg sod., 1g carb. (1g sugars, 0 fiber), 2g pro.

BIRTHDAY CAKE SHOOTERS

These festive shots are a fun way to get a birthday party started. Use chocolate cake-flavored vodka and chocolate liqueur for a super chocolaty treat.
—*Taste of Home* Test Kitchen

- -

Prep: 5 min. • **Makes:** 2 servings

  Ice cubes
- 2   oz. cake-flavored vodka
- 1   oz. white chocolate liqueur
  Sweetened whipped cream
  Sprinkles

Fill cocktail shaker three-fourths full with ice. Add vodka and white chocolate liqueur; cover and shake until condensation forms on outside of shaker, 10-15 seconds. Strain into 2 shot glasses. Top shooters with whipped cream and sprinkles.

1½ oz.: 181 cal., 0 fat (0 sat. fat), 0 chol., 3mg sod., 17g carb. (0 sugars, 0 fiber), 0 pro.

HONEY CINNAMON BUTTER

Here's a simple but special spread for toast and muffins. The sweet honey and warm cinnamon spice pair well together.
—Sue Seymour, Valatie, NY

- -

Takes: 5 min. • **Makes:** about 1⅓ cups

- 1   cup butter, softened
- ½   cup honey
- 1   tsp. ground cinnamon

Beat all ingredients until smooth. Store, tightly covered, in the refrigerator.

1 Tbsp.: 107 cal., 9g fat (6g sat. fat), 24mg chol., 73mg sod., 7g carb. (7g sugars, 0 fiber), 0 pro.

MINI ZUCCHINI PIZZAS

AIR-FRYER MINI
CHIMICHANGAS

MOM'S PICKLED CARROTS

My mom is the only other person I've known to make this recipe. In fact, whenever I take these carrots to a potluck or picnic, people are pleasantly surprised to try them for the first time. After that, they're hooked.
—Robin Koble, Fairview, PA

- -

Prep: 15 min. + chilling • **Cook:** 20 min.
Makes: 6 cups

- 2 **lbs. carrots, cut lengthwise into ¼-in.-thick strips**
- 1½ **cups sugar**
- 1½ **cups water**
- 1½ **cups cider vinegar**
- ¼ **cup mustard seed**
- 3 **cinnamon sticks (3 in.)**
- 3 **whole cloves**

1. Place the carrots in a large saucepan; add enough water to cover. Bring to a boil. Cook, covered, until crisp-tender, 3-5 minutes. Drain. Transfer to a large bowl. In another large saucepan, combine the remaining ingredients. Bring to a boil. Reduce heat; simmer, uncovered, for 20 minutes. Pour mixture over carrots. Refrigerate, covered, overnight to allow flavors to blend.
2. Transfer mixture to jars. Cover and refrigerate up to 1 month.
¼ cup: 30 cal., 0 fat (0 sat. fat), 0 chol., 170mg sod., 7g carb. (6g sugars, 1g fiber), 1g pro.

AIR-FRYER MINI CHIMICHANGAS

My family raves over my Mexican-inspired bites. Infused with green chile, these beefy snacks are guaranteed to liven up the party!
—Kathy Rogers, Hudson, OH

- -

Prep: 1 hour • **Cook:** 10 min./batch
Makes: 14 servings

- 1 **lb. ground beef**
- 1 **medium onion, chopped**
- 1 **envelope taco seasoning**
- ¾ **cup water**
- 3 **cups shredded Monterey Jack cheese**
- 1 **cup sour cream**
- 1 **can (4 oz.) chopped green chiles, drained**
- 14 **egg roll wrappers**
- 1 **large egg white, lightly beaten**
  Cooking spray
  Salsa

1. In a large skillet, cook beef and onion over medium heat until meat is no longer pink; drain. Stir in taco seasoning and water. Bring to a boil. Reduce heat; simmer, uncovered, for 5 minutes, stirring occasionally. Remove from the heat; cool slightly.
2. Preheat air fryer to 375°. In a large bowl, combine cheese, sour cream and chiles. Stir in beef mixture. Place an egg roll wrapper on work surface with 1 point facing you. Place ⅓ cup filling in center. Fold bottom one-third of wrapper over filling; fold in sides.
3. Brush top point with egg white; roll up to seal. Repeat with remaining wrappers and filling. (Keep the remaining egg roll wrappers covered with waxed paper to avoid drying out.)
4. In batches, place chimichangas in a single layer on greased tray in air-fryer basket; spritz with cooking spray. Cook until golden brown, 3-4 minutes on each side. Serve warm with salsa and additional sour cream.
1 chimichanga: 294 cal., 15g fat (8g sat. fat), 48mg chol., 618mg sod., 23g carb. (1g sugars, 1g fiber), 16g pro.

SOFT GIANT PRETZELS

My husband, friends and family love these soft, chewy pretzels. Let your machine mix the dough; then all you have to do is shape and bake these fun snacks.
—Sherry Peterson, Fort Collins, CO

Prep: 20 min. + rising • **Bake:** 10 min.
Makes: 8 pretzels

- 1 cup plus 2 Tbsp. water (70° to 80°)
- 3 cups all-purpose flour
- 3 Tbsp. brown sugar
- 1½ tsp. active dry yeast
- 2 qt. water
- ½ cup baking soda
   Coarse salt

1. In a bread machine pan, place 1 cup water and next 3 ingredients in order suggested by manufacturer. Select dough setting. Check dough after 5 minutes of mixing; if needed, add 1-2 Tbsp. water or flour.
2. When cycle is completed, turn dough onto a lightly floured surface. Divide dough into 8 balls. Roll each into a 20-in. rope; form into pretzel shape.
3. Preheat oven to 425°. In a large saucepan, bring 2 qt. water and the baking soda to a boil. Drop pretzels into boiling water, 2 at a time; boil for 10-15 seconds. Remove with a slotted spoon; drain on paper towels.
4. Place pretzels on greased baking sheets. Bake until golden brown, 8-10 minutes. Spritz or lightly brush with water. Sprinkle with salt.
1 pretzel: 193 cal., 1g fat (0 sat. fat), 0 chol., 380mg sod., 41g carb. (5g sugars, 1g fiber), 5g pro.

TEST KITCHEN TIP
Not sure what dip to serve with your pretzels? Consider these tasty ideas.
- Hot cheese dip
- Beer cheese dip
- Mustard dip
- Hummus
- Hot crab dip
- French onion dip
- Melted chocolate
- Chocolate chip dessert dip
- Nut butters

CHOCOLATE GANACHE PEANUT BUTTER CUPCAKES

I've been baking cakes and cupcakes for years and enjoy trying new flavors and textures. Here I blended the classic combo of chocolate and peanut butter. These treats are definitely worth the time it takes to make them.
—Ronda Schabes, Vicksburg, MI

Prep: 55 min. • **Bake:** 20 min. + cooling
Makes: 2 dozen

- 2 cups sugar
- 1¾ cups all-purpose flour
- ¾ cup baking cocoa
- ½ tsp. salt
- ½ tsp. baking soda
- ½ tsp. baking powder
- 1 cup buttermilk
- 1 cup strong brewed coffee, room temperature
- ½ cup canola oil
- 2 large eggs, room temperature
- 1 tsp. vanilla extract

FILLING
- ½ cup creamy peanut butter
- 3 Tbsp. unsalted butter, softened
- 1 cup confectioners' sugar
- 2 to 4 Tbsp. 2% milk

GANACHE
- 2 cups semisweet chocolate chips
- ½ cup heavy whipping cream

PEANUT BUTTER FROSTING
- 1 cup packed brown sugar
- 4 large egg whites
- ¼ tsp. salt
- ¼ tsp. cream of tartar
- 1 tsp. vanilla extract
- 2 cups unsalted butter, softened
- ⅓ cup creamy peanut butter
   Chocolate curls, optional

1. Preheat oven to 350°. In a large bowl, combine the first 6 ingredients. Whisk buttermilk, coffee, oil, eggs and vanilla until blended; add to the dry ingredients until combined. (Batter will be very thin.) Fill paper-lined muffin cups two-thirds full.
2. Bake 18-20 minutes or until a toothpick inserted in the center comes out clean. Cool 10 minutes before removing from pans to wire racks to cool completely.
3. In a small bowl, cream peanut butter, butter, confectioners' sugar and enough milk to achieve piping consistency. Cut a small hole in the corner of a pastry bag; insert a

small round tip. Fill bag with peanut butter filling. Insert tip into the top center of each cupcake; pipe about 1 Tbsp. filling into each.
4. Place chocolate chips in a small bowl. In a small saucepan, bring cream just to a boil. Pour over chocolate; whisk until smooth. Dip the top of each cupcake into ganache; place on wire racks to set.
5. In a large heavy saucepan, combine the brown sugar, egg whites, salt and cream of tartar over low heat. With a hand mixer, beat on low speed 1 minute. Continue beating on low over low heat until frosting reaches 160°, 8-10 minutes. Pour into a large bowl; add vanilla. Beat on high until stiff peaks form, about 5 minutes.
6. Add butter, 1 Tbsp. at a time, beating well after each addition. If mixture begins to look curdled, place frosting bowl in another bowl filled with hot water for a few seconds. Continue adding butter and beating until smooth. Beat in peanut butter 1-2 minutes or until smooth.
7. Place frosting in a pastry bag with large star tip; pipe onto each cupcake. If desired, top with chocolate curls. Store in an airtight container in the refrigerator. Let stand at room temperature before serving.
1 cupcake: 498 cal., 33g fat (16g sat. fat), 69mg chol., 196mg sod., 50g carb. (39g sugars, 2g fiber), 6g pro.

STRAWBERRY BASIL JAM

I make this sweet and savory jam with fresh-picked strawberries and fresh basil from my herb garden. The deep red jam, laced with flecks of green basil, is so pretty and makes a perfect gift. Just add a bright ribbon around the top with a gift tag.
—Julie O'Neil, Two Harbors, MN

- -

Prep: 25 min. • **Process:** 10 min./batch
Makes: 9 half-pints

- 5 cups crushed strawberries (about 3 lbs.)
- 1 tsp. butter
- 1 pkg. (1¾ oz.) powdered fruit pectin
- 7 cups sugar
- ½ cup minced fresh basil

1. In a Dutch oven, combine strawberries and butter. Stir in pectin. Bring to a full rolling boil over high heat, stirring constantly. Stir in sugar; return to a full rolling boil. Boil and stir 1 minute. Immediately stir in basil.
2. Remove from heat; skim off foam. Ladle hot mixture into 9 hot half-pint jars, leaving ¼-in. headspace. Remove air bubbles and adjust headspace, if necessary, by adding hot mixture. Wipe rims. Center lids on jars; screw on bands until fingertip tight.
3. Place jars into canner with simmering water, ensuring that they are completely covered with water. Bring to a boil; process for 10 minutes. Remove jars and cool.
2 Tbsp.: 81 cal., 0 fat (0 sat. fat), 0 chol., 1mg sod., 21g carb. (20g sugars, 0 fiber), 0 pro.

SPINACH-BASIL PESTO

SPINACH-BASIL PESTO

Toss this garlicky, rich pesto with pasta or use as a spread. It also freezes well.
—Jaye Beeler, Grand Rapids, MI

- -

Takes: 10 min. • **Makes:** 1¾ cups

- 6 garlic cloves, halved
- 3 cups fresh baby spinach
- 1½ cups loosely packed basil leaves
- ¾ cup chopped walnuts or pine nuts, toasted
- 1 cup grated Parmesan cheese
- ½ tsp. salt
- Dash pepper
- ¾ cup olive oil

Place garlic in a food processor; pulse until finely chopped. Add the spinach, basil and walnuts. Pulse until chopped. Add cheese, salt and pepper. Continue processing while gradually adding oil in a steady stream.
Freeze option: Freeze pesto in freezer containers. To use, thaw in refrigerator.
2 Tbsp.: 167 cal., 17g fat (3g sat. fat), 5mg chol., 177mg sod., 2g carb. (0 sugars, 1g fiber), 3g pro.

HOMEMADE STEAK SEASONING

Here's the perfect seasoning for your favorite cut.
—Sarah Farmer, Executive Culinary Director

- -

Takes: 5 min. • **Makes:** about ⅓ cup

- 2 Tbsp. coarsely ground pepper
- 2 Tbsp. kosher salt
- 2 tsp. onion powder
- 2 tsp. dried minced garlic
- 2 tsp. paprika
- 2 tsp. crushed coriander seeds
- 2 tsp. crushed red pepper flakes

In a small bowl, combine all ingredients. Store in an airtight container in a cool, dry place for up to 1 year.
½ tsp.: 3 cal., 0 fat (0 sat. fat), 0 chol., 360mg sod., 1g carb. (0 sugars, 0 fiber), 0 pro.

HOMEMADE PEANUT BUTTER CUPS

These irresistible homemade candies with gooey peanut butter centers are so easy to make. I choose pretty mini muffin liners and colored sprinkles to coordinate with whatever holiday we're celebrating.
—LaVonne Hegland, St. Michael, MN

Prep: 20 min. + chilling • **Makes:** 3 dozen

- 1 cup creamy peanut butter, divided
- ½ cup confectioners' sugar
- 4½ tsp. butter, softened
- ½ tsp. salt
- 2 cups semisweet chocolate chips
- 4 milk chocolate candy bars (1.55 oz. each), coarsely chopped
  Colored sprinkles, optional

1. In a bowl, combine ½ cup creamy peanut butter, confectioners' sugar, butter and salt until smooth.

2. In a microwave, melt chocolate chips, candy bars and remaining peanut butter; stir until smooth.

3. Drop 1 tsp. of chocolate mixture into paper-lined mini muffin cups. Drop a scant tsp. of peanut butter mixture into each cup; top with another tsp. of chocolate mixture. If desired, decorate with sprinkles. Refrigerate until set. Store in an airtight container.

1 piece: 123 cal., 8g fat (4g sat. fat), 2mg chol., 76mg sod., 12g carb. (10g sugars, 1g fiber), 3g pro.

ROASTED CURRY CHICKPEAS

We coated chickpeas with a few simple seasonings to make this low-fat snacking sensation. It rivals calorie-laden varieties sold in stores.
—*Taste of Home* Test Kitchen

Takes: 30 min. • **Makes:** 1 cup

- 1 can (15 oz.) chickpeas or garbanzo beans
- 2 Tbsp. olive oil
- 1 tsp. salt
- ¼ tsp. pepper
- 2 tsp. curry powder
- ½ tsp. crushed red pepper flakes

Rinse and drain chickpeas; place on paper towels and pat dry. Place in a greased 15x10x1-in. baking pan; drizzle with oil and sprinkle with seasonings. Toss to coat. Bake at 450° until crispy and golden brown, 25-30 minutes.

¼ cup: 162 cal., 9g fat (1g sat. fat), 0 chol., 728mg sod., 17g carb. (3g sugars, 5g fiber), 4g pro.

"In our family, we love snacks that have a little bit of heat. These seasoned chickpeas hit the spot."

—SARAH FARMER, EXECUTIVE CULINARY DIRECTOR

HOMEMADE PEANUT BUTTER CUPS

KEY LIME BLONDIE BARS
PAGE 202

Cookies, Brownies & Bars

Who doesn't love the first blissful bite into a warm, tender cookie or a rich brownie or bar? With these deliciously fun recipes and a few simple pantry staples, you can whip up batches of bite-sized yumminess the whole family is guaranteed to love!

CHOCOLATE CHIP
COOKIE BROWNIES

CHOCOLATE CHIP COOKIE BROWNIES

It was fun to experiment with this chippy brownie recipe. When my daughter tasted the final version, she told me she thought they were the best brownies ever. That sure does make a mom feel good.
—Dion Frischer, Ann Arbor, MI

- -

Prep: 15 min. • **Bake:** 50 min. + cooling
Makes: 1 dozen

- ¾ cup butter
- 1½ cups sugar
- ½ cup baking cocoa
- 3 large eggs, room temperature
- ¾ cup all-purpose flour
- ½ cup chopped walnuts

CHOCOLATE CHIP LAYER

- ½ cup butter
- 1 cup packed brown sugar
- 1 large egg, room temperature
- 1 cup all-purpose flour
- ½ tsp. baking soda
- 1 cup semisweet chocolate chips

1. Preheat oven to 350°. Line a 9-in. square baking pan with foil, letting ends extend up sides; grease foil.
2. In a microwave, melt butter in a large microwave-safe bowl. Stir in sugar and cocoa. Add the eggs, 1 at a time, whisking to blend after each addition. Add flour; stir just until combined. Stir in nuts. Spread into prepared pan. Bake 15 minutes.
3. Meanwhile, for chocolate chip layer, melt butter in another microwave-safe bowl. Stir in brown sugar. Whisk in egg. In a small bowl, whisk flour and baking soda; stir into butter mixture just until combined. Stir in chocolate chips. Spoon mixture over hot brownie layer.
4. Bake 35-40 minutes longer or until a toothpick inserted in center comes out with moist crumbs. Cool completely in pan on a wire rack. Lifting foil, remove brownies from pan. Cut into bars.

1 brownie: 536 cal., 29g fat (15g sat. fat), 113mg chol., 236mg sod., 69g carb. (51g sugars, 2g fiber), 6g pro.

PEANUT BUTTER KISS COOKIES

Everyone who tries these classic peanut butter gems is amazed that they only use five simple ingredients. Baking doesn't get much easier than this!
—Dee Davis, Sun City, AZ

- -

Prep: 20 min. • **Bake:** 10 min./batch + cooling
Makes: about 2½ dozen

- 1 cup peanut butter
- 1 cup sugar
- 1 large egg, room temperature
- 1 tsp. vanilla extract
- 30 milk chocolate kisses

1. Preheat oven to 350°. Cream peanut butter and sugar until light and fluffy. Beat in egg and vanilla.
2. Roll into 1¼-in. balls. Place 2 in. apart on ungreased baking sheets. Bake until tops are slightly cracked, 10-12 minutes. Immediately press 1 chocolate kiss into center of each cookie. Cool for 5 minutes before removing from pans to wire racks.

1 cookie: 102 cal., 6g fat (2g sat. fat), 7mg chol., 43mg sod., 11g carb. (10g sugars, 1g fiber), 2g pro.

> "I love the simplicity of these Peanut Butter Kiss Cookies at Christmastime. It's a welcomed recipe in the mix of more complex and time-consuming ones."
>
> —STEPHANIE MARCHESE, VISUAL PRODUCTION EXECUTIVE DIRECTOR

PEANUT BUTTER KISS COOKIES

GOOEY CARAMEL-TOPPED GINGERSNAPS

Making these cookies is therapeutic for me. These gingersnaps are quite popular at fundraisers. If you'd like, you can make variations by changing the cookie base or using different types of nuts.
—Deirdre Cox, Kansas City, MO

Prep: 30 min. + standing • **Makes:** 3½ dozen

- 42 **gingersnap cookies**
- 1 **pkg. (14 oz.) caramels**
- ¼ **cup 2% milk or heavy whipping cream**
- 1 **cup chopped honey-roasted peanuts**
- 12 **oz. white or dark chocolate candy coating, melted**
  Chocolate jimmies or finely chopped honey-roasted peanuts

1. Arrange cookies in a single layer on waxed paper-lined baking sheets. In a microwave, melt caramels with milk; stir until smooth. Stir in 1 cup chopped peanuts. Spoon about 1 tsp. caramel mixture over each cookie; refrigerate until set.
2. Dip each cookie halfway into candy coating; allow excess to drip off. Return to baking sheet; sprinkle with jimmies. Refrigerate until set.
1 cookie: 128 cal., 5g fat (3g sat. fat), 1mg chol., 70mg sod., 19g carb. (14g sugars, 0 fiber), 2g pro.

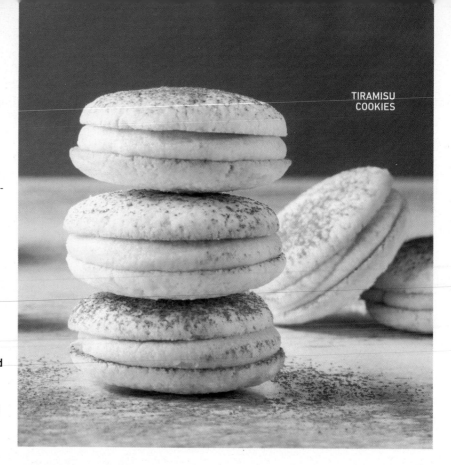

TIRAMISU COOKIES

TIRAMISU COOKIES

These tiramisu cookies bring out all the delicious flavors of tiramisu in sandwich style. Pack up these treats in a decorative container for an easy edible hostess gift.
—*Taste of Home* Test Kitchen

Prep: 30 min. • **Bake:** 15 min./batch + cooling
Makes: 1½ dozen

- 1 **cup butter, softened**
- ¾ **cup sugar**
- 2 **large eggs, room temperature**
- 1 **tsp. vanilla extract**
- ½ **tsp. rum extract**
- 2¼ **cups all-purpose flour**
- 1 **tsp. baking powder**
- ¼ **tsp. salt**
FILLING
- 1 **carton (8 oz.) mascarpone cheese**
- ¼ **cup butter, softened**
- 2 **tsp. instant coffee granules**
- 1 **tsp. vanilla extract**
- 3 **cups confectioners' sugar**
  Baking cocoa

1. Preheat oven to 350°. Cream butter and sugar until light and fluffy, 5-7 minutes. Beat in eggs and extracts. In another bowl, whisk flour, baking powder and salt; gradually beat into creamed mixture.

2. Drop dough by tablespoonfuls 2 in. apart onto parchment-lined baking sheets; flatten slightly with bottom of a glass dipped in sugar. Bake until the edges begin to brown slightly, 12-14 minutes. Remove from pans to wire racks; cool completely.
3. For the filling, in a large bowl, beat the mascarpone cheese and butter until smooth. In a small bowl, dissolve the instant coffee in vanilla; beat into mascarpone mixture. Gradually beat in confectioners' sugar until smooth. Pipe or spread filling on bottoms of half of the cookies; cover with remaining cookies. Dust cookies with cocoa. Store in the refrigerator.
1 sandwich cookie: 344 cal., 19g fat (11g sat. fat), 70mg chol., 176mg sod., 40g carb. (28g sugars, 0 fiber), 3g pro.

DID YOU KNOW?

Mascarpone is a soft fresh cheese with a milky white color. It has a rich, buttery, slightly sweet flavor and a smooth, thick, creamy texture.

SWEETHEART SLICES

You get the flavor of a snickerdoodle plus the texture of a shortbread in these fun cookies. Make them for your sweeties, or make them together for the memories!
—*Taste of Home* Test Kitchen

- -

Prep: 20 min. + freezing • **Bake:** 15 min./batch
Makes: about 2 dozen

- 1 cup butter, softened
- ¾ cup sugar
- 4 large egg yolks
- 3 tsp. vanilla extract
- 2½ cups all-purpose flour
- 1½ tsp. ground cinnamon
- ⅓ cup miniature semisweet chocolate chips
- Red or pink paste food coloring

1. Cream butter and sugar until light and fluffy, 5-7 minutes. Add egg yolks, 1 at a time, beating well after each addition. Beat in vanilla . Whisk flour and cinnamon; gradually add to the creamed mixture and mix well. Remove ⅔ of dough to another bowl; stir in chocolate chips. Tint remaining dough pink.

2. On a lightly floured surface, roll smaller portion to ½-in. thickness. Cut with a 1-in. heart-shaped cookie cutter. Brush 1 side of hearts with water and gently stack together to form two 5-in.-long logs, running a finger along sides to smooth edges. Refrigerate until firm, about 30 minutes.

3. Divide the chocolate chip dough into 10 portions. Roll each into a 5-in. coil. Brush outside of heart log with water; mold coils around heart logs, gently pressing to adhere. Wrap cookie logs tightly in plastic; roll to mold the dough into a smooth roll. Freeze until firm, about 2 hours.

4. Preheat oven to 350°. Cut into ¼-in. slices. Place 2 in. apart on parchment-lined baking sheets. Bake until edges are lightly browned, 12-14 minutes. Cool on pans for 2 minutes. Remove to wire racks to cool.

1 cookie: 162 cal., 9g fat (6g sat. fat), 51mg chol., 63mg sod., 18g carb. (8g sugars, 1g fiber), 2g pro.

CHOCOLATE PEANUT BUTTER NO-BAKE COOKIES

These peanut butter and chocolate cookies bring back fond memories of my mom. The no-bake recipe was her favorite, and she always made a batch whenever she knew company was coming.
—Jacquie McTaggart, Independence, IA

- -

Prep: 20 min. + chilling • **Makes:** 2½ dozen

- 2 cups sugar
- ½ cup butter or margarine, cubed
- ½ cup 2% milk
- 3 Tbsp. baking cocoa
- Dash salt
- ½ cup creamy peanut butter
- 1 tsp. vanilla extract
- 3 cups old-fashioned oats

1. In a large saucepan, combine the first 5 ingredients. Bring to a boil, stirring constantly. Cook and stir 3 minutes.

2. Remove from heat; stir in peanut butter and vanilla until blended. Stir in oats. Drop mixture by tablespoonfuls onto waxed paper-lined baking sheets. Refrigerate until set. Store in airtight containers.

1 cookie: 139 cal., 6g fat (3g sat. fat), 8mg chol., 50mg sod., 20g carb. (14g sugars, 1g fiber), 2g pro.

SWEETHEART SLICES

GLAZED ITALIAN FRUITCAKE COOKIES

I grew up in Italy and enjoyed these cookies every Christmas. Now I make them every year and give some to friends.
—Trisha Kruse, Eagle, ID

Prep: 25 min. + chilling • **Bake:** 10 min./batch
Makes: 4 dozen

- 1 cup butter, softened
- ⅓ cup half-and-half cream
- 1 tsp. vanilla extract
- 3 cups all-purpose flour
- ¾ cup sugar
- 4 tsp. baking powder
- ½ tsp. salt
- ½ cup chopped walnuts, toasted
- ½ cup chopped mixed dried fruit

GLAZE
- 1 oz. unsweetened chocolate
- 1½ tsp. butter
- 1 cup confectioners' sugar
- ½ tsp. vanilla extract
- 2 to 3 Tbsp. 2% milk

1. In a large bowl, beat butter, cream and vanilla until blended. In another bowl, whisk the flour, sugar, baking powder and salt; gradually beat into creamed mixture. Stir in the walnuts and dried fruit (mixture will be crumbly). Press the mixture together to form a ball.

2. Divide dough in half; shape each into an 8-in.-long roll. Wrap in plastic; refrigerate 1 hour or until firm.

3. Preheat oven to 350°. Unwrap and cut dough crosswise into ¼-in. slices. Place 1 in. apart on ungreased baking sheets. Bake 10-12 minutes or until edges are light brown. Remove cookies from pans to wire racks to cool completely.

4. Meanwhile, in a large heavy saucepan, melt chocolate and butter over low heat. Gradually stir in confectioners' sugar, vanilla extract and enough milk to reach drizzling consistency. Remove from heat; drizzle over cooled cookies.

Freeze option: Place wrapped logs in a freezer container and freeze. To use, unwrap frozen logs and cut into slices. If necessary, let dough stand 15 minutes at room temperature before cutting. Bake as directed.

1 cookie: 106 cal., 5g fat (3g sat. fat), 11mg chol., 100mg sod., 13g carb. (7g sugars, 0 fiber), 1g pro.

MANGO FUDGE REFRIGERATOR RIBBON COOKIES

These layered ribbon cookies taste like two or three different cookies rolled into one special treat. They have a rich chocolate layer balanced by a bright orange-mango layer—a special combination.
—Jeanne Holt, Mendota Heights, MN

Prep: 30 min. + chilling
Bake: 10 min./batch + cooling
Makes: 4 dozen

- 1 cup butter, softened
- 1 cup sugar
- 1 large egg, room temperature
- 2 Tbsp. 2% milk
- 1½ tsp. vanilla extract
- 3 cups all-purpose flour
- 1½ tsp. baking powder
- ½ tsp. salt
- ½ cup 60% cacao bittersweet chocolate baking chips, melted and cooled
- ⅓ cup miniature semisweet chocolate chips
- ½ cup finely chopped dried mango
- ⅓ cup finely chopped pistachios
- 2 tsp. grated orange zest

1. Cream the butter and sugar until light and fluffy, 5-7 minutes. Beat in the egg, milk and vanilla. In another bowl, whisk together flour, baking powder and salt; gradually add to the creamed mixture.

2. Divide the dough in half. Mix the melted chocolate into 1 half; stir in miniature chips. Mix mango, pistachios and orange zest into remaining half of dough.

3. Line an 8x4-in. loaf pan with plastic wrap, letting ends extend over sides. Press half of chocolate dough onto bottom of pan; top with half of the mango dough. Repeat layers.

4. Lifting with plastic, remove dough from pan; fold the plastic over dough to wrap completely. Refrigerate dough in pan until firm, 2 hours or overnight.

5. Preheat oven to 375°. Unwrap and cut dough crosswise into ½-in.-thick slices; cut each slice crosswise into thirds. Place 2 in. apart on ungreased baking sheets.

6. Bake until edges are light brown, 10-12 minutes. Remove from pans to wire racks to cool.

1 cookie: 104 cal., 5g fat (3g sat. fat), 14mg chol., 58mg sod., 13g carb. (7g sugars, 1g fiber), 1g pro.

GLAZED ITALIAN
FRUITCAKE COOKIES

MEXICAN CRINKLE COOKIES WITH A KICK

MEXICAN CRINKLE COOKIES WITH A KICK

For a new twist on an old favorite, we added the spicy chocolate cinnamon cane sugar blend to this tried-and-true cookie recipe originally submitted by Kim Kenyon of Greenwood, Missouri. It added pleasant cinnamon flavor with lingering warm heat.
—Josh Rink, Food Stylist

- -

Prep: 25 min. + chilling • **Bake:** 10 min./batch
Makes: about 2 dozen

¾ cup butter, cubed
2 oz. unsweetened chocolate, chopped
1 cup packed brown sugar
¼ cup light corn syrup
1 large egg, room temperature
2 cups all-purpose flour
2 tsp. baking soda
2 tsp. Gustus Vitae spicy chocolate cinnamon cane sugar
¼ tsp. salt
½ cup confectioners' sugar
½ tsp. ground cinnamon

1. In a microwave, melt the butter and chocolate; stir until smooth. Beat in brown sugar and corn syrup until blended. Beat in egg. In another bowl, whisk flour, baking soda, spicy chocolate cinnamon sugar and salt; gradually beat into the brown sugar mixture. Refrigerate, covered, until firm, about 1 hour.
2. Preheat oven to 350°. In a shallow bowl, mix confectioners' sugar and cinnamon. Shape dough into 1½-in. balls; roll in the confectioners' sugar mixture. Place 2 in. apart on greased baking sheets.
3. Bake until set and tops are cracked, 10-12 minutes. Cool on pans 2 minutes. Remove to wire racks to finish cooling.
1 cookie: 158 cal., 7g fat (4g sat. fat), 23mg chol., 184mg sod., 22g carb. (13g sugars, 1g fiber), 2g pro.

"I love a dessert with a little bite. These spicy cookies make a great finale to a Mexican meal."

—MAGGIE CONNERS, ART DIRECTOR

PEANUT BUTTER PRETZEL BARS

Pretzels are my secret to these rich no-bake bites. They add a salty crunch to the classic peanut butter and chocolate pairing.
—Jennifer Beckman, Falls Church, VA

Prep: 15 min. + chilling • Makes: 4 dozen

1 pkg. (16 oz.) miniature pretzels
1½ cups butter, melted
1½ cups peanut butter
3 cups confectioners' sugar
2 cups semisweet chocolate chips
1 Tbsp. shortening

1. Line a 13x9-in. baking pan with foil, letting ends extend up sides. Set aside 1½ cups pretzels for topping. Pulse remaining pretzels in a food processor until fine crumbs form. In a large bowl, mix butter, peanut butter, confectioners' sugar and pretzel crumbs.

2. Press into prepared pan. In a microwave, melt chocolate chips and shortening; stir until smooth. Spread over peanut butter layer. Break reserved pretzels and sprinkle over top; press down gently. Refrigerate, covered, until set, about 1 hour. Lifting with foil, remove from pan. Cut into 48 bars.

1 piece: 201 cal., 13g fat (6g sat. fat), 15mg chol., 233mg sod., 22g carb. (12g sugars, 1g fiber), 3g pro.

TEST KITCHEN TIP
Before putting peanut butter in a measuring cup, lightly coat the inside with water or oil. The peanut butter will slide right out without having to scrape the cup multiple times with a spatula.

CANNOLI WAFER SANDWICHES

My family loves to visit an Italian restaurant that has a wonderful dessert buffet. The cannoli are among our favorites, so I just had to come up with my own simple version. These are best served the same day so the wafers are still nice and crisp.
—Nichi Larson, Shawnee, KS

Prep: 35 min. + standing • Makes: 3½ dozen

1 cup whole-milk ricotta cheese
¼ cup confectioners' sugar
1 Tbsp. sugar
¼ tsp. vanilla extract
1 pkg. (12 oz.) vanilla wafers
12 oz. white candy coating, melted
½ cup miniature semisweet chocolate chips
Additional confectioners' sugar

1. In a small bowl, mix the ricotta cheese, confectioners' sugar, sugar and vanilla until blended. Spread 1 scant tsp. filling on the bottoms of half of the wafers; cover with remaining wafers.

2. Dip each sandwich cookie halfway into candy coating; allow excess to drip off. Place on waxed paper; sprinkle with chocolate chips. Let stand until set, about 10 minutes.

3. Serve within 2 hours or refrigerate until serving. Dust with additional confectioners' sugar just before serving.

1 sandwich cookie: 93 cal., 5g fat (3g sat. fat), 4mg chol., 38mg sod., 13g carb. (10g sugars, 0 fiber), 1g pro.

PEANUT BUTTER PRETZEL BARS

FROSTED WALNUT BROWNIE CUPS

Enjoy a little taste of heaven with these cute brownie cups. They're always a hit and are simple to make.

—Crystal Strick, Boyertown, PA

Prep: 30 min. • **Bake:** 20 min. + cooling
Makes: 32 brownie cups

- 2 cups semisweet chocolate chips
- 1 cup butter, cubed
- 1⅓ cups sugar
- 4 large eggs, room temperature
- 2 tsp. vanilla extract
- 1 cup all-purpose flour
- 1 cup chopped walnuts

GANACHE

- 2 cups semisweet chocolate chips
- ¾ cup heavy whipping cream

1. In a microwave, melt chocolate chips and butter; whisk until smooth. Cool slightly.
2. In a large bowl, beat sugar and eggs. Stir in vanilla and chocolate mixture. Gradually add flour; stir in walnuts. Fill paper-lined miniature muffin cups almost full.
3. Bake at 350° for 20-23 minutes or until a toothpick inserted in the center comes out clean. Cool for 5 minutes before removing from pans to wire racks to cool completely.
4. Place chocolate chips in a small bowl. In a small saucepan, bring cream just to a boil. Pour over chocolate; whisk until smooth. Cool for 30 minutes or until the ganache reaches a spreading consistency, stirring occasionally. Spread over brownies.

1 brownie cup: 353 cal., 24g fat (13g sat. fat), 49mg chol., 56mg sod., 39g carb. (32g sugars, 3g fiber), 4g pro.

APPLE-PEANUT BLONDIES

These blondies are mostly layers of apples, with a little bit of blondie mixed in, creating the perfect layered dessert. I started with a similar recipe and did a bit of tweaking to make it our family's own.

—Julie Peterson, Crofton, MD

Prep: 15 min. • **Bake:** 25 min. + cooling
Makes: 9 servings

- 1 cup packed brown sugar
- ½ cup butter, melted
- 1 large egg, room temperature
- 1 tsp. vanilla extract
- 1 cup all-purpose flour
- ½ tsp. baking powder
- ¼ tsp. baking soda
- ¼ tsp. salt
- 2 small apples (about 9 oz.), peeled and sliced
- ½ cup chopped salted peanuts

1. Preheat oven to 350°. Beat brown sugar and butter until light and fluffy, 5-7 minutes. Add egg and vanilla; beat until smooth. In a separate bowl, whisk together flour, baking powder, baking soda and salt; gradually beat into brown sugar mixture just until combined (batter will be thick).
2. Spread all but ¼ cup batter into a greased and floured 8-in. square baking dish. Layer with apple slices; dot with remaining batter. Sprinkle with chopped peanuts. Bake until the top is golden brown and center is set, 22-28 minutes. Cool on a wire rack.

1 blondie: 302 cal., 15g fat (7g sat. fat), 48mg chol., 256mg sod., 39g carb. (26g sugars, 1g fiber), 4g pro.

FROSTED WALNUT BROWNIE CUPS

SANTA'S ELF COOKIES

These rosy-cheeked elf cookies make a showstopping addition to your holiday cookie tray. Or set them atop cupcakes for an extra cute treat.
—Josh Rink, Food Stylist

Prep: 2 hours + standing
Bake: 10 min./batch + cooling
Makes: about 4 dozen

- 1¾ cups confectioners' sugar, divided
- 2 oz. almond paste
- 1¼ cups butter, softened
- 1 large egg, room temperature
- ¼ cup 2% milk
- 1 tsp. vanilla extract
- 4 cups all-purpose flour
- ½ tsp. salt

ROYAL ICING AND DECORATIONS
- 2 cups confectioners' sugar
- 2 Tbsp. water plus 2 tsp. water
- 4½ tsp. meringue powder
- ¼ tsp. cream of tartar
- Food coloring
- Edible food writing pen
- Black nonpareil sprinkles
- Pink luster dust, optional
- Chocolate frosting of your choice

1. In the bowl of a food processor fitted with the blade attachment, pulse ½ cup confectioner's sugar and almond paste until well mixed and texture resembles finely ground cornmeal. In a large bowl, cream butter and remaining 1¼ cups confectioners' sugar until light and fluffy, 5-7 minutes. Add almond paste mixture and beat until fully incorporated. Beat in egg, milk and vanilla. Combine flour and salt; gradually add to creamed mixture and mix well. Cover and refrigerate for 1 hour.

2. Preheat oven to 375°. On a lightly floured surface, roll out dough to ¼-in. thickness. Cut out using a floured 3½-in. elf cookie cutter. Place 1 in. apart on parchment-lined baking sheets. Bake until cookies are light golden brown and firm, 7-8 minutes. Let stand for 2 minutes before removing to wire racks to cool.

3. For icing, in a large bowl, combine confectioners' sugar, water, meringue powder and cream of tartar; beat on low speed just until blended. Beat on high until stiff peaks form, 4-5 minutes. Divide icing into thirds. Tint 1 portion of icing with red food coloring; tint second portion with

desired food coloring for face. Leave the remaining portion white. Place icings into piping bags fitted with fine round tips. Pipe icing onto cookies to create clothing, hat and face. While icing is still wet, place black sprinkles to create eyes. Let the icing dry completely. If desired, dip a small brush into pink luster dust; tap off excess and dab onto cookies to create pink cheeks. Using leaf tip #67, pipe frosting to create ears. Using a small round tip, pipe icing to create nose. Using edible pen or round tip, draw mouth. Place chocolate frosting into a piping bag fitted with #14 star tip; pipe along top of face and rim of hat to create hair. Store in an airtight container.

1 cookie: 134 cal., 6g fat (3g sat. fat), 18mg chol., 72mg sod., 19g carb. (10g sugars, 0 fiber), 2g pro.

DID YOU KNOW?

Royal icing is a specific type of icing. What sets it apart from other frostings and glazes is that it hardens when cooled, making it an ideal choice for decorated cookies, like these elf cookies, and gingerbread houses.

The secret ingredient in royal icing is meringue powder. This egg white substitute helps the icing achieve its glossy consistency. You can buy meringue powder at many grocery or craft stores or online.

GRAFFITI CUTOUT COOKIES

Talk about playing with your food! Edible color spray lets you create ombre and color blends unlike any other decorating technique. To re-create my ombre lines, hold a sheet of paper over desired sections as you spray to layer the color.
—Shannon Norris, Senior Food Stylist

- -

Prep: 30 min+ freezing
Bake: 15 min. + cooling
Makes: 15 cookies

- ¼   **cup butter, softened**
- ½   **cup sugar**
- 1   **large egg, room temperature**
- 1   **tsp. vanilla extract**
- 2   **cups almond flour**
- ¼   **tsp. salt**
- ¼   **tsp. baking soda**

ROYAL ICING

- 2   **cups confectioners' sugar**
- 2   **to 6 Tbsp. water**
- 5   **tsp. meringue powder**
      Food color spray, optional

1. In a bowl, cream butter and sugar until light and fluffy, 5-7 minutes. Beat in egg and vanilla. In another bowl, whisk almond flour, salt and baking soda; gradually beat into creamed mixture.

2. Preheat oven to 325°. Between 2 pieces of waxed paper, roll the dough to ¼-in. thickness. Place on a cutting board in the freezer until firm, about 20 minutes. Remove paper; cut with 3-in. cookie cutters. Place 2 in. apart on parchment-lined baking sheets.

3. Bake until lightly browned on the edges, about 12-15 minutes. Cool on baking sheets for 2 minutes. Remove cookies to wire racks to cool completely.

4. For the icing, in a large bowl, combine confectioners' sugar, 2 Tbsp. water and meringue powder; beat on low speed just until blended. Beat on high until stiff peaks form, 4-5 minutes. Add water as necessary to reach desired consistency. Keep unused icing covered at all times with a damp cloth. If necessary, beat again on high speed to restore texture.

5. Frost cookies and let stand at room temperature several hours or until frosting is dry and firm. Decorate if desired with color spray mist. Store in an airtight container.

1 cookie: 209 cal., 11g fat (3g sat. fat), 21mg chol., 103mg sod., 26g carb. (23g sugars, 2g fiber), 4g pro.

TRIPLE-CHOCOLATE CHEESECAKE BARS

What's better than a brownie crust layered with chocolate cheesecake and topped with chocolate ganache? These bars will satisfy even the biggest chocolate lovers.
—Andrea Price, Grafton, WI

- -

Prep: 35 min. • **Bake:** 25 min. + chilling
Makes: 2½ dozen

- ¼   **cup butter, cubed**
- ½   **cup sugar**
- 3   **Tbsp. baking cocoa**
- ½   **tsp. vanilla extract**
- 1   **large egg, room temperature**
- ¼   **cup all-purpose flour**
- ⅛   **tsp. baking powder**
- ⅛   **tsp. salt**

CHEESECAKE LAYER

- 2   **pkg. (8 oz. each) cream cheese, softened**
- ½   **cup sugar**
- 1½   **tsp. vanilla extract**
- ¾   **cup semisweet chocolate chips, melted and cooled**
- 2   **large eggs, room temperature, lightly beaten**

GANACHE

- 1½   **cups semisweet chocolate chips**
- ½   **cup heavy whipping cream**
- 1   **tsp. vanilla extract**

1. Preheat oven to 350°. Line a 13x9-in. pan with foil, letting ends extend up sides; grease foil. In a microwave, melt butter in a large microwave-safe bowl. Stir in sugar, cocoa and vanilla. Add egg; blend well. Add the flour, baking powder and salt; stir just until combined. Spread into a thin layer into prepared pan. Bake until top appears dry, 6-8 minutes.

2. Meanwhile, in a large bowl, beat cream cheese, sugar and vanilla until smooth. Beat in cooled chocolate chips. Add beaten eggs; beat on low speed just until combined. Spread over brownie layer. Bake until filling is set, 25-30 minutes. Cool 10 minutes on a wire rack.

3. For ganache, place chocolate chips in a small bowl. In a saucepan, bring cream just to a boil. Pour over chocolate; let stand for 5 minutes. Stir with a whisk until smooth. Stir in vanilla extract; cool slightly, stirring occasionally. Pour over cheesecake layer; cool in pan on a wire rack 1 hour. Refrigerate for at least 2 hours. Lifting with foil, remove brownies from pan. Cut into bars.

1 bar: 180 cal., 13g fat (7g sat. fat), 42mg chol., 81mg sod., 17g carb. (14g sugars, 1g fiber), 2g pro.

DID YOU KNOW?
Ganache is a French term for a smooth, velvety mixture of chocolate and cream.

TRIPLE-CHOCOLATE CHEESECAKE BARS

KEY LIME PIE BALLS

The classic creamy filling, graham-cracker crust and tart citrusy burst of lime are all mixed together in every bite of these easy rolled cookies.

—*Taste of Home* Test Kitchen

Prep: 25 min. + chilling
Makes: about 5 dozen

1	pkg. (8 oz.) cream cheese, softened
1	can (14½ oz.) sweetened condensed milk
3½	cups graham cracker crumbs
3	Tbsp. lime juice
2	tsp. grated lime zest
¼	tsp. salt
¼	tsp. ground cinnamon
½	cup confectioners' sugar

1. In a large bowl, beat the first 7 ingredients until blended. Shape into 1-in. balls. Roll the cookie balls in the confectioners' sugar. Refrigerate 30 minutes or until firm.

2. Store cookies between pieces of waxed paper in an airtight container and store in the refrigerator.

1 cookie: 72 calories, 3g fat (1g saturated fat), 7mg cholesterol, 60mg sodium, 11g carbohydrate (8g sugars, 0 fiber), 1g protein.

CHERRY-COCONUT SLICES

CHERRY-COCONUT SLICES

My mother loved to make this recipe from well-known home economist Emmie Oddie, who had a column in a Canadian farming newspaper. She would test reader recipes in her own kitchen and write about them. These tasty sweets are so rich that you only need a small piece.

—Judy Olson, Whitecourt, AB

Prep: 15 min. + chilling
Cook: 5 min. + cooling • **Makes:** 32 bars

3	cups graham cracker crumbs
1½	cups miniature marshmallows
1	cup unsweetened finely shredded coconut
½	cup chopped maraschino cherries
1	can (14 oz.) sweetened condensed milk
1	tsp. maple flavoring

FROSTING

1	cup packed brown sugar
⅓	cup butter, cubed
¼	cup 2% milk
1	cup confectioners' sugar

1. In a large bowl, mix cracker crumbs, marshmallows, coconut and cherries; stir in condensed milk and flavoring. Press into a greased 8-in. square baking pan.

2. For frosting, in a small saucepan, combine the brown sugar, butter and sweetened condensed milk. Bring to a boil, stirring constantly; cook and stir 3 minutes. Transfer to a small bowl; cool until lukewarm, about 15 minutes. Stir in confectioners' sugar until smooth. Spread over the crumb mixture; refrigerate until set, about 1½ hours.

3. Cut into bars. Store bars in an airtight container in the refrigerator.

1 bar: 169 cal., 6g fat (4g sat. fat), 9mg chol., 82mg sod., 28g carb. (22g sugars, 1g fiber), 2g pro.

DID YOU KNOW?

The darling of cocktails, fluffy fruit salads and vintage desserts like these bars, maraschino cherries can be made from any type of cherry.

SKILLET STOUT BROWNIES

These stout brownies are so rich and fudgy. I also love that you need only one bowl and a skillet to make this quick dessert, so it's perfect for busy weeknight.
—Mandy Naglich, New York, NY

Prep: 30 min. • **Bake:** 25 min. + cooling
Makes: 12 servings

- 8 oz. semisweet chocolate, chopped
- 1 cup butter, cubed
- 1 cup milk stout beer
- 1 large egg, room temperature
- 2 large egg yolks, room temperature
- ¾ cup sugar
- ¼ cup packed brown sugar
- ¾ cup all-purpose flour
- ⅓ cup baking cocoa
- ½ tsp. salt
  Vanilla ice cream, optional

1. Preheat oven to 350°. Place chocolate in a large bowl. In a 10-in. cast-iron or other ovenproof skillet, combine butter and stout. Bring to a boil; reduce heat. Simmer for 10 minutes, stirring constantly. Pour over the chocolate; stir with a whisk until smooth. Cool slightly. In another large bowl, beat egg, egg yolks and sugars until blended. Stir in chocolate mixture. In another bowl, mix the flour, baking cocoa and salt; gradually add to chocolate mixture, mixing well.
2. Spread into skillet. Bake until brownies are set, 25-30 minutes. Cool completely in skillet on a wire rack. If desired, serve with vanilla ice cream.

1 piece: 363 cal., 24g fat (14g sat. fat), 87mg chol., 229mg sod., 29g carb. (21g sugars, 1g fiber), 4g pro.

NO-BAKE CEREAL COOKIE BARS

We pull out all the goodies—like raisins and coconut—for these chewy bars. For more color, sprinkle the M&M's after the bars are in the pan. Then lightly press them into the cereal mixture.
—Connie Craig, Lakewood, WA

Prep: 10 min. • **Cook:** 15 min. + cooling
Makes: 3 dozen

- 4½ cups Rice Krispies
- 3¼ cups quick-cooking oats
- ½ cup cornflakes
- ½ cup sweetened shredded coconut
- ½ cup butter, cubed
- 1 pkg. (16 oz.) miniature marshmallows
- ¼ cup honey
- ½ cup M&M's minis
- ¼ cup raisins

1. Grease a 15x10x1-in. pan. In a large bowl, combine first 4 ingredients.
2. In a large saucepan, melt the butter over low heat. Add the marshmallows; stir until completely melted. Stir in the honey until blended. Pour over cereal mixture; stir until evenly coated. Cool 5 minutes.
3. Stir in M&M's minis and raisins; press into prepared pan using a greased spatula. Let stand for 30 minutes before cutting. Store bars between layers of waxed paper in an airtight container.

1 bar: 137 cal., 4g fat (3g sat. fat), 8mg chol., 58mg sod., 24g carb. (13g sugars, 1g fiber), 2g pro. **Diabetic exchanges:** 1½ starch, ½ fat.

SKILLET STOUT BROWNIES

KEY LIME
BLONDIE BARS

CINNAMON-CANDY COOKIES

I was trying to make a unique Christmas cookie inspired by my brother's love of Red Hots. I used the candies in these lacelike cookies for cinnamon flavor.
—Wendy Rusch, Cameron, WI

- -

Prep: 20 min. + chilling
Bake: 10 min./batch + cooling
Makes: about 5 dozen

- ⅔ cup Red Hots
- 2⅓ cups all-purpose flour
- 1 cup butter, softened
- 1 cup sugar
- 1 tsp. vanilla extract

FROSTING
- 2 cups confectioners' sugar
- ½ cup butter, softened
- ½ tsp. vanilla or cinnamon extract
- ⅛ tsp. salt
- 4 to 6 Tbsp. 2% milk

1. Place Red Hots in a food processor; process until fine and powdery. Add flour; pulse to combine.

2. In a large bowl, cream butter and sugar until light and fluffy, 5-7 minutes. Beat in vanilla. Gradually beat flour mixture into creamed mixture.

3. Shape dough into two 8-in. rolls; wrap each roll in waxed paper. Refrigerate until firm, about 1 hour.

4. Preheat oven to 350°. Unwrap rolls and cut into ¼-in. slices. Place 2 in. apart on ungreased baking sheets. Bake until edges are just light brown, 7-9 minutes. Cool on pans 2 minutes before removing to wire racks to cool completely.

5. For frosting, in a small bowl, beat the confectioners' sugar, butter, extract, salt and enough of the milk to reach desired consistency. Decorate cookies as desired.

Freeze option: Place wrapped logs in a freezer container; freeze. To use, unwrap frozen logs and cut into slices. If necessary, let the dough stand a few minutes at room temperature before cutting. Prepare, bake and decorate cookies as directed.

1 cookie: 98 cal., 5g fat (3g sat. fat), 12mg chol., 42mg sod., 14g carb. (9g sugars, 0 fiber), 1g pro.

KEY LIME BLONDIE BARS

Here's my tropical take on a beloved treat. These Key lime bars combine the taste of the classic pie with a blondie batter and cream cheese frosting. You can make a thicker crust if desired.
—Kristin LaBoon, Austin, TX

- -

Prep: 35 min. + chilling
Bake: 25 min. + cooling • **Makes:** 16 servings

- 1⅓ cups graham cracker crumbs, divided
- ⅓ cup plus 2 Tbsp. melted butter, divided
- 3 Tbsp. plus ¼ cup packed brown sugar, divided
- ⅔ cup butter, softened
- 1 cup plus 1 Tbsp. sugar, divided
- 2 large eggs, room temperature
- 1 large egg white, room temperature
- 3 Tbsp. Key lime juice
- 4½ tsp. grated Key lime zest
- 1 cup all-purpose flour
- ½ tsp. plus ⅛ tsp. salt, divided
- 1 tsp. vanilla extract
- ⅛ tsp. ground cinnamon

FROSTING
- ¼ cup butter, softened
- ¼ cup cream cheese, softened
- 4 cups confectioners' sugar
- 2 Tbsp. 2% milk
- 1 tsp. vanilla extract
  Key lime slices, optional

1. Preheat oven to 350°. Line a 9-in. square baking pan with parchment, letting ends extend up sides. Combine 1 cup cracker crumbs, ⅓ cup melted butter and 3 Tbsp. brown sugar; press onto bottom of prepared pan. Bake 10 minutes. Cool on a wire rack.

2. For blondie layer: In a large bowl, cream softened butter and 1 cup sugar until light and fluffy, 5-7 minutes. Beat in eggs, egg white, lime juice and zest. In a small bowl, mix flour and ½ tsp. salt; gradually add to creamed mixture, mixing well.

3. Spread over crust. Bake until a toothpick inserted in the center comes out clean, 25-30 minutes (do not overbake). Cool completely in pan on a wire rack.

4. For streusel, combine the remaining ⅓ cup cracker crumbs, 2 Tbsp. melted butter, ¼ cup brown sugar, 1 Tbsp. sugar and ⅛ tsp. salt, along with the vanilla and cinnamon, until crumbly. Reserve ½ cup for topping.

5. In a large bowl, combine all frosting ingredients; beat until smooth. Stir in the remaining ½ cup streusel. Spread over bars. Sprinkle with reserved topping. Refrigerate at least 4 hours before cutting. Lifting with the parchment, remove from pan. Cut into bars. Store in an airtight container in the refrigerator. If desired, garnish with sliced Key limes.

1 blondie: 422 cal., 19g fat (11g sat. fat), 69mg chol., 283mg sod., 62g carb. (51g sugars, 1g fiber), 3g pro.

BIG SOFT GINGER COOKIES

These nicely spiced, soft gingerbread cookies are perfect for folks who like the flavor of ginger but don't care for crunchy gingersnaps.
—Barbara Gray, Boise, ID

Prep: 20 min. • **Bake:** 10 min./batch
Makes: 2½ dozen

- ¾ cup butter, softened
- 1 cup sugar
- 1 large egg, room temperature
- ¼ cup molasses
- 2¼ cups all-purpose flour
- 2 tsp. ground ginger
- 1 tsp. baking soda
- ¾ tsp. ground cinnamon
- ½ tsp. ground cloves
- ¼ tsp. salt
- Additional sugar

1. In a large bowl, cream the butter and sugar until light and fluffy, 5-7 minutes. Beat in egg and molasses. Combine flour, ginger, baking soda, cinnamon, cloves and salt; gradually add to creamed mixture; mix well.
2. Roll into 1½-in. balls, then roll in sugar. Place 2 in. apart on ungreased baking sheets. Bake at 350° until puffy and lightly browned, 10-12 minutes. Remove to wire racks to cool.
1 cookie: 111 cal., 5g fat (3g sat. fat), 19mg chol., 98mg sod., 16g carb. (8g sugars, 0 fiber), 1g pro.

ASK SARAH

SHOULD I USE UNSALTED OR SALTED BUTTER WHEN BAKING COOKIES AND BARS?

The salt level makes a huge difference in baking. If a recipe calls for butter (neither unsalted nor salted) and salt, it's safe to assume the recipe has been precisely calibrated with unsalted butter in mind.

BIG SOFT
GINGER COOKIES

LEMON THYME ICEBOX COOKIES

I found this recipe at my grandmother's house, and I made them as soon as I got home. It's a very unique cookie that's almost savory because of the thyme, which pairs well with the lemon. It's a lovely melt-in-your-mouth butter cookie.
—Catherine Adams, Westwego, LA

Prep: 15 min. + chilling
Bake: 15 min./batch + cooling
Makes: about 2 dozen

- ½ cup butter, softened
- 5 Tbsp. sugar
- 1 Tbsp. minced fresh thyme
- 1 to 2 tsp. grated lemon zest
- 1 large egg yolk, room temperature
- 1 cup all-purpose flour
- ¼ tsp. baking powder
- ¼ tsp. salt

1. Cream the butter, sugar, thyme and lemon zest until light and fluffy, 5-7 minutes. Beat in egg yolk. In another bowl, whisk the flour, baking powder and salt; gradually beat into creamed mixture.

2. Roughly shape dough into a 12-in. roll along the edge of a 12x12-in. sheet of waxed paper. Tightly roll waxed paper over dough, using the paper to mold the dough into a smooth roll. Securely wrap roll in plastic; refrigerate 1 hour or overnight.

3. Preheat oven to 350°. Unwrap and cut dough crosswise into ½-in. slices. Place 2 in. apart on ungreased baking sheets. Bake until edges begin to brown, 12-15 minutes. Cool in pans 5 minutes. Remove to wire racks to finish cooling.

1 cookie: 65 cal., 4g fat (3g sat. fat), 18mg chol., 61mg sod., 7g carb. (3g sugars, 0 fiber), 1g pro.

S'MORES BROWNIES

Our family simply adores our daughter's fudgy s'mores brownies. The cinnamon graham cracker crust and dark chocolate brownies bring our passion for s'mores to a whole new level!
—Jennifer Gilbert, Brighton, MI

Prep: 20 min. • **Bake:** 30 min.
Makes: 2 dozen

- 1½ cups graham cracker crumbs (about 10 whole crackers)
- ¼ cup sugar
- 1 tsp. ground cinnamon
- ½ cup butter, melted

BROWNIES
- 1 oz. unsweetened baking chocolate
- ½ cup butter, softened
- 1¼ cups sugar
- 3 large eggs, room temperature
- 1 tsp. vanilla extract
- 1¼ cups all-purpose flour
- ⅓ cup dark baking cocoa
- ½ tsp. baking powder
- ¼ tsp. salt
- 1 cup miniature marshmallows

TOPPING
- 1 cup miniature marshmallows
- 5 whole graham crackers, broken into bite-sized pieces

1. Preheat oven to 350°. Combine cracker crumbs, sugar and cinnamon. Stir in melted butter. Press onto bottom of an ungreased 13x9-in. baking pan. Bake until lightly browned, 7-9 minutes. Cool on a wire rack.

2. For brownies, melt unsweetened baking chocolate on high in a microwave, stirring every 30 seconds. Cool slightly. Cream butter and sugar on medium speed until light and fluffy, 5-7 minutes. Add eggs and beat well; beat in melted chocolate and vanilla. In another bowl, whisk together the flour, baking cocoa, baking powder and salt; stir into creamed mixture. Fold in 1 cup of the miniature marshmallows.

3. Spread batter over graham cracker crust. Top with 1 cup marshmallows and broken graham crackers. Bake until center is set, 18-22 minutes (do not overbake).

1 brownie: 215 cal., 10g fat (6g sat. fat), 44mg chol., 157mg sod., 30g carb. (17g sugars, 1g fiber), 3g pro.

S'MORES BROWNIES

EASY SLICE & BAKE COOKIES

Anyone who loves a monster cookie will appreciate these large slice-and-bake treats. Since the dough is frozen, you can pull it out of the freezer and slice as many (or as few) cookies as you want to enjoy at one time.
—Heather Chambers, Largo, FL

Prep: 30 min. + freezing
Bake: 10 min./batch + cooling
Makes: about 4 dozen

- 1 cup unsalted butter, softened
- ⅓ cup Nutella
- ¾ cup sugar
- ¾ cup packed brown sugar
- 2 large eggs, room temperature
- 1 Tbsp. vanilla extract
- 2¾ cups all-purpose flour
- 1 tsp. baking soda
- 1 tsp. salt
- 1¼ cups white baking chips

1. Cream butter, Nutella and sugars until light and fluffy, 5-7 minutes. Beat in eggs and vanilla. In another bowl, whisk flour, baking soda and salt; gradually beat into creamed mixture. Stir in chips.

2. Divide dough in half. Roughly shape each portion into a 12-in. roll along the edge of a 12x12-in. sheet of waxed paper. Tightly roll waxed paper over dough, using it to mold the dough into a smooth roll. Freeze until firm, about 1 hour.

3. Preheat oven to 375°. Unwrap and cut dough crosswise into ½-in. slices. Place 2 in. apart on ungreased baking sheets. Bake until lightly browned, 10-12 minutes. Remove from pans to wire racks to cool.

1 cookie: 123 cal., 6g fat (3g sat. fat), 19mg chol., 85mg sod., 16g carb. (10g sugars, 0 fiber), 1g pro.

M&M & PRETZEL COOKIES

Kids and grown-ups alike adore these sweet and crunchy no-bake cookies. Add more candy for M&M's lovers, or toss in a few additional pretzels for an extra-salty bite.
—Madison Allen, Destrehan, LA

Prep: 20 min. + chilling • **Makes:** 6 dozen

- ½ cup butter, cubed
- 2 cups sugar
- ½ cup 2% milk
- 2 Tbsp. baking cocoa
- 1 cup creamy peanut butter
- 2 tsp. vanilla extract
- 3 cups quick-cooking oats
- 1 cup coarsely crushed pretzels
- 1 cup milk chocolate M&M's

1. In a large saucepan, combine the butter, sugar, milk and cocoa. Bring to a boil over medium heat, stirring constantly. Cook and stir 1 minute.

2. Remove from heat; stir in peanut butter and vanilla until blended. Stir in oats; let stand for 5 minutes to cool. Fold in pretzels and M&M's. Drop mixture by tablespoonfuls onto waxed paper-lined baking sheets. Refrigerate until set.

1 cookie: 87 cal., 4g fat (2g sat. fat), 4mg chol., 46mg sod., 12g carb. (8g sugars, 1g fiber), 2g pro.

CHEWY PEANUT BUTTER PAN SQUARES

With seven in our family, including two teenage boys, these peanut butter cookie bars never last long. I'm always amazed at how simple they are to prepare.
—Deb DeChant, Milan, OH

Prep: 10 min. • **Bake:** 30 min.
Makes: 2 dozen

- ½ cup butter, cubed
- ½ cup creamy peanut butter
- 1½ cups sugar
- 1 cup all-purpose flour
- 2 large eggs, room temperature, lightly beaten
- 1 tsp. vanilla extract

1. In a microwave-safe bowl, melt butter and peanut butter; stir until smooth. Combine sugar and flour; gradually add to the butter mixture and mix well. Beat in the eggs and vanilla extract.

2. Spread into a greased 13x9-in. baking pan. Bake at 350° until top is lightly browned and edges start to pull away from sides of pan, 28-32 minutes. Cool on a wire rack.

1 serving: 139 cal., 7g fat (3g sat. fat), 28mg chol., 69mg sod., 18g carb. (13g sugars, 0 fiber), 2g pro.

M&M &
PRETZEL COOKIES

CINNAMON BUN COOKIES

BUTTERSCOTCH-RUM RAISIN TREATS

I love making rum raisin rice pudding around the holidays—and those classic flavors inspired this confection. Crispy rice cereal adds crunch, but nuts, toasted coconut or candied pineapple could do the job, too.
—Crystal Schlueter, Northglenn, CO

- -

Takes: 20 min. • **Makes:** about 4½ dozen

- 1 pkg. (10 to 11 oz.) butterscotch chips
- 1 pkg. (10 to 12 oz.) white baking chips
- ½ tsp. rum extract
- 3 cups Rice Krispies
- 1 cup raisins

1. Line 56 mini muffin cups with paper liners. In a large bowl, combine butterscotch and white chips. Microwave, uncovered, on high for 30 seconds; stir. Microwave in additional 30-second intervals, stirring until smooth.
2. Stir in extract, Rice Krispies and raisins. Drop by rounded tablespoonfuls into prepared mini muffin cups. Chill until set.
Freeze option: Freeze treats in freezer containers, separating layers with waxed paper. Thaw before serving.
1 treat: 76 cal., 4g fat (3g sat. fat), 1mg chol., 21mg sod., 11g carb. (9g sugars, 0 fiber), 0 pro.

CINNAMON BUN COOKIES

I love cinnamon rolls, but working with yeast can be a little intimidating. These cookies give you the taste of a cinnamon roll in cookie form—no yeast required! They look like flattened cinnamon rolls and are pretty enough for special occasions.
—Erin Raatjes, New Lenox, IL

- -

Prep: 30 min. + chilling
Bake: 10 min./batch + cooling
Makes: about 4 dozen

- 1 cup unsalted butter, softened
- ¾ cup confectioners' sugar
- ⅓ cup sugar
- 1½ tsp. grated orange zest
- ½ tsp. salt
- 1 large egg, room temperature
- 1 tsp. vanilla extract
- 2¼ cups all-purpose flour

FILLING
- 5 Tbsp. unsalted butter, softened
- ¼ cup packed brown sugar
- 1½ tsp. light corn syrup
- ½ tsp. vanilla extract
- 2 Tbsp. all-purpose flour
- 1 Tbsp. ground cinnamon
- ½ tsp. salt

GLAZE
- 1 cup confectioners' sugar
- ¼ cup light corn syrup
- 2 tsp. vanilla extract
- 1 to 2 tsp. water

1. Cream first 5 ingredients until light and fluffy, 5-7 minutes. Beat in egg and vanilla. Gradually beat in flour. On a baking sheet, roll dough between 2 sheets of waxed paper into a 12-in. square. Refrigerate 30 minutes.
2. For filling, beat butter, brown sugar, corn syrup and vanilla. Add flour, cinnamon and salt; mix well. Remove top sheet of waxed paper; spread filling over dough to within ¼ in. of edges. Using waxed paper, roll up tightly jelly-roll style, removing paper as you roll. Wrap in plastic. Freeze until firm, about 30 minutes.
3. Preheat oven to 375°. Unwrap and cut dough crosswise into ¼-in. slices. Place slices 2 in. apart on parchment-lined baking sheets. Bake until edges are light brown, 10-12 minutes. Cool on pans 5 minutes. Remove to wire racks to cool completely.
4. For glaze, mix the confectioners' sugar, corn syrup, vanilla and enough water to reach desired consistency. Spread or drizzle over cookies. Let cookies stand at room temperature until set.
1 cookie: 103 cal., 5g fat (3g sat. fat), 17mg chol., 53mg sod., 13g carb. (8g sugars, 0 fiber), 1g pro.

BROWN SUGAR POUND CAKE
PAGE 214

FAVORITE

Cakes & Pies

A homemade cake or pie is the gateway to turning any gathering—whether it's a birthday, graduation or just a weeknight dinner—into a celebration. No matter what the occasion, rely on these wow-worthy cakes, from-scratch pies and tarts, and other nostalgic favorites when you want to whip up your best baked desserts.

FRENCH SILK PIE

I first prepared French silk pie when I was in high school. Years later, I experimented with the recipe until I came up with a version that was perfect. Now it's one of my husband's favorite desserts.
—Lisa Francis, Elba, AL

Prep: 40 min. • **Cook:** 10 min. + chilling
Makes: 6 servings

- 1 sheet refrigerated pie crust
- ⅔ cup sugar
- 2 large eggs, room temperature
- 2 oz. unsweetened chocolate, melted
- 1 tsp. vanilla extract
- ⅓ cup butter, softened
- ⅔ cup heavy whipping cream
- 2 tsp. confectioners' sugar
  Optional: Whipped cream and chocolate curls

1. Cut pie crust in half. Repackage and refrigerate 1 half for another use. On a lightly floured surface, roll remaining half into an 8-in. circle. Transfer to a 7-in. pie plate; flute edges.
2. Line shell with a double thickness of heavy-duty foil. Bake at 450° for 4 minutes. Remove foil; bake until the crust is golden brown, about 2 minutes longer. Cool on a wire rack.
3. In a small saucepan, combine sugar and eggs until well blended. Cook over low heat, stirring constantly, until mixture reaches 160° and coats the back of a metal spoon. Remove from the heat. Stir in chocolate and vanilla until smooth. Cool to lukewarm (90°), stirring occasionally.
4. In a small bowl, cream butter until light and fluffy. Add cooled chocolate mixture; beat on high speed until light and fluffy, about 5 minutes.
5. In another large bowl, beat cream until it begins to thicken. Add confectioners' sugar; beat until stiff peaks form. Fold whipped cream into the chocolate mixture.
6. Pour into cooled crust. Chill for at least 6 hours before serving. If desired, garnish with whipped cream and chocolate curls. Refrigerate leftovers.
1 piece: 450 cal., 33g fat (19g sat. fat), 139mg chol., 223mg sod., 38g carb. (24g sugars, 1g fiber), 5g pro.

LEMON RHUBARB TUBE CAKE

LEMON RHUBARB TUBE CAKE

Try my dessert for a taste of summer. The cake's fresh lemon flavor and tart rhubarb topping are so refreshing.
—Courtney Stultz, Weir, KS

Prep: 35 min. • **Bake:** 50 min. + cooling
Makes: 12 servings

- 3 medium lemons
- 1 cup butter, softened
- 2 cups sugar
- 3 large eggs, room temperature
- 3 cups all-purpose flour
- 1 tsp. baking powder
- ½ tsp. baking soda
- ½ tsp. salt
- 1 cup buttermilk

RHUBARB TOPPING
- 1 cup sugar
- 1 cup sliced fresh or frozen rhubarb
- 1 cup halved fresh strawberries
  Confectioners' sugar, optional

1. Preheat oven to 350°. Grease and flour a 10-in. fluted tube pan. Finely grate enough zest from lemons to measure 2 Tbsp. zest. Cut lemons crosswise in half; squeeze juice from lemons to measure ¼ cup juice. Save remaining juice for another use.
2. In a large bowl, cream butter and sugar until light and fluffy, 5-7 minutes. Add 1 egg at a time, beating well after each addition. Beat in lemon juice and zest. In another bowl, whisk flour, baking powder, baking soda and salt; add to creamed mixture alternately with buttermilk, beating well after each addition.
3. Transfer batter to prepared pan. Bake until a toothpick inserted in the the center comes out clean, 50-60 minutes. Cool in pan 10 minutes before removing to a wire rack to cool.
4. Meanwhile, for topping, combine sugar and rhubarb in a small saucepan. Bring to a boil; reduce heat. Simmer until rhubarb is almost tender, 8-10 minutes. Add halved strawberries; cook until strawberries and rhubarb are softened. Serve with cake. If desired, dust with confectioners' sugar.
1 slice with ¼ cup sauce: 481 cal., 17g fat (10g sat. fat), 88mg chol., 371mg sod., 78g carb. (53g sugars, 2g fiber), 6g pro.

CREAMY
BISCOFF PIE

DOUGHNUT HOLE CAKE

This is the easiest yet most impressive cake I have ever made! Feel free to use chocolate, lemon or strawberry cake mix in the place of red velvet.

—Robert Pickart, Chicago, IL

Prep: 15 min. • **Bake:** 35 min. + cooling
Makes: 16 servings

32 vanilla cake doughnut holes
1 pkg. red velvet cake
    mix (regular size)
1 can (16 oz.) vanilla frosting

1. Preheat oven to 350°. Place 16 doughnut holes in each of 2 greased 8-in. round baking pans. Prepare cake mix according to package directions. Pour batter over the doughnuts, dividing evenly.
2. Bake until a toothpick inserted in cake comes out clean, 35-40 minutes. Cool in pans 10 minutes before removing to a wire rack to cool completely. Spread frosting between layers and over top of cake.
1 piece: 420 cal., 20g fat (7g sat.fat), 38mg chol., 401mg sod., 57g carb. (36g sugars, 1g fiber), 4g pro.

CREAMY BISCOFF PIE

I tasted Biscoff cookie butter at a grocery store one day, and it was so delicious that I decided to create a no-bake pie with it. You can also use peanut butter or another kind of spread and matching toppings.
—Katrina Adams, Mount Olive, AL

Prep: 20 min. + freezing
Makes: 2 pies (8 servings each)

1 pkg. (8 oz.) cream cheese, softened
1 cup Biscoff cookie butter spread
¾ cup confectioners' sugar
2 cartons (8 oz. each) frozen
    whipped topping, thawed, divided
    Two 9-in. graham cracker crusts
    (about 6 oz. each)
¼ cup caramel sundae syrup
4 Biscoff cookies, crushed

In a large bowl, beat cream cheese, cookie spread and confectioners' sugar until combined. Fold in 1 carton whipped topping. Divide between crusts. Top with remaining container whipped topping. Drizzle with syrup; sprinkle with cookie crumbs. Freeze, covered, until firm, at least 4 hours.
1 piece: 367 cal., 21g fat (10g sat. fat), 14mg chol., 187mg sod., 40g carb. (31g sugars, 0 fiber), 3g pro.

TEST KITCHEN TIP
You'll find Biscoff cookie butter spread near the peanut butter at your store, or online. Biscoff cookies will be located in the cookie aisle.

PEANUT BUTTER CHOCOLATE POKE CAKE

When my family is planning a get-together, I can count on three or four people asking me if I'm bringing this cake. If you don't have a chocolate cake mix, you can use a white or yellow one; just stir in 3 tablespoons of baking cocoa.
—Fay Moreland, Wichita Falls, TX

Prep: 20 min. • **Bake:** 25 min. + chilling
Makes: 20 servings

- 1 pkg. chocolate cake mix (regular size)
- 2 tsp. vanilla extract, divided
  Dash salt
- ⅔ cup creamy peanut butter
- 2 cans (14 oz. each) sweetened condensed milk
- 1 cup confectioners' sugar
  Topping: Chopped peanut butter cups, peanut butter-filled sandwich cookies or a combination of the two

1. Preheat oven to 350°. Prepare cake mix according to package directions, adding 1 tsp. vanilla and salt before mixing batter. Transfer to a greased 13x9-in. baking pan. Bake and cool completely as package directs.
2. Whisk the peanut butter and milk until blended. Using the end of a wooden spoon handle, poke holes in cake 2 in. apart. Slowly pour 2 cups peanut butter mixture over cake, filling each hole. Refrigerate cake and remaining peanut butter mixture, covered, until cake is cold, 2-3 hours.
3. Combine remaining 1 tsp. vanilla and remaining peanut butter mixture; gradually beat in enough of the confectioners' sugar to reach a spreading consistency. Spread frosting over cake. Add toppings as desired. Refrigerate leftovers.

1 piece: 360 cal., 16g fat (4g sat. fat), 41mg chol., 312mg sod., 49g carb. (40g sugars, 1g fiber), 7g pro.

BREAD PUDDING PIE

This unique dessert is a bread pudding-pie combination. It was created by my paternal grandmother's family. They had a farm and made their own bread, which made this an economical dessert.
—Kelly Barnes, Lexington, IN

Prep: 15 min. • **Bake:** 55 min. + chilling
Makes: 8 servings

  Pastry for single-crust pie
- 1 cup cubed bread
- 2 large eggs, room temperature
- 2 cups 2% milk
- ¾ cup sugar
- ½ tsp. vanilla extract
- ¼ tsp. ground nutmeg
- 2 tsp. butter

PEANUT BUTTER CHOCOLATE POKE CAKE

1. Preheat oven to 425°. On a floured surface, roll dough to fit a 9-in. pie plate. Trim and flute edge. Arrange the bread in bottom of pie crust. In a large bowl, whisk eggs, milk, sugar and vanilla; pour over the bread. Sprinkle with nutmeg and dot with butter. Bake 10 minutes. Reduce oven setting to 350°.
2. Bake until a knife inserted in the center comes out clean, 45-50 minutes longer. Cover edges of pie crust with foil during the last 15 minutes to prevent overbrowning if necessary. Cool on a wire rack for 1 hour. Refrigerate for at least 3 hours before serving.

1 piece: 314 cal., 15g fat (9g sat. fat), 84mg chol., 230mg sod., 39g carb. (22g sugars, 1g fiber), 6g pro.

Pastry for single-crust pie (9 in.): Combine 1¼ cups all-purpose flour and ¼ tsp. salt; cut in ½ cup cold butter until crumbly. Gradually add 3-5 Tbsp. ice water, tossing with a fork until dough holds together when pressed. Cover and refrigerate 1 hour.

WINNIE'S MINI RHUBARB
& STRAWBERRY PIES

BROWN SUGAR POUND CAKE

This tender pound cake is the first one
I mastered. The browned butter icing
tastes like pralines.
—Shawn Barto, Winter Garden, FL

Prep: 20 min. • **Bake:** 55 min. + cooling
Makes: 16 servings

1½ cups unsalted butter, softened
2¼ cups packed brown sugar
5   large eggs, room temperature
2   tsp. vanilla extract
3   cups all-purpose flour
1   tsp. baking powder
¼   tsp. salt
1   cup sour cream

GLAZE

3   Tbsp. unsalted butter
¼   cup chopped pecans
1   cup confectioners' sugar
¼   tsp. vanilla extract
     Dash salt
2   to 3 Tbsp. half-and-half cream

1. Preheat oven to 350°. Grease and flour
a 10-in. fluted tube pan.
2. Cream butter and brown sugar until light
and fluffy, 5-7 minutes. Add 1 egg at a time,
beating well after each addition. Beat in the
vanilla. In another bowl, whisk flour, baking
powder and salt; add to creamed mixture
alternately with sour cream, beating after
each addition just until combined.
3. Transfer to prepared pan. Bake until
a toothpick inserted in center comes out
clean, 55-65 minutes. Cool cake in pan for
10 minutes before removing to a wire rack
to cool completely.
4. For glaze, combine butter and pecans in
a small saucepan over medium heat, stirring
constantly, until butter is light golden brown,
4-5 minutes. Stir into confectioners' sugar.
Add vanilla, salt and enough cream to reach
a drizzling consistency. Drizzle glaze over
cake, allowing some to drip down sides. Let
stand until set.
1 slice: 473 cal., 25g fat (15g sat. fat), 121mg
chol., 193mg sod., 57g carb. (38g sugars, 1g
fiber), 5g pro.

TEST KITCHEN TIP

To remove cakes easily, use solid
shortening to grease plain and
fluted tube pans.

WINNIE'S MINI RHUBARB & STRAWBERRY PIES

Every spring, we had strawberries and
rhubarb on our farm outside Seattle. These
fruity hand pies remind me of those times
and of Grandma Winnie's baking.
—Shawn Carleton, San Diego, CA

Prep: 25 min. + chilling • **Bake:** 15 min.
Makes: 18 mini pies

3   Tbsp. quick-cooking tapioca
4   cups sliced fresh strawberries
2   cups sliced fresh rhubarb
¾   cup sugar
1   tsp. grated orange zest
1   tsp. vanilla extract
¼   tsp. salt
¼   tsp. ground cinnamon
3   drops red food coloring, optional
     Pastry for double-crust pie (9 in.)
     Sweetened whipped cream,
     optional

1. Place tapioca in a small food processor
or spice grinder; process until finely ground.
2. In a large saucepan, combine the sliced
strawberries, rhubarb, sugar, orange zest,
vanilla, salt, cinnamon, ground tapioca and,
if desired, food coloring; bring to a boil.
Reduce heat; simmer, covered, until the
strawberries are tender, stirring occasionally,
15-20 minutes. Transfer to a large bowl;
cover and refrigerate overnight.
3. Preheat oven to 425°. On a lightly floured
surface, roll half of dough to an 18-in. circle.
Cut 12 circles with a 4-in. biscuit cutter,
rerolling scraps as necessary; press crust
onto bottom and up sides of ungreased
muffin cups. Repeat with remaining dough,
cutting 6 more circles. Spoon strawberry
mixture into muffin cups.
4. Bake until filling is bubbly and crust
golden brown, 12-15 minutes. Cool in pan
5 minutes; remove to wire racks to cool. If
desired, serve with whipped cream.
1 mini pie: 207 cal., 10g fat (6g sat. fat),
27mg chol., 171mg sod., 27g carb. (11g
sugars, 1g fiber), 2g pro.

BROWN SUGAR
POUND CAKE

CHOCOLATE CHESS PIE

This is one of my mother's go-to recipes. It's a yummy spin on classic chocolate chess pie.
—Ann Dickens, Nixa, MO

- -

Prep: 30 min. • **Cook:** 40 min. + chilling
Makes: 8 servings

1¼ cups all-purpose flour
¼ tsp. salt
¼ cup cold butter, cubed
¼ cup shortening
3 to 4 Tbsp. ice water

FILLING

2 large eggs, room temperature
1 cup packed brown sugar
½ cup sugar
1½ oz. unsweetened chocolate, melted and cooled
2 Tbsp. 2% milk
1 Tbsp. all-purpose flour
1 tsp. vanilla extract
½ cup butter, melted

1. Combine flour and salt; cut in butter and shortening until crumbly. Gradually add ice water, tossing with a fork until dough holds together when pressed. Shape the dough into a disk. Wrap and refrigerate for 1 hour or overnight.

2. On a floured surface, roll the dough to fit a 9-in. pie plate. Trim and flute edge. Refrigerate 30 minutes. Preheat oven to 425°. Line unpricked crust with a double thickness of foil. Fill with pie weights. Bake on a lower oven rack until light golden brown, 15-20 minutes. Remove foil and weights; bake until bottom is golden brown, 3-6 minutes. Cool on a wire rack. Reduce oven setting to 325°.

3. In a large bowl, whisk eggs, sugars, melted chocolate, milk, flour and vanilla. Gradually whisk in butter. Pour into crust. Cover edge with foil to prevent overbrowning.

4. Bake at 325° until a knife inserted in the center comes out clean, 35-40 minutes. Remove foil. Cool on a wire rack. Refrigerate, covered, for 3 hours or until chilled.

1 piece: 436 cal., 22g fat (13g sat. fat), 93mg chol., 240mg sod., 57g carb. (40g sugars, 1g fiber), 5g pro.

CHOCOLATE CHESS PIE

LEMON-BERRY ICE CREAM PIE

I love the combination of fresh strawberries and lemon curd. It's so refreshing, especially in an easy make-ahead dessert like this ice cream pie.
—Roxanne Chan, Albany, CA

Prep: 15 min. + freezing • **Makes:** 8 servings

 1 pint strawberry ice cream, softened
 1 graham cracker crust (9 in.)
 1 cup lemon curd
 2 cups frozen whipped topping, thawed
 1 pint fresh strawberries, halved

1. Spoon ice cream into pie crust; freeze 2 hours or until firm.
2. Spread lemon curd over ice cream; top with whipped topping. Freeze, covered, 4 hours or until firm.
3. Remove from freezer 10 minutes before serving. Serve with strawberries.
1 piece: 370 cal., 13g fat (7g sat. fat), 40mg chol., 171mg sod., 58g carb. (40g sugars, 1g fiber), 2g pro.

TEST KITCHEN TIP

When purchasing strawberries, look for brightly colored, plump and fragrant berries with the green hulls intact. Avoid any that are soft, shriveled or moldy. Wash berries before removing hulls. One pint of strawberries yields 1½-2 cups sliced.

YELLOW LAYER CAKE WITH CHOCOLATE BUTTERCREAM

This will become your go-to recipe for birthdays, but the tender yellow cake with flavorful chocolate buttercream is perfect for any occasion.
—*Taste of Home* Test Kitchen

Prep: 15 min. • **Bake:** 25 min. + cooling
Makes: 16 servings

 ⅔ cup butter, softened
 1¾ cups sugar
 2 large eggs, room temperature
 1½ tsp. vanilla extract
 2½ cups all-purpose flour
 2½ tsp. baking powder
 ½ tsp. salt
 1¼ cups 2% milk

CHOCOLATE BUTTERCREAM
 2 cups butter, softened
 4 cups confectioners' sugar, sifted
 ½ cup Dutch-processed cocoa, sifted
 1½ tsp. vanilla extract
 ⅛ tsp. salt
 ⅓ cup 2% milk

1. Preheat oven to 350°. Grease and flour two 9-in. round baking pans. In a large bowl, cream butter and sugar until light and fluffy, 5-7 minutes. Add eggs, 1 at a time, beating well after each addition. Beat in vanilla. In another bowl, whisk flour, baking powder and salt; add to creamed mixture alternately with milk, beating well after each addition.
2. Transfer to prepared pans. Bake until a toothpick inserted in the center comes out clean, 25-30 minutes. Cool in pans for 10 minutes before removing to wire racks to cool completely.
3. For buttercream, in a large bowl, beat butter until creamy. Gradually beat in confectioners' sugar and cocoa until smooth. Add vanilla and salt. Add milk; beat until light and fluffy, about 5 minutes.
4. Spread buttercream between layers and over top and sides of cake.
1 piece: 593 cal., 33g fat (21g sat. fat), 107mg chol., 432mg sod., 72g carb. (53g sugars, 4g fiber), 5g pro.

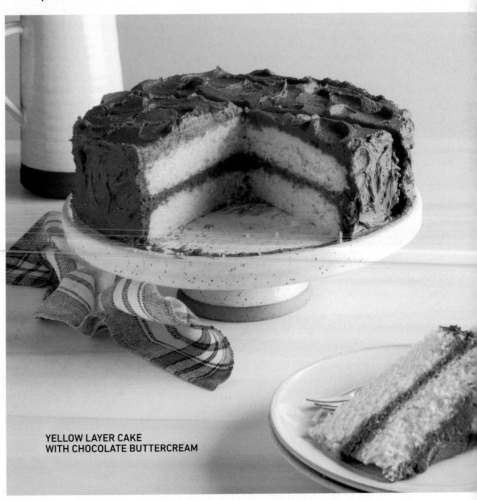

YELLOW LAYER CAKE WITH CHOCOLATE BUTTERCREAM

EASY PISTACHIO TUBE CAKE

Mixes make this light cake a breeze to bake, and a Bundt pan gets it party-ready. Go for the pistachios on top—the extra crunch is worth it.
—Dina Crowell, Fredericksburg, VA

- -

Prep: 15 min. • **Bake:** 35 min. + cooling
Makes: 12 servings

- 1 pkg. yellow cake mix (regular size)
- 1 pkg. (3.4 oz.) instant pistachio pudding mix
- 4 large eggs, room temperature
- 1½ cups water
- ¼ cup canola oil
- ½ tsp. almond extract
  Confectioners' sugar
  Finely chopped pistachios, optional

1. Preheat oven to 350°. Grease and flour a 10-in. fluted tube pan.
2. In a large bowl, combine the first 6 ingredients; beat on low speed 30 seconds. Beat on medium 2 minutes. Transfer to prepared pan. Bake until a toothpick inserted in center comes out clean, 35-40 minutes. Cool in pan 10 minutes before removing to a wire rack to cool completely.
3. Dust with confectioners' sugar. If desired, sprinkle with pistachios.
1 slice: 266 cal., 10g fat (2g sat. fat), 62mg chol., 416mg sod., 41g carb. (24g sugars, 0 fiber), 4g pro.

EASY BOURBON PECAN PIE

This pecan pie has a mellow bourbon flavor—not too strong and not too sweet. It's crunchy, chewy and easy to make.
—Nick Iverson, Denver, CO

- -

Prep: 10 min. + freezing
Bake: 1¼ hours + cooling
Makes: 10 servings

- 12 oz. toasted pecan halves, divided
- 4 large eggs, room temperature
- ½ cup packed dark brown sugar
- ¼ cup sugar
- 1 cup dark corn syrup
- 8 Tbsp. unsalted butter, melted
- ¼ cup bourbon
- 2 tsp. vanilla extract
- ¼ tsp. salt
- 1 sheet refrigerated pie crust
  Vanilla ice cream, optional

1. In a food processor, pulse half the pecans until coarsely chopped; reserve remaining pecans. Combine eggs and sugars until well mixed. Add the next 5 ingredients and the chopped pecans.
2. Unroll crust into a 9-in. metal pie plate; flute edge. Pour filling into crust. Arrange reserved pecan halves over filling. Place filled pie in freezer for 30 minutes.
3. Preheat oven to 425°. Bake until crust is set, about 15 minutes. Reduce oven setting to 350°; continue baking until pie is puffed and set in the middle, about 1 hour (tent loosely with aluminum foil if needed to prevent overbrowning). Cool. If desired, serve with vanilla ice cream.
1 piece: 600 cal., 41g fat (11g sat. fat), 103mg chol., 221mg sod., 56g carb. (43g sugars, 3g fiber), 7g pro.

EASY BOURBON PECAN PIE

**RASPBERRY MOSCOW
MULE CAKE**

CHOCOLATE
CHEESECAKE PIE

Guests always ask for seconds of this rich but simple pie. I top it with fresh raspberries or cherry pie filling.
—Sandy Schwartz, Brooklyn, NY

Takes: 30 min. • **Makes:** 8 servings

- 1 pkg. (8 oz.) cream cheese, softened
- ¼ cup butter, softened
- ⅓ cup sugar
- 1½ tsp. vanilla extract
- 1½ cups milk chocolate chips, melted and cooled
- 1 carton (8 oz.) frozen whipped topping, thawed
- 1 graham cracker crust (9 in.) Chocolate curls, optional

In a large bowl, beat cream cheese, butter, sugar and vanilla until smooth. Beat in cooled chocolate. Fold in whipped topping. Spoon filling into crust. Refrigerate until serving. Decorate with chocolate curls as desired.
1 piece: 535 cal., 35g fat (20g sat. fat), 53mg chol., 270mg sod., 48g carb. (38g sugars, 1g fiber), 6g pro.

TEST KITCHEN TIP

To speed up the softening process for cream cheese, place the sealed package in a bowl of warm water.

RASPBERRY MOSCOW
MULE CAKE

This cake was inspired by my favorite cocktail—the Moscow mule. It's so moist and flavorful, and the best cake I have ever made from scratch.
—Becky Hardin, St. Peters, MO

Prep: 25 min. • **Bake:** 70 min. + cooling
Makes: 16 servings

- 1½ cups unsalted butter, softened
- 2¾ cups sugar
- 5 large eggs, room temperature
- 1 Tbsp. vanilla extract
- 3 cups cake flour
- ½ tsp. salt
- 1 cup alcoholic raspberry ginger beer or nonalcoholic plain ginger beer
- 2 cups fresh raspberries

SYRUP
- ½ cup alcoholic raspberry ginger beer or nonalcoholic plain ginger beer
- ½ cup sugar
- ¼ cup lime juice

GLAZE
- 1½ cups confectioners' sugar
- 2 to 3 Tbsp. lime juice

1. Preheat oven to 325°. Grease and flour a 10-in. fluted tube pan.
2. In a large bowl, cream the butter and sugar until light and fluffy, 5-7 minutes. Add eggs, 1 at a time, beating well after each addition. Beat in vanilla. In another bowl, whisk cake flour and salt; add to the creamed mixture alternately with ginger beer, beating well after each addition (the mixture may appear curdled).
3. Gently fold raspberries into batter; pour into prepared pan. Bake until a toothpick inserted in center comes out clean, 70-80 minutes. Meanwhile, for syrup, in a small saucepan, bring ginger beer, sugar and lime juice to a boil. Reduce the heat; simmer 10 minutes. Cool slightly.
4. Poke holes in warm cake using a fork or wooden skewer. Slowly spoon syrup over cake. Cool 15 minutes before removing from pan to a wire rack; cool completely. For the glaze, in a small bowl, mix the confectioners' sugar and enough lime juice to reach desired consistency; pour over cake. Let stand until set. If desired, top the cake with additional fresh raspberries.
1 piece: 488 cal., 19g fat (11g sat. fat), 104mg chol., 100mg sod., 75g carb. (53g sugars, 1g fiber), 5g pro.

COOKIE CAKE

COOKIE CAKE

This oversized cookie "cake" is so easy and quick, I'm tempted to make it my go-to cookie treat. I won't miss portioning out batter for individual cookies or shuffling pans in and out of the oven. Store leftovers in an airtight container for up to a week.
—Lisa Kaminski, Associate Digital Editor

Prep: 15 min. • **Bake:** 20 min. + cooling
Makes: 8 servings

- ¾ cup butter, softened
- ½ cup sugar
- ½ cup packed brown sugar
- 1 large egg plus 1 large egg yolk, room temperature
- 2 tsp. vanilla extract
- 2 cups all-purpose flour
- 2 tsp. cornstarch
- 1 tsp. baking soda
- ¼ tsp. salt
- 1 cup semisweet chocolate chips

FROSTING
- ½ cup butter, softened
- 4½ cups confectioners' sugar
- 1½ tsp. vanilla extract
- 5 to 6 Tbsp. 2% milk
  Optional: Food coloring and sprinkles

1. Preheat oven to 350°. Line the bottom of a 9-in. springform pan with parchment. In a large bowl, cream butter and sugars until light and fluffy, 5-7 minutes. Beat in egg, egg yolk and vanilla. In another bowl, whisk flour, cornstarch, baking soda and salt; gradually beat into creamed mixture. Stir in chips. Press onto the bottom of prepared pan.
2. Bake until golden brown, 20-25 minutes. Cool on a wire rack 10 minutes. Loosen sides from pan with a knife; cool completely. Remove rim from pan. Carefully remove cookie cake from bottom pan; transfer to serving platter.
3. In a large bowl, beat softened butter, confectioners' sugar, vanilla and enough milk to reach piping consistency. If desired, beat in food coloring. Pipe around edge of cookie cake. If desired, garnish with sprinkles.
1 piece: 861 cal., 37g fat (23g sat. fat), 123mg chol., 482mg sod., 132g carb. (104g sugars, 2g fiber), 6g pro.

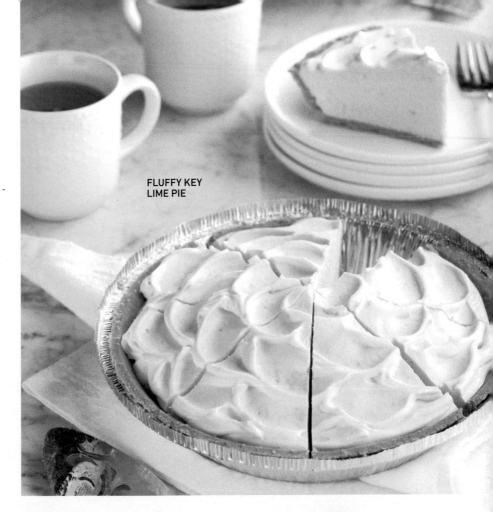

FLUFFY KEY LIME PIE

FLUFFY KEY LIME PIE

For a taste of paradise, try this light and creamy tropical confection. It's low in fat, sugar and fuss. Dessert doesn't get any better than that!
—Frances VanFossan, Warren, MI

Prep: 20 min. + chilling • **Makes:** 8 servings

- ¼ cup boiling water
- 1 pkg. (0.3 oz.) sugar-free lime gelatin
- 2 cartons (6 oz. each) Key lime yogurt
- 1 carton (8 oz.) frozen fat-free whipped topping, thawed
- 1 reduced-fat graham cracker crust (8 in.)

1. In a large bowl, add boiling water to the gelatin; stir 2 minutes to completely dissolve. Whisk in yogurt. Fold in whipped topping. Pour into crust.
2. Refrigerate, covered, until set, about 2 hours.
1 piece: 194 cal., 3g fat (1g sat. fat), 2mg chol., 159mg sod., 33g carb. (18g sugars, 0 fiber), 3g pro. **Diabetic exchanges:** 2 starch, ½ fat.

ASK SARAH

WHAT EXTRA GARNISHES CAN I ADD TO THIS NO-BAKE KEY LIME PIE?

After that stay in the fridge, this Key lime pie is ready for some final touches. To give it extra tropical flair, sprinkle toasted coconut over the top to give the pie some crunch and extra color. If you have fresh Key limes, garnish with a few slices and some stemmed maraschino cherries. And don't forgot everyone's favorite finishing touch—whipped cream!

OLIVE OIL CAKE

A good olive oil cake isn't overly sweet, so it can just as easily be a breakfast treat or an afternoon snack as a dessert.
—Lisa Kaminski, Associate Digital Editor

- -

Prep: 15 min. • **Bake:** 45 min. + cooling
Makes: 16 servings

  3 **large eggs, room temperature**
1½ **cups sugar**
 ¾ **cup extra virgin olive oil**
 ¾ **cup ground almonds**
 ½ **cup 2% milk**
  4 **tsp. grated orange zest**
  1 **tsp. vanilla extract**
1¾ **cups all-purpose flour**
  2 **tsp. baking powder**
 ½ **tsp. salt**
 ¾ **cup confectioners' sugar**
  2 **to 3 Tbsp. orange juice**
     Sliced almonds, toasted, optional

1. Preheat oven to 350°. Grease and flour a 10-in. fluted tube pan. In a large bowl, beat eggs on high speed 3 minutes. Gradually add sugar, beating until thick and lemon-colored. Gradually beat in olive oil. Beat in ground almonds, milk, orange zest and vanilla.
2. In another bowl, whisk flour, baking powder and salt; fold into egg mixture. Transfer batter to prepared pan, spreading evenly. Bake until a toothpick inserted in the cake comes out clean, 45-50 minutes. Cool in pan 15 minutes before removing to a wire rack to cool completely.
3. For icing, in a small bowl, whisk the confectioners' sugar and enough orange juice to achieve a drizzling consistency. Drizzle over cake. If desired, sprinkle with toasted almonds.
1 piece: 279 cal., 14g fat (2g sat. fat), 35mg chol., 152mg sod., 37g carb. (25g sugars, 1g fiber), 4g pro.

> ### TEST KITCHEN TIP
> For a fun flavor twist, try this cake with ground pistachios and lemon zest instead of the almonds and orange zest.

EASY PEANUT BUTTER & PRETZEL PIE

Crispy, salty pretzel crust is just begging for a creamy no-bake peanut butter filling and a layer of chocolate ganache.
—Gina Nistico, Denver, CO

- -

Prep: 10 min. • **Bake:** 15 min. + chilling
Makes: 8 servings

2¾ **cups crushed pretzel sticks**
  1 **cup sugar, divided**
 ¾ **cup butter, melted**
  1 **envelope unflavored gelatin**
 ¼ **cup cold water**
  1 **cup creamy peanut butter**
 ¼ **cup butter, softened**
  2 **oz. cream cheese, softened**
 ¾ **cup heavy whipping cream, divided**
 ½ **cup milk chocolate chips**
     Additional crushed pretzel sticks, optional

1. Preheat oven to 350°. Combine crushed pretzels and ⅓ cup sugar with melted butter. Using the bottom of a glass, press onto bottom and up the sides of a greased 9-in. deep-dish pie plate. Bake until set, 12-15 minutes. Cool completely on a wire rack.
2. Meanwhile, sprinkle gelatin over cold water; let stand 5 minutes. Beat peanut butter, softened butter, cream cheese and remaining sugar until smooth. Gradually beat in ½ cup cream. Microwave gelatin on high until melted, about 10 seconds; stir into peanut butter mixture. Transfer to crust.
3. Microwave milk chocolate chips and remaining cream on high; stir until smooth. Cool slightly. Spread chocolate mixture over peanut butter mixture. If desired, top with additional crushed pretzels. Refrigerate, covered, until set, about 3 hours.
1 piece: 750 cal., 54g fat (26g sat. fat), 96mg chol., 738mg sod., 60g carb. (36g sugars, 3g fiber), 13g pro.

PLUM UPSIDE-DOWN CAKE

The delicate flavor of plums is a pleasing change of pace in this upside-down cake.
—Bobbie Talbott, Veneta, OR

Prep: 15 min. • **Bake:** 40 min.
Makes: 10 servings

⅓   cup butter
½   cup packed brown sugar
1¾ to 2 lbs. medium plums, pitted and halved
2   large eggs, room temperature
⅔   cup sugar
1   cup all-purpose flour
1   tsp. baking powder
¼   tsp. salt
⅓   cup hot water
½   tsp. lemon extract
    Whipped cream, optional

1. Melt the butter in a 10-in. cast-iron or other ovenproof skillet. Sprinkle brown sugar over butter. Arrange the plum halves, cut side down, in a single layer over sugar; set aside.

2. In a large bowl, beat eggs until thick and lemon-colored; gradually beat in sugar. Combine the flour, baking powder and salt; add to egg mixture and mix well. Blend water and lemon extract; beat into batter. Pour over plums.

3. Bake at 350° until a toothpick inserted in the center comes out clean, 40-45 minutes. Immediately invert onto a serving plate. Serve warm, with whipped cream if desired.

1 piece: 245 cal., 7g fat (4g sat. fat), 53mg chol., 173mg sod., 43g carb. (32g sugars, 1g fiber), 3g pro.

FRESH RASPBERRY ICEBOX CAKE

Layered icebox cakes are so fun because they look impressive but couldn't be easier. Fresh raspberries make this one extra special. If you can find them at your grocer, use Anna's Ginger Thins with scalloped edges. Regular gingersnaps are fine, too.
—Elisabeth Larsen, Pleasant Grove, UT

Prep: 25 min. + chilling • **Makes:** 12 servings

1   carton (8 oz.) mascarpone cheese
3   cups cold heavy whipping cream
2   Tbsp. sugar
2   Tbsp. grated lemon zest (about 2 lemons)
2   pkg. (5¼ oz. each) thin ginger cookies
5   cups fresh raspberries (about 20 oz.), divided

1. Stir mascarpone cheese; let stand at room temperature 30 minutes. Meanwhile, beat cream until it begins to thicken. Add sugar; beat until soft peaks form. Reserve ½ cup thickened cream; cover and refrigerate. Add lemon zest and mascarpone to remaining whipped cream; beat until stiff peaks form, 30-60 seconds.

2. On a serving plate, spread ½ cup of the cream mixture in a 7-in.-diameter circle. Arrange 6 cookies in a circle on top of the cream, placing a seventh cookie in the center. Gently fold 4 cups of raspberries into remaining cream mixture. Spoon about 1 cup raspberry cream mixture over the cookies. Repeat layers 6 times, ending with cookies (there will be 8 cookie layers in all). Spread reserved whipped cream over the cookies; top with remaining raspberries. Refrigerate, covered, overnight.

1 piece: 421 cal., 35g fat (21g sat. fat), 91mg chol., 132mg sod., 25g carb. (13g sugars, 3g fiber), 4g pro.

PLUM
UPSIDE-DOWN CAKE

BLUEBERRIES & CREAM COFFEE CAKE

Growing up, my boys enjoyed this blueberry coffee cake as a Saturday morning tradition. It's also my go-to recipe for all of our holiday parties because it's perfect for brunch or dessert. It's easy to make and so delicious.
—Susan Ober, Franconia, NH

- -

Prep: 20 min. • **Bake:** 55 min. + cooling
Makes: 12 servings

- 1 **cup butter, softened**
- 2 **cups sugar**
- 2 **large eggs, room temperature**
- 1 **tsp. vanilla extract**
- 1¾ **cups all-purpose flour**
- 1 **tsp. baking powder**
- ¼ **tsp. salt**
- 1 **cup sour cream**
- 1 **cup fresh or frozen unsweetened blueberries**
- ½ **cup packed brown sugar**
- ½ **cup chopped pecans, optional**
- 1 **tsp. ground cinnamon**
- 1 **Tbsp. confectioners' sugar**

1. In a large bowl, cream butter and sugar until light and fluffy, 5-7 minutes. Add eggs, 1 at a time, beating well after each addition. Beat in vanilla. Combine the flour, baking powder and salt; add to the creamed mixture alternately with sour cream, beating well after each addition. Fold in blueberries.
2. Spoon half of batter into a greased and floured 10-in. fluted tube pan. In a small bowl, combine the brown sugar, pecans if desired, and cinnamon. Sprinkle half over the batter. Top with the remaining batter; sprinkle with the remaining brown sugar mixture. Cut through batter with a knife to swirl the brown sugar mixture.
3. Bake at 350° until a toothpick inserted in center comes out clean, 55-60 minutes. Cool for 10 minutes before removing from pan to a wire rack to cool completely. Just before serving, dust with confectioners' sugar.
1 slice: 428 cal., 20g fat (12g sat. fat), 76mg chol., 233mg sod., 60g carb. (45g sugars, 1g fiber), 4g pro.

EASY LEMON PIE

EASY LEMON PIE

I've had this one-bowl lemon pie recipe for years. It's my twist on chocolate French silk pie, and it's easy to make with refrigerated pie pastry.
—Glenna Tooman, Boise, ID

- -

Prep: 15 min. • **Bake:** 40 min. + chilling
Makes: 8 servings

- 1 **sheet refrigerated pie crust**
- ½ **cup sugar**
- 2 **Tbsp. all-purpose flour**
- 4 **large eggs, room temperature**
- 1 **cup light corn syrup**
- 1 **tsp. grated lemon zest**
- ⅓ **cup lemon juice**
- 2 **Tbsp. butter, melted**
WHIPPED CREAM
- 1 **cup heavy whipping cream**
- 2 **Tbsp. confectioners' sugar**

1. Preheat oven to 350°. Unroll crust into a 9-in. pie plate; flute edge. Refrigerate while preparing filling.
2. In a bowl, mix the sugar and flour until blended. Whisk in eggs, corn syrup, lemon zest, lemon juice and melted butter until blended. Pour into crust.
3. Bake on a lower oven rack until filling is golden brown and thickened, 40-45 minutes; cover edge loosely with foil during the last 15 minutes if needed to prevent overbrowning. Remove foil; cool for 1 hour on a wire rack. Refrigerate, covered, 2 hours or until cold.
4. For whipped cream, in a bowl, beat cream until it begins to thicken. Add confectioners' sugar; beat until soft peaks form. Serve pie with whipped cream.
1 piece: 475 cal., 23g fat (13g sat. fat), 147mg chol., 197mg sod., 65g carb. (50g sugars, 0 fiber), 5g pro.

BLUEBERRIES &
CREAM COFFEE CAKE

TASTE OF HOME
TEST
KITCHEN
RECIPE OF THE YEAR
★★★★★

CHOCOLATE-PEANUT BUTTER DUMP CAKE

I am a huge fan of the chocolate-peanut butter combination. I'm also a fan of easy recipes, including dump cakes. On occasion, I've omitted the peanut butter chips from this recipe and used 1½ cups semisweet chocolate chips with delicious results.
—Lisa Varner, El Paso, TX

Prep: 15 min. • **Bake:** 20 min. + cooling
Makes: 15 servings

1 pkg. (3.9 oz.) instant chocolate pudding mix
1¾ cups 2% milk
1 pkg. chocolate cake mix or devil's food cake mix (regular size)
6 pkg. (1½ oz. each) peanut butter cups, chopped
¾ cup peanut butter chips
¾ cup semisweet chocolate chips
½ cup chopped unsalted peanuts
    Vanilla ice cream or sweetened whipped cream, optional

1. Preheat oven to 350°. Grease a 13x9-in. baking pan. In a large bowl, combine the pudding mix and milk until blended. Stir in cake mix (batter will be thick). Fold in the peanut butter cups, peanut butter chips and chocolate chips. Spread into prepared pan. Sprinkle with peanuts.
2. Bake until a toothpick inserted in the center comes out with moist crumbs, 20-25 minutes. Cool completely in pan on a wire rack. Serve with ice cream or whipped cream if desired.
1 piece: 349 cal., 14g fat (6g sat. fat), 3mg chol., 373mg sod., 51g carb. (33g sugars, 3g fiber), 7g pro.

TEST KITCHEN TIP
The toothpick test is the easiest way to test a cake to see if it's done. If you can't find a toothpick, get creative! Try a bamboo skewer or a sharp paring knife. If you don't have anything to pierce your cake, try pressing the top of the cake. If it springs back, it's ready to come out of the oven.

CHOCOLATE-PEANUT BUTTER DUMP CAKE

PATCHWORK QUILT CAKE

This cake has a great homemade flavor. The buttery frosting adds a burst of vanilla.
—Aria Thornton, Milwaukee, WI

Prep: 55 min. • **Bake:** 40 min. + cooling
Makes: 15 servings

- ⅔ cup butter, softened
- 1¾ cups sugar
- 1 Tbsp. vanilla extract
- 2 large eggs, room temperature
- 2½ cups all-purpose flour
- 2½ tsp. baking powder
- ½ tsp. salt
- 1¼ cups 2% milk

FROSTING

- 1 cup butter, softened
- 3 cups confectioners' sugar
- 4 tsp. vanilla extract
- 3 to 4 Tbsp. heavy whipping cream
  Assorted fresh berries

1. Preheat oven to 350°. Grease a 13x9-in. baking dish.
2. Cream butter and sugar until light and fluffy, 5-7 minutes. Add vanilla and eggs, 1 at at time, beating well. In another bowl, whisk together flour, baking powder and salt; beat into creamed mixture alternately with milk. Transfer to prepared dish.
3. Bake until a toothpick inserted in center comes out clean, 40-45 minutes. Place on a wire rack; cool completely.
4. For frosting, beat butter until creamy; gradually beat in confectioners' sugar until smooth and light in color, about 3 minutes. Beat in vanilla and 3 Tbsp. cream until light and fluffy, about 2 minutes; thin frosting with additional cream if desired. Spread over cake. Before serving, top with berries in a patchwork quilt pattern.
1 piece: 477 cal., 23g fat (14g sat. fat), 84mg chol., 342mg sod., 65g carb. (48g sugars, 1g fiber), 4g pro.

DOUBLE BUTTERSCOTCH COCONUT CAKE

I got this recipe for coconut cake from a co-worker years ago, then I changed it up a bit by adding a family favorite: butterscotch. It's easy to throw together and makes a perfect accompaniment to coffee or tea.
—Marina Castle Kelley, Canyon Country, CA

Prep: 20 min. • **Bake:** 40 min. + cooling
Makes: 16 servings

- 1 pkg. yellow cake mix (regular size)
- 1 pkg. (3.4 oz.) instant butterscotch pudding mix
- 4 large eggs, room temperature
- 1 cup canned coconut milk
- ¼ cup canola oil
- 1 cup sweetened shredded coconut
- ½ cup butterscotch chips

GLAZE

- ½ cup butterscotch chips
- 2 Tbsp. heavy whipping cream
- ⅓ cup sweetened shredded coconut, toasted

1. Preheat oven to 350°. Grease and flour a 10-in. fluted tube pan.
2. In a large bowl, combine the cake mix, pudding mix, eggs, coconut milk and canola oil; beat on low speed 30 seconds. Beat on medium speed for 2 minutes. Stir in the coconut and butterscotch chips. Transfer to prepared pan.
3. Bake until a toothpick inserted in center comes out clean, 40-45 minutes. Cool in pan 10 minutes before removing to a wire rack to cool completely. For glaze, in a microwave, melt butterscotch chips and cream; stir until smooth. Drizzle over cake; sprinkle with toasted coconut.
1 slice: 327 cal., 15g fat (10g sat. fat), 49mg chol., 359mg sod., 42g carb. (30g sugars, 1g fiber), 4g pro.

"This Bundt cake takes five seconds to whip together and has a solid—not too sweet—butterscotch flavor."

—MARGARET KNOEBEL, CULINARY ASSISTANT

DOUBLE BUTTERSCOTCH COCONUT CAKE

DOUBLE-CRUST RHUBARB PIE

Old-fashioned and delicious, rhubarb pie is springtime comfort food. The first time I made this pie was when my husband and I started dating. He loved it, and I've made it many times since. I recommend placing a baking sheet under this pie while bakes as the filling sometimes runs over.
—Lavonn Bormuth, Westerville, OH

Prep: 20 min. • **Bake:** 45 min. + cooling
Makes: 8 servings

- 1 cup sugar
- 3 Tbsp. all-purpose flour
- ½ tsp. ground cinnamon
- 2 large eggs, lightly beaten, room temperature
- 4 cups chopped fresh rhubarb or frozen rhubarb
   Pastry for double-crust pie (9 in.)
- 1 Tbsp. butter

1. In a large bowl, combine sugar, flour and cinnamon. Add eggs; whisk until smooth. Gently stir in rhubarb. Line a 9-in. pie plate with pastry; add filling. Dot with butter.
2. Roll out remaining pastry to fit top of pie; place over filling. Trim, seal and flute edges. Cut slits in top.
3. Bake at 400° until crust is golden brown and filling is bubbly, 45-50 minutes. Cool on a wire rack. Store in the refrigerator.
1 piece: 392 cal., 17g fat (7g sat. fat), 67mg chol., 233mg sod., 56g carb. (28g sugars, 1g fiber), 4g pro.

TEST KITCHEN TIP
Buy fresh rhubarb in season, cut it up and freeze it so you can enjoy this pie any time of year. If using frozen rhubarb, measure the fruit while still frozen, then thaw completely. Drain in a colander, but do not press liquid out.

EASY STRAWBERRY LEMONADE FREEZER PIE

EASY STRAWBERRY LEMONADE FREEZER PIE

Three simple ingredients mixed together and spread into a graham crust make magic while your freezer does the all the work. Make this pie ahead and freeze it overnight or even longer. Feel free to vary the fruit.
—Debbie Glasscock, Conway, AR

Prep: 15 min. + freezing • **Makes:** 8 servings

- 1 container (23.2 oz.) frozen sweetened sliced strawberries, thawed (2½ cups thawed)
- 1 pkg. (3.4 oz.) instant lemon pudding mix
- 1 carton (8 oz.) frozen whipped topping, thawed
   One 9-in. graham cracker crust (about 6 oz.)
   Optional: Additional whipped topping and fresh strawberries

1. In a large bowl, combine the strawberries (with juices) and pudding mix; let stand until slightly thickened, about 5 minutes. Fold in the whipped topping. Spread into graham cracker crust.
2. Freeze at least 8 hours or overnight. Let stand 5-10 minutes before serving. If desired, serve with additional whipped topping and fresh strawberries.
1 piece: 306 cal., 10g fat (6g sat. fat), 0 chol., 273mg sod., 51g carb. (45g sugars, 2g fiber), 1g pro.

CONFETTI BIRTHDAY CAKE

Here's a moist and fluffy vanilla cake with lots of sprinkles and a whipped vanilla buttercream. It's almost impossible not to feel happy when you see the fun pop of rainbow confetti!
—Courtney Rich, Highland, UT

- -

Prep: 30 min. • **Bake:** 35 min. + cooling
Makes: 16 servings

- 1 cup unsalted butter, room temperature
- ⅓ cup vegetable oil
- 1¾ cups sugar
- 3 large eggs, room temperature
- 3 large egg whites, room temperature
- 1 Tbsp. vanilla extract
- 3 cups cake flour
- 2 tsp. baking powder
- 1 tsp. salt
- 1 cup buttermilk, room temperature
- ¼ cup rainbow sprinkles

BUTTERCREAM

- 1½ cups unsalted butter, softened
- 4½ cups confectioners' sugar, sifted
- 3 Tbsp. heavy whipping cream
- 2 tsp. clear vanilla extract
  Soft pink paste food coloring

1. Preheat oven to 325°. Grease a 13x9-in. baking dish. In a large bowl, cream butter, oil and sugar until light and fluffy, 5-7 minutes. Add eggs, then egg whites, 1 at a time, beating well after each addition. Beat in vanilla. In another bowl, whisk flour, baking powder and salt; add to creamed mixture alternately with buttermilk, beating well after each addition. Fold in sprinkles.

2. Transfer to prepared pan. Bake until a toothpick inserted in center comes out clean, 35-40 minutes. Cool completely on a wire rack.

3. For buttercream, in a large bowl, beat butter until creamy. Gradually beat in the confectioners' sugar until smooth. Add cream, vanilla and food coloring. Beat until light and fluffy, 5-7 minutes. Frost top of cake with frosting, and top with additional sprinkles if desired.

1 piece: 823 cal., 47g fat (26g sat. fat), 138mg chol., 279mg sod., 97g carb. (75g sugars, 0 fiber), 6g pro.

EASY GRASSHOPPER ICE CREAM PIE

This quick pie is such an ego booster! My family gives me compliments the entire time they're eating it. A big hit at work potlucks, too, it's good to the last crumb.
—Kim Murphy, Albia, IA

- -

Prep: 15 min. + freezing • **Makes:** 8 servings

- 4 cups mint chocolate chip ice cream, softened
- 1 chocolate crumb crust (8 in.)
- 5 Oreo cookies, chopped
- ⅓ cup chocolate-covered peppermint candies
  Chocolate hard-shell ice cream topping

Spread ice cream into crust. Sprinkle with cookies and candies; drizzle with ice cream topping. Freeze until firm. Remove from the freezer 15 minutes before serving.
Note: This recipe was tested with Junior Mints chocolate-covered peppermint candies.
1 piece: 374 cal., 19g fat (9g sat. fat), 25g chol., 182g sod., 47g carb. (35g sugar, 1g fiber), 4g pro.

CONFETTI BIRTHDAY CAKE

Desserts

There's always room for dessert! Whether you need a homemade tart for an upcoming potluck, a velvety cheesecake to contribute to a dinner party or a no-fuss sweet specialty to surprise your family, you're sure to find the perfect grand finale among these knock-'em-dead desserts.

STRAWBERRY BUTTERMILK
SKILLET SHORTCAKE
PAGE 246

PRETTY
PEACH TART

PRETTY PEACH TART

When ripe peaches finally arrive at local fruit stands, this is the first recipe I reach for. The tart is perfection—a delightful way to celebrate spring's arrival. You can make the tart with other varieties of fruit, too.
—Lorraine Caland, Shuniah, ON

- -

Prep: 30 min. • **Bake:** 40 min. + cooling
Makes: 8 servings

- ¼ cup butter, softened
- 3 Tbsp. sugar
- ¼ tsp. ground nutmeg
- 1 cup all-purpose flour

FILLING
- 2 lbs. peaches (about 7 medium), peeled and sliced
- ⅓ cup sugar
- 2 Tbsp. all-purpose flour
- ¼ tsp. ground cinnamon
- ⅛ tsp. almond extract
- ¼ cup sliced almonds
  Whipped cream, optional

1. Preheat oven to 375°. Cream the butter, sugar and nutmeg until light and fluffy, 5-7 minutes. Beat in the flour until blended (mixture will be dry). Press the dough firmly onto bottom and up sides of an ungreased 9-in. fluted tart pan with removable bottom.
2. Place on a baking sheet. Bake on a middle oven rack until the crust is lightly browned, 10-12 minutes. Cool on a wire rack.
3. In a large bowl, toss peaches with sugar, flour, cinnamon and extract; add to crust. Sprinkle with almonds.
4. Bake tart on a lower oven rack until the crust is golden brown and the peaches are tender, 40-45 minutes. Cool on a wire rack. If desired, serve with whipped cream.
1 piece: 222 cal., 8g fat (4g sat. fat), 15mg chol., 46mg sod., 36g carb. (21g sugars, 3g fiber), 4g pro.

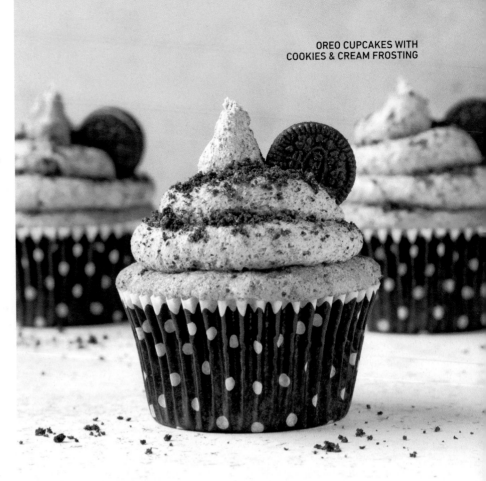

OREO CUPCAKES WITH COOKIES & CREAM FROSTING

OREO CUPCAKES WITH COOKIES & CREAM FROSTING

No one will be able to resist these Oreo cupcakes. If you want to pipe the frosting, be sure to thoroughly crush the Oreos.
—*Taste of Home* Test Kitchen

- -

Prep: 20 min. • **Bake:** 20 min. + cooling
Makes: 2 dozen

- ⅔ cup butter, softened
- 1¾ cups sugar
- 2 large eggs, room temperature
- 1½ tsp. vanilla extract
- 2½ cups all-purpose flour
- 2½ tsp. baking powder
- ½ tsp. salt
- 1¼ cups 2% milk
- 2 cups coarsely crushed Oreo cookies

FROSTING
- 1 cup butter, softened
- 3 cups confectioners' sugar
- 2 Tbsp. 2% milk
- 1 tsp. vanilla extract
- 1½ cups finely crushed Oreo cookie crumbs
  Optional: Additional Oreo cookie crumbs and mini Oreo cookies

1. Preheat oven to 350°. Line 24 muffin cups with paper liners.
2. In a large bowl, cream butter and sugar until light and fluffy, 5-7 minutes. Add eggs, 1 at a time, beating well after each addition. Beat in vanilla. In another bowl, whisk flour, baking powder and salt; add to the creamed mixture alternately with milk, beating well after each addition. Fold in crushed cookies.
3. Fill prepared cups three-fourths full. Bake 20-22 minutes or until a toothpick inserted in the center comes out clean. Cool in pans 10 minutes before removing to wire racks to cool completely.
4. In a large bowl, combine the butter, confectioners' sugar, milk and vanilla; beat until smooth. Fold in cookie crumbs. Pipe or spread frosting over cupcakes. If desired, sprinkle with additional cookie crumbs and garnish with mini Oreo cookies.
1 cupcake: 411 cal., 19g fat (10g sat. fat), 51mg chol., 346mg sod., 58g carb. (40g sugars, 2g fiber), 4g pro.

SKILLET CARAMEL APRICOT GRUNT

Here's an old-fashioned pantry dessert made with items you can easily keep on hand. To save a few minutes the next time you prepare it, mix a second batch of the dry ingredients for the dumplings now.
—Shannon Norris, Senior Food Stylist

Prep: 20 min. + standing • **Bake:** 20 min.
Makes: 8 servings

- 2 cans (15¼ oz. each) apricot halves, undrained
- 2 tsp. quick-cooking tapioca
- ⅓ cup packed brown sugar
- 1 Tbsp. butter
- 1 Tbsp. lemon juice

DUMPLINGS
- 1½ cups all-purpose flour
- ½ cup sugar
- 2 tsp. baking powder
- 2 Tbsp. cold butter
- ½ cup 2% milk

TOPPING
- ¼ cup packed brown sugar
- 1 Tbsp. water
- Half-and-half cream, optional

1. In a large saucepan, combine the apricots and tapioca; let stand for 15 minutes. Add the brown sugar, butter and lemon juice. Cook and stir until mixture comes to a full boil. Reduce heat to low; keep warm.
2. For dumplings, in a large bowl, combine the flour, sugar and baking powder; cut in butter until crumbly. Add milk; mix just until combined. Pour warm fruit mixture into an ungreased 9- or 10-in. cast-iron skillet. Drop the batter in 6 mounds onto fruit mixture.
3. Bake, uncovered, at 425° until a toothpick inserted into a dumpling comes out clean, about 15 minutes. Stir together the brown sugar and water; microwave until sugar is dissolved, stirring frequently, about 30 seconds. Spoon over dumplings; bake 5 minutes longer. Serve with the cream if desired.

1 serving: 336 cal., 5g fat (3g sat. fat), 13mg chol., 170mg sod., 71g carb. (51g sugars, 2g fiber), 4g pro.

PEACH CREAM PUFFS

PEACH CREAM PUFFS

On a sizzling day, we crave something light, airy and cool. Nothing says summer like cream puffs stuffed with peaches and whipped cream.
—Angela Benedict, Dunbar, WV

Prep: 55 min. + cooling
Bake: 25 min. + cooling
Makes: 16 servings

- 1 cup water
- ½ cup butter, cubed
- ⅛ tsp. salt
- 1 cup all-purpose flour
- 4 large eggs, room temperature

FILLING
- 4 medium peaches, peeled and cubed (about 3 cups)
- ½ cup sugar
- ½ cup water
- ½ cup peach schnapps liqueur or peach nectar
- ½ tsp. ground cinnamon
- ¼ tsp. ground nutmeg

WHIPPED CREAM
- 2 cups heavy whipping cream
- ½ cup confectioners' sugar
- 3 Tbsp. peach schnapps liqueur, optional
- Additional confectioners' sugar

1. Preheat oven to 400°. In a large saucepan, bring water, butter and salt to a rolling boil. Add flour all at once and beat until blended. Cook over medium heat, stirring vigorously until mixture pulls away from sides of pan and forms a ball. Transfer dough to a large bowl; let stand 5 minutes.
2. Add the eggs, 1 at a time, beating well after each addition until smooth. Continue beating until mixture is smooth and shiny.
3. Cut a ½-in. hole in tip of a pastry bag. Transfer dough to bag; pipe sixteen 2-in. mounds 3 in. apart onto parchment-lined baking sheets.
4. Bake on a low oven rack 25-30 minutes or until puffed, firm and golden brown. Pierce side of each puff with a knife to allow steam to escape. Cool completely on wire racks.
5. Meanwhile, in a large saucepan, combine filling ingredients; bring to a boil, stirring occasionally. Reduce the heat; simmer, uncovered, 25-30 minutes or until the mixture is slightly thickened and peaches are tender. Cool completely.
6. In a bowl, beat cream until it begins to thicken. Add confectioners' sugar and, if desired, peach schnapps; beat until soft peaks form.
7. Cut top third off each cream puff. Pull out and discard soft dough from inside tops and bottoms.
8. To serve, spoon 2 Tbsp. whipped cream into each bottom; top with 2 Tbsp. filling and 2 Tbsp. additional whipped cream. Replace the tops. Dust with additional confectioners' sugar.

1 cream puff with ¼ cup whipped cream and 2 Tbsp. filling: 256 cal., 18g fat (11g sat. fat), 103mg chol., 94mg sod., 21g carb. (14g sugars, 1g fiber), 3g pro.

BLUEBERRY RHUBARB COUNTRY TART

When rhubarb comes in, mix it with blueberries for a rustic and bubbly tart. Offer it to a friend with a warm cup of tea.
—Jeanne Ambrose, Milwaukee, WI

- -

Prep: 15 min. • **Bake:** 40 min.
Makes: 8 servings

    Dough for single-crust pie
¾ **cup sugar**
¼ **cup all-purpose flour**
4 **cups chopped fresh or frozen rhubarb, thawed**
1 **cup fresh or frozen blueberries, thawed**
2 **Tbsp. 2% milk**
1 **Tbsp. coarse sugar**

1. Preheat oven to 400°. On a lightly floured surface, roll the dough into a 14-in. circle. Transfer to a parchment-lined baking sheet.
2. In a large bowl, mix sugar and flour. Add rhubarb and blueberries; toss to coat. Spoon filling over crust to within 2 in. of edge. Fold crust edge over filling, pleating as you go and leaving a 4-in. opening in the center. Brush folded crust with milk; sprinkle with coarse sugar. Bake 40-45 minutes or until crust is golden. Transfer to a wire rack to cool.
1 piece: 290 cal., 12g fat (7g sat. fat), 30mg chol., 159mg sod., 44g carb. (23g sugars, 2g fiber), 3g pro.
Dough for single-crust pie: Combine 1¼ cups all-purpose flour and ¼ tsp. salt; cut in ½ cup cold butter until crumbly. Gradually add 3-5 Tbsp. ice water, tossing with a fork until dough holds together when pressed. Cover and refrigerate 1 hour.

LEMON COCONUT STREUSEL ICE CREAM CAKE

Here's a cool treat my family loves anytime, but we find it especially refreshing on a hot summer day. The sweet cream of coconut and the tart lemon juice make a delicious combo, and the streusel adds a nice crunch. You can use any crunchy sugar, lemon or coconut cookie in place of the shortbreads, as long as each cookie is about 2 inches.
—Janet Gill, Canton, OH

- -

Prep: 30 min. + freezing • **Makes:** 16 servings

1 **pkg. (11.2 oz.) shortbread cookies**
½ **cup sweetened shredded coconut, toasted**
¼ **cup macadamia nuts, coarsely chopped and toasted**
1 **tsp. grated lemon zest**
1 **can (15 oz.) cream of coconut**
½ **cup lemon juice**
1½ **qt. vanilla ice cream, softened**
1 **carton (8 oz.) frozen whipped topping, thawed, divided**
    Optional: Fresh blueberries, raspberries and strawberries

1. Reserve 10 cookies for decoration. Crush remaining cookies; transfer to a bowl. Stir in coconut, macadamia nuts and lemon zest. Reserve 2 Tbsp. crumb mixture for topping. In a large bowl, whisk the cream of coconut and lemon juice until combined. Stir in the softened ice cream until smooth. Fold in 1 cup whipped topping.
2. Sprinkle 1 cup crumb mixture onto the bottom of a greased 9-in. springform pan. Top with half the ice cream mixture. Layer with remaining 1 cup crumbs and ice cream mixture. Place the reserved whole cookies around edge of pan. Top with remaining 2½ cups whipped topping; sprinkle with reserved 2 Tbsp. crumb mixture. Freeze, covered, until firm, at least 8 hours or overnight. If desired, serve with berries.
1 piece: 384 cal., 21g fat (13g sat. fat), 29mg chol., 149mg sod., 45g carb. (35g sugars, 1g fiber), 4g pro.

BLUEBERRY RHUBARB COUNTRY TART

ROASTED BANANA & PECAN CHEESECAKE

We keep bananas on hand, but with just two of us in the house, they ripen faster than we can eat them. They soon become perfect for roasting and baking into this cheesecake.
—Patricia Harmon, Baden, PA

Prep: 45 min. + cooling
Bake: 45 min. + chilling • **Makes:** 12 servings

- 3 medium ripe bananas, unpeeled
- 1¾ cups crushed pecan shortbread cookies
- 3 Tbsp. butter, melted

FILLING

- 2 pkg. (8 oz. each) cream cheese, softened
- 1 pkg. (8 oz.) reduced-fat cream cheese
- ½ cup sugar
- ¼ cup plus 2 Tbsp. packed brown sugar, divided
- 1 tsp. vanilla extract
- 2 Tbsp. spiced rum, optional
- 4 large eggs, lightly beaten
- ½ cup chopped pecans
- ½ tsp. ground cinnamon
- 12 pecan halves, toasted
  Chocolate syrup

1. Preheat the oven to 400°. Place unpeeled bananas in an 8-in. square baking dish. Bake until banana peels are black, 10-12 minutes. Cool to room temperature. Reduce oven setting to 325°.

2. Place a greased 9-in. springform pan on a double thickness of heavy-duty foil (about 18 in. square). Wrap foil securely around pan. Place on a baking sheet.

3. In a small bowl, mix cookie crumbs and melted butter. Press onto bottom and 1 in. up sides of prepared pan. Bake until set, 8-10 minutes. Cool on a wire rack.

4. In a large bowl, beat cream cheese, sugar and ¼ cup brown sugar until smooth. Beat in vanilla and, if desired, rum. Add eggs; beat on low speed just until blended. Remove ½ cup cream cheese mixture to a small bowl. Pour remaining filling into crust.

5. Peel and place roasted bananas in a food processor; process until smooth. Add to the reserved cream cheese mixture; stir in the chopped pecans, cinnamon and remaining brown sugar. Pour over plain cream cheese mixture. Cut through cream cheese mixture with a knife to swirl.

6. Place springform pan in a larger baking pan; add 1 in. of hot water to the larger pan. Bake until center is just set and top appears dull, 45-55 minutes. Remove springform pan from water bath. Cool cheesecake on a wire rack 10 minutes. Loosen sides from the pan with a knife; remove the foil. Cool 1 hour longer. Refrigerate overnight, covering when completely cooled.

7. Remove the rim from the pan. Top the cheesecake with pecan halves; drizzle with chocolate syrup.

1 slice: 430 cal., 30g fat (14g sat. fat), 126mg chol., 308mg sod., 33g carb. (24g sugars, 2g fiber), 8g pro.

UPSIDE-DOWN PEAR PANCAKE

There's a pear tree in my yard that inspires me to bake with its fragrant fruit. This upside-down pancake works best with a firm pear, not one that is fully ripe.
—Helen Nelander, Boulder Creek, CA

Takes: 30 min. • **Makes:** 2 servings

- ½ cup all-purpose flour
- ½ tsp. baking powder
- 1 large egg, room temperature
- ¼ cup 2% milk
- 1 Tbsp. butter
- 1 tsp. sugar
- 1 medium pear, peeled and thinly sliced lengthwise
  Confectioners' sugar

1. Preheat the oven to 375°. In a large bowl, whisk flour and baking powder. In a separate bowl, whisk the egg and milk until blended. Add to the dry ingredients, stirring just until combined.

2. Meanwhile, in a small ovenproof skillet, melt butter over medium-low heat. Sprinkle with sugar. Add pear slices in a single layer; cook 5 minutes. Spread prepared batter over pears. Cover and cook until top is set, about 5 minutes.

3. Transfer pan to oven; bake until edges are lightly brown, 8-10 minutes. Invert onto a serving plate. Sprinkle with confectioners' sugar. Serve warm.

½ pancake: 274 cal., 9g fat (5g sat. fat), 111mg chol., 197mg sod., 41g carb. (12g sugars, 4g fiber), 8g pro. **Diabetic exchanges:** 2 starch, 1½ fat, 1 medium-fat meat, ½ fruit.

"I love these light and fruity pancakes. I sprinkle mine with a cinnamon-sugar mixture, and when I'm feeling really indulgent, I add a dollop of whipped cream or ice cream on top!"

—AMY GLANDER, EDITOR

ROASTED BANANA & PECAN CHEESECAKE

UPSIDE-DOWN
PEAR PANCAKE

DUTCH OVEN CHERRY CHOCOLATE DUMP CAKE

Looking for a super quick dessert that will make people think you spent all day in the kitchen? This easy dessert will wow your guests. Feel free to use your favorite pie filling in place of cherry.

—Rashanda Cobbins, Food Editor

- -

Prep: 5 min. • **Bake:** 35 min.
Makes: 8 servings

- 1 can (21 oz.) cherry pie filling
- 1 can (12 oz.) evaporated milk
- 1 pkg. chocolate cake mix (regular size)
- ⅓ cup sliced almonds
- ¾ cup butter, melted
  Vanilla ice cream, optional

Preheat oven to 350°. Line 4-qt. Dutch oven with parchment; lightly spray with cooking spray. Combine pie filling and evaporated milk; spread filling mixture into bottom of Dutch oven. Sprinkle with the cake mix (unprepared) and almonds; drizzle with butter. Bake, covered, until cake springs back when touched, 35-40 minutes. If desired, serve with ice cream.

1 cup: 515 cal., 24g fat (15g sat. fat), 61mg chol., 605mg sod., 68g carb. (44g sugars, 3g fiber), 7g pro.

ASK SARAH

SHOULD I INSPECT MY DUTCH OVEN BEFORE I BAKE IN IT?

Yes! Before you put it in the oven, check the inside for chips and cracks. Be sure to clean off any burnt-on bits inside the pan, too, as they can add an unsavory flavor to baked goods. Finally, check that the lid is oven-safe. Some less expensive models have plastic handles, which can melt at high oven temperatures.

DUTCH OVEN CHERRY
CHOCOLATE DUMP CAKE

RED, WHITE & BLUE BERRY TRIFLE

This luscious trifle tastes best if you make it the day before serving. I always keep extra blueberries and raspberries on hand to garnish the top.

—Kaia McShane, Munster, IN

Prep: 20 min. + chilling • **Makes:** 12 servings

1 can (14 oz.) sweetened condensed milk
1½ cups 2% milk
2 pkg. (3.4 oz. each) instant lemon pudding mix
½ cup sour cream
2 cups fresh blueberries
2 cups fresh raspberries
1 Tbsp. lemon juice
1 loaf (16 oz.) frozen pound cake, thawed and cubed
1 container (8 oz.) frozen whipped topping, thawed
   Optional: Additional blueberries and raspberries

1. In a large bowl, whisk condensed milk, 2% milk and pudding mix 2 minutes. Fold in the sour cream. In another bowl, toss the blueberries and raspberries with lemon juice.
2. In a greased 9-in. springform pan, layer half each of the following: pound cake cubes, berry mixture and pudding mixture. Repeat layers. Refrigerate, covered, at least 2 hours before serving.
3. To serve, remove the rim from the pan. Serve with whipped topping and, if desired, additional berries.
1 piece: 418 cal., 15g fat (10g sat. fat), 74mg chol., 397mg sod., 65g carb. (48g sugars, 2g fiber), 7g pro.

QUICK & EASY BAKLAVA SQUARES

I love baklava but rarely indulge because it takes so much time to make. Then a friend gave me this simple recipe. I've made it for family, friends and co-workers—they can't get enough! I am always asked to bring these squares to special gatherings and parties, and I even give them as gifts during the holidays.

—Paula Marchesi, Lenhartsville, PA

Prep: 20 min. • **Bake:** 25 min. + cooling
Makes: 2 dozen

1 lb. (4 cups) chopped walnuts
1½ tsp. ground cinnamon
1 pkg. (16 oz., 14x9-in. sheets) frozen phyllo dough, thawed
1 cup butter, melted
1 cup honey

1. Preheat oven to 350°. Coat a 13x9-in. baking dish with cooking spray. Combine walnuts and cinnamon.
2. Unroll phyllo dough. Layer 2 sheets of phyllo in prepared pan; brush with butter. Repeat with 6 more sheets of the phyllo, brushing every other 1 with butter. (Keep the remaining phyllo covered with a damp towel to prevent it from drying out.)
3. Sprinkle ½ cup nut mixture in the pan; drizzle with 2 Tbsp. honey. Add 2 more phyllo sheets, brushing with the butter; sprinkle another ½ cup nut mixture and 2 Tbsp. honey over phyllo. Repeat layers 6 times. Top with remaining phyllo sheets, brushing every other 1 with butter.
4. Using a sharp knife, score the surface to make 24 squares. Bake until golden brown and crisp, 25-30 minutes. Cool on a wire rack 1 hour before serving.
1 piece: 294 cal., 21g fat (6g sat. fat), 20mg chol., 145mg sod., 26g carb. (13g sugars, 2g fiber), 5g pro.

QUICK & EASY BAKLAVA SQUARES

WINTER WISHES TRIFLE

I created this light, fluffy trifle for a dear friend who was looking for a stunning dessert. This recipe hit the mark.
—Susan Stetzel, Gainesville, NY

Prep: 20 min. + chilling • **Makes:** 12 servings

- 1 prepared angel food cake (8 to 10 oz.)
- 4 oz. white baking chocolate
- 4 cups heavy whipping cream, divided
- ½ tsp. peppermint extract
- 12 peppermint candies, crushed

1. Place mixer beaters in a large metal bowl; refrigerate 30 minutes. Cut or tear cake into bite-sized pieces; set aside.
2. Break the white chocolate into smaller pieces; microwave at 70% power, stirring after 45 seconds. Microwave until melted, about 30 seconds more. Stir until smooth.

Let stand 5 minutes; stir ¼ cup heavy cream into white chocolate until smooth.
3. In the chilled bowl, beat remaining heavy cream until soft peaks form. Gently fold two-thirds of whipped cream into white chocolate. Stir extract into remaining whipped cream.
4. In a trifle bowl, layer cake and white chocolate mixture, repeating layers. Top with peppermint-flavored whipped cream. Refrigerate, covered, until serving. Sprinkle with crushed candies.
1 serving: 392 cal., 32g fat (20g sat. fat), 90mg chol., 173mg sod., 25g carb. (12g sugars, 0 fiber), 4g pro.

TEST KITCHEN TIP

If you want a touch of color, add a couple of drops of red food coloring to the whipped cream.

EASY LEMON BERRY TARTLETS

These fruity, flaky tartlets filled with raspberries and topped with lemon-tinged cream cheese are a sweet ending to any weeknight meal. They are elegant yet come together quickly and easily.
—Elizabeth Dehart, West Jordan, UT

Takes: 15 min. • **Makes:** 15 tartlets

- ⅔ cup frozen unsweetened raspberries, thawed and drained
- 1 tsp. confectioners' sugar
- 1 pkg. (1.9 oz.) frozen miniature phyllo tart shells
- 4 oz. reduced-fat cream cheese
- 2 Tbsp. lemon curd
  Fresh raspberries, optional

1. In a small bowl, combine the thawed raspberries and the confectioners' sugar; mash with a fork. Spoon into tart shells.
2. In another small bowl, combine cream cheese and lemon curd. Pipe or spoon over filling. Top with fresh raspberries if desired.
1 tartlet: 51 cal., 3g fat (1g sat. fat), 7mg chol., 43mg sod., 5g carb. (2g sugars, 0 fiber), 1g pro. **Diabetic exchanges:** ½ starch, ½ fat.

WINTER WISHES TRIFLE

UPSIDE-DOWN
PUMPKIN PECAN TARTS

PEACH MELBA TRIFLE

This dream of a dessert tastes extra good on a busy day because you can make it ahead of time. If you don't have fresh peaches handy, use canned peaches.
—Christina Moore, Casar, NC

Prep: 20 min. + chilling • **Makes:** 12 servings

- 2 pkg. (12 oz. each) frozen unsweetened raspberries, thawed
- 1 Tbsp. cornstarch
- 1½ cups fat-free peach yogurt
- ⅛ tsp. almond extract
- 1 carton (8 oz.) frozen reduced-fat whipped topping, thawed
- 2 prepared angel food cakes (8 to 10 oz. each), cut into 1-in. cubes (about 8 cups)
- 4 small peaches, peeled and sliced (about 2 cups)

1. In a large saucepan, mix the raspberries and cornstarch until blended. Bring to a boil; cook and stir 1-2 minutes or until thickened. Strain seeds; cover and refrigerate.

2. In a large bowl, mix yogurt and extract; fold in the whipped topping. In a 4-qt. bowl, layer half each of the cake cubes, yogurt mixture and peaches. Repeat the layers. Refrigerate, covered, at least 3 hours before serving. Serve with raspberry sauce.

⅔ cup: 201 cal., 3g fat (2g sat. fat), 1mg chol., 298mg sod., 41g carb. (10g sugars, 3g fiber), 4g pro.

UPSIDE-DOWN PUMPKIN PECAN TARTS

These flaky treats with a creamy filling are a fantastic twist on pumpkin pie and can be prepared a day before they are needed.
—Darlene Buerger, Peoria, AZ

Prep: 45 min. • **Bake:** 45 min. + cooling
Makes: 12 servings

- 1¼ cups melted butter, divided
- ⅓ cup packed brown sugar
- ¼ cup maple syrup
- ½ cup chopped pecans
- 12 oz. cream cheese, softened
- ½ cup sugar
- 1 tsp. vanilla extract
- 2 large eggs, room temperature
- ¾ cup canned pumpkin
- 2 Tbsp. all-purpose flour
- 2 tsp. pumpkin pie spice
- 36 sheets phyllo dough (14x9-in. size)
  Optional: Whipped cream and additional pumpkin pie spice

1. Preheat the oven to 325°. In a bowl, combine ¼ cup melted butter, brown sugar and maple syrup. Divide between 12 greased jumbo muffin cups. Sprinkle with pecans; set aside.

2. In a large bowl, beat cream cheese, sugar and vanilla until smooth. Add eggs, 1 at a time, until blended. Remove 1 cup for filling. Stir in the pumpkin, flour and pie spice to remaining cream cheese mixture; set aside.

3. Place 1 sheet of phyllo dough on a work surface; brush with melted butter. Layer with 5 additional phyllo sheets, brushing each layer. (Keep remaining phyllo covered with a damp towel to prevent it from drying out.) Cut sheets into a 9x7-in. rectangle. Carefully press the stack into a prepared muffin cup. Repeat with remaining phyllo.

4. Spoon 1 heaping Tbsp. plain cream cheese mixture into each phyllo cup. Top with 3 Tbsp. pumpkin mixture. Pinch corners of phyllo together and twist to seal; brush with remaining butter. Bake until golden brown, 45-50 minutes. Cool 5 minutes before inverting onto wire racks to cool completely. If desired, serve with whipped cream and sprinkle with additional pumpkin pie spice.

1 tart: 487 cal., 34g fat (18g sat. fat), 111mg chol., 392mg sod., 42g carb. (22g sugars, 2g fiber), 7g pro.

**SLOW-COOKER
PEACH COBBLER**

SLOW-COOKER PEACH COBBLER

Unlike most cobblers, the "topping" of this simple dessert is on the bottom. Placing the batter underneath the peaches helps it cook through evenly in the slow cooker.
—*Taste of Home* Test Kitchen

- -

Prep: 15 min. • **Cook:** 2 hours
Makes: 8 servings

1¼ cups all-purpose flour, divided
2 Tbsp. sugar
1 tsp. baking powder
¼ tsp. ground cinnamon
⅛ tsp. salt
1 large egg, room temperature
¼ cup 2% milk, warmed
2 Tbsp. butter, melted
6 cups sliced peeled
   fresh peaches (about 6 large)
2 Tbsp. brown sugar
1 Tbsp. lemon juice
1 Tbsp. vanilla extract
   Vanilla ice cream, optional

1. Whisk together 1 cup flour, the sugar, baking powder, cinnamon and salt. In another bowl, whisk together egg, milk and butter; add to dry ingredients, stirring just until moistened (batter will be thick). Spread onto bottom of a greased 5-qt. slow cooker.
2. Combine peaches, the remaining ¼ cup flour, brown sugar, lemon juice and vanilla; spoon over batter. Cook, covered, on high until peach mixture is bubbly, 1¾-2 hours. If desired, serve with vanilla ice cream.
1 serving: 198 cal., 6g fat (3g sat. fat), 35mg chol., 145mg sod., 33g carb. (17g sugars, 2g fiber), 4g pro.

TEST KITCHEN TIP
Fresh peaches are in season June to September. If you can't find fresh, you can substitute frozen peaches (thawed and drained) or well-drained canned peaches in an equal amount. You could also try this cobbler with other fruits, such as nectarines or plums. Both are a little tarter than peaches, so you'd maybe want to add a touch more sugar.

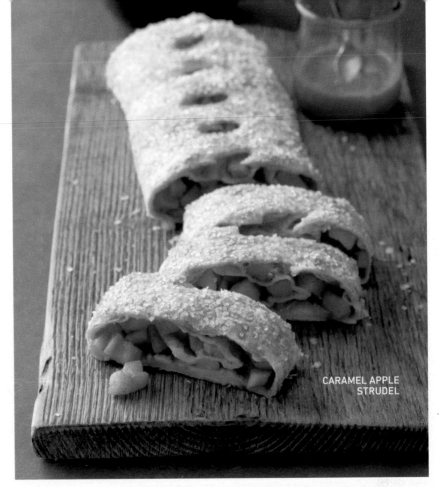

CARAMEL APPLE STRUDEL

CARAMEL APPLE STRUDEL

My father, who was born and raised in Vienna, Austria, would tell us stories about how his mother covered all of the kitchen counters with dough whenever she made apple strudel. This recipe is a modern, delicious way to carry on part of my family's heritage.
—Sarah Haengel, Bowie, MD

- -

Prep: 35 min. + cooling • **Bake:** 25 min
Makes: 8 servings

5 medium apples,
   peeled and chopped (5 cups)
¾ cup apple cider or juice
¼ cup sugar
½ tsp. ground cinnamon
¼ tsp. ground allspice
¼ tsp. ground cloves
1 frozen puff pastry sheet, thawed
¼ cup fat-free caramel
   ice cream topping
1 large egg
1 Tbsp. water
1 Tbsp. coarse sugar
   Optional Sweetened
   whipped cream and additional
   caramel ice cream topping

1. Preheat the oven to 375°. In a large saucepan, combine the first 6 ingredients. Bring to a boil. Reduce the heat; simmer, uncovered, 15-20 minutes or until the apples are tender, stirring occasionally. Cool completely.
2. Unfold puff pastry onto a large sheet of parchment; roll into a 16x12-in. rectangle. Transfer paper and pastry to a baking sheet, placing a short side of the rectangle facing you. Using a slotted spoon, arrange apples on bottom half of pastry to within 1 in. of edges. Drizzle the apples with the caramel topping. Roll up jelly-roll style, starting with the bottom side. Pinch seams to seal, and tuck ends under.
3. In a small bowl, whisk egg with water; brush over pastry. Sprinkle with coarse sugar. Cut slits in top. Bake 25-30 minutes or until golden brown. If desired, serve with whipped cream and additional caramel topping.
1 slice: 270 cal., 9g fat (2g sat. fat), 26mg chol., 140mg sod., 46g carb. (24g sugars, 4g fiber), 3g pro.

YOGURT-RICOTTA CHEESECAKE

I love Italian ricotta cheesecakes, but they have too much sugar for me. I created a diabetic version, and my family could not tell the difference! I serve mine with sugar-free strawberry ice cream topping and fresh strawberries.
—Diane Shipley, Mentor, OH

- -

Prep: 35 min. • **Bake:** 1 hour 20 min. + chilling
Makes: 16 servings

- 2 pkg. (8 oz. each) reduced-fat cream cheese
- 2 cups reduced-fat ricotta cheese
  Sugar substitute blend (made with sucralose) equivalent to 1½ cups sugar
- 2 cups vanilla yogurt
- ½ cup butter, melted
- ¼ cup cornstarch
- 3 Tbsp. all-purpose flour
- 2 Tbsp. lemon juice
- 1 tsp. vanilla extract
- 4 large eggs, room temperature, lightly beaten
  Halved fresh strawberries, optional

1. Preheat oven to 325°. In a large bowl, beat cream cheese, ricotta and sugar blend until smooth. Beat in yogurt, butter, cornstarch, flour, lemon juice and vanilla. Add eggs; beat on low speed just until blended. Pour into a greased 9-in. springform pan. Place pan on a baking sheet.

2. Bake 80-85 minutes, until center is almost set. Cool on a wire rack for 10 minutes. Loosen sides from pan with a knife. Cool 1 hour longer. Refrigerate the cheesecake overnight, covering when completely cooled.

3. Remove rim from pan. If desired, serve cheesecake with strawberries.

1 slice: 246 cal., 15g fat (9g sat. fat), 91mg chol., 231mg sod., 19g carb. (16g sugars, 0 fiber), 9g pro.

TEST KITCHEN TIP

It is best to cut a cheesecake right after you remove it from the refrigerator. Dip a clean knife in a glass of hot water and wipe it dry before cutting. Wipe the knife clean and dip in warm water again after each cut.

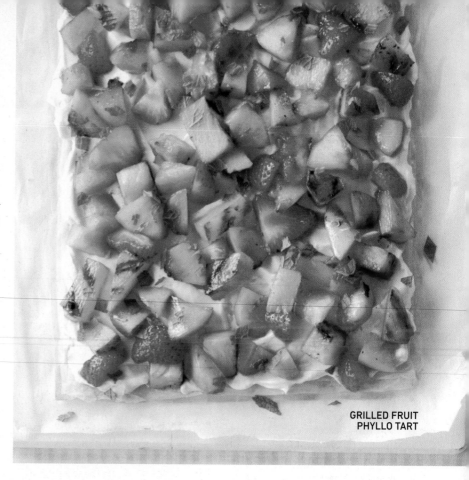

GRILLED FRUIT PHYLLO TART

GRILLED FRUIT PHYLLO TART

This tart was a hit at my friend's baby shower. It reminds me of a fruit salad my mother used to make with cream cheese and whipped topping. Everyone loves the flaky crust, and the bright colors make it a pretty addition to any spread.
—Laura McAllister, Morganton, NC

- -

Prep: 30 min. • **Grill:** 10 min.
Makes: 12 servings

- 3 Tbsp. butter, melted
- 4 tsp. canola oil
- 8 sheets phyllo dough (14x9-in. size)
- 1 large lemon
- 3 medium peaches, peeled and halved
- 2 cups large fresh strawberries, stems removed
- 4 slices fresh pineapple (½ in. thick)
- ⅓ cup packed brown sugar
- ½ tsp. salt
- ½ cup heavy whipping cream
- 1 pkg. (8 oz.) cream cheese, softened
- ⅓ cup confectioners' sugar
- 2 Tbsp. chopped fresh mint

1. Preheat oven to 400°. In a small bowl, mix butter and oil. Brush a 15x10x1-in. baking pan with some of the butter mixture. Place 1 sheet of phyllo dough into prepared pan; brush with the butter mixture. Layer with 7 additional phyllo sheets, brushing each layer. (Keep the remaining phyllo covered with a damp towel to prevent it from drying out.) Bake 5-7 minutes or until golden brown (phyllo will puff up during baking). Cool completely.

2. Finely grate enough zest from lemon to measure 1 Tbsp. zest. Cut lemon crosswise in half; squeeze out juice. In a large bowl, toss peaches, strawberries, pineapple, brown sugar, salt, lemon zest and juice. Remove strawberries; thread fruit onto 3 metal or soaked wooden skewers.

3. Place fruit on oiled grill rack. Grill, covered, over medium heat until fruit is tender, turning once, 8-10 minutes for pineapple slices and peaches, 4-5 minutes for strawberries. Remove and set aside.

4. In a small bowl, beat the cream until soft peaks form. In another bowl, beat the cream cheese and confectioners' sugar until smooth. Fold in whipped cream. Spread over phyllo crust. Slice grilled fruit; arrange over filling. Sprinkle with mint; cut into pieces.

1 piece: 233 cal., 15g fat (8g sat. fat), 38mg chol., 216mg sod., 24g carb. (18g sugars, 2g fiber), 3g pro.

CHERRY FUDGE TRUFFLE COCONUT CHEESECAKE

Cherries and chocolate come together in this dazzling coconut cheesecake. It's a holiday showstopper!
—Jeanne Holt, Mendota Heights, MN

Prep: 40 min. • **Bake:** 1 hour 20 min. + chilling
Makes: 16 servings

- 1⅔ cups crushed Oreo cookies (about 17 cookies)
- ⅔ cup sweetened shredded coconut, toasted
- ¼ cup butter, melted

FILLING
- 4 pkg. (8 oz. each) cream cheese, softened, divided
- 1 cup sugar
- ¾ cup cream of coconut
- 1 tsp. coconut extract
- 3 large eggs, lightly beaten
- ¼ cup chopped maraschino cherries
- 1 cup 60% cacao bittersweet chocolate baking chips, melted and cooled
- ⅓ cup cherry preserves, finely chopped

TOPPING
- ½ cup 60% cacao bittersweet chocolate baking chips, melted and cooled
- 1 cup sweetened whipped cream
- ⅓ cup sweetened shredded coconut, toasted
- 16 maraschino cherries with stems, patted dry

1. Preheat oven to 375°. Place a greased 10-in. springform pan on a double thickness of heavy-duty foil (about 18 in. square). Wrap foil securely around the pan. Place on a baking sheet.
2. In a small bowl, mix crushed cookies and coconut; stir in butter. Press onto bottom and ½ in. up sides of prepared pan. Bake 10 minutes. Cool on a wire rack. Reduce oven setting to 325°.
3. In a large bowl, beat 3 pkg. cream cheese and sugar until smooth. Beat in cream of coconut and extract. Add eggs; beat on low speed just until blended. Stir in chopped cherries. Pour 3 cups batter into crust. In another bowl, beat remaining 8 oz. cream cheese until smooth. Beat in the cooled chocolate and cherry preserves. Drop by tablespoonfuls over the coconut batter. Carefully spoon remaining coconut batter over top. Place springform pan in a larger baking pan; add 1 in. hot water to larger pan.
4. Bake until the center is just set and top appears dull, 80-85 minutes. Remove the springform pan from the water bath. Cool the cheesecake on a wire rack 10 minutes. Loosen sides from pan with a knife; remove foil. Cool 1 hour longer. Once completely cool, cover and refrigerate overnight.
5. Remove rim from pan. Top cheesecake with chocolate, whipped cream, toasted coconut and cherries.
1 piece: 545 cal., 37g fat (22g sat. fat), 108mg chol., 290mg sod., 52g carb. (44g sugars, 2g fiber), 6g pro.

CHOCOLATE-FILLED CRESCENTS

I always get compliments on these rich, flaky rolls drizzled with chocolate.
—Carol Patterson, Deltona, FL

Prep: 25 min. • **Bake:** 15 min.
Makes: 16 servings

- 3 Tbsp. butter, softened
- 1 cup confectioners' sugar
- 1 Tbsp. 2% milk
- 1 tsp. vanilla extract
- ¼ cup baking cocoa
- 3 Tbsp. finely chopped pecans
- 2 tubes (8 oz. each) refrigerated crescent rolls

CHOCOLATE GLAZE
- 1 cup confectioners' sugar
- 2 Tbsp. baking cocoa
- 2 Tbsp. plus 1 tsp. water
- 2 Tbsp. butter, melted
- ½ tsp. vanilla extract

1. In a small bowl, cream the butter and confectioners' sugar until light and fluffy, 5-7 minutes. Beat in the milk and vanilla. Gradually add cocoa; mix well. Stir in pecans.
2. Unroll crescent dough and separate into triangles. Spread 2 rounded tsp. of filling over each triangle to within ¼ in. of edges. Roll up each from the wide end. Place point sides down, 2 in. apart on ungreased baking sheets. Curve ends to form crescent shapes.
3. Bake at 375° for 12-15 minutes or until golden brown. Remove to wire racks; cool slightly. In a bowl, whisk glaze ingredients until smooth; drizzle over crescents.
1 crescent roll: 208 cal., 10g fat (2g sat. fat), 10mg chol., 242mg sod., 29g carb. (18g sugars, 1g fiber), 3g pro.

CHERRY FUDGE TRUFFLE COCONUT CHEESECAKE

PEANUT BUTTER & JELLY ICE CREAM

What could be better than peanut butter and jelly ice cream? You'll love the sweet-salty combination. Use your favorite flavor of jelly and switch to crunchy peanut butter if you like extra texture.
—*Taste of Home* Test Kitchen

Prep: 30 min. + freezing • **Makes:** 1¼ qt.

- 1½ cups whole milk
- ⅔ cup packed brown sugar
- ½ tsp. salt
- 1 large egg, lightly beaten
- ⅔ cup creamy peanut butter
- 2 cups heavy whipping cream
- 2 tsp. vanilla extract
- ½ cup grape jelly or strawberry jelly

1. In a large heavy saucepan, heat the milk, brown sugar and salt until bubbles form around sides of pan. Whisk a small amount of hot mixture into the egg. Return all to the pan, whisking constantly.
2. Cook and stir over low heat until mixture is thickened and coats the back of a spoon. Remove from heat; whisk in peanut butter. Quickly transfer to a bowl; place in ice water and stir for 2 minutes. Stir in cream and vanilla. Press waxed paper onto surface of custard. Refrigerate for several hours or overnight.
3. Fill the cylinder of ice cream freezer two-thirds full; freeze according to the manufacturer's directions.
4. When ice cream is frozen, spoon into a freezer container, layering with jelly; freeze for 2-4 hours before serving.
½ cup: 393 cal., 28g fat (14g sat. fat), 77mg chol., 231mg sod., 32g carb. (29g sugars, 1g fiber), 7g pro.

LOVELY LEMON CHEESECAKE

Listen for the oohs and aahs when you present this luxurious cheesecake. The lemon flavor gives it a bright and tangy flair.
—Margaret Allen, Abingdon, VA

Prep: 25 min. • **Bake:** 70 min. + chilling
Makes: 14 servings

- ¾ cup graham cracker crumbs
- 2 Tbsp. sugar
- 3 tsp. ground cinnamon
- 2 Tbsp. butter, melted

FILLING
- 5 pkg. (8 oz. each) cream cheese, softened
- 1⅔ cups sugar
- ⅛ tsp. salt
- ¼ cup lemon juice
- 1½ tsp. vanilla extract
- 5 large eggs, room temperature, lightly beaten
  Thin lemon slices, optional

1. Preheat oven to 325°. Place a greased 10-in. springform pan on a double thickness of heavy-duty foil (about 18 in. square). Wrap foil securely around pan.
2. In a small bowl, mix the cracker crumbs, sugar and cinnamon; stir in butter. Press onto bottom of prepared pan; refrigerate while preparing filling.
3. In a large bowl, beat cream cheese, sugar and salt until smooth. Beat in lemon juice and vanilla. Add eggs; beat on low speed just until blended. Pour over crust. Place the springform pan in a larger baking pan; add 1 in. of hot water to larger pan.
4. Bake 70-80 minutes or until center is just set and top appears dull. Remove springform pan from water bath. Cool cheesecake on a wire rack 10 minutes. Loosen sides from the pan with a knife; remove foil. Cool 1 hour longer. Refrigerate overnight, covering when completely cooled.
5. Remove rim from pan. If desired, top the cheesecake with lemon slices.
1 slice: 444 cal., 32g fat (19g sat. fat), 169mg chol., 325mg sod., 32g carb. (27g sugars, 0 fiber), 9g pro.

STRAWBERRY BUTTERMILK SKILLET SHORTCAKE

This scratch-made buttermilk shortcake is a family favorite. It's become tradition for my grandmother to make it every summer.
—Claudia Lamascolo, Melbourne, FL

Prep: 25 min. • **Bake:** 50 min.
Makes: 10 servings

- 10 Tbsp. shortening
- ¼ cup butter, softened
- 1 cup sugar
- 2 large eggs, room temperature
- 2½ cups all-purpose flour
- 3 tsp. baking powder
- ½ tsp. salt
- ⅔ cup buttermilk

STREUSEL TOPPING
- ⅔ cup all-purpose flour
- ½ cup sugar
- 1 tsp. ground cinnamon
- ¼ tsp. ground allspice
- ½ cup butter, softened
- 2 cups sliced fresh strawberries
  Whipped cream

1. Preheat oven to 350°. In a large bowl, cream shortening, butter and sugar until light and fluffy, 5-7 minutes. Add eggs, 1 at a time, beating well after each addition. In another bowl, whisk flour, baking powder and salt; add to creamed mixture alternately with the buttermilk, beating well after each addition. Transfer to a 12-in. cast-iron or other ovenproof skillet.
2. For streusel topping, in a small bowl, mix the flour, sugar, cinnamon and allspice; cut in the butter until crumbly. Sprinkle over batter. Top with the strawberries. Bake 50-60 minutes or until center is puffed and edges are golden brown. Serve warm with whipped cream.
1 slice: 526 cal., 27g fat (12g sat. fat), 74mg chol., 418mg sod., 64g carb. (33g sugars, 2g fiber), 6g pro.

STRAWBERRY BUTTERMILK
SKILLET SHORTCAKE

TASTE OF HOME
TEST
KITCHEN
RECIPE OF THE YEAR
★ ★ ★ ★ ★

NO-BAKE CHOCOLATE CHIP CANNOLI CHEESECAKE

I make this cheesecake in the summer for a flavorful and refreshing treat. I love the added bonus of not having to turn on the oven in hot weather.
—Kristen Heigl, Staten Island, NY

Prep: 25 min. + chilling • **Makes:** 8 servings

- 1 pkg. (4 oz.) cannoli shells
- ½ cup sugar
- ½ cup graham cracker crumbs
- ⅓ cup butter, melted

FILLING

- 2 pkg. (8 oz. each) cream cheese, softened
- 1 cup confectioners' sugar
- ½ tsp. grated orange zest
- ¼ tsp. ground cinnamon
- ¾ cup part-skim ricotta cheese
- 1 tsp. vanilla extract
- ½ tsp. rum extract
- ½ cup miniature semisweet chocolate chips
  Chopped pistachios, optional

1. Pulse the cannoli shells in a food processor until coarse crumbs form. Add sugar, cracker crumbs and melted butter; pulse just until combined. Press onto bottom and up sides of a greased 9-in. pie plate. Refrigerate until firm, about 1 hour.

2. Beat the first 4 filling ingredients until blended. Beat in ricotta cheese and extracts. Stir in chocolate chips. Spread into crust.

3. Refrigerate, covered, until set, about 4 hours. If desired, top with pistachios.

1 piece: 548 cal., 36g fat (20g sat. fat), 88mg chol., 292mg sod., 51g carb. (38g sugars, 1g fiber), 8g pro.

TEST KITCHEN TIP

Pistachios are classic in cannoli, but if you don't have them, you can still add crunch by topping the pie with additional crumbled cannoli shells. Or add a sprinkle of chocolate shavings. If you don't have mini chocolate chips, you can coarsely chop regular chocolate chips.

NO-BAKE CHOCOLATE CHIP CANNOLI CHEESECAKE

PEANUTTY CREAM-FILLED PASTRY SHELLS

These cream-filled pastries are indulgent, but they couldn't be easier to make. Prepare and freeze them for an upcoming event.
—Teri Rasey, Cadillac, MI

- -

Prep: 15 min. + freezing • **Bake:** 20 min.
Makes: 12 servings

- 2 pkg. (10 oz. each) frozen puff pastry shells
- 1 pkg. (8 oz.) cream cheese, softened
- 1 cup creamy peanut butter
- 1 can (14 oz.) sweetened condensed milk
- 1 tsp. lemon juice
- 1½ cups whipped topping
   Chocolate hard-shell ice cream topping
- ¼ cup chopped unsalted peanuts

1. Bake puff pastry shells according to the package directions. Cool completely. Meanwhile, in a large bowl, beat the cream cheese until light and fluffy. Add the peanut butter, milk and lemon juice. Fold in the whipped topping.

2. Place the shells on a waxed paper-lined baking sheet. Remove the tops; save for another use. Pour 1 tsp. hard-shell topping into each pastry shell. Mound ⅓ cup cream cheese mixture over the topping. Drizzle with an additional 1 tsp. topping; sprinkle with peanuts. Freeze for 30 minutes or until firm.

3. Let stand at room temperature for 5 minutes before serving.
1 serving: 601 cal., 42g fat (16g sat. fat), 32mg chol., 436mg sod., 47g carb. (28g sugars, 3g fiber), 15g pro.

MINT CHOCOLATE CHEESECAKE

I created this mint chocolate cheesecake for our high school's annual fundraiser. We learned it brought a hefty price and was one of the first desserts to go! If desired, you can stir the cookie pieces into the batter instead of adding them in a layer. Keep the pieces fairly small, because otherwise they have a tendency to rise to the top.
—Sue Gronholz, Beaver Dam, WI

- -

Prep: 20 min. • **Bake:** 1¼ hours + chilling
Makes: 16 servings

- 1 cup Oreo cookie crumbs
- 3 Tbsp. sugar
- 2 Tbsp. butter, melted

FILLING
- 4 pkg. (8 oz. each) cream cheese, softened
- 1 cup sugar
- 1 cup white baking chips, melted and cooled
- 6 Tbsp. creme de menthe
- ¼ cup all-purpose flour
- 2 Tbsp. creme de cacao
- ½ tsp. peppermint extract
- 4 large eggs, lightly beaten
- 1 cup coarsely crushed Oreo cookies (about 10 cookies)

GANACHE
- ¾ cup semisweet chocolate chips
- 6 Tbsp. heavy whipping cream

1. Preheat oven to 325°. Place a greased 9-in. springform pan on a double thickness of heavy-duty foil (about 18 in. square). Wrap foil securely around pan. In a small bowl, mix cookie crumbs and sugar; stir in butter. Press onto bottom of prepared pan.

2. In a large bowl, beat cream cheese and sugar until smooth. Beat in the cooled chips, creme de menthe, flour, creme de cacao and extract. Add the eggs; beat on low speed just until blended. Pour half the batter over crust; sprinkle with crushed Oreos. Carefully spoon remaining batter over top. Place springform pan in a larger baking pan; add 1 in. hot water to larger pan.

3. Bake until the center is just set and the top appears dull, 75-80 minutes. Remove the springform pan from water bath. Cool the cheesecake on a wire rack 10 minutes. Loosen sides from the pan with a knife; remove foil. Cool 1 hour longer. Refrigerate overnight, covering when completely cooled.

4. Remove rim from pan. Place chocolate chips in a bowl. In a saucepan, bring cream just to a boil. Pour over chocolate; stir with a whisk until smooth. Spread over cheesecake.
1 slice: 518 cal., 33g fat (18g sat. fat), 116mg chol., 296mg sod., 46g carb. (38g sugars, 1g fiber), 7g pro.

MINT CHOCOLATE CHEESECAKE

STRAWBERRY
BLISS

STRAWBERRY BLISS

You'll love this homemade puff pastry crust topped with a soft-set pudding layer that has a hint of strawberry flavor. This dessert needs to chill for at least an hour, so it's a fabulous make-ahead dish.
—Candace Richter, Stevens Point, WI

- -

Prep: 30 min. • **Bake:** 20 min. + chilling
Makes: 12 servings

- 1 cup water
- ½ cup butter, cubed
- 1 cup all-purpose flour
- 4 large eggs, room temperature
- 1 pkg. (8 oz.) cream cheese, softened
- ½ cup sugar
- 5 Tbsp. seedless strawberry jam
- 3 cups cold whole milk
- 1 pkg. (5.1 oz.) instant vanilla pudding mix
- ½ cup heavy whipping cream
- 3 cups quartered fresh strawberries

1. Preheat oven to 400°. In a large saucepan, bring water and butter to a rolling boil. Add flour all at once and beat until blended. Cook over medium heat, stirring vigorously until mixture pulls away from sides of pan and forms a ball. Remove from heat; let stand 5 minutes.
2. Add 1 egg at a time, beating well after each addition. Continue beating until the mixture is smooth and shiny.
3. Spread into a greased 15x10x1-in. baking pan. Bake 20-25 minutes or until puffed and golden brown (surface will be uneven). Cool completely in pan on a wire rack.
4. In a large bowl, beat cream cheese, sugar and jam until smooth. Beat in the milk and pudding mix until smooth. In a small bowl, beat cream until stiff peaks form; fold into the pudding mixture. Spread over crust. Refrigerate at least 1 hour.
5. Just before serving, top dessert with strawberries.
1 piece: 377 cal., 22g fat (13g sat. fat), 131mg chol., 332mg sod., 40g carb. (27g sugars, 1g fiber), 7g pro.

CHOCOLATE & FRUIT TRIFLE

This pretty dessert layered with devil's food cake, a creamy pudding mixture, red berries and green kiwi is perfect for the holidays. I make it in a clear glass trifle bowl to show off its festive colors.
—Angie Dierikx, State Center, IA

- -

Prep: 20 min. + chilling
Bake: 20 min. + cooling
Makes: 16 servings

- 1 pkg. devil's food cake mix (regular size)
- 1 can (14 oz.) sweetened condensed milk
- 1 cup cold water
- 1 pkg. (3.4 oz.) instant vanilla pudding mix
- 2 cups heavy whipping cream, whipped
- 2 Tbsp. orange juice
- 2 cups fresh strawberries, chopped
- 2 cups fresh raspberries
- 2 kiwifruit, peeled and chopped

1. Prepare cake batter according to package directions; pour into a greased 15x10x1-in. baking pan. Bake at 350° for 20 minutes or until a toothpick inserted in the center comes out clean. Cool completely on a wire rack. Crumble enough cake to measure 8 cups; set aside. (Save remaining cake for another use.)
2. In a large bowl, whisk the milk, water and pudding mix for 2 minutes. Let stand for 2 minutes or until soft-set. Fold in the whipped cream.
3. To assemble, spread 2½ cups pudding mixture in a 4-qt. glass bowl. Top with half the crumbled cake; sprinkle with 1 Tbsp. orange juice. Arrange half the berries and kiwi over cake.
4. Repeat pudding and cake layers; sprinkle with remaining orange juice. Top trifle with the remaining pudding mixture. Spoon the remaining fruit around edge of bowl. Cover and refrigerate until serving.
1 cup: 419 cal., 22g fat (10g sat. fat), 77mg chol., 362mg sod., 51g carb. (35g sugars, 2g fiber), 6g pro.

FIGGY APPLE BRIE TART

Our family gatherings often included baked Brie. I transformed it into a dessert that's savory and sweet. It makes a wonderful appetizer, too.
—Kristie Schley, Severna Park, MD

- -

Prep: 25 min. • **Bake:** 15 min. + cooling
Makes: 8 servings

- 3 Tbsp. butter, softened
- ¾ cup sugar
- 2 large apples
- 1 cup dried figs, halved
- ½ lb. Brie cheese, rind removed, sliced
- 1 sheet refrigerated pie crust

1. Preheat oven to 425°. Spread butter over bottom of a 10-in. ovenproof skillet; sprinkle evenly with sugar.
2. Peel, quarter and core apples; arrange in a circular pattern over sugar, rounded side down. Place figs around apples. Place skillet over medium heat; cook until the sugar is caramelized and apples have softened slightly, 10-12 minutes. Remove from heat; top with cheese.
3. Unroll the crust; place over the apples, tucking under edges. Place the skillet in oven on an upper rack; bake until crust is golden brown, 15-18 minutes. Let cool in skillet 5 minutes. Carefully invert onto a serving plate; serve warm.
1 piece: 394 cal., 19g fat (11g sat. fat), 45mg chol., 315mg sod., 50g carb. (33g sugars, 2g fiber), 8g pro.

Recipe Index

A

Air-Fryer Candied Acorn
  Squash Slices 157
Air-Fryer Crumb-Topped Sole 119
Air-Fryer Ham & Egg Pockets 55
Air-Fryer Mini Chimichangas 181
Apple Butter Biscuit
  Breakfast Bake 61
Apple Cinnamon Overnight Oats 61
Apple Quinoa Spoon Bread 75
Apple-Peanut Blondies 196
Apricot & Macadamia
  Eggnog Bread 76
Artichoke Cod with Sun-Dried
  Tomatoes 103
Asian Chicken Thighs 132
Asian Salmon Tacos 105

B

Bacon & Garlic Sugar
  Snap Peas 167
Bacon Mac & Cheese
  Cornbread Skillet 151
Bacon-Wrapped
  Avocado Wedges 17
Badger State Stuffing 167
Baked Asparagus Dip 41
Balsamic Brussels Sprouts 162
Banana Blueberry
  Oatmeal Bake 55
Banana-Orange Sweet
  Potato Bake 156
Bang Bang Shrimp
  Cake Sliders 40
Banh Mi Skewers 35
Basil-Lemon Crab Linguine 120
Beef Suya 146
Beer Dip 28
Berry Ricotta Puff Pancake 51
Berry Smoothie Bowl 57
Best Ever Veggie Burger 116
Best Italian Sausage
  Sandwiches 84
Best Vanilla Buttercream 19
Best-Ever Crescent Rolls 72
Big Soft Ginger Cookies 204
Birthday Cake Shooters 180
Black Bean & Sweet
  Potato Rice Bowls 118
Black Bean Burgers with
  Chipotle Slaw 104

BLT Bites 41
Blueberries & Cream
  Coffee Cake 224
Blueberry Cornmeal
  Pancakes 54
Blueberry Rhubarb
  Country Tart 235
Bread Pudding Pie 213
Brown Rice & Vegetables 159
Brown Rice with Almonds
  & Cranberries 161
Brown Sugar Pound Cake 214
Buffalo Chicken Enchiladas 128
Buffalo Chicken Stuffed Poblano
  Peppers 140
Butterscotch-Rum
  Raisin Treats 207

C

Canned Blueberry Jam 178
Cannoli Wafer Sandwiches 195
Caramel Apple Strudel 243
Caramel-Scotch Cream Cheese
  Coffee Cake 59
Carrot Raisin Couscous 161
Cashew Cheese 30
Cast-Iron Chocolate Chip Banana
  Bread 75
Cast-Iron Skillet Steak 125
Cauliflower & Tofu Curry 111
Cheddar Corn Dog Muffins 77
Cheese-Filled Garlic Rolls 73
Cheesy Caramelized Onion
  Skillet Bread 38
Cherry Fudge Truffle Coconut
  Cheesecake 245
Cherry-Coconut Slices 200
Chewy Peanut Butter
  Pan Squares 206
Chicken Fries 37
Chicken Piccata Meatballs 37
Chicken Potpie Galette with
  Cheddar-Thyme Crust 138
Chicken with Peach-Avocado
  Salsa 14
Chickpea Potpies 109
Chiles Rellenos Breakfast Bake 45
Chilled Pea Soup Shooters 32
Chipotle Sweet Potato Salad 94
Chipotle-Orange Chicken 137
Chocolate & Fruit Trifle 251

Chocolate Babka 18
Chocolate Cheesecake Pie 219
Chocolate Chess Pie 216
Chocolate Chip Cookie
  Brownies 189
Chocolate Ganache Peanut Butter
  Cupcakes 183
Chocolate-Filled Crescents 245
Chocolate-Peanut Butter
  Dump Cake 226
Chocolate Peanut Butter No-Bake
  Cookies 191
Cinnamon Blueberry
  French Toast 47
Cinnamon Bun Cookies 207
Cinnamon-Candy Cookies 202
Classic Crab Boil 104
Coastal Carolina Muffin-Tin
  Frittatas 54
Coconut-Macadamia Sheet-Pan
  Pancakes 52
Confetti Birthday Cake 229
Contest-Winning Chicken Wild Rice
  Casserole 141
Cookie Cake 221
Crab-Topped Tomato Slices 119
Cranberry & Bacon
  Swiss Cheese Dip 26
Creamy Biscoff Pie 212
Crispy Fried Onion Rings 154
Crudite Dip 33
Crunchy Chili Cilantro Lime
  Roasted Shrimp 116
Crunchy Lemon-Pesto
  Garden Salad 88
Crusty Homemade Bread 71
Curry Coconut Chicken 136
Curry-Rubbed Roast Chicken 143

D

Dad's Famous Stuffies 109
Dilly Chickpea Salad
  Sandwiches 83
Dog Biscuits 174
Double Butterscotch
  Coconut Cake 227
Double-Crust Rhubarb Pie 228
Doughnut Hole Cake 212
Down East Blueberry Buckle 65
Dry-Rub Grilled Pork Chops over
  Cannellini Greens 126

Dutch Oven Cherry
  Chocolate Dump Cake 238
Dutch-Oven Barbecued Pork
  Sandwiches 81
Dutch-Oven Bread................................. 13
Dutch-Oven Raisin Walnut Bread ... 13

E

Easy Bourbon Pecan Pie 218
Easy Butternut Squash Soup........... 93
Easy Cast-Iron Peach
  Biscuit Rolls 68
Easy Cheesy Cauliflower
  Breakfast Casserole 50
Easy Chicken Pesto
  Stuffed Peppers 127
Easy Chocolate Souffles................... 10
Easy Grasshopper Ice
  Cream Pie..229
Easy Grilled Corn with
  Chipotle-Lime Butter 166
Easy Lemon Berry Tartlets 240
Easy Lemon Pie 224
Easy Morning Waffles 48
Easy Peanut Butter
  & Pretzel Pie.................................222
Easy Pistachio Tube Cake 218
Easy Puppy Chow 36
Easy Slice & Bake Cookies............206
Easy Slow-Cooker Pot Roast 133
Easy Slow-Cooker Potato Soup 87
Easy Strawberry Lemonade
  Freezer Pie.....................................228
Egg Roll Noodle Bowl 147
Epiphany Ham 131
Everything Breakfast Sliders........... 47

F

Farmers Market Enchiladas........... 121
Feta Asparagus Frittata 58
Figgy Apple Brie Tart.......................251
Fluffy Key Lime Pie.......................... 221
French Silk Pie 211
Fresh Corn & Tomato
  Fettuccini...................................... 114
Fresh Raspberry Icebox Cake.......223
Fresh Shrimp & Avocado
  Nachos 25
Fried Chicken & Pulled Pork
  Cornbread Poppers 27
Fried Lemon-Pepper Wings............ 31
Frosted Walnut Brownie Cups 196
Frozen Brandy Old-Fashioneds....... 31

G

Garlicky Chicken Dinner 138
Giardiniera.. 176
Glazed Italian Fruitcake Cookies...192

Golden Beet Curry Risotto with
  Crispy Beet Greens........................158
Gooey Caramel-Topped
  Gingersnaps 190
Graffiti Cutout Cookies.................... 199
Grandma's Onion Squares.............. 68
Granola Blueberry Muffins.............. 66
Greek Chicken & Rice 133
Greek Salad-Inspired Quiche........... 57
Green Onion Rolls 67
Grilled Basil Chicken
  & Tomatoes.................................... 142
Grilled Cheese &
  Avocado Sandwich 87
Grilled Fruit Phyllo Tart 244
Grilled Mediterranean
  Zucchini Salad 164
Grilled Salmon with Chorizo-Olive
  Sauce 114
Gulf Coast Jambalaya Rice.............. 120

H

Ham & Green Onion Biscuits............ 75
Ham & Swiss Baked Penne 132
Hasselback Tomato Clubs................. 94
Healthy Gazpacho for 2 89
Heirloom Tomato Galette with
  Pecorino.. 153
Homemade Butterfinger Bites 175
Homemade Eggnog 174
Homemade Peanut Butter Cups ...185
Homemade Sauerkraut.................... 173
Homemade Steak Seasoning......... 184
Honey Cinnamon Butter 180
Honey-Squash Dinner Rolls 65
Hot Shrimp Dip.................................... 28

I

I Like to Eat Apples &
  Bananas Bread 66

J

Jalapeno Buttermilk
  Cornbread 73

K

Kale Caesar Salad............................... 82
Key Lime Blondie Bars.....................202
Key Lime Pie Balls 200
Kimchi Fried Rice............................. 108
Kohlrabi, Cucumber
  & Tomato Salad 92

L

Larb Gai 130
Layered Hummus Dip 27
Lemon Coconut Streusel
  Ice Cream Cake..............................235

Lemon Popovers with Pecan Honey
  Butter... 71
Lemon Rhubarb Tube Cake 211
Lemon Ricotta Fritters....................... 70
Lemon Thyme Icebox Cookies.......205
Lemon-Basil Grilled Shrimp &
  Couscous... 103
Lemon-Berry Ice Cream Pie 217
Linguine with Broccoli
  Rabe & Peppers............................. 106
Loaded Huevos Rancheros with
  Roasted Poblano Peppers............ 58
Loaded Mashed Potato Bites 152
Lovely Lemon Cheesecake............246

M

M&M & Pretzel Cookies...................206
Makeover Cheddar Biscuits............. 19
Makeover Hash & Eggs 51
Makeover Manicotti Crepes............ 17
Makeover Meatless Lasagna 113
Mango Chicken Thighs with
  Basil-Coconut Sauce..................... 128
Mango Fudge Refrigerator
  Ribbon Cookies............................. 192
Maple Pulled Pork Buns 36
Marinated Tenderloin &
  Avocado on Baguette Toasts........82
Mashed Cauliflower 158
Meat Lover's Pizza Rice Skillet......146
Meatball Alphabet Soup 91
Meatballs with
  Chimichurri Sauce 41
Melon-Berry Salad............................. 93
Mexican Crinkle Cookies
  with a Kick....................................... 194
Mexican Street Corn Chowder........... 9
Michigan Cherry Salad...................... 91
Mini Cheese Balls 28
Mini Zucchini Pizzas 180
Mint Chocolate Cheesecake...........249
Miso Butter Roasted
  Chicken.. 125
Mixed Greens with Orange-Ginger
  Vinaigrette.. 98
Moist Corn Spoon Bread 152
Moist Irish Soda Bread 65
Mom's Pickled Carrots 181
Muffin-Tin Lasagnas......................... 111
Mushroom & Olive
  Bruschetta.. 32
Mushroom Marsala with Barley.... 159

N

Nashville BBQ Sauce 179
No-Bake Cereal Cookie Bars.........201
No-Bake Chocolate Chip Cannoli
  Cheesecake....................................248

O

Oktoberfest Casserole 142
Old-Fashioned Ermine Frosting....179
Olive Oil Cake 222
One-Pot Bacon Cheeseburger
    Pasta 136
One-Pot Salsa Chicken 135
Orange-Fennel Salsa 33
Oreo Cupcakes with
    Cookies & Cream Frosting 233

P

Patchwork Quilt Cake 227
Peach Cream Puffs 234
Peach Melba Trifle.........................241
Peanut Butter &
    Jelly Ice Cream 246
Peanut Butter & Jelly
    Overnight Oats 59
Peanut Butter Chocolate
    Poke Cake 213
Peanut Butter Kiss Cookies............189
Peanut Butter Pretzel Bars 195
Peanut Butter Pretzel Shake 12
Peanutty Cream-Filled
    Pastry Shells.........................249
Pear & Pomegranate Salad..............97
Pepper Jack Hash
    Brown Casserole......................168
Perfect Sushi Rice........................ 151
Pesto Corn Salad with Shrimp 113
Pesto Pinwheel Buns...................... 76
Pickled Green Beans 175
Plum Upside-Down Cake 223
Pomegranate Short Ribs.................135
Pork & Asparagus
    Sheet-Pan Dinner 143
Pork & Cheesy Macaroni Sliders 9
Potato & Chorizo Casserole............162
Pressure-Cooker Chicken & Bacon
    White Chili 99
Pressure-Cooker
    Chili con Carne.........................97
Pretty Peach Tart..........................233

Q

Quick & Easy Baklava Squares......239
Quick Cheesy Broccoli....................164
Quick Ham & Bean Soup..................86
Quick Jalapeno Hush Puppies 174
Quick Stovetop Granola 45
Quinoa & Black Bean-Stuffed
    Peppers..................................104

R

Raspberry Moscow Mule Cake 219
Red, White & Blue Berry Trifle.......239
Roasted Asparagus & Leeks..........154

Roasted Banana & Pecan
    Cheesecake..............................236
Roasted Beet Salad with Orange
    Vinaigrette..............................84
Roasted Brussels Sprouts with
    Sriracha Aioli 38
Roasted Curry Chickpeas 185
Roasted Radishes 162
Roasted Vegetable Strata 52
Rustic Tomato Pie 168

S

S'mores Brownies, ...205
Salmon & Artichoke
    Quiche Squares 46
Salsa Steak Garlic Toasts 147
Salty Dog Sangria...........................25
Santa's Elf Cookies........................197
Seared Scallops with Citrus
    Herb Sauce 106
Shaved Fennel Salad.........................99
Sheet-Pan Honey
    Mustard Chicken 131
Shiitake & Butternut Risotto 163
Simple Biscuits 72
Skillet Caramel Apricot Grunt.......234
Skillet Stout Brownies....................201
Slim Bloody Mary Deviled Eggs 26
Slow-Cooker Breakfast
    Burritos 48
Slow-Cooker Mongolian Beef 126
Slow-Cooker Peach Cobbler 243
Slow-Cooker Polenta......................164
Smoky Macaroni & Cheese.............154
Socca 77
Soft Giant Pretzels 183
Spanish-Style Paella 103
Spice-Crusted Steaks
    with Cherry Sauce.....................145
Spiced Sweet Potato Fries..............153
Spicy Chuck Wagon Beans 169
Spicy Peruvian Potato Soup............89
Spicy Plum Pork Meatballs
    with Bok Choy 145
Spinach-Basil Pesto 184
Spring Onion Pimiento
    Cheese Grits.............................163
Sticky Cinnamon-Sugar
    Monkey Bread 46
Strawberry Basil Jam.....................184
Strawberry Bliss............................251
Strawberry Buttermilk Skillet
    Shortcake.................................246
Surf & Turf 110
Sweet & Tangy Beets.......................169
Sweet Club Sandwich.......................98
Sweet Hoosier Dog Sauce 173
Sweet Italian Holiday Bread............67

Sweetheart Slices 191
Swiss Chard Bean Soup 96

T

Thai Sloppy Joe Chicken &
    Waffles 141
That Good Salad............................81
The Best Ever Chili 11
The Best Hummus..........................16
The Best Marinara Sauce.............176
The Best Pizza Dough 21
The Best Quiche Lorraine 60
The Best Sausage Pizzas.................21
The Best Sweet Potato Pie 14
The Ultimate Chicken
    Noodle Soup..............................83
Tiramisu Cookies 190
Toasted Ravioli 38
Tomato Fritters 35
Tomato-Garlic Lentil Bowls...........115
Triple-Chocolate
    Cheesecake Bars 199
Triple-Citrus Steaks with
    Jicama & Mango 137
Tuna Cakes with Mustard Mayo 115
Turkey Pitas with Creamy Slaw 94
Turkey Wafflewiches 88

U

Upside-Down Pear Pancake 236
Upside-Down Pumpkin
    Pecan Tarts..............................241

V

Vegan Mac & Cheese 116
Vegan Peanut Butter Cookies 10
Vegetable Barley Saute 157
Vegetarian Farro Skillet.................105
Veggie-Cashew Stir-Fry 110
Vietnamese Crunchy
    Chicken Salad 92

W

Weeknight Goulash 127
White Beans & Bow Ties.................121
Winnie's Mini Rhubarb
    & Strawberry Pies 214
Winter Wishes Trifle.......................240

Y

Yellow Layer Cake with Chocolate
    Buttercream.............................217
Yogurt-Ricotta Cheesecake...........244
Yummy Corn Chip Salad.................81

Equivalents & Substitutions

3 teaspoons = 1 tablespoon		**16 tablespoons** = 1 cup	
4 tablespoons = ¼ cup		**2 cups** = 1 pint	
5⅓ tablespoons = ⅓ cup		**4 cups** = 1 quart	
8 tablespoons = ½ cup		**4 quarts** = 1 gallon	

Macaroni	1 cup (3½ ounces) uncooked = 2½ cups cooked
Noodles, Medium	3 cups (4 ounces) uncooked = 4 cups cooked
Popcorn	⅓-½ cup unpopped = 8 cups popped
Rice, Long Grain	1 cup uncooked = 3 cups cooked
Rice, Quick-Cooking	1 cup uncooked = 2 cups cooked
Spaghetti	8 ounces uncooked = 4 cups cooked

Bread	1 slice = ¾ cup soft crumbs or ¼ cup fine dry crumbs
Graham Crackers	7 squares = ½ cup finely crushed
Buttery Round Crackers	12 crackers = ½ cup finely crushed
Saltine Crackers	14 crackers = ½ cup finely crushed

Bananas	1 medium = ⅓ cup mashed
Lemons	1 medium = 3 tablespoons juice + 2 teaspoons grated zest
Limes	1 medium = 2 tablespoons juice + 1½ teaspoons grated zest
Oranges	1 medium = ¼-⅓ cup juice + 4 teaspoons grated zest

Cabbage	1 head = 5 cups shredded	**Green Pepper**	1 large = 1 cup chopped
Carrots	1 pound = 3 cups shredded	**Mushrooms**	½ pound = 3 cups sliced
Celery	1 rib = ½ cup chopped	**Onions**	1 medium = ½ cup chopped
Corn	1 ear fresh = ⅔ cup kernels	**Potatoes**	3 medium = 2 cups cubed

Almonds	1 pound = 3 cups chopped	**Pecan Halves**	1 pound = 4½ cups chopped
Ground Nuts	3¾ ounces = 1 cup	**Walnuts**	1 pound = 3¾ cups chopped

WHEN YOU NEED...		USE...
Baking Powder	1 teaspoon	½ teaspoon cream of tartar + ¼ teaspoon baking soda
Buttermilk	1 cup	1 tablespoon lemon juice or vinegar + enough milk to measure 1 cup (let stand 5 minutes before using)
Cornstarch	1 tablespoon	2 tablespoons all-purpose flour
Honey	1 cup	1¼ cups sugar + ¼ cup water
Half-and-Half Cream	1 cup	1 tablespoon melted butter + enough whole milk to measure 1 cup
Onion	1 small, chopped (⅓ cup)	1 teaspoon onion powder or 1 tablespoon dried minced onion
Tomato Juice	1 cup	½ cup tomato sauce + ½ cup water
Tomato Sauce	2 cups	¾ cup tomato paste + 1 cup water
Unsweetened Chocolate	1 square (1 ounce)	3 tablespoons baking cocoa + 1 tablespoon shortening or oil
Whole Milk	1 cup	½ cup evaporated milk + ½ cup water

Cutting Techniques

MINCING AND CHOPPING

Holding the handle of a chef's knife with one hand, rest the fingers of your other hand on the top of the blade near the tip. Using the handle to guide and apply pressure, move knife in an arc across the food with a rocking motion until pieces of food are the desired size. Mincing results in pieces no larger than ⅛ in., and chopping produces ¼- to ½-in. pieces.

DICING AND CUBING

Using a utility knife, trim each side of the fruit, vegetable or other food, squaring it off. Cut lengthwise into evenly spaced strips. The narrower the strips, the smaller the pieces will be. Stack the strips and cut lengthwise into uniformly sized strips. Arrange the square-shaped strips into a pile and cut widthwise into uniform pieces.

MAKING BIAS OR DIAGONAL CUTS

Holding a chef's knife at an angle to the length of the food, slice as thick or thin as desired. This technique is often used in stir-fry recipes.

MAKING JULIENNE STRIPS

Using a utility knife, cut a thin strip from one side of vegetable. Turn so flat side is down. Cut into 2-in. lengths, then cut each piece lengthwise into thin strips. Stack the strips and cut lengthwise into thinner strips.

CUTTING WEDGES

Using a chef's knife or serrated knife, cut the produce in half from stem end to blossom end. Lay halves cut side down on a cutting board. Set knife at the center of one the halves and cut in half vertically, then cut each quarter in half vertically. Repeat with other half.

ZESTING

Pull a citrus zester across limes, lemons or oranges, being careful not to remove the bitter white pith. The small holes in the zester will yield thin, narrow strips of zest. Use full strips to garnish or, if recipe instructs, chop into fine pieces and use as directed.

▲ **Mincing**
Pieces no larger than ⅛ in.

▼ **Chopping**
¼- to ½-in. pieces

▼ **Dicing**
⅛- to ¼-in. uniform pieces

▶ **Cubing**
½- to 1-in. uniform pieces

▼ **Bias/Diagonal Cuts**
Size of pieces based on desired length and thickness

▲ **Julienne Strips**
Pieces roughly 2 in. long

▲ **Wedges**
Size of wedges based on desired thickness

▲ **Zesting**
Size of strips or chopped zest based on desired preference